ANALOGIES IN INT1
INVESTMENT LAW AND
ARBITRATION

Although investment treaty arbitration has become the most common method for settling investor–state disputes, some scholars and practitioners have expressed concern regarding the magnitude of decision-making power allocated to investment treaty tribunals. Many of the recent arbitral awards have determined the boundary between two conflicting values: the legitimate sphere for state regulation in the pursuit of public goods, on the one hand, and the protection of foreign investments from state interference on the other. Can comparative reasoning help adjudicators in interpreting and applying broad and open-ended investment treaty provisions? Can the use of analogies contribute to the current debate over the legitimacy of investor–state arbitration, facilitating the consideration of the commonweal in the same? How should comparisons be made? What are the limits, if any, of comparative approaches to investment treaty law and arbitration? This book scrutinises the impact a comparative approach can have on investment law, and identifies methods for drawing sound analogies.

VALENTINA VADI is Professor of International Economic Law at Lancaster University. She is the author of *Public Health in International Investment Law and Arbitration* (Routledge, 2012) and *Cultural Heritage in International Investment Law and Arbitration* (Cambridge University Press, 2014).

ANALOGIES IN INTERNATIONAL INVESTMENT LAW AND ARBITRATION

VALENTINA VADI

Lancaster University

CAMBRIDGE
UNIVERSITY PRESS

University Printing House, Cambridge CB2 8BS, United Kingdom

One Liberty Plaza, 20th Floor, New York, NY 10006, USA

477 Williamstown Road, Port Melbourne, VIC 3207, Australia

314-321, 3rd Floor, Plot 3, Splendor Forum, Jasola District Centre, New Delhi - 110025, India

79 Anson Road, #06-04/06, Singapore 079906

Cambridge University Press is part of the University of Cambridge.

It furthers the University's mission by disseminating knowledge in the pursuit of education, learning and research at the highest international levels of excellence.

www.cambridge.org
Information on this title: www.cambridge.org/9781107472105

First published 2016
First paperback edition 2018

A catalogue record for this publication is available from the British Library

Library of Congress Cataloging in Publication data
Vadi, Valentina, author.
Analogies in international investment law and arbitration / Valentina Vadi.
pages   cm
ISBN 978-1-107-09331-7 (hardback)
1. Investments, Foreign – Law and legislation.   2. International commercial arbitration.   I. Title.
K3830.V33   2016
346′.092–dc23
2015030773

ISBN 978-1-107-09331-7 Hardback
ISBN 978-1-107-47210-5 Paperback

To the memory of my beloved grandmother, Lora

CONTENTS

PREFACE

The original idea for this book came about in 2009 when I was completing my doctoral thesis at the European University Institute, Florence. Coming across a large number of comparisons and instances of judicial borrowing in investment treaty arbitrations, I began to wonder *why, when, how* and *what* kind of analogies are made by investment treaty tribunals. Finding no conclusive answers to these questions in the available literature, I started investigating the matter. Comparisons may play a crucial role in legitimising (and/or increasing the perception of legitimacy of) the investment treaty system. At the same time, critical analysis is needed to provide a sound theoretical framework to comparative analysis. It is my belief that a study of this kind may contribute to making investment treaty arbitration more consistent, fair and predictable.

ACKNOWLEDGEMENTS

In writing this book, I have benefitted from the inspiration of many people. I thank Antonietta Di Blase, Francesco Francioni, Alisdair Gillespie, Amanda Perry Kessaris, Hildegard Schneider, Sigrun Skogly, Gus Van Harten, Ana Filipa Vrdoljak and Bruno De Witte for their mentorship, guidance and support. The book was largely written while I was an Emile Noël Fellow at the Jean Monnet Center for International and Regional Economic Law of New York University, and I would like to thank that institution, the staff and my temporary colleagues in New York, for providing a thought-provoking and ideal space for writing. In particular, I would like to thank José Alvarez, Gráinne de Burca, Ester Herlin-Karnell, Lauri Mälksoo, Christopher McCrudden, Wojciek Sadurski, Victoria Schultz and Sivan Schlomo-Agon for many stimulating conversations.

The book was completed during the period in which I lectured at Lancaster Law School. I could not have found a more welcoming environment for conducting my research, and I would like to thank the Law School and my colleagues for their encouragement and support. In particular, I would like to thank Agata Fijalkowski, Sophia Kopela and Steve Wheatley for many conversations in the field of international law. The book reflects my views only and the usual disclaimer applies.

Parts of this book were presented at conferences and seminars held in: Beijing, Bristol, Granada, Keele, Leiden, London, Maastricht, New York, Rome, Sevilla and Warwick. Convening an international conference on international economic law at the University of Edinburgh also helped me to frame the discourse. I greatly benefitted from the comments received on these occasions. In particular, I thank the anonymous reviewers, John Bell, Andrea Bjorklund, Judith Carter, Claire Cutler, Emily Den, Paula Gilliker, Sead Kadic, Fabrizio Sanna, Stephan W. Schill, Fiona Smith, M. Sornarajah, Vito Velluzzi and the late Thomas Wälde for their comments on earlier parts of my research.

I am grateful to Elizabeth Spicer, Jeevitha Baskaran and Sarah Green for accompanying this book from proposal to its publication.

On a personal note, I thank my husband, Gianluca, for his love and support, my parents, Lidiana and Carlo, for encouraging me in every possible way, and my daughter, Esther Susanna, for being a bundle of joy.

V.V.
Florence, August 2015

~

Introduction

Why compare? Not only is comparison a mode of thinking,[1] 'central to all legal analysis',[2] but it 'has always been a major technique in the development of law'.[3] In legal systems in general, and international investment law in particular, comparisons are consistently being made; the phenomenon is far from new. Why then does it need to be scrutinised? There are two main reasons for doing so. First, it seems that when comparisons are made, they are often done implicitly without spelling out their rationale and/or their systemic implications. Second, although investment treaty arbitration has become the most common method for settling investor–state disputes, nonetheless it has been harshly criticised by some authors because of its alleged legitimacy crisis.[4] This book explores whether a wider use of analogies can undermine or rather foster the legitimacy of investment treaty arbitration.

Under most investment treaties, states have agreed to give arbitrators comprehensive jurisdiction over what are essentially regulatory

---

[1] G. Swanson, 'Frameworks for Comparative Research: Structural Anthropology and the Theory of Action', in I. Vallier (ed.), *Comparative Methods in Sociology* (Berkeley: University of California Press, 1971), pp. 141–202, at 145 (stating that 'Thinking without comparison is unthinkable. And, in the absence of comparison, so is all scientific thought and scientific research'), quoted by J.H. Merryman, 'The Loneliness of the Comparative Lawyer', in J.H. Merryman (ed.), *The Loneliness of the Comparative Lawyer And Other Essays in Foreign and Comparative Law* (The Hague/London/Boston: Kluwer Law International, 1999), p. 2.

[2] V. Grosswald Curran, 'Cultural Immersion, Difference and Categories in U.S. Comparative Law', *American Journal of Comparative Law* 46 (1998), 43, 45.

[3] D. Barak-Erez, 'The Institutional Aspects of Comparative Law', *Columbia Journal European Law* 15 (2008–2009), 477, 478.

[4] See, for example, S.D. Franck, 'The Legitimacy Crisis in Investment Treaty Arbitration: Privatizing Public International Law Through Inconsistent Decisions', *Fordham Law Review* 73 (2005), 1521–1625, at 1571 (noting that 'decisions about public issues with economic and political consequences are resolved in private before different sets of individuals who can and do come to conflicting decisions on the same points of law – and no single body has the capacity to resolve these inconsistencies').

disputes. Some scholars and practitioners have expressed concern regarding the magnitude of decision-making power allocated to investment treaty tribunals. Many of the recent arbitral awards have determined the boundary between two conflicting values: the legitimate sphere for state regulation in the pursuit of public goods, on the one hand, and the protection of foreign investments from state interference, on the other. Can comparative reasoning help adjudicators in interpreting and applying broad and open-ended investment treaty provisions? Can the use of analogies contribute to the current debate over the legitimacy of investor–state arbitration, facilitating the consideration of the commonweal in the same? How should comparisons be made? What are the limits, if any, of comparative approaches to investment treaty law and arbitration?

Comparative or analogic reasoning is a technique of legal reasoning based on similarities/differences between cases or rules (either within investment law or outside the formal rules of investment law, such as human rights). Comparative or analogic reasoning, that is, borrowing from cases or rules belonging to other jurisdictions, should follow certain methodological criteria. For instance, before borrowing cases, the arbitrators may well investigate whether the system they would like to refer to is truly comparable. The gist of the argument is that while analogies are at the core of legal reasoning, hermeneutical rules, that is, the rules of construction or interpretation, as discussed *inter alia*, in the comparative law literature, help select the available comparators.

Against this background, this book aims at scrutinising the role that comparative reasoning plays in international investment law and arbitration and identifying a method for drawing sound analogies. This investigation is of the utmost theoretical and practical relevance for investment law scholars and practitioners. It can also attract comparative lawyers' interests, proposing international investment law as a new frontier of investigation for comparative law.

The underlying hypothesis of this book is that comparative reasoning may play an important role in 'legitimising' investment treaty arbitration. A theoretical discussion of the role of comparative reasoning in international investment law and arbitration will contribute to the existing literature on investment law and other values in that it offers practical tools to solve policy-related dilemmas. For instance, in the current arbitrations concerning plain packaging of tobacco products,[5] it will be interesting to see whether the arbitrators will refer to national or regional or even international law cases concerning analogous issues.

However, the use of analogies requires the elaboration of a sound methodology to contribute to the further development of the field in a manner compatible with public international law. While other authors have clarified *what* kind of analogies are drawn, *why* and *who* makes them,[6] the time is ripe for further investigation on *how* analogies are drawn and whether there is a suitable and reliable method for drawing them. As Cassese puts it, 'comparative lawyers establish a transnational legal discourse and act as merchants of law'. According to this paradigm, analogies are '"goods" or "merchandise" imported from the outside into a different legal order'.[7] Are there rules to govern this 'market'? Should such rules exist? How should interpretation by comparison be governed? Determining a clear methodology for drawing sound analogies can help scholars, practitioners and arbitrators to reach sound awards.

Both private and public law are often used as the relevant benchmarks for the analysis of international investment law, as the traditional distinction between public and private law is becoming blurred and investor–state arbitration itself presents hybrid features. This may have repercussions on many practical issues, such as the choice of legal orders. However, at both the macro- and micro-levels, analogies based on public international law sources should be preferred to a private law paradigm because international investment arbitration is a creature of public international law. This does not exclude public law sources provided that they are embodied in international law in the form of general principles of law or constitute evidence of state practice. In this

---

[5] *Philip Morris Brands Sàrl, Philip Morris Products S.A. and Abal Hermanos S.A. v. Oriental Republic of Uruguay*, ICSID Case No. ARB/10/7, ICSID Case No. ARB/10/7 Request for Arbitration, 19 February 2010; *Philip Morris Asia Limited v. The Commonwealth of Australia*, UNCITRAL, PCA Case No. 2012-12, Notice of Arbitration, 21 November 2011.

[6] J.E. Alvarez, 'Beware: Boundary Crossing', in T. Kahana and A. Scolnicov (eds.), *Boundaries of Rights, Boundaries of State (forthcoming 2015)*; S. Schill (ed.), *International Investment Law and Comparative Public Law* (Oxford: Oxford University Press, 2010); A. Roberts, 'Clash of Paradigms: Actors and Analogies shaping the Investment Treaty System', *American Journal of International Law* 107 (2013), 45–94.

[7] S. Cassese, 'Beyond Legal Comparison', *Annuario di diritto comparato e di studi legislativi* (2012), 387, 388.

context, awareness of sound comparative methods helps in identifying state practice and general principles of law. In this respect, adopting principled hermeneutics may enhance the perceived legitimacy of the system.

Although the use of comparative legal reasoning in international investment law and arbitration seems to offer concrete solutions to emerging conceptual dilemmas – such as the definition of investment, the notion of legitimate expectations and others – and is forcefully presented by reputed scholars, one may question whether a more critical approach to the use of comparative reasoning should be adopted. It is often assumed that comparative reasoning is a neutral process, but this is not always the case. For instance, the *Lauder* case[8] and the *CME* case[9] – which were parallel proceedings over the same underlying dispute – had different outcomes because different bilateral investment treaties (BITs) governed the substantive law, and the arbitral tribunals weighted the comparative method differently. While the *Lauder* Tribunal referred to a human rights case for establishing the expropriation standards,[10] the other tribunal did not. Unsurprisingly, the two tribunals came to opposite decisions. In fact, depending on the selected perspective, comparisons may have completely different outcomes. Furthermore, textual differences need to be taken into account, as interpretation cannot be used to transpose obligations from one field to another or to create new obligations. The major risk consists in adopting an ideology of free decision-making. The inadvertent use of analogies may determine the abuse of the same and ultimately lead to undesirable outcomes. Arbitrators risk acting as 'bricoleurs' rather than as 'engineers' of legal norms. 'As engineers, they would sort through the concepts and assemble them into a constitutional design that made sense according to some overarching conceptual scheme. As bricoleurs, though, they . . . use the first thing that happens to fit the immediate problem they are facing.'[11]

---

[8] *Ronald S. Lauder* v. *Czech Republic*, Final Award, 3 September 2001, available at http://italaw. com/documents/LauderAward.pdf.

[9] *CME Czech Republic B.V.* v. *Czech Republic*, Final Award, 14 March 2003, available at http://italaw.com/documents/CME-2003-Final_001.pdf.

[10] *Ronald S. Lauder* v. *Czech Republic*, Final Award, para. 200.

[11] The metaphor is borrowed from Lévi-Strauss, cited by M. Tushnet, 'The Possibilities of Comparative Law', *Yale Law Journal* 108 (1998–1999), 1225, 1286.

As investment law scholars, arbitrators and practitioners often recur to analogies, it seems crucial to map the current dimension of the phenomenon and to propose a more critical use of the comparative method. Since the use of analogies in investment treaty law and arbitration can shape the development of the field, this book aims to fill a lacuna in legal studies focusing on the methodology for drawing sound analogies. By furthering the judicial dialogue among international courts and tribunals, comparative reasoning may help insert non-economic considerations into investment treaty arbitration and has the potential for ultimately promoting the humanisation of international (investment) law. At the same time, this book highlights that only by knowing the merits and limits of the comparative method can adjudicators and practitioners make appropriate use of it.

This book examines the use of comparative legal reasoning in international investment law and arbitration in a comprehensive and analytical fashion, drawing on international law and comparative law literature as well as legal theory. At the same time, it has lines of continuity with the available literature that can be placed in five broad categories: (1) literature on international investment law;[12] (2) literature on international investment law and other values;[13] (3) literature on

---

[12] See, for example, M. Sornarajah, *The International Law on Foreign Investment* (Cambridge: Cambridge University Press, 2010); J.W. Salacuse, *The Law of Investment Treaties* (Oxford: Oxford University Press, 2010); C. Binder, U. Kriebaum, A. Reinisch and S. Wittich (eds.), *International Investment Law for the 21st Century* (Oxford: Oxford University Press, 2009); C. Dugan, N. Rubins, D. Wallace, B. Sabahi, *Investor–State Arbitration* (Oxford: Oxford University Press, 2008); A. Reinisch, *Standards of Investment Protection* (Oxford: Oxford University Press, 2008); R. Dolzer and C. Schreuer, *Principles of International Investment Law*, 2nd ed. (Oxford: Oxford University Press, 2012).

[13] See, for instance, T. Treves, F. Seatzu, S. Trevisanut (eds.), *Foreign Investment, International Law and Common Concerns* (London: Routledge, 2014); F. Baetens (ed.), *Investment Law Within International Law: Integrationist Perspectives* (Cambridge: Cambridge University Press, 2013); L. Cotula, *Human Rights, Natural Resources and Investment Law in a Globalised World* (London: Routledge, 2013); O. De Schutter, J. Swinnen, J. Wouters (eds.), *Foreign Direct Investment and Human Development* (London: Routledge, 2012); P.-M. Dupuy, F. Francioni and E.-U. Petersmann (eds.), *Human Rights in International Investment Law and Arbitration* (Oxford: Oxford University Press, 2009); S. Subedi, *International Investment Law: Reconciling Policy and Principle* (Oxford: Hart Publishing, 2008); G. Van Harten, *Investment Treaty Arbitration and Public Law* (Oxford: Oxford University Press, 2007); K. Tienhaara, *The Expropriation of Environmental Governance* (Cambridge: Cambridge University Press, 2009); S.F. Puvimanasinghe, *Foreign Investment, Human Rights and the Environment* (Leiden: Martinus Nijhoff, 2007).

multinational corporations and the law;[14] (4) comparative law scholarship;[15] and (5) legal theory.[16]

This book differs from and complements the available literature in several ways. First, by presenting a complete and systematic framework of the use of analogies in international investment law and arbitration, it maps and structures the debate.[17] Second, it relies on a public international law approach, while other scholars have relied mainly on a public law approach.[18] Third, this book does not draw merely on international (investment) law or public law sources, but it relies also on comparative law and legal theory.[19] Therefore, on the one hand, this book contributes

[14] See, for instance, S. Picciotto, *Regulating Global Corporate Capitalism* (Cambridge: Cambridge University Press, 2011); P. Muchlinski, *Multinational Enterprises and the Law*, 2nd ed. (Oxford: Oxford University Press, 2007).

[15] See, for example, M. Bogdan, *Concise Introduction to Comparative Law* (Amsterdam: Europa Law Publishing, 2013); P.G. Monateri (ed.), *Methods of Comparative Law* (Cheltenham: Edward Elgar, 2012); M. Bussani and U. Mattei (eds.), *The Cambridge Companion to Comparative Law* (Cambridge: Cambridge University Press, 2012); M. Adams, J. Bomhoff (eds.), *Practice and Theory in Comparative Law* (Cambridge: Cambridge University Press, 2012); W. Butler, O.V. Kresin and I.S. Shemshuchenko, *Foundations of Comparative Law: Methods and Typologies* (London: Wildy, Simmonds & Hill Publishing, 2011); E. Örücü, *The Enigma of Comparative Law* (Leiden: Martinus Nijhoff, 2004); M. Reimann and R. Zimmerman (eds.), *The Oxford Handbook of Comparative Law* (Oxford: Oxford University Press, 2006); J. Smits, *Elgar Encyclopedia of Comparative Law*, 2nd ed. (Cheltenham, UK: Edward Elgar, 2012); M. Van Hoecke (ed.), *Epistemology and Methodology of Comparative Law* (Oxford/Portland: Hart Publishing, 2004); K. Zweigert and H. Kotz, *Introduction to Comparative Law*, 3rd ed. (Oxford: Oxford University Press, 1998); O. Kahn-Freund, *Comparative Law as an Academic Subject* (Oxford: Clarendon Press, 1965).

[16] See, for example, A. Larry and E. Sherwin, *Demystifying Legal Reasoning* (Cambridge: Cambridge University Press, 2008); L.L. Weinreb, *Legal Reason: The Use of Analogy in Legal Argument* (Cambridge: Cambridge University Press, 2005); C.R. Sunstein, 'On Analogical Reasoning', *Harvard Law Review* 106 (1993), 741.

[17] There are very few, albeit excellent, contributions concerning the linkage between comparative law and international investment law. Apart from an edited volume, other contributions to the topic under discussion are in the form of long articles or book chapters. See Schill, *International Investment Law and Comparative Public Law*; See Roberts, 'Clash of Paradigms: Actors and Analogies Shaping the Investment Treaty System'; V. Vadi, 'Critical Comparisons: The Role of Comparative Law in Investment Treaty Arbitration', *Denver Journal of International Law and Policy* 39 (2010), 67–100; M. Paparinskis, 'Analogies and Other Regimes of International Law', in Z. Douglas, J. Pauwelyn and J.E. Viñuales (eds.), *The Foundations of International Investment Law: Bringing Theory into Practice* (Oxford: Oxford University Press, 2014).

[18] See, for example, S. Schill, 'Enhancing International Investment Law's Legitimacy: Conceptual and Methodological Foundations of a New Public Law Approach', *Virginia Journal of International Law* 52 (2011), 57–102.

[19] In the process of borrowing concepts and categories from comparative law, inevitably such concepts will have lost some of their initial meaning from their source discipline.

to the existing investment law scholarship by going beyond purely functionalist approaches. While constant reference will be made to the relevant awards, the theoretical framework provided by the book may be of help to both practitioners and scholars alike who are interested in the legitimacy of international investment law and arbitration. On the other hand, it complements comparative law literature transposing the current debate on the methodology of analogic reasoning from traditional fields of study to international investment law. Therefore, the book presents some elements of cross-disciplinary analysis. This is a novelty as most investment law scholars have relied only on investment law sources, while comparative law scholars have not paid much attention to the selected topic. Finally, this book does not merely describe what kinds of analogies are made, but it also investigates whether a sound methodology exists and/or should be adopted and provides the reader with a complete analytical framework of the issues involved. Therefore, such theoretical framework may be of help to both practitioners and scholars alike.

This book is written by an international law scholar and primarily for international lawyers. While the use of comparative reasoning in international law may be studied from a variety of different perspectives and institutional settings,[20] this book adopts an 'internal' approach with respect to international investment law and arbitration. Given the wealth of arbitral decisions that have been handed down in recent years, an analysis and critical assessment of this emerging field of study is necessary. Looking at the use of analogies in international investment law and arbitration allows a reflection on this emerging area of international law.

In order to make the analysis relevant to different audiences, the language will deliberately be kept technical, but efforts will be taken to achieve clarity and cohesion. As a result, this study will be of relevance for a wide audience, including but not limited to international scholars, investment law arbitrators and practitioners, state officials, as well as comparative law experts and other interested audiences.

Chapter plan

The book will proceed as follows. Part I of the book (which constitutes its *pars generalis*) sets the scene and introduces the main theoretical

---

The author, however, has tried to be fair to the original context of comparative law, highlighting its main features and dilemmas in a comprehensive fashion.

[20] See, for example, M. Bobek, *Comparative Reasoning in European Supreme Courts* (Oxford: Oxford University Press, 2013).

and practical questions posed by the topic. Chapter 1 scrutinises some essential features of comparative law, comparative reasoning and the comparative method. Only by knowing the merits and limits of the comparative method can interpreters and adjudicators make an appropriate use of it. Chapter 2 examines the main features of international investment law and arbitration. Chapter 3 focuses on the use of comparative reasoning and international investment law. Brief reference will be made to comparative investment law (i.e. the study of national laws governing foreign direct investment and how comparative studies can influence treaty-making practices); comparative arbitration law (i.e. the use of comparisons in international arbitration); legal doctrine (i.e. how legal scholars discussing international investment law and arbitration refer to national and other regional and international legal systems); and judicial borrowing or cross-judging (i.e. how investment arbitral tribunals borrow concepts from the jurisprudence of other international, regional and national courts and tribunals). The analysis then highlights the role played by comparative reasoning in the process of treaty interpretation and the consideration of the various sources of international law such as customary law and general principles of law.

Part II, the *pars specialis* of the book, investigates the use of analogies in investment treaty arbitration. Chapter 4 considers the use of micro-comparisons (i.e. analogies dealing with specific institutions or specific problems) in investment treaty arbitration. For instance, the chapter will consider whether and, if so, how given concepts such as proportionality and reasonableness can (or have) migrate(d) from domestic legal systems to international investment arbitration. The use of comparative surveys as a legitimating factor of policy measures and as evidence of state practice is also considered. Extensive reference will be made to the jurisprudence of the relevant arbitral tribunals.

Chapter 5 examines the use of macro-comparisons (i.e. analogies between entire legal systems) in relation to international investment law and arbitration. Given its hybrid features, investment treaty law and arbitration has been analogised to different systems of law.[21] First, given the fact that under most investment treaties, states have agreed to give arbitrators comprehensive jurisdiction over what are essentially regulatory disputes, such an investment review has been compared to a

[21] Roberts, 'Clash of Paradigms: Actors and Analogies Shaping the Investment Treaty System', 45.

sort of administrative review.[22] Second, it has been argued that access to investor–state arbitration shares many characteristics of the direct right of action before human rights courts.[23] Third, because of the procedural rules which govern it, investor–state arbitration has been analogised to commercial arbitration. Finally, arbitral tribunals have been analogised to other public international law tribunals.

Chapters 4 and 5 scrutinise and critically assess the merits and limits of such comparative endeavours and conclude that international investment law is part of international law. Therefore, it is submitted that the best analogue is not that of national courts (whose selection might be arbitrary) or commercial arbitration (which is seldom concerned with public law aspects); rather, the most appropriate framework is given by public international law. Therefore, the use of micro-comparisons should be governed by the traditional interpretative tools available to international law scholars. Comparative reasoning plays an important role in the ascertainment of general principles of law and state practice as evidence of customary international law. It also helps with interpreting international law.

Chapter 6 concludes by examining how comparative reasoning can (and does) contribute to the development of international investment law, highlighting the pros and cons of using analogies in the field and identifying methods for drawing sound analogies. The aim is to make explicit what is often implicit in the jurisprudence of arbitral tribunals; to map the ways analogies are made in the literature and in the awards; and to identify some methodological problems along the way. This chapter maps an ongoing phenomenon and identifies possible methodological tools which may help adjudicators and practitioners. On the one hand, analogies can supplement fragmentary or contradictory materials so as to ensure systemic unity and consistency. Moreover, comparative reasoning

---

[22] G. Van Harten and M. Loughlin, 'Investment Treaty Arbitration as a Species of Global Administrative Law', *European Journal of International Law* 17 (2006), 121; Van Harten, *Investment Treaty Arbitration and Public Law*; S. Montt, *State Liability in Investment Treaty Arbitration: Global Constitutional Law and Administrative Law in the BIT Generation* (Portland: Hart Publishing, 2009); D. Schneiderman, *Constitutionalizing Economic Globalization: Investment Rules and Democracy's Premise* (Oxford: Oxford University Press, 2008).

[23] See G. Bastid Burdeau, 'Nouvelles perspectives pour l'arbitrage dans le contentieux économique intéressant l'Etat', *Revue de l'Arbitrage* 1 (1995), 16; C. Reiner and C. Schreuer, 'Human Rights and International Investment Arbitration', in P.-M. Dupuy, F. Francioni and E.-U. Petersmann (eds.), *Human Rights in International Investment Law and Arbitration* (Oxford: Oxford University Press, 2008), pp. 82–96.

may play an important role in 'legitimising' investment treaty arbitration. On the other hand, methodology matters, and uncritical use of analogies may lead to undesirable outcomes. At both the macro- and micro-levels, the public international law paradigm should be preferred to a private law paradigm because international investment arbitration is a creature of public international law. This does not exclude public law sources provided that they are embodied in international law in the form of general principles of law or constitute evidence of state practice. Adopting a principled hermeneutics and comparative reasoning may enhance the perceived legitimacy of the system. The conclusions will then sum up the key findings of the study.

PART I

Comparative reasoning and international
investment law

Introductory note

Investment treaty arbitration has moved 'from a matter of peripheral academic interest to a matter of vital international concern'.[1] By signing international investment treaties, states grant certain substantive and procedural rights to foreign investors. In a typical investment treaty, substantive provisions cover matters such as prohibition against unlawful expropriation, full protection and security, fair and equitable treatment and non-discrimination, among others. Most contemporary investment treaties include investor–state arbitration for the settlement of disputes which may arise between the foreign investor and the host state. Under this mechanism, foreign investors may bring claims against the host state before international arbitral tribunals. This development has transformed the landscape of modern investment protection, as customary international law did not confer such a right to individuals. The internationalisation of investment disputes has been conceived as an important mechanism for adequately protecting the assets of foreign investors from expropriation or other forms of regulation by the host state by guaranteeing a neutral forum.

However, some scholars and practitioners have expressed concern regarding the magnitude of decision-making power allocated to investment treaty tribunals. Many of the recent arbitral awards have determined the boundary between two conflicting values: the regulatory autonomy of the host state, on the one hand, and the protection of foreign investments from state interference, on the other. According to some authors, investment treaty law and arbitration is facing a 'legitimacy crisis', as arbitral awards seem to affect public policy 'in a vacuum'.[2] There is uncertainty over the relevance

---

[1] S.D. Franck, 'Development and Outcomes of Investment Treaty Arbitration', *Harvard International Law Journal* 50 (2009), 435.

[2] S.D. Franck, 'The Legitimacy Crisis in Investment Treaty Arbitration: Privatizing Public International Law Through Inconsistent Decisions', *Fordham Law Review* 73 (2005), at

(or irrelevance) of norms external to investment law, such as human rights law, within investment treaty arbitration.[3] Furthermore, while developing countries have deemed investment treaty arbitration politically biased against them,[4] even emerging economies and industrialised countries alike have expressed some concerns about this mechanism. Being fearful of becoming respondents in investment disputes, states have increasingly felt the need to protect their regulatory space and to limit arbitral discretion. While a few countries have withdrawn from the International Convention on the Settlement of Investment Disputes between states and nationals of other states (ICSID Convention),[5] the investment chapter of the Australia–US Free Trade Agreement does not include provisions on investor–state dispute resolution. A growing number of states are recalibrating their model bilateral investment treaties to include general exceptions and/or to enhance the regulatory power of governments.[6]

Against this background, this book scrutinises the role of comparative reasoning in international investment law and arbitration. Can comparative reasoning help adjudicators in interpreting and applying broad and open-ended investment treaty provisions? Can the use of analogies contribute to the current debate over the legitimacy of investor–state arbitration? Can comparative reasoning help facilitate the consideration of the commonweal, thus contributing to the humanisation of international (investment) law? How should comparisons be made? What are the limits, if any, of comparative approaches to investment treaty law and arbitration?

Comparative reasoning may play an important role in 'legitimising' international investment law and arbitration. 'The eyes of the rest of mankind' can help with understanding whether a given regulatory

---

1571. See also C.N. Brower and S.W. Schill, 'Is Arbitration a Threat or a Boon to the Legitimacy of International Investment Law?', *Chicago Journal of International Law* 9 (2008–2009), 471, 473; M. Sornarajah, 'A Coming Crisis: Expansionary Trends in Investment Treaty Arbitration', in K.P. Sauvant (ed.), *Appeals Mechanism in International Investment Disputes Law* (Oxford: Oxford University Press, 2008), p. 39.

[3] See generally P.-M. Dupuy, F. Francioni and E.-U. Petersmann (eds.), *Human Rights in International Investment Law and Arbitration* (Oxford: Oxford University Press, 2009).

[4] A. Shalakany, 'Arbitration and the Third World: A Plea for Reassessing Bias Under the Specter of Neoliberalism', *Harvard International Law Journal* 41 (2000), 419–468.

[5] M. Clark, 'Venezuela's Withdrawal from the ICSID Convention', *Association for International Arbitration Bulletin*, October 2012, 2.

[6] J.E. Alvarez, 'The Evolving BIT', in I.A. Laird and T. Weiler (eds.), *Investment Treaty Arbitration and International Law* (New York: Juris, 2010), p. 1.

measure appears reasonable.[7] Comparative reasoning can promote adaptive responses evolving over the course of time, making the investment law system both perceptive of changing circumstances and responsive to a multiplicity of challenges and to community needs and demands. Comparative reasoning enables a panoply of responses and a rich diversity of outputs.

However, the use of analogies requires the elaboration of a sound methodology to contribute to the further development of the field in a manner compatible with public international law. The time is ripe for investigating *how* analogies are drawn and whether there is a suitable and reliable method for drawing them. As Cassese puts it, 'comparative lawyers establish a transnational legal discourse and act as *merchants of law*'.[8] Accordingly, analogies are 'goods' or 'merchandise imported from the outside into a different legal order'.[9] Are there rules to govern the 'marketplace of ideas'? Should there be?

This book aims at exploring the role that comparative reasoning plays in investment treaty arbitration and addresses the question as to whether the use of comparative reasoning can help solve some aspects of the 'legitimacy crisis' of investment treaty arbitration. In order to unpack the role of comparative reasoning in investor–state arbitration and add shade and texture to existing understandings and debates, Part I of this book defines and connects the two fields of comparative legal reasoning and international investment law.

---

[7] A. Smith, *Lectures on Jurisprudence* (1762–3) (R.L. Meek et al., eds., Oxford: Oxford University Clarendon Press, 1978), p. 104, quoted by A. Sen, *The Idea of Justice* (Boston, MA: Harvard University Press, 2009), p. 405.

[8] S. Cassese, 'Beyond Legal Comparison', *Annuario di diritto comparato e di studi legislativi* (2012), 387, 388 (emphasis added).

[9] *Ibid.*

1

Comparative law, methods and reasoning

There is almost nothing right or wrong which does not alter with a change in clime. A shift of three degrees of latitude is enough to overthrow jurisprudence. One's location on the meridian decides the truth ... Strange justice that is bounded by a river or mountain! The truth on this side of the Pyrenees, error on the other.[10]

Introduction

With growing economic and political integration, globalisation and ongoing migration processes, there has been extensive interest in (and scholarship on) comparative law, methods and reasoning. The existence of legal pluralism in both vertical and horizontal senses;[11] the phenomenon of 'judicial globalization';[12] the shifting boundaries of legal traditions; the increasing 'migration of constitutional ideas';[13] and harmonisation processes driven by international law in general[14]

---

[10] Pascal, *Pensées*, quoted in J.H. Merryman, 'On the Convergence (and Divergence) of the Civil Law and the Common Law', in M. Cappelletti (ed.), *New Perspectives for a Common Law of Europe* (Leyden: Sijthoff, 1978), p. 195 ('On ne voit rien de juste ou d'injuste qui ne change de qualité en changeant de climat. Trois degrés d'élévation du pole renversent toute la jurisprudence; un méridien décide de la verité ... Plaisance justice qu'une rivière borne! Vérité au deçà des Pyrénées, erreur au de là ... ').

[11] See, for example, G. De Burca, R.O. Keohane and C. Sabel, 'New Modes of Pluralist Global Governance', *New York University Journal of International Law and Politics* 45 (2013), 723–786; P.S. Berman, 'A Pluralist Approach to International Law', *Yale Journal of International Law* 32 (2007), 301; W.W. Burke-White, 'International Legal Pluralism', *Michigan Journal of International Law* 25 (2004), 963; G. Teubner, 'Global Bukowina: Legal Pluralism in the World Society', in G. Teubner (ed.), *Global Law Without a State* (Aldershot: Dartmouth Publishing, 1997).

[12] A.M. Slaughter, 'Judicial Globalization', *Virginia Journal of International Law* 40 (2000), 1103–1124.

[13] S. Choudry (ed.), *The Migration of Constitutional Ideas* (Cambridge: Cambridge University Press, 2006).

[14] P. Legrand, 'On the Singularity of Law', *Harvard International Law Journal* 47 (2006), 517–530, 518 (pinpointing that 'Whether one has in mind ... the Agreement on Trade Related Aspects of Intellectual Property Rights (TRIPS), or the World Heritage

and international economic governance in particular[15] have furthered comparative legal studies to an extent unknown before.[16]

On the one hand, comparative reasoning has traditionally been instrumental in harmonisation attempts – being conceptualised as: (1) a legislative tool to elaborate common standards on a variety of issues; (2) a jurisprudential tool to ensure consistency and path coherence; and (3) a theoretical tool to defragment fragmentation and map the landscape of international organisations, courts and tribunals with partially complementary, but also partially competing, goals, embodying different values and ultimately different cultures.[17] On the other hand, comparative reasoning is an essential instrument for understanding legal pluralism and cultural diversity.[18] Despite the fact that eminent authors forcefully alleged the end of comparative legal studies,[19] the recent proliferation of studies in the field narrates a quite different story of success.[20]

In addition to being an element of general legal culture,[21] comparative reasoning has been perceived in a functional fashion, as a tool for understanding the current forces which shape the development of law – in both

Convention, "global" rules of governance are understood as ... being implemented irrespective of the legal traditions and the economic and political conditions of the countries in which they are to be applied'). [Internal citations omitted.]

[15] *Ibid.*, at 520 (highlighting 'the development of supranational capital markets which have joined many of the world's various peoples and societies into a new polity, a single virtual metropolis ... [and determined] a great deal of shared and legally enforceable culture').

[16] R. Banakar, 'Power, Culture and Method in Comparative Law', *International Journal of Law in Context* 5 (2009), 69–85, 86.

[17] On the different cultures of international organisations, see C. Picker, 'International Investment Law: Some Legal Cultural Insights', in L. Trakman and N. Ranieri (eds.), *Regionalism in International Investment Law* (Oxford: Oxford University Press, 2013), pp. 27–58; A. Bjorklund, 'The Emerging Civilization of Investment Arbitration', *Penn State Law Review* 113 (2009), 1269; D. Steger, 'The Culture of the WTO: Why It Needs to Change', *Journal of International Economic Law* 10 (2007), 483–495.

[18] See, for example, H.P. Glenn, *Legal Traditions of the World: Sustainable Diversity in Law*, 4th ed. (Oxford: Oxford University Press, 2010).

[19] M. Siems, 'The End of Comparative Law', *Journal of Comparative Law* 2 (2007), 133–150, at 133 and 148.

[20] See, for example, P. Legrand and R. Munday, *Comparative Legal Studies: Traditions and Transitions* (Cambridge: Cambridge University Press, 2003); W. Menski, *Comparative Law in a Global Context*, 2nd ed. (Cambridge: Cambridge University Press, 2006); H.P. Glenn, *Legal Traditions of the World: Sustainable Diversity in Law*, 4th ed. (Oxford: Oxford University Press, 2010); P. De Cruz, *Comparative Law in Changing World* (Abingdon/New York: Routledge-Cavendish, 2007).

[21] R. David, 'Le droit comparé enseignement de culture générale', *Revue internationale de droit comparé* 2 (1950), 682–685, 683.

a legislative and jurisprudential sense – at national, regional and international levels. It enriches lawyers' perspectives, equipping them with
the necessary flexibility (and relativity) to deal with an increasingly
globalised legal profession and map the global legal landscape. The
borrowing of foreign legal concepts is continuing unabashed,[22] 'building
bridges' between different legal systems, but also allowing 'investigations
into the legitimacy of global governance'.[23]

The legitimising force of comparative reasoning works at two different
levels: on the one hand, it establishes parameters for international
adjudication about the legitimacy of a given state measure.[24] Arbitral
tribunals have adopted a *comparative approach* holding that 'a rule
cannot be said to be unfair, inadequate, inequitable or discriminatory
when it has been adopted by many countries around the world'.[25] This
comparative approach can build coherence at the international law level,
helping adjudicators to reach results in harmony with what may have
achieved the status of general principles of international law or even
customary law.

On the other hand, the reference to cases and scholarly writings brings
the given case into a 'circuit of legitimation', so that reference to a leading
case lends dignity to more recent cases.[26] This mechanism of 'cultured
allusions and analogies endlessly point[ing] to other analogies'[27] tends
not to justify itself by stating the basis of the analogy it performs; rather, it
weaves a complex tapestry of references, each replying to and reinforcing
all the others, which in turn creates a global jurisprudence. Comparative
reasoning allows the interpreter a fresh approach to her own system,[28]

---

[22] C. McCrudden, 'A Common Law of Human Rights? Transnational Judicial Conversations
on Constitutional Rights', *Oxford Journal of Legal Studies* 20 (2000), 499–532.

[23] P. Zumbansen, 'Transnational Comparisons: Theory and Practice of Comparative Law as
a Critique of Global Governance', Osgoode Hall Law School, Research Paper No. 1/2012,
1–20, 13.

[24] On the need of comparative surveys of best regulatory practices, see P. Eeckhout, 'The
Scales of Trade – Reflections on the Growth and Functions of the WTO Adjudicative
Branch', *Journal of International Economic Law* 13 (2010), 3–26.

[25] *Lemire, Joseph Charles* v. *Ukraine*, ICSID Case No. ARB/06/18, Decision on Jurisdiction
and Liability, 14 January 2010, para. 506.

[26] P. Bourdieu, *Distinction – A Social Critique of the Judgment of Taste* (R. Nice, trans.,
Cambridge, MA: Harvard University Press, 1984), p. 53.

[27] *Ibid.* (referring to analogous referencing process in paintings).

[28] H.E. Yntema, 'Comparative Research. Some Remarks on "Looking out of the Cave"',
Michigan Law Review 54 (1956), 899–928 (suggesting that comparative law scholars
should look out of the cave, emancipating themselves from the constraints of domestic
law and widening their horizons through comparative legal research).

and it can be perceived as an 'instrument of progress',[29] mutual under-standing and dialogue among civilisations.

Comparative law and international law share the idea that certain fundamental principles go beyond national borders – that there are 'common elements in human experience', thus presupposing a 'huma-nist conception of universal justice'.[30] Comparative reasoning is instrumental in deciphering and mapping general principles of law and the practice of states, which is an element of customary law. Yet, just as with analogies in general, analogies in international (invest-ment) law still reveal a great degree of methodological uncertainty. To examine the role of comparative reasoning in international investment law, some preliminary understanding of comparative law, methods and reasoning is necessary.

The argument of this chapter shall proceed as follows. First, a few essential features of comparative law and the comparative method will be scrutinised. Only by knowing the merits and limits of the comparative method can interpreters and adjudicators make appropriate use of it. Second, the chapter considers analogy as a key tool of legal interpretation: distinguishing between the two different albeit related concepts of *ana-logia legis* (analogy from statute) and *analogia juris* (analogy from legal systems). Third, the use of analogies in international law will be briefly explored. The chapter concludes with some final remarks.

Comparative law

Comparative law can and has been regarded as 'an oxymoron', juxtapos-ing apparently contradictory elements.[31] While comparison is 'a purely descriptive process', law is 'a normative process', describing the way something ought to be done. Identifying this apparent paradox, Glenn asks, 'How can one do both at the same time?'[32] Comparative law has thus been defined as 'an intellectual activity with law as its object and comparison as its process'[33] or 'the study of how and why legal systems

---

[29] David, 'Le droit comparé enseignement de culture générale', 685.

[30] H.E. Yntema, 'Le droit comparé et l'humanisme', *Revue international de droit comparé* 10 (1958), 693–700, 698.

[31] P. Glenn, 'Comparative Law: Problems and Prospects', *American University International Law Review* 26 (2010–2011), 935–968, 943.

[32] Id.

[33] K. Zweigert and H. Kötz, *Introduction to Comparative Law* (Tony Weir, trans., 3rd ed., Oxford: Oxford University Press, 1998), p. 2.

differ or are the same'.[34] The Latin roots of 'com-paring' – *cum*, in
English 'with', and *par*, in English 'peer' – suggest 'the process of living
together', forming in pairs, bringing together different items.[35]
Therefore, the logic of comparing is not that of separation; rather, it is
one of synthesis of differences.[36] Comparative law has a wider scope of
analysis than positive law, because it brings together two or more systems
of law. However, comparative law has a narrower scope than legal theory
as it can be regarded as the part of legal theory that investigates legal
structures in different contexts.[37] Comparative law includes the process
and outcome of comparing different legal systems (macro-comparisons) and/or concepts and institutions belonging to such systems
(micro-comparisons).

For decades, scholars have debated the very existence of comparative
law as a legal field. While some authors have qualified comparative law as
an autonomous discipline,[38] others have contended that comparative
law consists of the mere utilisation of the comparative method.[39] For
instance, Gutteridge, then Emeritus Professor of comparative law at
the University of Cambridge, contended that comparative law is not a
distinct body of law but a method, while acknowledging that the term
'comparative law' '[wa]s too deeply rooted to be dislodged'.[40]

Yet, the autonomy of comparative law as a science is now well established.[41] Today, comparative law is generally acknowledged as 'a science

---

[34] S. Choudry, 'Globalization in Search of a Justification: Toward a Theory of Comparative
Constitutional Interpretation', *Indiana Law Journal* 74 (1999), 819, 829.

[35] Glenn, 'Comparative Law: Problems and Prospects', 944.

[36] H.P. Glenn, 'Com-paring', in E. Örücü and D. Nelken (eds.), *Comparative Law: A
Handbook* (Oxford: Hart Publishing, 2007), pp. 91–108, p. 92.

[37] O. Pfersmann, 'Le droit comparé comme interprétation et comme théorie du droit', *Revue
Internationale de Droit Comparé* (2001), 275–288, 275.

[38] *Ibid.*, at 277 ('Le droit comparé n'est pas un ordre juridique du tout, mais une discipline. Il
suppose une pluralité d'ordres juridiques entre lesquels on établit des "comparisons"').

[39] O. Kahn-Freund, 'Comparative Law as an Academic Subject', *Law Quarterly Review* 82
(1966), 41 (explaining that comparative law 'has by common consent the somewhat
unusual characteristic that it does not exist' and that comparative law indicates a variety
of methods of looking at law).

[40] H.C. Gutteridge, 'Comparative Law and the Law of Nations', *British Yearbook of
International Law* 21 (1944), 1, 1 (stating that 'there is, of course, no such thing as
"comparative law" ... The stages of analysis and synthesis of the rules of two or more
systems of law which constitute the comparative process cannot and do not result in the
formulation of any independent body of law').

[41] See, among others, M. Schmitthoff, 'The Science of Comparative Law', *Cambridge Law
Journal* 7 (1939), 94–110; Rodolfo Sacco, 'Legal Formants: A Dynamic Approach to
Comparative Law', *American Journal of Comparative Law* 39 (1991), 1–34, 4 ('Like

and academic discipline, and as a scientific method for the study of different legal systems'.[42] Metaphors[43] and comparisons[44] are essential to comprehend new concepts and organise thought. Therefore, the dilemma – whether comparative law is a discipline or a method – is a false dichotomy, because comparative law is an autonomous discipline based on the comparative method.[45] Arguably, 'those who view comparative law as a method and those who regard it as a science look at comparative law from different angles'.[46] Furthermore, 'a sharp dichotomy between science and method can be epistemologically dangerous. There is no science without method'.[47] More importantly, keeping in mind the coexistence of both discipline and method helps the scholar apply the comparative method to new subject areas, eventually contributing to the expansion of comparative law.

Although comparative law scholars and practitioners have different views on the objectives, methods and prerogatives of comparative law, the controversial nature of such law does not eliminate its legal nature; by way of contrast, the awareness of its controversies may only benefit legal analysis. This section aims to offer some insights on the origins of comparative law, its *modus operandi* and its objectives.

Comparative law became an autonomous legal discipline at the end of the nineteenth century.[48] The ascent of comparative law was precipitated

---

other sciences, comparative law remains a science'); D. Kiekbaev, 'Comparative Law: Method, Science or Educational Discipline?', *Electronic Journal of Comparative Law* 7 (2003), 1–7, 4 (defining comparative law as a legal method and a scientific discipline).

[42] G. Mousourakis, 'How Comparative Law Can Contribute to the Development of a General Theory on Legal Evolution', *Tilburg Law Review* 14 (2008), 272–297, 276.

[43] Metaphor is a way of thinking or cognitive method for translating abstract ideas into concrete form. See G. Lakoff, 'Contemporary Theory of Metaphor', in A. Ortony (ed.), *Metaphor and Thought* (Cambridge: Cambridge University Press, 1993), pp. 202–251, 243 (highlighting that '[l]aw is a major area where metaphor is made real'), and G. Watt, 'Comparison as Deep Appreciation', in P.G. Monateri (ed.), *Methods of Comparative Law* (Cheltenham, UK: Edward Elgar, 2012), pp. 82–99, 91 (stressing the need to explore 'the poetic dimension', the persuasive rhetorical power and the 'aesthetic appeal' of metaphors).

[44] *See* E. Örücü, *The Enigma of Comparative Law – Variations on a Theme for the Twenty-First Century* (Leiden: Martinus Nijhoff Publishers, 2004), p. 11 (stating that 'Comparison is the essence of understanding').

[45] *Ibid.*, at p. 1.

[46] Mousourakis, 'How Comparative Law Can Contribute to the Development of a General Theory on Legal Evolution', 277.

[47] *Ibid.*, at 278, footnote 8.

[48] A. Pizzorusso, *Sistemi Giuridici Comparati*, 2nd ed. (Milano: Giuffré, 1998), p. 145; M. Ancel, 'Comment aborder le droit comparé (A propos d'une nouvelle "Introduction au droit comparé")', in *Études offertes à René Rodière* (Paris: Dalloz, 1981), p. 3.

by the development of international commercial relations and the growth of codification processes to modernise the state and facilitate the Industrial Revolution.[49] By the early twentieth century, comparative legal studies aimed at 'the unification of law or the development of a common law of mankind (*droit commun de l'humanité*)'[50] or 'common legislative law (*droit commun legislatif*)'.[51] At the first International Congress of Comparative Law, which was held in Paris in 1900, an eminent comparativist, Raymond Saleilles, asserted that the principal aim of comparative law is 'the discovery, through the study of different national laws, of . . . universal concepts and principles that constitute a relatively ideal law'.[52] In this regard, the more successful comparative lawyers became in detecting these principles, 'the less visible comparative law w[ould] be as a discipline'.[53]

The German *Begriffsjurisprudenz* (jurisprudence of concepts), a school of thought which then dominated European legal science, favoured the construction of 'grand schemes of systematization' by identifying general conceptual categories. The members of this school aimed at revealing 'the common core or essence (*Wesen*)' of legal concepts.[54] Scholars believed that 'a universal truth, hidden in historical and national variations', 'could be uncovered through legal comparison'.[55] Universalist threads appear in the writings of early comparativists, who saw many legal concepts as the 'common heritage of mankind'.[56] Following the tradition

---

[49] Mousourakis, 'How Comparative Law Can Contribute to the Development of a General Theory on Legal Evolution', 273.

[50] See generally C.W. Jenks, *The Common Law of Mankind* (New York: Frederick A. Praeger, 1958).

[51] Mousourakis, 'How Comparative Law Can Contribute to the Development of a General Theory on Legal Evolution', 274.

[52] R. Saleilles, 'Conception et Objet de la Science Juridique du Droit Comparé', in *Procès-Verbaux des Séances et Documents du Congrès International de Droit Comparé* 1900, vol. 1 (Paris: LGDJ, 1905–1907), p. 173.

[53] P. Glenn, 'Comparative Law: Problems and Prospects', *American University International Law Review* 26 (2010–2011), 935–968, 944 (noting that 'there is a clear parallel with Alice in Wonderland's Cheshire Cat who would slowly disappear while smiling . . . Perhaps the last comparative lawyer in the world will disappear leaving only a smile').

[54] Mousourakis, 'How Comparative Law Can Contribute to the Development of a General Theory on Legal Evolution', 275.

[55] A. Peters, 'New Approaches to Comparative Law', *American Society of International Law. Proceedings of the Annual Meeting* (1999), 366–369, 366.

[56] G. Del Vecchio, 'L'Unité de l'Esprit Humain Comme Base de la Comparaison Juridique', *Revue Internationale de Droit Comparé* 2 (1950), 686–691, 688 (claiming that 'une grande partie des principes et des institutions juridiques est le patrimoine commun de l'humanité tout entière de tous les temps').

of the *jus commune*,[57] comparative law was perceived as an expression of the universality of justice, seeking, in other words, to identify and map the common elements of human experience relating to law and justice.[58]

Functionalist approaches emerged later, emphasising that the starting point of comparative endeavours is the analysis of a concrete social problem.[59] The assumption is that every society faces the same problems and the role of law is to address these analogous challenges.[60] Finally, cultural/critical studies, considering rules against their cultural and social background, have recently emerged.[61]

Comparative legal studies focus on two or more systems of law[62] and can endorse different rationales and aims. Their primary aim is the knowledge of a plurality of legal systems.[63] This does not necessarily imply that comparative law is a mere theoretical exercise. On the contrary, comparative law can (and often does) adopt a functionalist approach and may have very concrete outcomes. By exploring how a concrete problem is solved in different jurisdictions, comparative law can constitute a useful tool for the construction or amendment of legal systems. Comparative law has an evolutionary or dynamic dimension in that it may stimulate change, eventually promoting the unification or harmonisation of different legal systems.[64] For instance, as mentioned, already at the end of the nineteenth century, legal scholars Lambert and Saleilles aspired at the unification of law and supported the search for the 'common stock of legal solutions' from the various legal

---

[57] The *jus commune*, in its historical meaning, was a hybrid of Roman law and canon law which formed the basis of a common system of legal thought in Western Europe during the Middle Ages. See J.H. Merryman, 'On the Convergence (and Divergence) of the Civil Law and the Common Law', *Stanford Journal of International Law* 17 (1981), 357–388, 359 (pointing out that 'Lawyers . . . attended the same universities, studied the same books in the same language (Latin), and taught in the same way, using the same authorities, to their own students. There was a common law of Europe, a common literature and language of the law, and an international community of lawyers').

[58] H.E. Yntema, 'Le Droit Comparé et l'Humanisme', *Revue internationale de droit comparé* 10 (1958), 693, 698.

[59] Peters, 'New Approaches to Comparative Law', 367.

[60] F.F. Stone, 'The End to be Served by Comparative Law', *Tulane Law Review* 25 (1950–1951), 325–335, 326.

[61] Peters, 'New Approaches to Comparative Law', 368.

[62] Örücü, *The Enigma of Comparative Law*, p. 1.

[63] R. Sacco, *La Comparaison juridique au service de la connaissance du droit* (Paris: Economica, 1991), p. 8.

[64] See, for example, M. Sarfatti, 'Comparative Law and the Unification of Law', *Tulane Law Review* 26 (1952), 317.

families.[65] Later attempts to use comparative law for unifying purposes include the research of a 'common core of legal systems' by Rudolf Schlesinger[66] and research for the unification of some aspects of European law.[67] These attempts at unifying laws and finding common principles may (but not necessarily) have underlying political motivation – for instance, to promote economic integration, 'create a greater feeling of solidarity among peoples'[68] and 'contribut[e] ... toward a better community of nations'.[69]

There are three main criticisms which come into play regarding comparative law: (1) the presumption of similitude (*praesumptio similitudinis*); (2) the term of comparison (*tertium comparationis*); and (3) state sovereignty. The first relates to the presumption of similarity. To compare two elements, comparative lawyers often assume their similarity or comparability. However, questions arise with regard to the scientific rigour of the presumption.[70] On the one hand, some authors highlight that comparative law may be superficial, as it necessarily investigates two or more legal systems rather than focusing on one:[71] 'It is hard enough to know in detail one branch of the law of one system, but to know ... its relationship with that of some other system ... is well-nigh impossible.'[72] On the other hand, grand comparative law projects risk collapsing into 'an infinite facticity'.[73] Furthermore, authors have

[65] C. Jamin, 'Saleilles and Lambert's Old Dream Revisited', *American Journal of Comparative Law* 50 (2002), 701–718.
[66] See R.B. Schlesinger, 'The Common Core of Legal Systems – An Emerging Subject of Comparative Study', in K.H. Nadelmann, A.T. von Mehren and J.N. Hazard (eds.), *Twentieth Century Comparative and Conflicts Law – Legal Essays in Honour of Hessel E. Yntema* (Leiden: A. W. Sijthoff, 1961), p. 65.
[67] See, for example, M. Bussani and U. Mattei (eds.), *The Common Core of European Private Law – Essays on the Project* (The Hague/London/New York: Kluwer Law International, 2002). For a critical approach, see, for instance, P. Legrand, 'European Legal Systems are not Converging', *International and Comparative Law Quarterly* 45 (1996), 52.
[68] R.B. Schlesinger, 'Research on the General Principles of Law Recognized by Civilized Nations', *American Journal of International Law* 51 (1957), 734–753, 749.
[69] *Ibid.*, at 753.
[70] M.S. McDougal, 'The Comparative Study of Law for Policy Purposes: Value Clarification as an Instrument of World Order', *American Journal of Comparative Law* 1 (1952), 24, 28–9.
[71] See, for example, M. Reimann, 'The End of Comparative Law as an Autonomous Subject', *Tulane European and Civil Law Forum* 11 (1996), 49 at 53.
[72] A. Watson, *Legal Transplants: An Approach to Comparative Law*, 2nd ed. (Athens/London: University of Georgia Press, 1994), p. 10.
[73] A. Riles, 'Wigmore's Treasure Box: Comparative Law in the Era of Information', *Harvard International Law Journal* 40 (1999), 221–464, 239.

highlighted the possible ethnocentric bias of any comparative endeavour,[74] questioning whether a lawyer trained in a certain legal system can truly understand another system without pre-judging it according to the legal categories that constitute her legal imprinting.[75] According to this line of thought, the fact of being raised in a certain legal culture determines certain procedural or substantive choices.[76] Comparatists risk considering their own legal system as the golden standard or normal point of reference. They risk considering 'the similarities that surface' as 'mirror images of the categories ... of law in the[ir] own culture'.[77] More fundamentally, the presumption of similitude 'violates requirements of ideological neutrality...: the comparavist should not favour similarity over difference'.[78]

The second criticism relates to the term of comparison (*tertium comparationis*) and the alleged unpredictability of the comparative method. Analytically, comparison requires 'two or more variables that are commensurable along a dimension (the *tertium comparationis*)'.[79] For instance, A is taller than B.[80] The neutral referent or term of comparison may seem attractive in theory, but may become misleading in practice. Multiple standpoints can be simultaneously valid, and depending on the perspective adopted, comparisons may have completely different outcomes. In other words, where one stands on any particular issue

[74] N. Demleitner, 'Combating Legal Ethnocentrism: Comparative Law Sets Boundaries', *Arizona State Law Journal* 31 (1999), 737.

[75] F.J.M. Feldbrugge, 'Sociological Research Methods and Comparative Law', in M. Rotondi (ed.), *Buts et Methods du Droit Compare/Aims and Methods of Comparative Law* (Padua: CEDAM, 1973) pp. 211, 214; G. Frankenberg, 'Critical Comparisons: Rethinking Comparative Law', *Harvard International Law Journal* 26 (1985), 415 (referring to the 'sceptical assumption that objective comparison is impossible because the comparatist's vision is totally determined by her specific historical and social experience and perspective').

[76] *See* V. Grosswald Curran, 'Comparative Law and the Legal Origins Thesis', *American Journal of Comparative Law* 57 (2009), 863, 866.

[77] Frankenberg, 'Critical Comparisons', 423.

[78] R. Michaels, 'The Functional Method of Comparative Law', in M. Reimann and R. Zimmermann (eds.), *The Oxford Handbook of Comparative Law* (Oxford: Oxford University Press, 2006), pp. 340, 369.

[79] J.H. Merryman, 'The Loneliness of the Comparative Lawyer', in J.H. Merryman, *The Loneliness of the Comparative Lawyer and other Essays in Foreign and Comparative Law* (The Hague/London/Boston: Kluwer Law International, 1999), pp. 1, 2.

[80] *Ibid.*

nearly always depends upon where one sits. Furthermore, in comparing two elements, scholars may confuse the two instead of keeping them separate.[81]

An example may clarify the issue at stake. Let us imagine a debate on the shade of colour *alpha* which is neither black nor red. Is *alpha* a *red* colour with a black glance or a *black* colour with a red glance? Some may even hypothesise that the essence of *alpha* is purple. Whatever the shade, it is evident that if *alpha* is compared to other red colours, it will look black; if it is compared to black colours, it will look red. Instead, if *alpha* is compared to black and red colours all together, its shade will appear similar to purple. In conclusion, depending on the particular perspective adopted, the results of the comparative process may be very different. Another parallel risk is given by cherry-picking: that is, using analogies only when they agree with one's own thinking, or 'to deliver additional arguments for what has politically already been decided'.[82]

The third criticism relies on state sovereignty. Comparative law scholars have sometimes promoted ambitious normative projects for the uniformity of law.[83] For instance, some 'proposed to look to the majority solution of legal orders to find a "droit idéal relatif", but why should majority suggest superiority?'[84] Perhaps the most famous articulation of this critique is the argument that courts should not impose 'foreign moods, fads, or fashions' on their audiences, as this would infringe the principle of separation of power, state sovereignty and regulatory autonomy, ultimately undermining the very legitimacy of the adjudicators.[85]

These criticisms have the merit of showing certain limits and risks of any comparative endeavour. The interpreter must be aware of the perspective selected to avoid the risks mentioned above. For instance, with regard to the breadth of the discipline, one may well focus on certain aspects, leaving other aspects to subsequent studies. In any

---

[81] Talking about comparisons, Wittgenstein pointed out the great risk of confusing the prototype with the object of comparison, which we are viewing in its light. L. Wittgenstein, *Culture and Value* (G.H. Von Wright, ed., Peter Winch, trans., Oxford: Basil Blackwell, 1980), p. 14.

[82] Siems, 'The End of Comparative Law', 136.

[83] Michaels, 'The Functional Method of Comparative Law', 373.   [84] *Ibid.*

[85] *Lawrence* v. *Texas*, 123 Ct 2472, 2495 (2003) (Scalia J), and *Foster* v. *Florida*, 537 US 990 (2002) (Thomas J.).

case, law – as any other social science – cannot be conceived as a 'mathematically organized system of jurisprudence'.[86] Instead, as one comparative lawyer put it, comparative legal studies have accepted their 'inevitable imprecision', and admitted their own 'fuzziness born of intuition and insight'.[87]

With regard to the cognitive bias of any legal scholar trained in a certain legal system, this question may have become moot in practice. It is not rare that scholars are trained in two or more jurisdictions and are therefore exposed to more than one legal culture. Globalisation has globalised legal careers.[88] The fact that scholars often speak one or more foreign languages facilitates access to primary sources and legal databases. Furthermore, not only can the willingness to understand and to appreciate the particular features of a foreign system contribute to the development of comparative law, but it can also further reflection on the examined legal systems themselves.

With regard to the methodological problem of confusing the *elementa comparationis*, this does not exist in comparative law alone, rather it appears as soon as analogies are drawn in different fields of study. Finally with regard to the sovereignty-related critique, harmonisation projects should not be confused with comparative legal studies; while comparative studies have accompanied harmonisation projects, and the historical origins of comparative law were characterised by the search for an ideal universal law, harmonisation projects do not capture the varied essence of comparative reasoning.

In conclusion, to argue that comparative law is useless because it is a risky enterprise would be going too far. Comparative law requires both audacity and carefulness: the mapping of foreign lands requires certain methodological choices and the selection of a particular scale and perspective. What seems important is not the adoption of a particular perspective, but the awareness that the comparative reasoning may lead to different results, and therefore, the perspective adopted needs to be spelled out at the outset.

---

[86] Grosswald Curran, 'Comparative Law and the Legal Origins Thesis', 865 [internal citations omitted].

[87] *Ibid.*

[88] T. Ginsburg, 'The Culture of Arbitration', *Vanderbilt Journal of Transnational Law* 36 (2003), 1335, 1337.

Comparative methods

Methodological concerns[89] have been featured prominently as 'the stock in trade' of comparative legal studies.[90] The debate on the methods and theories of comparative legal research has been particularly vivid in the past decades. Reflection about one's own method is an essential precondition for serious comparative research. This section distils a number of methodological dilemmas faced by comparative legal research, clarifies that there is no fixed one-size-fits-all method and identifies several diverging yet legitimate methods of comparative legal research.

Comparative legal studies face a number of methodological dilemmas. First, comparing different legal systems may require the crossing of linguistic borders;[91] 'every comparative legal study inevitably requires an act of translation'.[92] Yet, as English has become the *lingua franca* of international relations, materials in other languages are rarely taken into account.[93] Furthermore, each legal system uses language in its own way, using, for instance, a particular level of abstraction.[94] Some expressions may not be translatable or may assume different meanings in different legal contexts.[95] More substantively, the written

---

[89] The word method comes from Greek and is a combination of two words: along (μετά) and way (οδός). Literally method indicates 'way to go along the road' or 'certain manner to follow the way'. See J. Husa, 'Methodology of Comparative Law Today: From Paradoxes to Flexibility?' *Revue Internationale de droit comparé* 4 (2006), 1095–1117, 1096.

[90] M. Schor, 'Mapping Comparative Judicial Review', *Washington University Global Studies Law Review* 7 (2008), 257–287, 258 (noting that 'perhaps no field of legal inquiry faces deeper unresolved methodological problems'). See also A. Riles, 'Wigmore's Treasure Box: Comparative Law in the Era of Information, *Harvard International Law Journal* 40 (1999) 221, 224 (noting that 'a collective crisis of methodological confidence is something of a defining genre of comparative legal scholarship, as each commentator outdoes the next with dire critiques of the field and timid solutions for its reconfiguration').

[91] See, for example, S. Glanert (ed.), *Comparative Law: Engaging Translation* (London: Routledge, 2014).

[92] S. Glanert, 'The Challenge of Translation', in M. Palmer (ed.), *ADR and Legal Practice in Comparative Perspective* (Beijing: China University of Political Science and Law Press, 2013), pp. 370–380, p. 370 (highlighting the most important problems arising from translation in the context of comparative legal studies).

[93] Siems, 'The End of Comparative Law', 137.

[94] See, for example, A. Kocbek, 'Language and Culture in International Legal Communication', *Managing Global Transitions* 4 (2006), 231–247.

[95] R. Sacco, 'Legal Formants: A Dynamic Approach to Comparative Law', *American Journal of Comparative Law* 39 (1991), 1–34, 12 (pinpointing that 'Not only can two codes in different countries use the same words with different meanings, but two codes in the same

text, Rabel argued, does not suffice for a sound comparative study; rather, the comparative lawyer should consider the context of a given norm and its actual application.[96]

Second, one may wonder whether a methodology is needed at all. Famously, the philosopher of science Paul Feyerabend contends that

> the idea of a method which contains firm, unchanging, and absolutely binding principles for conducting the business of science meets considerable difficulty when confronted with the result of historical research. We find, then, that there is no single rule – however plausible and however firmly grounded in epistemology – that is not violated at some time or other ... [Such violations] are necessary for progress.[97]

The Copernican revolution, the development of the quantum theory and the emergence of the wave theory of light among others 'occurred only because some thinkers either *decided* not to be bound by certain "obvious" methodological rules, or because they *unwittingly broke* them'.[98] Feyerabend argues that scientists should adopt 'a pluralistic methodology', 'compar[ing] ideas with other ideas', 'trying to improve rather than discard[ing] the views that have failed in the competition'.[99]

Some scholars contend that Feyerabend's ideas are not necessarily transposable in the legal field,[100] where the principle of legality requires judges to interpret and apply the law rather than create it. If international judges deliberately admitted that they create the law, they would undermine their legitimacy, because of an implicit separation of power between the legislative and adjudicative functions. While there is no single parliament at the international law level, the sources of international law are well delimited. Yet, Feyerabend's ideas have their merit as they show that 'all methodologies ... have their limits'.[101] This is not to say

---

country may give different meanings to the same words ... Words do not, in fact, have absolute permanent meanings').

[96] D.J. Gerber, 'Sculpting the Agenda of Comparative Law: Ernst Rabel and the Façade of Language', in A. Riles (ed.), *Rethinking the Masters of Comparative Law* (Oxford and Portland, Oregon: Hart Publishing, 2001), p. 199. See also D.J. Gerber, 'Towards a Language of Comparative Law', *American Journal of Comparative Law* 46 (1998), 719.

[97] P. Feyerabend, *Against Method* (3rd edition, London: Verso, 1993), p. 14.   [98] *Ibid.*

[99] *Ibid.* p. 21.

[100] See H.G. Gadamer, *Truth and Method*, 2nd ed., trans. J. Weinsheimer and D. G. Marshall (New York: Crossroad, 2004) (distinguishing the methodology of social sciences from that of natural sciences).

[101] Feyerabend, *Against Method*, p. 23

that 'anything goes', 'but a recognition that the comparison of laws has always varied in its methods according to circumstance'.[102]

Third, there is no single comparative method;[103] rather, several methods have developed over time.[104] The reason for this is rather straightforward: there are as many methods as research questions.[105] As the latter are varied, contingent and possibly infinite, countless methods can be envisaged and attuned to the variables of each research project.[106] In a sliding scale, the various comparative methods range from wholly functionalist approaches to purely cultural ones. Lying in between these extremes, several comparative methods include in diverse proportions different elements of these major approaches to the field.

Despite scholarly attempts to identify the best method for comparative research, comparative legal research remains under siege, surrounded by theoretical uncertainties and methodological dilemmas. What seems clear is that there is no best method *a priori*:[107] one method can be better than another with regard to a specific investigation; but this is not necessarily true in abstract terms and does not necessarily apply to every possible circumstance.

---

[102] H. Patrick Glenn, 'Against Method?', in P. G. Monateri (ed.), *Methods of Comparative Law* (Cheltenham, UK: Edward Elgar, 2012), pp. 177–188, 186.

[103] M. Adams and J. Griffiths, 'Against "Comparative Method": Explaining Similarities and Differences', in M. Adams and J. Bomhoff (eds.), *Practice and Theory in Comparative Law* (Cambridge: Cambridge University Press, 2012), pp. 279–301, 280.

[104] M.C. Ponthoreau, 'Le droit comparé en question(s) entre pragmatism et outil épistémologique', *Revue internationale de droit comparé* 57 (2005), 7–27, 23 (highlighting the existence of 'plusieurs methods'). See also P.G. Monateri, *Methods in Comparative Law* (Chelternham: Edward Elgar, 2012); V.V. Palmer, 'From Lerotholi to Lando: Some Examples of Comparative Law Methodology', *American Journal of Comparative Law* 53 (2005), 261–290 (pinpointing that 'there should be a sliding scale of methods and the best approach will always be adapted in terms of the specific purposes of the research, the subjective abilities of the researcher . . . '); Husa, 'Methodology of Comparative Law Today', 115 ('the idea of scale or methodological toolbox is relevant – there are a number of tools in the tool-box, however, which tools ought to be taken from that tool-box depend on the purpose of a given study'); Siems, 'The End of Comparative Law', 147–8 (stressing that 'there can be different approaches to comparative law research depending on its aim . . . exchanges and mergers of these different approaches . . . are also possible').

[105] Palmer, 'From Lerotholi to Lando', 290 (stating that 'there is not, and indeed cannot be, a single exclusive method that comparative law research should follow').

[106] *Ibid.*, 283 (suggesting the existence of 'a sliding scale of methods' and stressing, at p. 262, that 'the possibilities are endless').

[107] *Ibid.*, 290.

The functional approach – which has been regarded by some as the mainstream orthodoxy[108] – relies on the assumption that law addresses social problems and that all societies confront essentially the same challenges.[109] The functional approach thus presupposes similarity among legal systems (*praesumptio similitudinis*),[110] potentially reflecting epistemological optimism, that is, the belief that legal systems are comparable.[111] Concepts and institutions are compared because of their analogous function. This approach allows a great – yet arguably loose – methodological freedom.[112]

By contrast, cultural approaches reject a purely functionalist vision of law and contend that law expresses the cultural features of a society. Therefore, not only do comparativists need to consider the functions of legal concepts, but they should also take into account 'the respective legal systems and the broader cultures of which they are part'.[113] Meaningful comparisons require understanding the social, economic and cultural context of legal rules.[114] Cultural differences are presumed; cultural diversity is deemed worthy of protection; and legal unification is considered an undesirable outcome.

The battle of concepts between functionalism and cultural approaches to comparative legal research is epitomised by the famous 1974 dispute between two comparatists, Alan Watson and Otto Kahn-Freund. Alan Watson contended that there is no inherent relationship between law and society; being autonomous from any social structure, law develops by transplanting.[115] A legal concept can be moved from a context and

---

[108] Husa, 'The Methodology of Comparative Law Today', 1113; D. Gerber, 'System Dynamics: Toward a Language of Comparative Law?', *American Journal of Comparative Law* 46 (1998), 719–732, 722.

[109] See, for example, K. Zweigert, 'Méthodologie du droit comparé', in *Mélanges J. Maury* (Paris: Dalloz-Sirey, 1960), pp. 579–596.

[110] J. Husa, 'Methodology of Comparative Law Today: From Paradoxes to Flexibility?', *Revue Internationale de droit comparé* 4 (2006), 1095–1117, 1107.

[111] M. Van Hoecke, 'Deep Level Comparative Law', in M. Van Hoecke (ed.), *Epistemology and Methodology of Comparative Law* (Oxford: Hart Publishing, 2004), pp. 172–174.

[112] R. Michaels, 'The Functional Method of Comparative Law', in M. Reimann and R. Zimmermann (eds.), *The Oxford Handbook of Comparative Law* (Oxford: Oxford University Press, 2006).

[113] J.C. Reitz, 'How to do Comparative Law', *American Journal of Comparative Law* 46 (1998), 617–36, 626.

[114] P. Legrand, 'How to Compare Now?', *Legal Studies* 16 (1996), 232. See also M. Van Hoecke, 'Deep Level Comparative Law', in M. Van Hoecke (ed.), *Epistemology and Methodology of Comparative Law* (Oxford: Hart Publishing, 2004), pp. 165, 172.

[115] See generally A. Watson, *Legal Transplants: An Approach to Comparative Law* (Athens and London: University of Georgia Press, 1974).

applied elsewhere.[116] Inevitably, the concept will adapt to the new context. However, according to Watson, the adaptation does not imply the failure of the transplant; rather, it is a natural process.[117]

Kahn-Freund disagreed, believing that law cannot be separated from its context.[118] Kahn-Freund noted the 'far reaching free trade in legal ideas'[119] and that 'legal ideas are now moving freely around the world'.[120] He also recognised 'the flattening of economic and cultural diversity' due to 'industrialization, urbanization and the development of communication', as well as migration processes.[121] Yet, he pinpointed that legal systems are also embedded in given cultures. Kahn-Freund identified different degrees of transferability depending on sociological and geographical factors[122] and set out a two-step process to ascertain if a legal transplant was feasible. First, one should consider the connection between the legal rule that she wants to transplant and the socio-political structure of the donor state. Second, one should compare the socio-political structure of donor and receiving states.[123] Therefore, not only should one verify whether the item that would be borrowed has proven satisfactory in its country of origin, but she should consider whether it would be suitable to the potentially recipient country.

More recently, Pierre Legrand gave new emphasis to the cultural approach, arguing that law is a cultural phenomenon and legal rules are embedded in a given culture. As social, economic and political factors are in constant interaction with law, each legal system is unique.[124] Even the interpreter's epistemological assumptions, Legrand argues, are culturally conditioned.[125] The cultural turn of comparative legal studies, that is,

---

[116] See A. Watson, 'Comparative Law and Legal Change', *Cambridge Law Journal* 37 (1978), 313, at 314–5.

[117] Watson, *Legal Transplants: An Approach to Comparative Law*, pp. 19–20.

[118] O. Kahn-Freund, 'On Uses and Misuses of Comparative Law', *Modern Law Review* 37 (1974), 1–27.

[119] *Ibid.* 10.   [120] *Ibid.*   [121] *Ibid.* 9.

[122] *Ibid.* 13 (pinpointing that 'The question is in many cases no longer how deeply [a rule] is embedded, how deep its roots are in the soil of the country, but who has planted the roots and who cultivates the garden. Or in non-metaphorical language: how closely it is linked with the foreign power structure, whether that be expressed in the distribution of formal constitutional functions or in the influence of [interested] groups . . . ').

[123] *Ibid.*, 6 (questioning: 'are there any principles which may assist us in measuring the degree to which a foreign institution can be "naturalized"? Can we do something to trace the line which separates the use of the comparative method . . . from its misuse?').

[124] P. Legrand, 'On the Singularity of Law', *Harvard International Law Journal* 47 (2006), 517.

[125] P. Legrand, 'What "Legal Transplants"?' In D. Nelken and J. Feest (eds.), *Adapting Legal Cultures* (Oxford: Hart Publishing, 2001), p. 58.

considering law as a 'cultural expression', contextualises law; 'what happens to legal rules ... depends to a great extent on the institutional settings in which they are used'.[126]

In its most radical form, the cultural approach suggests that comparing legal systems is comparing different worldviews. This argument recalls Savigny's view that law is an expression of the people's spirit (*Volksgeist*).[127] As the entire context of law can never be perfectly understood, legal systems become unknowable, the laws under comparisons incommensurable[128] and legal transplants impossible.[129] Unavoidably, Legrand's hermeneutical discourse implies the necessity of 'an organic method of comparison' to 'contextualize every object of comparison and thus capture its essence as a unique manifestation of the community'.[130] Yet, authors contend that cultural approaches constitute a deconstructive 'postmodern critique'[131] (*pars destruens*) rather than offering a constructive structured method (*pars construens*).

Both functional and postmodern methods have merits and pitfalls; whatever the approach adopted by the interpreter, methodological awareness should accompany her choices. In fact, the apparently diametrically opposed methods constitute a case of agreement to disagree (*concordia discors*), in which diverging opinions converge in stressing the importance of methodological awareness.

One could argue that an overly sophisticated methodology risks rendering comparative reasoning so complicated as to jeopardise further engagement. Yet, the standards of proper comparative research must be maintained.[132] Comparative legal research is 'a variant form of legal research'.[133] Therefore, for several aspects, it follows the methodological

---

[126] Banakar, 'Power, Culture and Method in Comparative Law', 78 and 93 (stressing the dialectical nature of the relationship between law and society).

[127] Palmer, 'From Lerotholi to Lando', 271.

[128] Siems, 'The End of Comparative Law', 140–141.

[129] P. Legrand, 'The Impossibility of Legal Transplants', *Maastricht Journal of European and Comparative Law* 4 (1997), 111.

[130] Palmer, 'From Lerotholi to Lando', 272.   [131] *Ibid.* 264.

[132] See, for example, K. Lemmens, 'Comparative Law as an Act of Modesty: A Pragmatic and Realistic Approach to Comparative Legal Scholarship', in M. Adams and J. Bomhoff (eds.), *Practice and Theory in Comparative Law* (Cambridge: Cambridge University Press, 2012), pp. 302–326, 305 (stressing that 'nuclear physics is beyond the intellectual faculties of most, but would anyone suggest that, as a corollary, the methodological standards of nuclear physics should be lowered?').

[133] J. Bell, 'Legal Research and the Distinctiveness of Comparative Law', in M. Van Hoecke (ed.), *Methodologies of Legal Research. Which Kind of Method for What Kind of Discipline?* (Oxford: Hart Publishing, 2011), p. 167.

patterns and adopts the methodological tools of cognate legal disciplines.[134] Yet, it also differs, as it presupposes the comparison between two or more fields of study. Therefore a larger number of variables must be taken into account. In this regard, as Merryman pointed out, 'In our domestic work we can be hedgehogs, but in our foreign law work we must be foxes.'[135]

In particular, differences between legal systems should be detected and taken into account; the cultural context of given norms should be considered; and the understanding of the borrowed items should be proper, accurate and contextual. More importantly, the comparatist should be aware of and make explicit her own perspective and selected methodological choices.[136] The selection of the use of certain countries as examples should be justified. If comparisons are made, these should be explicit rather than implicit. Some scholars warn that comparatists should consider 'the law in action',[137] that is, as it functions in practice and 'as opposed to the law in the books'.[138] Other scholars stress the need for a 'cultural immersion' as a prerequisite for effective comparative analysis[139] and adequately verified information.[140]

[134] F. Feldbrugge, 'Sociological Research Methods and Comparative Law', in M. Rotondi (ed.), *Inchieste di diritto comparato* (Padova: Cedam, 1973) p. 215 (noting that 'When lawyers indulge in what they consider scientific work, their method is usually to take up a subject, read and think about it ... and hope vaguely that all this will result in conclusions which are in some ways interesting, useful ... [T]here are almost no rules concerning research methods, except the one which says that the more legal provisions, cases and other pertinent material you read, the better the research').

[135] J.H. Merryman, 'The Loneliness of the Comparative Lawyer', in J.H. Merryman, *The Loneliness of the Comparative Lawyer And Other Essays in Foreign and Comparative Law* (The Hague/London/Boston: Kluwer Law International, 1999), p. 11, referring to a line by the Greek poet Archilochus: 'The fox knows many things but the hedgehog knows one thing', quoted in Isaiah Berlin's famous essay: 'The Hedgehog and the Fox' (1953), which is included in *The Proper Study of Mankind* (London: Chatto, 1998), a collection of his essays.

[136] Lemmens, 'Comparative Law as an Act of Modesty', 312–314.

[137] E. Erlich, 'Judicial Freedom of Decision: Its Principles and Objects', in *Science of Legal Method: Selected Essays by Various Authors*, transl. E. Bruncken and L.B. Register (New York: A.M. Kelley, 1969) (1917), pp. 47, 51–53.

[138] M. Rheinstein, 'Comparative Law and Conflict of Laws in Germany', *University of Chicago Law Review* 2 (1934), 232.

[139] V. Grosswald Curran, 'Cultural Immersion: Differences and Categories in US Comparative Law', *American Journal of Comparative Law* 46 (1998), 43.

[140] For instance, adjudicators should be wary of relying on sources provided by the parties without further research as to whether the case mentioned by one of the parties has not been appealed and/or reversed and/or constitutes an authority in the relevant system.

Analogies as a tool of legal interpretation

Described as 'the core of cognition',[141] analogy – from Greek αναλογία, proportion – is the comparison between similar objects for the purpose of illuminating their understanding.[142] Analogy is the process through which people 'learn about a new situation (the target analogue) by relating it to a more familiar situation (the source analogue) that can be viewed as structurally parallel'.[143] In legal reasoning, the classic use of analogy is the argument that, 'because A and B are analogues, a rule X which ... is applicable to A is also applicable to B'.[144] The interpreter transfers meaning (X) from one context (A, i.e., the source) to another context (B, i.e., the target).[145] The target is supposed to be incomplete and in need for completion using the source.

Analogical reasoning indicates a cognitive process moving from the specific (in our example, A) to the general (in our example, X), and then back to the specific (in our example, B). Yet, it does not seem to be inductive nor deductive. While induction tries to achieve general conclusions, analogy looks for particular ones. While deduction moves from the general to the specific, the starting point of analogical reasoning is a specific case. Rather, analogy can be a case of imperfect induction (from A to X) or a case of hidden deduction (from X to B).

Whatever approach one adopts, unavoidably analogies include an evaluative component, that is, the search of the specific legal aim of a given norm (*ratio* or *anima legis*) which allows the same treatment of two analogous situations.[146] Analogies do not provide certainties: rather they are based on probabilistic reasoning.[147] Therefore, analogical thinking is a matter of controversy; sceptics contend that it may be

---

[141] D. Hofstadter, 'Analogy as the Core of Cognition', in D. Gentner, K. Holyoak and B. Kokinov (eds.), *The Analogical Mind: Perspectives from Cognitive Science* (Cambridge, MA: The MIT Press/Bradford Book, 2001), pp. 499–538.

[142] If two items are identical, there is no analogy but identity. See L.C. Becker, 'Analogy in Legal Reasoning', *Ethics* 83 (1973), 248–255, 248.

[143] K.J. Holyoak and P. Thagard, 'The Analogical Mind', *American Psychologist* 52 (1997), 35–44.

[144] Becker, 'Analogy in Legal Reasoning', 249.

[145] A. Juthe, 'Argument by Analogy', *Argumentation* 19 (2005), 1–27, 4.

[146] L. Gianformaggio, 'L'analogia giuridica', in L. Gianformaggio, *Studi sulla giustificazione giuridica* (Torino: Giappichelli, 1986), pp. 131–147.

[147] P. Borsellino, 'L'analogia nella logica del diritto: un contributo di Norberto Bobbio alla metodologia giuridica', *Rivista internazionale di filosofia del diritto* LXII (1985), 3–39, 35.

theoretically unsound and practically dangerous,[148] maintaining that the use of analogies is not a form of 'reasoning' at all[149] and that, at best, it is a method for 'querying (or quarrying)' previous cases for ideas, information and/or persuasion in settling analogue cases.[150] Others have cautioned against forms of 'legal romanticism'.[151] For instance, Ronald Dworkin stated that 'an analogy is a way of stating a conclusion, not a way of reaching one'.[152]

Certainly analogy is 'the basic pattern of legal reasoning'[153] and constitutes a complex type of argumentation.[154] Philosophers and lawyers have discussed analogical reasoning since antiquity. For instance, analogies and metaphors are at the heart of Plato and Aristotle's writings.[155] Analogical reasoning entails a great deal of judicial discretion; the adjudicator ultimately decides the question as to whether two issues are similar and deserve the same legal treatment. Therefore, legal systems have governed analogical reasoning in different fashions. For instance, in Roman law, the Justinian's *Codex* prohibited reasoning by analogy, requiring adjudicators to rule by law rather than by example.[156]

In civil law systems, however, analogies are a familiar tool of legal interpretation. When a given provision does not address a specific issue, judges are entitled to identify an analogous provision whose *ratio* applies to the case at hand (*analogia legis*). *Analogia legis* indicates the application of a particular provision aimed at governing a given A-type cases to similar B-type cases which are not governed by the given provision but are nonetheless considered to be similar to A.[157] The similarity is based

---

[148] G.J. Postema, 'A Similibus ad Similia—Analogical Thinking in Law', in D.E. Edlin (ed.), *Common Law Theory* (Cambridge: Cambridge University Press, 2010), pp. 102–133, at 107.

[149] R.A. Posner, *The Problems of Jurisprudence* (Cambridge, MA: Harvard University Press, 1990), p. 93.

[150] R.A. Posner, *Overcoming Law* (Cambridge, MA: Harvard University Press, 1995), p. 518.

[151] N. Bobbio, *L'analogia nella logica del diritto* (Torino: Istituto Giuridico della Regia Università di Torino, 1938), p. 134.

[152] R. Dworkin, 'In Praise of Theory' *Arizona State Law Journal* 29 (1997), 353, 371.

[153] E.H. Levi, *An Introduction to Legal Reasoning* (Chicago, IL: University of Chicago Press, 1949), p. 1.

[154] Postema, 'A Similibus ad Similia', p. 117; Bobbio, *L'analogia nella logica del diritto*, p. 87.

[155] See G.E.R. Lloyd, *Polarity and Analogy, Two Types of Argumentation in Early Greek Thought* (Cambridge: Cambridge University Press, 1966).

[156] *Justinian Code*, Book VII, title 45, para. 13 (stating that '*Non exemplis sed legibus iudicandum est*', i.e. adjudicators should rule by law rather than by example), cited by Postema, 'A Similibus ad Similia', p. 102.

[157] Becker, 'Analogy in Legal Reasoning', 249.

on the same reason of the law (*ratio legis*). When an analogous specific provision is not found to fill a given gap in the law (*lacuna legis*), several provisions are examined to detect an underlying purpose that might be applied generally (*analogia juris*). This process leads to the identification of general principles of law which are a source of law. Analogy from previous judicial decisions is also common, although these decisions are not binding authorities.

Analogously, the common law has recognised a significant role for analogies.[158] Precedents are a source of law. The courts are presented with 'a range of competing analogies – that is, competing candidates for source analogues that may pull in different directions'.[159] The courts have to ascertain whether and, if so, why a given case is more like one case than another.

Analogical thinking can lead to different outcomes depending on the selected comparator.[160] The requirements for analogy – that is, similarity and purpose – do not operate rigidly; rather they allow different combinations. Therefore, analogy has a 'multiplying effect', functioning like the technical constraints which inspire architects to develop different creative designs.[161] A classic example can clarify the issues at stake.[162] In *Hynes v. New York Central Railway Co.*,[163] a young man who had been swimming in the Hudson River died after climbing up on a springboard attached to the railroad's property and being struck by a falling high-tension wire. The plaintiff's lawyers argued that Hynes had the right to swim in a public river, that the trespass was purely incidental and that the railroad owed him duty of care. The railroad's lawyers countered that Hynes was a trespasser and therefore no duty of care was owed to him. Depending on the selected analogy – that is, comparing Hynes to cases concerning landowners' duties to trespassers or rather to cases concerning landowners' duty of care towards those exercising public rights – the outcome of the case would be different.[164] Justice Cardozo

---

[158] H. de Bracton, *Bracton on the Laws and Customs of England* (1250/1259) (S.E. Thorne ed.) vol. 2 (Cambridge, MA: Harvard University Press, 1976), pp. 21, 25 (stating that 'if like matters arise, let them be decided by like, since the occasion is a good one for proceeding from like to like'), cited by Postema, 'A Similibus as Similia', p. 102.

[159] Postema, 'A Similibus as Similia', p. 105.

[160] Posner, *The Problems of Jurisprudence*, p. 86.

[161] P. Legrand, *Le droit comparé* (Paris: Presses Universitaires de France, 1999), pp. 36–37.

[162] See R. Cross, *Precedent in English Law*, 2nd ed. (Oxford: Clarendon Press, 1968), p. 188; Becker, 'Analogy in Legal Reasoning', 249–250.

[163] *Hynes v. New York Central Railway Co.* (1921) 231 NY 229; 131 NE 898.

[164] Cross, *Precedent in English Law*, p. 188.

noted this[165] and concluded: 'The truth is that every act of Hynes from his first plunge into the river until the moment of his death was in the enjoyment of the public waters.'[166] *Mutatis mutandis*, the same considerations apply in other areas of law.

Analogia legis

Analogia legis indicates the application of a particular provision aimed at governing a given A-type cases to similar B-type cases, which are not governed by the given provision but are nonetheless judged by the interpreter to be similar to A. The similarity is based on the same *ratio legis*. The essence of legal analogies has often been distilled and summarised in the maxim: *ubi eadem ratio legis ibi eadem legis dispositio* (where the same reason exists, there the same law prevails).[167] The *ratio legis* or *ratio decidendi* – the principle underlying a given statute or a given case respectively[168] – allows the interpreter to evaluate commonalities and differences among different (but potentially analogous) circumstances.[169] Analogic reasoning has an evaluative nature.[170]

Yet, it is doubtful whether the distinction between *ratio decidendi* and *obiter dicta* matters in international law and/or applies to international courts and tribunals. On the one hand, there is no doctrine of binding precedent in international law. On the other hand, certain *obiter dicta* have played a major role in the development of international law. In this regard, Judge Anzilotti argued that 'there is no need to distinguish between essential and non-essential grounds, a more or less arbitrary distinction which rests on no solid basis and which can only be regarded

---

[165] *Hynes v. New York Railway Co.* 131 NE 898, at 899 (pinpointing that 'Jumping from a boat or a barrel, the boy would have been a bather in the river. Jumping from the end of a springboard, he was no longer, it is said, a bather, but a trespasser . . . ').

[166] *Hynes v. New York Railway Co.* 131 NE 898, at 899.

[167] R. Ross Perry, *Common Law Pleading: Its History and Principles* (Boston: Little Brown, 1897), p. 11

[168] See H.L.A. Hart, *The Concept of Law* (Oxford: Oxford University Press, 1961), p. 126, 128–9 (illustrating the concept of *ratio decidendi* with reference to a prohibition on the use of cars in public parks. If a lawyer considers whether this norm is to apply by analogy to bicycles, she examines cars and bicycles in the light of the *ratio* of the statutory rule. In particular, she asks whether the purpose of the norm, that is, the safety of pedestrian also requires the prohibition on the use of bicycles).

[169] V. Velluzzi, 'Osservazioni sull'analogia giuridica', in V. Velluzzi, *Tra Teoria e dogmatica* (Pisa: Edizioni ETS, 2012), pp. 65–84, p. 71.

[170] L. Gianformaggio, 'L'analogia giuridica', in L. Gianformaggio, *Studi sulla giustificazione giuridica* (Torino: Giappichelli, 1986), pp. 131–147.

as an inaccurate way of expressing the different degree of importance
which the various grounds of a judgment may possess . . .'[171] For instance,
the reference to *erga omnes* obligations may be the most often cited
element of the *Barcelona Traction* case,[172] even though this element did
not belong to the *ratio decidendi* of the case; rather, it was an *obiter dictum*.

Very often arbitrators make use of *analogia legis* when they interpret a
given provision expansively so as to include cases that were not envisaged
by the treaty makers. For instance, in *Maffezini v. Spain*, the Most
Favoured Nation Treaty clause was expanded to include procedural
safeguards.[173] This type of interpretation is not uncontroversial: in fact
while several subsequent tribunals have followed the *Maffezini* Tribunal,
adopting the same line of reasoning, others have preferred a more
conservative approach.[174]

Analogia juris

Analogia juris indicates that the norm to be applied is not explicitly
codified; rather, it is inferred from a whole group of norms expressing
a general principle.[175] General principles of law have long been debated
due to the methodological issue of how to distil them. Some have questioned whether judges are making law rather than interpreting it when
they rely on general principles.[176] There is a concern that adjudicators
will impose erratic rulings rather than following legal norms. However,
general principles of law are a source of international law[177] and may be
part of the applicable law.[178]

---

[171] *Factory at Chorzów* (*Germany* v. *Poland*), Interpretation of Judgments Nos. 7 and 8, 1927
PCIJ (ser. A) No 13, 16 December 1927, at para. 60. Dissenting Opinion by Judge
Anzilotti.

[172] *Barcelona Traction, Light and Power Company Ltd* (*Belgium* v. *Spain*) (Second Phase),
Judgment of 5 February 1970, ICJ Rep. 1970, 32.

[173] *Maffezini (Emilio Augusto) v. Kingdom of Spain* (Jurisdiction), 13 November 2000,
ICSID Case No ARB/97/7, 5 ICSID Rep 387.

[174] See, for example, *Salini Costruttori S.p.A. and Italstrade S.p.A. v. Hashemite
Kingdom of Jordan*, ICSID Case No. ARB/02/13, Decision on Jurisdiction, 9
November 2004.

[175] Bobbio, *L'analogia nella logica del diritto*; N. Bobbio, 'Analogia', in N. Bobbio, *Contributi
a un dizionario giuridico* (Torino: Giappichelli, 1994), p. 1.

[176] J.N. Hazard, 'Briefer Notice', *American Journal of International Law* 63 (1969), 179–180,
180 (noting the distrust of 'general principles' as 'spring[ing] from a feeling among
international lawyers that the term is used to mask capricious law-making').

[177] ICJ Statute, Article 38.

[178] ICSID Convention, Article 42(1) ('The Tribunal shall decide a dispute in accordance
with such rules of law as may be agreed by the parties. In the absence of such agreement,

The main function of general principles of law is to fill gaps in the law, and they are often used in emerging areas of international law.[179] As stated in an early case:

> International law, as well as domestic law, may not contain, and generally does not contain, express rules decisive of particular cases; but the function of jurisprudence is to resolve the conflict of opposing rights and interests by applying, in default of any specific provision of law, the corollaries of general principles, and so to find ... the solution of the problem.[180]

General principles help the interpreter to enlighten the silence, obscurity or vagueness of customary and treaty law. In identifying the rules applicable to a given problem, one should first look for any existing treaty provisions. In the event that any such obligations should not exist, one should then look to any applicable custom. Failing a sufficient solution being found in customary law, one should have recourse to general principles of law to avoid *non liquet*.[181] *Non liquet* expresses the idea that 'international courts have the duty never to refuse to give a decision on the grounds that the law is non-existent, controversial, or uncertain, or lacking in clarity'.[182] Since most investment conflicts are settled before becoming disputes, and disputes can be settled before or after registration at a relevant arbitral institution,[183] arguably, the cases that reach arbitral tribunals are difficult cases where treaty norms or the facts of a given case are ambiguous and several interpretations are possible.

The legal basis for applying general principles of law is multilayered. On the one hand, Article 38(1)(c) of the ICJ Statute requires the consideration of general principles of law as a source of international

---

the Tribunal shall apply the law of the Contracting State party to the dispute (including its rules on the conflict of laws) and such rules of international law as may be applicable'). Convention on the Settlement of Investment Disputes between States and Nationals of Other States (ICSID Convention), Washington, 18 March 1965, in force 14 October 1966, 575 UNTS 159.

[179] W. Friedmann, 'The Uses of "General Principles" in the Development of International Law', *American Journal of International Law* 57 (1963), 279, 279–280.

[180] *Eastern Extension, Australasia and China Telegraph Company Ltd* v. *US*, 6 RIAA 112, 114–115, 9 November 1923.

[181] ICSID Convention, Article 42(2) (stating that 'The Tribunal may not bring in a finding of *non liquet* on the ground of silence or obscurity of the law').

[182] See, for example, J. Stone, 'Non Liquet and the Function of Law in the International Community', *British Yearbook of International Law* 35 (1959), 124, 124.

[183] W.M. Reisman, 'International Investment Arbitration and ADR: Married but Best Living Apart', *ICSID –Foreign Investment Law Journal* 24 (2009), 185–192, at 187.

COMPARATIVE LAW, METHODS AND REASONING   41

law. It is generally assumed that this provision reflects customary international law.[184] On the other, treaty interpretation 'may require the
application of general principles of law recognized by civilized nations'
especially in those cases in which treaty provisions are vague.[185]

In order to clarify the content of general principles of law, it is apposite
to scrutinise the various components of this expression. The fact that
general principles are described as 'principles of *law*' shows that they do
not authorise adjudicators to proceed on the basis of non-legal considerations. Rather, recourse to general principles of law is conceptually
different from adjudication *ex aequo et bono* which requires the agreement of the parties, frees the adjudicator from the rigidities of positive
law and allows considerations of equity.[186] General principles of law are a
source of law and thus imply adjudication on the basis of law. In addition,
the fact that general principles are merely 'recognised' by nations
indicates that they are *existing* legal concepts, although they have not
necessarily been enacted or consented to on the plane of international
law.[187] The recognition of general principles is by nations and not by
states. This indicates that these principles are recognised worldwide,
constituting the common law of mankind.

Analogies in international law

Comparative reasoning lies at the heart of international law and takes
place in a number of areas. International law scholars have always relied
to a considerable extent on comparative reasoning to identify customary law and general principles of law.[188] The determination of state
practice – one of the constitutive elements of customary law – and
general principles of law rely on the comparison of the legal systems

---

[184] J. Ellis, 'General Principles and Comparative Law', *European Journal of International Law* 22 (2011), 949–971, 950.

[185] Schlesinger, 'Research on the General Principles of Law Recognized by Civilized Nations', 734.

[186] ICSID Convention, Article 42(2) (authorising adjudicators to decide cases *ex aequo et bono* if the parties agree).

[187] E. Lauterpacht (ed.), *International Law – The Collected Papers of Hersch Lauterpacht*, vol I (Cambridge: Cambridge University Press, 1970), p. 91 (acknowledging that although general principles of law are a source of law 'recognized to a large extent by the practice of States', they are 'essentially independent of it and ow[e] [their] validity to the very existence of the international community').

[188] See Schlesinger, 'Research on the General Principles of Law Recognized by Civilized Nations', 735.

from many countries in the world.[189] For instance, in the *Lotus* case, the Permanent Court of International Justice (PCIJ) surveyed decisions from a number of countries to ascertain whether a Turkish court could exercise jurisdiction over the officer of a French ship after collision on the high seas.[190]

Comparative reasoning has also played a pivotal role in the making of international law. Legal transplantation is a technique often adopted by treaty makers. For instance, the provisions against indirect expropriation in a number of international investment treaties derive from US constitutional law, specifically, the *Penn Central* test, articulated by the US Supreme Court.[191] In parallel, as the US Model BIT is often used as a template by a number of countries in their investment treaty negotiations, the *lex Americana* has become the gold standard in the area.[192] Other recent international investment treaties borrow the general exceptions provisions for the protection of public goods – including public health, environment and cultural heritage – from international trade law, especially Article XX of the General Agreement on Tariffs and Trade 1994[193] and Article XIV of the General Agreement on Trade in Services.[194] For instance, Canada has included a GATT-type Article XX exception in a number of investment treaties.[195]

With regard to interpretation, comparative reasoning plays an important role, as adjudicators do refer to the cases of other jurisdictions – be they national, regional or even international. As most international conflicts are settled before being brought before international courts and tribunals, cases that do reach international *fora* are often difficult cases relating to ambiguous rules or involving complex factual evidence. In the context of interpretation, comparative and international jurisprudence has been used to illuminate specific treaty provisions and analogical reasoning has been very common in the arbitral jurisprudence.

[189] *Ibid.*, 734.   [190] *S.S. Lotus Case (France v. Turkey)*, 1927 PCIJ (ser. A) No. 10.
[191] *Penn Central Transportation Co. v. New York City*, 438 U.S. 104, 124 (1978).
[192] J.E. Alvarez, 'The Evolving BIT', in I.A. Laird and T. Weiler (eds.), *Investment Treaty Arbitration and International Law* (New York: Juris, 2010), pp. 12–13.
[193] General Agreement on Tariffs and Trade 1994 (GATT 1994), 15 April 1994, Marrakesh Agreement Establishing the World Trade Organization, Annex 1A, 33 ILM 1153 (1994).
[194] General Agreement on Trade in Services (GATS), 15 April 1994, Marrakesh Agreement Establishing the World Trade Organization, Annex 1B to the WTO Agreement, 33 ILM 1167 (1994).
[195] C. Lévesque, 'Influences on the Canadian FIPA Model and the U.S. Model BIT: NAFTA Chapter 11 and Beyond', *Canadian Yearbook of International Law* 44 (2006), 249, 271.

Conclusions

In an evolving and increasingly interdependent transnational legal order, comparative reasoning has come to the fore, becoming a paradigm for legal analysis. Although the use of comparative reasoning is on the rise, the field remains beleaguered by a number of methodological dilemmas and theoretical uncertainties. While earlier comparative studies remained implicit about the methods they relied upon, more recent studies have addressed the question 'how to compare' with varied results.

There is no single method in comparative law; rather there are as many methods as research questions. As the latter are varied, contingent and possibly infinite, countless methods can be envisaged and attuned to the variables of each research project. This chapter has illustrated the most prominent approaches to the discipline, focusing on the functional and cultural methodologies. On the one hand, functional analysis helps in clarifying the multifold uses of comparative reasoning. However, it risks adopting an ideological approach. On the other hand, a cultural approach to comparative reasoning has the merit of highlighting the cultural wealth of various legal systems and their unique – at times converging and at times diverging – features. Yet, the extreme version of the cultural approach – contending that each legal culture is unique, culturally contingent and thus incommensurable – entails the impossibility of comparative reasoning. Therefore, this chapter highlights that both methods have merits and pitfalls and concludes that whatever the approach adopted by the interpreter, methodological awareness should accompany her choices. Both methods constitute a paradigmatic case of agreement to disagree (*concordia discors*). In fact, the apparently diametrically opposed methodologies converge in stressing the importance of methodological awareness.

One could argue that an overly sophisticated methodology risks rendering comparative reasoning unattainable. Yet, the standards of proper comparative research must be maintained. Comparative research is a type of legal research. Therefore, for some aspects, it follows the methodological patterns and adopts the methodological tools of cognate legal disciplines. Yet, for other aspects, it differs from other fields, as it presupposes the comparison between two or more areas of study. In particular, differences between legal systems should be detected and taken into account; the cultural context of given norms should be considered; and, more importantly, the comparatist should be aware of and make explicit her own perspective and selected approach.

After a brief scrutiny of the main characteristics of comparative law, methods and reasoning, this chapter has illustrated a number of constructive methodological choices. It then examined analogy as a tool of legal interpretation and the distinction between *analogia legis* and *analogia juris*. It then illustrated the use of analogies in international law.

The emergence of a transnational legal order has been seen as the next phase in the theory of comparative law,[196] while comparative analysis has been seen as the next phase in the theory of international investment law. The emergence of norm creation and enforcement outside the boundaries of the state; the increasingly important role of private actors; and the intermingling of private and public, and national and international dimensions of law which characterise international investment law constitute a new frontier which deserves further scrutiny. In this context, comparative studies may offer a useful lens through which to deepen the analysis of the emerging field of study. These intradisciplinary intersections may prove to be a fertile ground for methodological consolidation and offer opportunities for addressing issues in a new fashion. After briefly exploring the main features of international investment law, the following chapters will explore the role of comparative reasoning in this field of study.

---

[196] P. Zumbansen, 'Transnational Comparisons: Theory and Practice of Comparative Law as a Critique of Global Governance', in M. Adams and J. Bomhoff (eds.), *Practice and Theory in Comparative Law* (Cambridge: Cambridge University Press, 2012), pp. 186–211, p. 200.

2

International investment law and arbitration

The Kaleidoscope of Justice shows the different peoples of the world in all times and climes perpetually engaged in this perennial process of seeking to administer justice, in one or another fashion. The same recurring elements are found combining again and again in new designs.[1]

Introduction

International investment law constitutes an important part of public international law governing foreign direct investment (FDI).[2] The sources of international investment law include international investment treaties; customary rules of international law protecting the rights of aliens; general principles of law; and – as subsidiary means for the determination of rules of law – previous awards, judicial decisions and legal scholarship. As there is still no single comprehensive global treaty, investor rights are mainly defined by almost 3,000 international investment agreements (IIAs) that are signed by two or more states and are governed by public international law.[3] Under such treaties, state parties agree to provide a certain degree of protection to investors who are nationals of contracting states, including compensation in case of expropriation, fair and equitable treatment, most favoured nation treatment and full protection and security, among others.

---

[1] A. Riles, 'Wigmore's Treasure Box: Comparative Law in the Era of Information', *Harvard International Law Journal* 40 (1999), 221–464, quoting J.H. Wigmore, *A Kaleidoscope of Justice* (Washington, DC: Washington Law Books Co., 1941).

[2] J.E. Alvarez, *The Public International Law Regime Governing International Investment* (The Hague: Hague Academy of International Law, 2011). For an historical overview, see A. Lowenfeld, *International Economic Law*, 2nd ed. (Oxford: Oxford University Press, 2008), pp. 469–494; J.W. Salacuse, *The Law of Investment Treaties* (Oxford: Oxford University Press, 2010); M. Sornarajah, *The International Law on Foreign Investment*, 3rd ed. (Cambridge: Cambridge University Press, 2010), pp. 19–28; A. Newcombe and L. Paradell, *Law and Practice of Investment Treaties* (Alphen aan den Rijn: Kluwer Law International, 2009), pp. 3–57.

[3] UNCTAD, *World Investment Report 2011* (Geneva: UN, 2011), p. 100.

FDI can be defined as 'the transfer of tangible or intangible assets from one country into another for the purpose of their use in that country to generate wealth under the total or partial control of the owner of the assets'.[4] As contained in investment treaties, investment is an all-encompassing concept, including almost any kind of business activity. All assets of an enterprise, such as movable and immovable property, contractual rights, intellectual property rights, concessions, licenses and similar rights, are included. Given the broad scope of the concept, some investment provisions include both a general clause and an illustrative list of covered investments, as well as a negative list of areas specifically excluded from the scope of the agreements.[5]

The reason for protecting and promoting FDI is two-fold. On the one hand, historically foreigners have been amongst the vulnerable sectors of societies – easy objects of reprisal, without a vote or a voice in local political affairs.[6] Fundamentally, investment treaties aim at establishing a level playing field for foreign investors and a sort of shield against discrimination and mistreatment by the host state. On the other hand, the majority of economists and policy-makers see FDI as an engine for promoting economic growth and development.[7]

At the procedural level, most investment treaties allow foreign investors to file arbitral claims directly against the host state. This is a major novelty in international law as investors are not required to exhaust local remedies and no longer depend on diplomatic protection to defend their interests against the host state. Investment treaty arbitration is often selected as the adjudicatory model to settle investment disputes. The claims are heard by *ad hoc* arbitral tribunals whose arbitrators are selected by the disputing parties and/or appointing institutions. Depending on the arbitral rules chosen, the proceedings occur *in camera* and the very existence of the claim and the final award may never become public.

Due to its specific features and the recent boom of investment treaty arbitrations, international investment law has come to the forefront of legal debate. Once deemed to be an 'exotic and highly specialised'

---

[4] Sornarajah, *The International Law on Foreign Investment*, p. 8.

[5] See, for example, North American Free Trade Agreement (NAFTA), 17 December 1992, in force 1 January 1994 (1993) 32 ILM 289, Article 1101(2).

[6] See generally J. Paulsson, *Denial of Justice in International Law* (Cambridge: Cambridge University Press, 2005).

[7] J. Bhagwati, 'Why Multinationals Help Reduce Poverty', *World Economy* 30 (2007), 211–228.

domain,[8] it is now moving mainstream.[9] At the same time, investment treaty law and arbitration has raised a storm of criticism mainly due to the alleged lack of democratic insight and its impact on the host state's sovereignty. Investors have increasingly challenged regulatory measures in key sectors relating to a number of public goods, including but not limited to water services, cultural heritage and public health.[10] The recent boom of investment treaty arbitrations has attracted the increasing attention of the media and the public, not to mention the ever-growing academic focus on the field.

This chapter proceeds as follows. First, after briefly providing historical background, it explores the normative framework which governs FDI. Second, it highlights the most salient features of investor–state arbitration referring to the different paradigms through which this mechanism can be scrutinised. Third, the chapter briefly explores the backlash against investment treaty law and arbitration.[11] It then concludes that, albeit still undertheorised, this area of law promises to develop in conformity with and has the potential of contributing to the further development of international law.

Multilateral failures and bilateral successes

Efforts to constitute a set of global rules to protect investor rights and to settle potential disputes between host countries and investors have been pursued by industrialised countries for a long time.[12] A first attempt to create a unified global investment law was made at the Bretton Woods Conference in 1944. At the conference, the major international actors agreed on the importance of establishing international economic institutions to foster peace and economic growth, adhering to the charters of the International Monetary

---

[8] International Law Commission, *Fragmentation of International Law: Difficulties Arising from the Diversification and Expansion of International Law*, Report of the Study Group (Martti Koskenniemi) UN Doc. A/CN.4/L.682 (13 April 2006) para. 8.

[9] S.W. Schill, 'W(h)ither Fragmentation? On the Literature and Sociology of International Investment Law', *European Journal of International Law* 22 (2011), 875.

[10] See, for example, V. Vadi, *Public Health in International Investment Law and Arbitration* (Abingdon: Routledge, 2012).

[11] See generally M. Waibel, A. Kaushal, K.-H. Chung and C. Balchin (eds.), *The Backlash Against Investment Arbitration* (the Netherlands: Kluwer Law International, 2010).

[12] See, for example, R. Dattu, 'A Journey from Havana to Paris: The Fifty Year Quest for the Elusive Multilateral Agreement on Investment', *Fordham International Law Journal* 24 (2000–2001), 275–316.

Fund (IMF)[13] and the International Bank for Reconstruction and Development (IBRD).[14] Although the participants at the conference contemplated the establishment of an International Trade Organization (ITO), the Havana Charter – which included rules on investment – never came into force.[15] While the World Trade Organization (WTO)[16] in some ways has become 'the missing leg' of the Bretton Woods 'stool',[17] it does not include a comprehensive regulation of FDI.

The moves to adopt multilateral investment rules initiated at the first Ministerial Conference of the WTO, which was held in Singapore in 1996, had to be abandoned at the Ministerial Conference in Cancun in 2003, due to the growing opposition from developing countries and strong criticism from the NGO community. Similarly, the Organisation for Economic Co-operation and Development (hereinafter OECD),[18] a forum of thirty-four industrialised countries, attempted to establish a Multilateral Agreement on Investments (MAI),[19] but this effort collapsed because of the opposition from civil society. The MAI was a one-sided instrument, unilaterally prepared by OECD countries to ensure higher standards of protection and legal security for foreign investors. It did not adequately take into account the developmental needs of the host states, omitting crucial environmental and social issues.[20]

However, according to some authors, there are global rules on foreign investment.[21] On the one hand, several WTO instruments deal directly with areas of foreign investment. While the Agreement

---

[13] Articles of Agreement of the International Monetary Fund (IMF), 22 July 1944, in force 27 December 1945, 2 UNTS 40.

[14] Articles of Agreement of the International Bank for Reconstruction and Development (IBRD) as amended in 1965, 606 UNTS 294.

[15] Charter for an International Trade Organization (Havana Charter), Final Act of the United Nations Conference on Trade and Employment, held at Havana, Cuba, from 21 November 1947 to 24 March 1948, UN Document E/Conf. 2/78.

[16] Agreement Establishing the World Trade Organization, 15 April 1994, 33 ILM 1994.

[17] See J. Jackson, *The World Trading System* (Cambridge: MIT Press, 2002), p. 32.

[18] The Convention on the Organisation for Economic Co-operation and Development (OECD) was signed in Paris on 14 December 1960 and came into force on 30 September 1961.

[19] OECD Multilateral Agreement on Investment, Consolidated Text and Commentary, Draft DAFFE/MAI/NM(97)2.

[20] See S. Picciotto, 'Linkages in International Investment Regulation: The Antinomies of the Draft Multilateral Agreement on Investment', *University of Pennsylvania Journal of International Economic Law* 19 (1998), 731–768.

[21] See generally S.W. Schill, *The Multilateralization of International Investment Law* (Cambridge: Cambridge University Press, 2009).

on Trade Related Aspects of Intellectual Property Rights (TRIPS Agreement)[22] covers intellectual property, which is deemed to be a form of investment, the General Agreement on Trade in Services (GATS)[23] covers the provision of services through a commercial presence in another country. While the Agreement on Trade Related Investment Measures (TRIMS Agreement)[24] deals with performance requirements associated with foreign investment, the Agreement on Subsidies and Countervailing Measures (SCMs)[25] covers other investment-related issues as 'a variety of subsidies are often offered to foreign investors'.[26] Not only have 'investment issues' been 'explicitly raised in WTO disputes',[27] but even those WTO disputes that do not technically address investment-related issues have had investment-related implications.[28]

On the other hand, notwithstanding the persistent failures at the multilateral level, successful negotiations on investment protection have been undertaken at the bilateral and regional levels and a growing number of wider economic agreements establishing free trade areas (FTAs) have incorporated BIT-style provisions into an investment chapter. All these treaties are designed to clarify what standards of protection will apply to investments from one country into another and to provide a stable environment for such investments. Because of the similarities among these different investment treaties and the fact that they tend to be negotiated from a limited set of model BITs, it has been argued that investment treaties are incrementally building a *de facto* global investment regime.[29] While some consider investment treaties as evidence of

---

[22] Agreement on Trade Related Aspects of Intellectual Property Rights (TRIPS Agreement), 15 April 1994, Marrakesh Agreement establishing the World Trade Organization, Annex 1C, 33 ILM 1997 (1994).

[23] General Agreement on Trade in Services (GATS), 15 April 1994, Marrakesh Agreement Establishing the World Trade Organization, Annex 1B, 33 ILM 1167 (1994).

[24] Agreement on Trade-Related Investment Measures (TRIMS Agreement), 15 April 1994, Annex 1A to the Marrakesh Agreement Establishing the World Trade Organization (WTO Agreement), 1868 UNTS 186.

[25] Agreement on Subsidies and Countervailing Measures, 15 April 1994, Marrakesh Agreement Establishing the World Trade Organization, Annex 1A, 1869 UNTS 14.

[26] T.L. Brewer and S. Young, 'Investment Issues at the WTO: The Architecture of Rules and the Settlement of Disputes', *Journal of International Economic Law* 1 (1998), 457, 462.

[27] *Ibid.*, 457.   [28] *Ibid.*, 466.

[29] J.W. Salacuse, 'The Emerging Global Regime for Investment', *Harvard International Law Journal* 51 (2010), 431.

customary law,[30] others argue that such treaties are best seen as creating a *lex specialis* between the parties.[31]

As investment treaties are 'the most important instruments for the protection of foreign direct investment',[32] there is a general expectation that the conclusion of such treaties will encourage FDI.[33] Therefore, investment treaties are being strategically pushed by both developed and developing countries albeit for different reasons. On the one hand, host countries – generally developing and least developed countries – assume broad obligations for the protection of foreign investors in order to attract foreign investments. According to Guzman, least developed countries (LDCs) sign BITs because they 'face a prisoner's dilemma in which it is optimal for them, as a group, to reject the Hull Rule, requiring "prompt, adequate and effective" compensation in case of expropriation, but in which each individual LDC is better off "defecting" from the group by signing a BIT that gives it an advantage over other LDCs in the competition to attract foreign investment'.[34] On the other hand, developed countries have adhered to these dealings to protect the economic interests of their nationals and to possibly obtain favourable standards. The inception of modern investment treaties began in the late 1950s, when industrialised countries selected this mechanism to protect their nationals in response to waves of expropriation in developing countries as newly independent states emerged due to the decolonisation process.

---

[30] J.E. Alvarez, 'A BIT on Custom', *New York University Journal of International Law & Policy* 42 (2010), 63; A. Lowenfeld, 'Investment Agreements and International Law', *Columbia Journal of Transnational Law* 42 (2003–2004), 123–130. *Contra* see M. Sornarajah, 'A Coming Crisis: Expansionary Trends in Investment Treaty Arbitration', in K. Sauvant (ed.), *Appeals Mechanism in International Investment Disputes* (Oxford: Oxford University Press, 2008), p. 44.

[31] Sornarajah, *The International Law on Foreign Investment*, pp. 176–177.

[32] UNCTAD, *Bilateral Investment Treaties: 1959–1999* (Geneva: UNCTAD, 2000), p. 1.

[33] Earlier work did not provide support for such a positive impact. See M. Hallward-Driemeier, 'Do Bilateral Investment Treaties Attract Foreign Direct Investment? Only a Bit ... And They Could Bite', Policy Research Working Paper No 3121 (Washington, DC: World Bank, 2003). However, more recent research suggests that the empirically identified impact is positive. See A. Bénassy-Quéré, M. Coupet and T. Mayer, 'Institutional Determinants of Foreign Direct Investment', *World Economy* 30 (2007), 764–782; J. Tobin and S. Rose-Ackerman, 'Foreign Direct Investment and the Business Environment in Developing Countries: The Impact of Bilateral Investment Treaties', Yale Law and Economics Research Paper No. 293 (2005).

[34] See A. Guzman, 'Explaining the Popularity of Bilateral Investment Treaties: Why LDCs Sign Treaties that Hurt Them', *Virginia Journal of Transnational Law* 38 (1997), 667.

Recently, investment treaties have increasingly been signed not only among industrialised countries on the one hand and developing countries on the other, but also among LDCs and emerging economies. Therefore, the traditional distinction between capital importers and capital exporters has become blurred as emerging economies – like India and China – have become capital exporters.[35] As the primary objective of would-be investors is to obtain the effective guarantee that the host state will not act opportunistically once the investment has been made, investment treaties have come to play a major role in the growing competition to attract FDI and to provide conditions regarded as necessary to attract foreign investment.

Substantive standards of protection

While investment treaties differ in their details, their scope and content have been standardised over the years, as negotiations have been characterised by an ongoing sharing and borrowing of concepts.[36] The inclusion of the most favoured nation clause in most BITs drives convergence in treaty interpretation. Moreover, arbitral tribunals have constantly drawn upon earlier cases – which, albeit not binding, constitute *de facto* persuasive precedents – leading to the coalescence of a *jurisprudence constante*.[37] Therefore, some authors have highlighted the development of a *common lexicon* of investment treaty law.[38]

Typically, investment treaty provisions deal with the scope and definition of foreign investment, non-discrimination (both national treatment and most favoured nation treatment), expropriation and fair and equitable treatment. Other common provisions in investment treaties concern the repatriation of profits and other investment-related funds or the promise to freeze the existing regulatory regime for the duration of

---

[35] V. Vadi, 'Converging Divergences: The Rise of Chinese Outward Foreign Investment and Its Implications for International (Investment) Law', *Yearbook of International Investment Law* (2012), 705–724.

[36] C. McLachlan, 'The Principle of Systemic Integration and Article 31(3)(c) of the Vienna Convention', *International and Comparative Law Quarterly* 54 (2005), 284.

[37] See A.K. Bjorklund, 'Investment Treaty Arbitral Decisions as Jurisprudence Constante', in C. Picker, I. Bunn and D. Arner (eds.), *International Economic Law: The State and Future of the Discipline* (Oxford: Hart Publishing, 2008), p. 265; G. Kaufmann-Kohler, 'Arbitral Precedent: Dream, Necessity or Excuse?', *Arbitration International* 23 (2007), 357.

[38] C. McLachlan, L. Shore and M. Weiniger, *International Investment Arbitration* (Oxford: Oxford University Press, 2007), p. 6.

the investment (stabilisation clauses). A small number of investment treaties also include provisions prohibiting certain forms of performance requirements, that is, obligations on investors to act in ways considered beneficial for the host economy, mostly relating to local content, joint ventures, technology transfer and employment of nationals.

Investment treaties rarely mention the specific consequences in the case of non-compliance, when the host state violates a substantive standard of treatment. In practice, arbitral tribunals have held states liable to compensate investors for breaches of treaty standards that result in injury, relying on the *Chorzow Factory Case*.[39] In this case, the PCIJ held that 'reparation must, as far as possible, wipe out all the consequences of the illegal act and re-establish the situation which would in all probability, have existed if that act had not been committed'.[40]

Protection against unlawful expropriation and guarantees of compensation in the event of expropriation constitutes the core of investment treaties. In general terms, states can expropriate private property; such expropriations are lawful provided that certain conditions are met.[41] For instance, according to Article 1110 of the North American Free Trade Agreement (NAFTA), 'No Party may directly or indirectly nationalise or expropriate an investment of an investor of another Party in its territory or take a measure tantamount to nationalisation or expropriation of such an investment, except: (a) for a public purpose; (b) on a non-discriminatory basis; (c) in accordance with due process of law and Article 1105(1); and (d) on payment of compensation.'[42]

The concept of expropriation is broadly construed in investment treaties which protect foreign assets not only from the direct and full taking of property, but also from *de facto* or *indirect* expropriation. While direct and overt expropriations have become rare – after the nationalisations that marked the 1960s and 1970s[43] – indirect expropriation now

---

[39] The *Chorzow Factory* case involved the German government seeking damages for harm sustained by two German companies caused by acts of the Polish government. *Case Concerning the Factory at Chorzów*, Judgment on the Merits, 13 September 1928, 1928 PCIJ (Ser. A) No. 17, at 27–28.

[40] See also *MTD Equity Sdn. Bhd & MTD Chile S.A.* v. *Republic of Chile*, Award, 24 May 2004, ICSID Case No. ARB/01/7, para. 238.

[41] P. Comeaux and N. Kinsella, *Protecting Foreign Investment under International Law* (New York: Oceana Publications, 1997), pp. 77–78.

[42] NAFTA, Article 1110.

[43] See A. Akinsanya, 'International Protection of Foreign Direct Investments in the Third World', *International and Comparative Law Quarterly* 36 (1987), 58–75.

constitutes the typical form in which expropriations take place. Indirect expropriation refers to measures that do not directly take investment property, but which interfere with its use, depriving the owner of its economic benefits. As Professor Stern highlights, 'The prism of indirect expropriation includes a broad array of very different measures that do not involve a transfer of the investment but result in a serious interference with it.'[44] Treaty provisions lack precise definitions of indirect expropriation and their language encompasses a wide variety of state activity that could potentially interfere with investor property.[45] States tend to achieve the same result (of expropriation) by indirect means, interfering in the use of property or with the enjoyment of its benefits even where the property has not been seized and the legal title of the property is not affected.[46] For instance, the host state may target a foreign investor by imposing very high taxes or regulatory requirements which may make the foreign investment economically unviable. In *Starrett Housing v. Iran*, the Iran–US Claims Tribunal held that '[m]easures taken by a state can interfere with property rights to such an extent that these rights are rendered so useless that they must be deemed to have been expropriated, even though the State does not purport to have expropriated them and the legal title to the property formally remains with the original owner'.[47]

In particular, the central question raised by the so-called indirect expropriation is how to draw the line between legitimate regulations that do not give rise to compensation and regulatory takings that do.[48] States have an inherent right to regulate domestic affairs,[49] including private property and business activities. Moreover, 'due to the proliferation of treaties, states are increasingly becoming subject to international

---

[44] B. Stern, 'In Search of the Frontiers of Indirect Expropriation', in A. Rovine (ed.), *Contemporary Issues in International Arbitration and Mediation* (Leiden: Martinus Nijhoff Publishers, 2008), p. 35.

[45] L.Y. Fortier and S.L. Drymer, 'Indirect Expropriation in the Law of International Investment: I Know It When I See It, or *Caveat Investor*', *ICSID Review-Foreign Investment Law Journal* 19 (2004), 293–327.

[46] OECD, 'Indirect Expropriation and the Right to Regulate in International Investment Law', Working Paper on International Investment No. 4, (2004), pp. 3–4.

[47] *Starrett Housing Corp. v. Iran*, 16 Iran–US CTR (1983), at 112, 154.

[48] V. Lowe, 'Regulation or Expropriation?', *Current Legal Problems* 55 (2002), 447.

[49] *ADC Affiliate Ltd and ADC & ADMC Management Ltd v. Hungary*, Award, ICSID No. ARB/03/16, 2 October 2006, at para. 423.

obligations that require states to regulate'.[50] However, the exercise of such regulatory powers 'is not unlimited and must have its boundaries'.[51] There is no settled approach to cases where investors allege that certain regulatory measures constitute a compensable form of expropriation. Thus, as Professor Schreuer points out, today, the most difficult question for an arbitrator faced with an allegation of expropriation is not so much whether the requirements for a legal expropriation have been met, but whether there has been an expropriation in the first place.[52] Useful criteria to distinguish regulatory measures from indirect expropriation include the degree of interference (the extent, gravity and duration of the deprivation) and the character of the governmental measure (i.e. the purpose and the context of such measure). Principles like proportionality, reasonableness, non-discrimination and due process of law are seen as interpretative tools in assessing whether a regulatory measure amounts to a taking.[53]

For instance, after recognising that the identification of an indirect expropriation requires 'a case-by-case, fact-based inquiry', Annex B of the 2012 US Model BIT sets out a tripartite test to identify an indirect expropriation: (i) 'the economic impact of the government action …; (ii) the extent to which the government action interferes with distinct, reasonable investment-backed expectations; and (iii) the character of the government action'.[54] At the same time, the same Annex acknowledges that 'Except in rare circumstances, non-discriminatory regulatory actions by a Party that are designed and applied to protect legitimate public welfare objectives, such as public health, safety, and the environment, do not constitute indirect expropriations.'[55] This formulation was also present in the previous 2004 US Model BIT and has been imported into the text of other investment treaties due to the perceived authority of its source.[56]

---

[50] S. Olynyk, 'A Balanced Approach to Distinguishing Between Legitimate Regulation and Indirect Expropriation in Investor–State Arbitration', *International Trade and Business Law Review* 15 (2012), 269.

[51] *ADC* v. *Hungary*, Award, at 423.

[52] C.H. Schreuer, 'The Concept of Expropriation under the ETC and other Investment Protection Treaties', *Transnational Dispute Management* 2 (2005), 3.

[53] A. Newcombe, 'The Boundaries of Regulatory Expropriation in International Law', *ICSID Review–Foreign Investment Law Journal* 20 (2005), 1–57, and S. Ratner, 'Regulatory Takings in Institutional Context: Beyond the Fear of Fragmented International Law', *American Journal of International Law* 102 (2008), 475–528.

[54] 2012 US Model BIT, Annex B, 4(a).   [55] *Ibid.*, p. 4(b).

[56] See, for example, 2004 Canada Model BIT, Article 10. 2004 Canadian Model BIT (Foreign Investment Protection Agreement or FIPA), available at http://italaw.com/documents/Canadian2004-FIPA-model-en.pdf.

Doctrinal studies have attempted to clarify the distinction between indirect expropriation and the right to regulate. Notably, some authors and arbitrators have elaborated a two-fold test to verify whether regulatory measures may be deemed to be indirect expropriation or a legitimate exercise of police power. According to the proposed procedure, first, it must be ascertained whether a deprivation of property has occurred because of the effect of the measure taken. The answer to this question would be given through an essentially quantitative approach. Second, the conclusion that a given measure is potentially expropriatory may be modified through an essentially qualitative approach. One should take into account both quantitative and qualitative aspects, and 'the challenge is precisely to know where to draw the line in balancing the conflicting interests of investors and states'.[57] In conclusion, the identification of indirect expropriation depends on the case-by-case analysis of the specific facts.

The settlement of disputes between foreign investors and states

Investment treaty arbitration has moved 'from a matter of peripheral academic interest to a matter of vital international concern'.[58] When the International Centre for the Settlement of Investment Disputes (ICSID) was first established in 1966,[59] it was hardly foreseen that it would in due course become one of the most active international tribunals.[60] Investor–state arbitration has become a standard feature in international investment treaties since the 1980s, and such mechanism has been used increasingly. The ICSID renaissance is probably due to economic globalisation and the proliferation of investment treaties. The ICSID is not a permanent court: rather it is an arbitral centre offering dispute settlement

---

[57] Stern, 'In Search of the Frontiers of Indirect Expropriation', p. 44.

[58] S.D. Franck, 'Development and Outcomes of Investment Treaty Arbitration', *Harvard International Law Journal* 50 (2009), 435.

[59] Convention on the Settlement of Investment Disputes between States and Nationals of Other States, 18 Mar. 1965, 575 UNTS 159 [hereinafter ICSID Convention]. For commentary, see A. Parra, *History of ICSID* (Oxford: Oxford University Press, 2012); S. Puig, 'Emergence and Dynamism in International Organizations: ICSID, Investor–State Arbitration and International Investment Law', *Georgetown Journal of International Law* 44 (2013), 531.

[60] There are now 204 cases pending before ICSID. See *List of Pending Cases*, International Centre for Settlement of Investment Disputes, http://icsid.worldbank.org/ICSID (last visited 6 August 2015).

mechanisms, such as conciliation and arbitration to settle investment disputes. It keeps a list of arbitrators, from which the parties can select their arbitrators for the settlement of specific disputes.

Most contemporary investment treaties include investor–state arbitration for the settlement of disputes which may arise between the foreign investor and the host state.[61] Under this mechanism, foreign investors may bring claims against the host state before international arbitral tribunals. This development has transformed the landscape of modern investment protection as customary international law did not confer such a right to individuals.[62] Similarly, Friendship, Commerce and Navigation (FCN) treaties and investment treaties that predated the establishment of the ICSID only provided for state-to-state dispute resolution mechanisms.[63] In contrast with this traditional paradigm of states as the only subjects of international law and the only ones having the capacity to raise international claims against other states in legal proceedings, modern investment treaties do not require the intervention of the home state in the furtherance of the dispute.[64] Private companies no longer depend on the discretion of their home states in the context of diplomatic protection as to whether a claim should be raised against another state.[65]

Suggestively described as 'arbitration without privity',[66] the internationalisation of investment disputes has been conceived as an important tool for adequately recognising and protecting the assets of foreign investors from expropriation or other forms of state interference. Through arbitration clauses, the host state signatory to the treaty agrees

[61] See D. Sedlak, 'ICSID's Resurgence in International Investment Arbitration: Can the Momentum Hold?', *Penn State International Law Review* 23 (2004), 147.

[62] See J. Collier and V. Lowe, *The Settlement of Disputes in International Law: Institutions and Procedures* (Oxford: Oxford University Press, 1999), pp. 1–10; P. Muchlinski, *The Diplomatic Protection of Foreign Investors: A Tale of Judicial Caution*, in C. Binder, U. Kriebaum, A. Reinisch and S. Wittich (eds.), *International Investment Law for the 21st Century: Essays in Honour of Christoph Schreuer* (Oxford: Oxford University Press, 2009), p. 341.

[63] H. Walker, Jr., 'Modern Treaties of Friendship, Commerce, and Navigation', *Minnesota Law Review* 42 (1957), 805.

[64] See Newcombe and Paradell, *Law and Practice of Investment Treaties*, pp. 44–45.

[65] See M. Sornarajah, *The Settlement of Foreign Investment Disputes* (Aalphen aan den Rijn: Kluwer Law International, 2000), pp. 61–84; K.-H. Böckstiegel, 'Arbitration of Foreign Investment Disputes – An Introduction', in A.J. van den Berg (ed.), *New Horizons in International Commercial Arbitration and Beyond* (Kluwer Law International, 2005), pp. 125–131, p. 125.

[66] J. Paulsson, 'Arbitration Without Privity', *ICSID Review – Foreign Investment Law Journal* 10 (1995), 232, 256.

in advance to arbitrate disputes over the treaty meaning and application, at the investor's initiative. Such clauses are to some degree necessary to render meaningful the more substantive investment treaty provisions. As the late Professor Thomas Wälde once stated, 'it is the ability to access a tribunal outside the sway of the host state which is the principal advantage of a modern investment treaty ... The effectiveness of substantive rights is ... linked to the availability of an effective enforcement ... Right and procedural remedy, are, in practical and effective terms, one.'[67]

Arbitral tribunals constitute not only an additional forum with respect to state courts, but also an alternative to the same. Thus, not only can foreign investors seek another decision after recourse to the national courts, but they are not required to exhaust local remedies prior to pursuing an international legal claim. This is in stark contrast to international human rights treaties which require that claimants exhaust local remedies first. Even where contracts between an enterprise and a state expressly limit recourse to local dispute settlement options, claimants can directly bypass national jurisdictions and bring investment claims to arbitral tribunals in situations where the investor's home state and the host state have a BIT in place.[68]

Main characteristics of investor–state arbitration

Procedurally, the arbitral process in investment arbitration presents characteristics similar to those in a typical international commercial

---

[67] T. Wälde, 'The "Umbrella" (or Sanctity of Contract/Pacta Sunt Servanda) Clause in Investment Arbitration: A Comment on Original Intentions and Recent Cases', *Transnational Dispute Management* 1 (2004), 13; K.-H. Böckstiegel, 'Enterprise v. State: The New David and Goliath? – The Clayton Utz Lecture', *Arbitration International* 23 (2007), 93 (noting that the traditional David–Goliath relationship between private investors and states has been replaced, at least procedurally, by a level playing field and that in some circumstances, private claimants, as large multinational companies, may well have more resources available than a small state that is a respondent).

[68] Several ICSID cases have upheld jurisdiction to hear treaty claims, notwithstanding the fact that the foreign investor was party to a contract which specified that contract claims would be the exclusive province of a given domestic court. See *Compañia de Aguas del Aconquija S.A. & Vivendi Universal v. Argentine Republic*, ICSID Case No. ARB/97/3, Annulment Decision, 3 July 2002, para. 119, 41 ILM 1135, 1159 (2002); *CMS Gas Transmission Co. v. Argentine Republic*, ICSID Case No. ARB/01/8, Decision on Jurisdiction, 17 July 2003, 42 ILM 788, 808 (2003); *Noble Ventures, Inc. v. Romania*, ICSID Case No. ARB/01/11, Award, 12 October 2005, paras. 40–62.

arbitration.[69] The composition of the tribunal is determined by the parties who generally choose law scholars or professionals.[70] Arbitral rules require that arbitrators be independent.[71] While 'arbitrators ... are expected to be both independent of the party appointing them and impartial ... it is usually conceded that without violating in any way this theoretical obligation of independence, the arbitrator may quite acceptably share the political or economic philosophy, or "legal culture" of the party who has nominated him – and may therefore be assumed from the very beginning to be "sympathetic" to that party's contentions or favourably disposed to its positions ...'[72] Arbitrators have clear incentives to adopt a high level of standard of conduct because of reputation:[73] the arbitrator has an obligation to disclose potential con-flicts of interest; and the parties can challenge him or her if a conflict of interest is deemed to have arisen.

Confidentiality is one of the main features of the proceedings as generally hearings are held *in camera* and the documents submitted by the parties remain confidential in principle. Final awards may not be published, depending on the will of the parties. Even the names of the parties and the details of the dispute may not be disclosed.[74] While confidentiality may suit commercial disputes well, it may be problematic in investor–state arbitration because investment arbitrations can deal with regulatory disputes involving public policy matters. The lack of transparency may hamper efforts to track investment treaty disputes,

---

[69] N. Blackaby, 'Investment Arbitration and Commercial Arbitration (or the Tale of the Dolphin and the Shark)', in J. Lew and L. Mistelis (eds.), *Pervasive Problems in International Arbitration* (The Hague/London/New York: Kluwer Law International, 2006), pp. 217–233.

[70] J.A. Fontoura Costa, 'Comparing WTO Panelists and ICSID Arbitrators: The Creation of International Legal Fields', *Onati Socio-Legal Series* 1 (2011), 14 (highlighting that 'Virtually all ICSID arbitrators and *ad hoc* committee members have some legal back-ground, since only 0.4% of the whole population is composed of individuals who had not at least studied law. On the other hand, WTO figures are very different: 45% of panelists and 10% of AB members have no links to any legal background or professional activity').

[71] Salacuse, 'The Emerging Global Regime for Investment', 466.

[72] A.S. Rau, 'Integrity in Private Judging', *South Texas Law Review* 38 (1997), 507.

[73] See A. Lowenfeld, 'The Party-Appointed Arbitrator in International Controversies: Some Reflections', *Texas International Law Journal* 30 (1995), 59–72.

[74] For instance, Article 46 of the 2010 Arbitration Rules of the Arbitration Institute of the Stockholm Chamber of Commerce (SCC Institute) provides that unless otherwise agreed by the parties, the SCC Institute and the Arbitral Tribunal shall maintain the confidenti-ality of the arbitration and the award. The new arbitration rules entered into force on 1 January 2010. The text is available at http://www.sccinstitute.com.

monitor their frequency and settlement and assess the policy implications involved.

In recent years, efforts to make investment arbitration more transparent have been undertaken in different *fora*. In response to calls from civil society groups, the three parties to the NAFTA – Canada, the United States and Mexico – have pledged to disclose all NAFTA arbitrations and to open future arbitration hearings to the public.[75] Similarly, the ICSID Regulations provide for the public disclosure of the dispute proceedings under their auspices.[76] The ICSID Arbitration Rules now also grant ICSID Tribunals discretion to allow interested third parties to make written submissions in arbitral proceedings.[77] More recently, the United Nations Commission on International Trade Law (UNCITRAL) has enacted the UNCITRAL Rules on Transparency in Treaty-based Investor–State Arbitration, a procedural framework that provides for transparency and accessibility to the public of treaty-based investor–state arbitration.[78] The recent adoption of the United Nations Convention on Transparency in Treaty-based Investor–State Arbitration (the 'Mauritius Convention on Transparency'),[79] by which Parties to investment treaties concluded before 1 April 2014 express their consent to apply the UNCITRAL Rules on Transparency in Treaty-based Investor–State Arbitration, may increase the transparency of such disputes. Increasingly, investment arbitration tribunals have allowed public interest groups to present *amicus curiae* briefs or to have access to the arbitral process.[80] However, the vast majority of

---

[75] NAFTA Free Trade Commission, *Statement of the Free Trade Commission on Non-Disputing Party Participation*, 7 October 2003, 16 WTAM (2004).

[76] ICSID Regulation 22. The Administrative and Financial Regulations of ICSID are available at http://icsid.worldbank.org/ICSID/ICSID/RulesMain.jsp.

[77] ICSID Rules of Procedure for Arbitration Proceedings (ICSID Arbitration Rules), Arbitration Rule 37.

[78] The UNCITRAL Rules on Transparency in Treaty-based Investor–State Arbitration came into effect on 1 April 2014.

[79] United Nations Convention on Transparency in Treaty-based Investor–State Arbitration (the 'Mauritius Convention on Transparency'), adopted 10 December 2014, and opened for signature in Port Louis, Mauritius, on 17 March 2015, and thereafter at the United Nations Headquarters in New York. The Convention will enter into force six months after the deposit of the third instrument of ratification. The list of the parties to the Convention as well as signatories is available at http://www.uncitral.org/uncitral/en/uncitral_texts/arbitration/2014Transparency_Convention_status.html (accessed on 28 July 2015).

[80] See, for example, A. Kawharu, 'Participation of Non-Governmental Organizations in Investment Arbitration as Amici Curiae', in M. Waibel, A. Kaushal, K.-H.L. Chung and C. Balchin (eds.), *The Blacklash Against Investment Arbitration: Perceptions and Reality* (the Netherlands: Kluwer Law International, 2010), pp. 275–295.

existing treaties do not mandate such transparency and most of the proceedings are resolved behind closed doors.

Finally and perhaps more importantly, awards rendered against host states are, in theory, readily enforceable against host state property worldwide, due to the widespread adoption of the New York[81] and Washington Conventions[82] which provide for the prompt enforceability of foreign arbitral awards and ICSID awards, respectively. The awards have only limited avenues for revision and cannot be amended by the domestic courts.[83] Furthermore, ICSID arbitrations are wholly exempted from the supervision of local courts, with awards being subject only to an internal annulment process.[84] The ICSID annulment process provides for a very limited review. ICSID annulment committees only have the ability to annul awards and send them back to the tribunal or to a new tribunal for a new decision, but cannot replace the decision with their own. The grounds for annulment are very narrow and concern due process issues: that is, the tribunal was not properly constituted; it manifestly exceeded its powers; corruption on the part of a member; fundamental serious departure from a procedural rule; or the award did not state the reasons on which it was based.[85]

The different conceptualisations of investment treaty arbitration

Given its hybrid features, investment treaty law and arbitration has been analogised to different legal systems.[86] *First*, arbitral tribunals have been analogised to other public international law tribunals. For instance, due to the transfer of adjudicative authority from national courts to arbitral tribunals, it has been argued that access to investor–state arbitration shares many characteristics of the direct right of action before human rights courts. However, arbitral tribunals constitute not only an additional forum with respect to state courts, but also an alternative to the same. Thus, not only can foreign investors seek another decision after

---

[81] Convention on the Recognition and Enforcement of Foreign Arbitral Awards (New York Convention), 10 June 1958, in force 7 June 1959, 330 UNTS 38.

[82] Convention on the Settlement of Investment Disputes between States and Nationals of Other States (Washington Convention), 18 March 1965, in force 14 October 1966, 575 UNTS 159.

[83] New York Convention, Article V.   [84] ICSID Convention, Article 53.   [85] *Ibid.*

[86] See A. Roberts, 'Clash of Paradigms: Actors and Analogies Shaping the Investment Treaty System', *American Journal of International Law* 107 (2013), 45–94.

recourse to the national courts, but they are not required to exhaust local remedies prior to pursuing an international legal claim.[87] This is in stark counterpoint to international human rights treaties which oblige the claimants to exhaust local remedies in the first instance.

Arbitral tribunals have also been analogised to the WTO panels and the Appellate Body.[88] The case for drawing such an analogy is evident. On the one hand, arbitral tribunals and WTO dispute settlement panels essentially share the same functions by settling international disputes in accordance with international economic law. Like WTO panels and the Appellate Body, arbitral tribunals are asked to strike a balance between economic and non-economic concerns. Certain international trade treaties present an articulated regime that the investment treaties presuppose.[89] For instance, the subject matter of investment treaties and the TRIMS Agreement coincide to a certain extent.[90] Moreover, analogising international investment law to international trade law would impede the dilution of multilateral norms while providing predictability.[91] However, while only states can file claims before the WTO panels and the Appellate Body, foreign investors can pursue investor–state arbitration without any intervention of the home state. Furthermore, arbitral tribunals can authorise damages to the foreign investors, while remedies at the WTO only have prospective character and involve states only.

Second, given the fact that under most investment treaties, states have waived their sovereign immunity and have agreed to give arbitrators a comprehensive jurisdiction over what are essentially regulatory disputes, such review has been compared to a sort of administrative review.[92] Authors postulate the existence of a 'global

---

[87] However, denial of justice claims require the exhaustion of local remedies. See Paulsson, *Denial of Justice in International Law*, chapter 5.

[88] See generally T. Weiler (ed.), 'Intersections: Dissemblance or Convergence between International Trade and Investment Law', *Transnational Dispute Management* 3 (2011).

[89] C. Pfaff, 'Alternative Approaches to Foreign Investment Protection', *Transnational Dispute Management* 3 (2006), 1–16.

[90] Agreement on Trade-Related Investment Measures (TRIMS Agreement), 15 April 1994, Marrakesh Agreement Establishing the World Trade Organization, Annex 1A, 1868 UNTS 186.

[91] L. Hsu, 'Applicability of WTO Law in Regional Trade Agreements: Identifying the Links', in L. Bartels and F. Ortino (eds.), *Regional Trade Agreements and the WTO Legal System* (Oxford: Oxford University Press, 2006), p. 551.

[92] G. Van Harten, *Investment Treaty Arbitration and Public Law* (Oxford: Oxford University Press, 2007); D. Schneiderman, *Constitutionalizing Economic Globalization: Investment Rules and Democracy's Premise* (Oxford: Oxford University Press, 2008).

administrative space': 'a space in which the strict dichotomy between domestic and international has been largely broken down, in which administrative functions are performed in often complex interplays between ... institutions on different levels ... '.[93] Under this theoretical framework, investor–state arbitration has been conceptualised as a creature of global administrative law (GAL),[94] which impels states to conform to GAL principles and to adopt principles of good governance.

In particular, Van Harten and Loughlin claim that investment arbitration can be analogised to domestic administrative review since most investment disputes arise from the exercise of public authority by the state and arbitral tribunals are given the power to review and control such an exercise of public authority.[95] While investment treaty arbitration structurally resembles a private model of adjudication, substantively, it can be viewed as public law adjudication as it centres on the state's regulatory relations with foreign investors.[96] Adjudication over a state's *acta jure imperii* implies a significant departure from the conventional use of international arbitration in the commercial sphere.[97] Arbitral awards ultimately shape the relationship between a state, on the one hand, and private individuals on the other,[98] determining matters such as the legality of governmental activity, the degree to which individuals should be protected from regulation and the appropriate role of the state.[99] Many of the recent arbitral awards have concerned the determination of the appropriate boundary between two conflicting values: the legitimate sphere for state regulation in the pursuit of public goods, on the one hand, and the protection of private property from state interference, on the other.

---

[93] N. Krisch and B. Kingsbury, 'Introduction: Global Governance and Global Administrative Law in the International Legal Order', *European Journal of International Law* 17 (2006), 1.

[94] G. Van Harten and M. Loughlin, 'Investment Treaty Arbitration as a Species of Global Administrative Law', *European Journal of International Law* 17 (2006), 121.

[95] *Ibid.*, pp. 121–123.

[96] G. Van Harten, 'The Public-Private Distinction in the International Arbitration of Individual Claims Against the State', *International and Comparative Law Quarterly* 56 (2007), 372.

[97] Z. Douglas, 'The Hybrid Foundations of Investment Treaty Arbitration', *The British Yearbook of International Law* 74 (2003), 221–222.

[98] Van Harten, *Investment Treaty Arbitration and Public Law*, p. 70.

[99] M. Sornarajah, 'The Clash of Globalizations and the International Law on Foreign Investment', *Canadian Foreign Policy* 12 (2003), 17.

However, the fact that international investment treaty arbitration currently addresses the diagonal relationship between the host state and the foreign investors reflects an evolution which is present in other sectors of international law such as human rights law. Therefore, if this mechanism parallels the local judicial review of the courts of the host state, it should not be conceived as a substitute of the same, but as a different and additional venue expressly provided by international investment treaties. Investor–state arbitration is a creature of international law established by a treaty, and as such it constitutes a consensual delimitation of state power.

Third, because of the procedural rules which govern it, investor–state arbitration has been analogised to commercial arbitration. As mentioned above, arbitrators are selected by the parties and/or an appointing institution and the hearings are held *in camera*. However, the distinction between international commercial arbitration and investment treaty arbitration is clear: while the former generally involves private parties and concerns disputes of a commercial nature, the latter involves states and private actors and may concern disputes of a public law nature.[100] This 'diagonal' dispute settlement mechanism is a major novelty in international law since international disputes have traditionally involved states only. In this sense, investment arbitration represents a successful means to ensure access to justice at the international level.[101]

These paradigms for categorising investment treaty arbitrations all have merits and weaknesses and may diverge and converge on specific aspects. Most notably, none of them – but perhaps the international law and public law paradigms due to their comprehensive nature – fully encapsulates the complex phenomenon of investor–state arbitration. Although no single paradigm is hereby singled out for analysis as the leading paradigm, the author mainly relies on the public international law paradigm. As Crawford puts it, '[i]nvestment law . . . is about the way in which we bring the state under some measure of control, which is the main aspiration of general international law'.[102] Moreover, compelling

---

[100] See J. Paulsson, 'International Arbitration is not Arbitration', *Stockholm International Arbitration Review* 2 (2008), 1–20.

[101] F. Francioni, 'Access to Justice, Denial of Justice, and International Investment Law', *European Journal of International Law* 20 (2009), 729–747.

[102] J. Crawford, 'International Protection of Foreign Direct Investment: Between Clinical Isolation and Systematic Integration', in R. Hofmann and C.J. Tams (eds.), *International Investment Law and General International Law – from Clinical Isolation to Systemic Integration?* (Baden/Baden: Nomos, 2011), p. 22.

arguments stand in favour of assimilating arbitrators to international judges. From a historical perspective, adjudication traces its roots to arbitration. From a functional perspective, both judges and arbitrators 'exercise the ultimate decision-making authority of the juridical sovereign in public law'.[103] Like judges, arbitrators are asked to safeguard vital community interests as well as to settle disputes in conformity with 'principles of justice and international law'.[104]

In conclusion, these paradigms are not normative; rather they are descriptive in nature and emphasise some aspects of investment treaty arbitration over others. They are useful theoretical tools to better configure and understand investment treaty arbitration. While investment treaty arbitration is a relatively recent phenomenon and remains undertheorised, awareness of the existence of different paradigms promotes a better understanding and functioning of the same. Depending on the selected perspective the outcome of a given dispute can be different.[105]

International investment law and its discontents

The rise in investment treaty arbitration and its impact on public goods have raised a number of criticisms. On the one hand, investor–state tribunals are constituted *ad hoc*, under different arbitral rules and without an appellate court to ensure consistency in *dicta*. The resulting inconsistent awards have caused concern leaving many observers with the impression that international investment arbitration lacks structure and coherence.[106] On the other hand, given the fact that a number of arbitrations have affected public goods, ranging from access to water to tobacco control to cultural heritage management, some commentators contend that international investment law and arbitration is constraining the regulatory autonomy of the state, potentially privileging foreign investors over the public interest and/or imprudently using private commercial dispute resolution tools to resolve

---

[103] Van Harten, 'The Public-Private Distinction in the International Arbitration of Individual Claims against the State', 379–380.
[104] VCLT, Preamble.
[105] V. Vadi, 'Critical Comparisons: The Role of Comparative Law in Investment Treaty Arbitration', *Denver Journal of International Law & Policy* 39 (2010), 78.
[106] See S. Franck, 'The Legitimacy Crisis in Investment Treaty Arbitration: Privatizing Public International Law through Inconsistent Decisions', *Fordham Law Review* 73 (2005), 1537–1538.

public disputes.[107] According to some authors, investment treaty law and arbitration would be facing a 'legitimacy crisis' as arbitral tribunals consider important public policy issues; yet, there is uncertainty over the relevance or irrelevance of norms external to investment law within investment treaty arbitration. Have IIAs 'become a charter of rights for foreign investors, with no concomitant responsibilities or liabilities, no direct legal links to promoting development objectives, and no protection for public welfare in the face of environmentally or socially destabilizing foreign investment'?[108] Has international investment law become a 'corporate bill of rights'[109] or a 'system of corporate rights without responsibility'?[110]

Against this background, states have increasingly felt the need to protect their regulatory space and to limit arbitral discretion. While a few developing countries have withdrawn from the ICSID system,[111] others have omitted investor–state arbitration from the provisions of their treaties. For instance, the 2005 Australia–United States FTA does not include investor–state arbitration.[112] More recently, the prospect of including investor–state arbitration into the Transatlantic Trade and Investment Partnership (TTIP), a proposed free trade agreement between the European Union (EU) and the United States of America, has resulted in a polarised debate in the EU.[113] Others have adopted a preventive stance and have introduced general exceptions clauses in their investment treaties.

Such criticisms, however, do not play only a negative role indicating dissatisfaction with how the system works. They can also have a positive

---

[107] See generally M. Waibel, A. Kaushal, K.-H.L. Chung and C. Balchin, 'The Blacklash against Investment Arbitration: Perceptions and Reality', in M. Waibel, A. Kaushal, K.-H.L. Chung and C. Balchin (eds.), *The Blacklash against Investment Arbitration: Perceptions and Reality* (The Netherlands: Kluwer Law International, 2010), p. xxxviii.

[108] H. Mann, 'The Right of States to Regulate and International Investment Law: A Comment', in UNCTAD, *The Development Dimension of FDI: Policy and Rule-Making Perspectives* (New York; Geneva: UN, 2003), p. 212.

[109] T. Weiler, 'Balancing Human Rights and Investor Protection: A New Approach for a Different Legal Order', *Transnational Dispute Management* 1 (2004), 2.

[110] Mann, 'The Right of States to Regulate and International Investment Law', p. 215.

[111] For instance, Bolivia, Ecuador and Venezuela have withdrawn from the ICSID Convention. See S. Ripinsky, 'Venezuela's Withdrawal from ICSID: What it Does and Does Not Achieve', *Investment Treaty News*, 13 April 2012.

[112] See L.E. Peterson, 'In Policy Switch, Australia Disavows Need for Investor-State Arbitration Provisions in Trade and Investment Agreements', *Investment Arbitration Reporter*, 14 April 2011.

[113] I. Traynor, 'TTIP Divides a Continent as EU Negotiatiors Cross the Atlantic', *The Guardian*, 8 December 2014.

function in that they can be perceived as the necessary corollary to the vitality of the system shown by the recent boom of investment arbitrations as well as the willingness of states to participate in the system. Such criticisms can strengthen the system's legitimacy by raising important issues, stimulating debate and spurring novel approaches. They should be taken into account to allow the investment treaty system to develop properly. For instance, due to the increasingly widespread publication of arbitral awards and sustained commentary, some elements of a *jurisprudence constante* have emerged.

With regard to the criticism that international investment law and arbitration constitutes a charter of corporate rights without responsibilities, it is worth pointing out that in protecting foreign investors and their investments, international investment treaties do not have a revolutionary character. After the Second World War, property rights and the parallel right to compensation for expropriation were enshrined in the Universal Declaration of Human Rights,[114] the first Protocol of the European Convention on Human Rights (ECHR),[115] the American Human Rights Convention (ACHR)[116] and the African Charter on Human and Peoples' Rights (Banjul Charter),[117] as well as in the constitutions of many states.[118]

The balance between private interests and public interests at large is intrinsic to the same concept of property. The owner has the power to use what she owns, but she must use it lawfully. If one accepts an absolutist conception of property, interference with the use of property becomes *ipso facto* a breach of the relevant BIT. However, this absolutist view is a misconception of property. Comparative reasoning can make it easier for the public good to be taken into account in investment treaty arbitration, as most constitutional systems and even human rights

---

[114] Universal Declaration of Human Rights (UDHR), GA Res. 217(III) UNGAOR UN Doc A/810 (1948), 10 December 1948, Article 17.

[115] Article 1(1) of the First Protocol to the European Convention on Human Rights. Convention for the Protection of Human Rights and Fundamental Freedoms (the European Convention on Human Rights or ECHR), 4 November 1950, in force 3 September 1953, 213 UNTS 222.

[116] Article 21.1 of the American Convention on Human Rights, 22 November 1969, 9 ILM 673 (1970).

[117] Article 14 of the African Charter on Human and Peoples' Rights, 27 June 1981, in force 21 October 1986, 1520 UNTS 217.

[118] See V. Vadi, 'Through the Looking Glass: International Investment Law through the Lenses of a Property Theory', *Manchester Journal of International Economic Law* 8 (2011), 47.

systems which protect property as a human right also recognise the limits of property and the need for its regulation. For instance, the ECHR recognises 'the right of the state to enforce such laws as it deems necessary to control the use of property in accordance with the general interest or to secure the payment of taxes or other contributions or penalties'.[119] The ACHR similarly states that 'the law may subordinate [the] use and enjoyment [of property] to the interest of society'.[120]

Final remarks

By signing investment treaties, countries seek to make the regulatory framework for FDI more transparent, stable and predictable and, thus, more attractive to foreign investors. The ratification of treaties necessarily involves the surrender of a part of their sovereignty as states limit their regulatory autonomy in exchange for certain benefits.[121] In this regard, however, investment treaties are more intrusive than trade agreements as foreign investment takes place within the borders of a state. As one author puts it, 'While [investment] treaties may be a useful bulwark against egregious interference or expropriation of foreign-owned property, they may condition more subtle measures taken by governments . . . in the realm of regulation, taxation, legislation and judicial decision making.'[122] In addition, investment treaties provide foreign investors with direct access to the investor–state dispute settlement mechanism.

However, the right to regulate is a basic attribute of sovereignty under international law.[123] Traditionally, the sovereign powers of the state include the authority to adopt legislation, enforce judgments and adopt welfare policies. In certain cases, states have not only a right to regulate but also a duty to do so because of international obligations. In these cases, regulation has the function of safeguarding internationally or regionally recognised values, and international institutions that have

---

[119] First Protocol to the European Convention on Human Rights, Article 1.2.
[120] American Convention on Human Rights, Article 21.1.
[121] See generally W. Shan, P. Simons and D. Singh (eds.), *Redefining Sovereignty in International Economic Law* (Oxford: Hart Publishing, 2008).
[122] L.E. Peterson, *The Global Governance of Foreign Direct Investment: Madly Off in All Directions* (Geneva: Friedrich Ebert Stiftung Publisher, 2005), p. 4.
[123] M. Sornarajah, 'Right to Regulate and Safeguards', in UNCTAD, *The Development Dimension of FDI: Policy and Rule Making Perspectives* (New York/Geneva: UN, 2003), p. 205.

'rendered the erosion of sovereignty more legible, actually serve as a means to reassert sovereignty'.[124]

Therefore, according to some authors, investment treaty law and arbitration is facing a 'legitimacy crisis', as arbitral awards can affect public policy, but there is uncertainty over the relevance or irrelevance of norms external to investment law within investment treaty arbitration. Furthermore, while developing countries have deemed investment treaty arbitration politically biased against them, even industrialised countries have expressed some concerns about this mechanism. The criticisms on the functioning of investment treaty arbitration in relation to public goods should be taken into account to allow the investment treaty system to develop in accordance with public international law. Against this background, this study now explores the use of analogies in international investment law and arbitration.

---

[124] K. Raustiala, 'Rethinking the Sovereignty Debate in International Economic Law', *Journal of International Economic Law* 6 (2003), 841.

3

Comparative reasoning and international investment law

The more one became lost in unfamiliar quarters of distant cities, the more he understood the other cities he had crossed to arrive there, thus retracing the stages of his journeys. And he came to know the port from which he had set sail, and the familiar places of his youth; the surroundings of home, and a little square of Venice where he gamboled as a child.[1]

Introduction

Both comparativists and internationalists have largely neglected the role that comparative reasoning plays in international law. While '[i]nternationalists seem comfortable with power and uncomfortable with culture ... comparativists are eager for cultural understanding and wary of involvement with governance'.[2] Comparative lawyers do not usually focus on international law, perceiving it as a uniform system providing little opportunity to compare anything.[3] Rather, they are devoted to exploring the specificities of national systems.[4] In parallel, international lawyers' attitude towards municipal law has been one of caution: 'it would mean the end of international law if the municipal courts of a single country could create international law'.[5]

However, this attitude is gradually changing. On the one hand, due to the manifest increase in transnational relations, some comparativists

---

[1] I. Calvino, *Le città invisibili* [Torino: Einaudi, 1972], (W. Weaver Transl., London: Penguin, 1997), p. 28.

[2] D. Kennedy, 'New Approaches to Comparative Law: Comparativism and International Governance', *Utah Law Review* 2 (1997), 545–637, 633.

[3] M. Reimann, 'Comparative Law and Neighbouring Disciplines', in M. Bussani and U. Mattei (eds.), *The Cambridge Companion to Comparative Law* (Cambridge: Cambridge University Press, 2012), pp. 13–34, p. 18.

[4] But see the seminal W.E. Butler, 'Comparative Approaches to International Law', *Recueil des Cours* 190 (1985), 9, 58–61.

[5] H. Lauterpacht, 'Decisions of Municipal Courts as a Source of International Law', *British Yearbook of International Law* 10 (1929), 65, 85.

have highlighted the need for comparative legal studies to keep fulfilling their traditional role while, at the same time, adapting to new circumstances and integrating the most important transnational regimes.[6] In fact, domestic law is no longer self-contained; rather, it is responding to the top-down pressures of international law.[7] On the other hand, internationalists have similarly emphasised that 'the internationalist and comparativist share more than they realize'.[8]

Both comparative law and international law have long appeared as vague in their boundaries from other disciplines: legal positivists contended that 'international law is not really law',[9] and the autonomy and legitimacy of comparative law as a legal discipline has been contested.[10] Until recently, both comparative law and international law had a Westphalian,[11] if not Eurocentric, character.[12] For a long time, comparative studies (have) focused on European legal systems;[13] the law of former colonies, with the exception of US law, was largely overlooked. In other words, by limiting their focus to Western legal traditions, comparative legal studies contributed to the legitimisation of an order in which peripheral countries received limited, if any, recognition for their contribution to the market of legal ideas.[14] Comparativists (have)

---

[6] M. Reimann, 'Beyond National Systems: A Comparative Law for the International Age', *Tulane Law Review* 75 (2001), 1103, 1119.

[7] K. Lane Scheppele, 'Comparative Law: Problems and Prospects', *American University International Law Review* 26 (2010–2011), 950.

[8] Kennedy, 'New Approaches to Comparative Law', 557.

[9] J. Austin, *The Province of Jurisprudence Determined* (1832) (Wilfred E. Rumble ed.) (Cambridge: Cambridge University Press, 1995), pp. 164–293 (arguing that international law is not really law because it has no enforcement mechanism).

[10] H. Cooke Gutteridge, *Comparative Law: An Introduction to the Comparative Method of Legal Study and Research*, 2nd edn (Cambridge: Cambridge University Press, 1949), p. 41 (opining that '"Comparative law" denotes a method of study and research and not a distinct branch or department of law').

[11] Treaty of Westphalia: Peace Treaty between the Holy Roman Empire and the King of France and their respective Allies, 24 October 1648, available at http://www.yale.edu/lawweb/avalon/westphal.htm.

[12] W. Twining, 'Globalization and Comparative Law', *Maastricht Journal of European and Comparative Law* 6 (1999), 217–243, 233.

[13] H. Muir Watt, 'Globalization and Comparative Law', in M. Reimann and R. Zimmermann (eds.), *The Oxford Handbook of Comparative Law* (Oxford: Oxford University Press, 2006), p. 583 (arguing that 'if comparative legal studies are to retain their relevance in understanding the impact of global changes on existing local traditions . . . their focus needs adjusting').

[14] J. González Jácome, 'El uso del derecho comparado como forma de escape de la subordinación colonial', *International Law: Revista Colombiana de Derecho Internacional* 7 (2006), 295–338, 301 (affirming that 'se está contribuyendo a la legitimación de un orden

assumed that law is almost completely of European making, unfolded throughout nearly the entire world via colonialism, imperialism, trade and more recent neo-liberal structural adjustment programmes in developing countries, post-conflict reconstruction[15] and reform in countries in transition.

In parallel, international law has been characterised as having a predominantly Western character.[16] Former colonies played no part in the development of a number of rules of international law; rather, to a large extent, these rules were imposed on them and reflected 'the vested interests of the colonial era'.[17] Some authors have even questioned just how international is international law.[18] The origins of international law are imbued in civil law ideas; the fathers of international law, such as Gentili, Grotius and others, borrowed concepts from their domestic traditions which, in turn, regarded Roman law as the standard by which justice should be measured.[19] Furthermore, international law mainly governed relations among states, despite the fact that some treaties also regulated the interaction between states and indigenous peoples.[20] After the Second World War, common law has increasingly influenced the development of international law.[21] Therefore, according to some scholars, international law mainly reflects Western culture and attempts to universalise the values that it conveys.[22]

---

geopolítico en donde a los países periféricos se les atribuye poca posibilidad creativa en el mercado de las ideas jurídicas').

[15] See, for example, D. Zartner, 'The Culture of Law: Understanding the Influence of Legal Tradition on Transitional Justice in Post-Conflict Societies', *Indiana International & Comparative Law Review* 22 (2012), 297.

[16] A. Anghie, *Imperialism, Sovereignty and the Making of International Law* (Cambridge: Cambridge University Press, 2005); C.B. Picker, 'International Law's Mixed Heritage: A Common/Civil Law Jurisdiction', *Vanderbilt Journal of Transnational Law* 41 (2008), 1083–1140, 1095.

[17] L.C. Green, 'Comparative Law as a "Source" of International Law', *Tulane Law Review* 42 (1967–1968), 52.

[18] K.T. Gaubatz and M. MacArthur, 'How International is International Law?' *Michigan Journal of International Law* 22 (2001), 239.

[19] See generally B. Kingsbury and B. Straumann (eds.), *The Roman Foundations of the Law of Nations* (Oxford: Oxford University Press, 2010).

[20] A notable example is the Treaty of Waitangi, signed on 6 February 1840 by representatives of the British Crown and various Māori chiefs from New Zealand.

[21] Picker, 'International Law's Mixed Heritage: A Common/Civil Law Jurisdiction', 1105.

[22] E. Jouannet, 'Universalism and Imperialism: The True False Paradox of International Law?', *European Journal of International Law* 18 (2007), 379. See also J. Alvarez, 'Contemporary Foreign Investment Law: An Empire of Law or the Law of Empire?', *Alabama Law Review* 60 (2009), 943.

In the post-colonial era, however, there is an emergent awareness that diffusion of law does not necessarily lead to convergence, harmonisation, or unification of laws.[23] On the one hand, Koschaker and a number of comparativists contend that the reception of Roman law in Europe and the spreading of the *Code Napoleon* were more a matter of imperial power than of superior quality.[24] Others point out the multicultural genealogy of the Western legal tradition.[25] On the other hand, the imported law did not remain the same; legal transplants undergo meaning transformation once they are implanted into a new legal system and are 'transformed by the new context'.[26] For instance, Japanese scholar Masaji Chiba contends that 'The whole structure of law in a non-Western society is, seen from a cultural point of view, formed in the interaction between received law and indigenous law.'[27] Furthermore, in a number of countries, the so-called mixed jurisdictions, the Romano-Germanic tradition and the common law have met and mingled for historical reasons with varied outcomes.[28] Finally, economic globalisation has spurred the constant interaction among legal cultures, facilitating processes of mutual borrowing, cross-fertilisation and learning.[29] Therefore, many characteristics which define and shape legal

---

[23] See, for example, *Maritime International Nominees Establishment (MINE)* v. *Government of Guinea*, ICSID Case No. ARB/84/4, decision of the Annulment Committee, 14 December 1989, para. 6.39 (stating that 'French laws and regulations were not automatically applicable in the colonies in these matters. They had to be introduced in accordance with the principle of "specialité legislative". In this matter, the "Code Civil" was introduced, and the modifications locally enacted were not necessarily the same as those applicable in France. Consequently, certain discrepancies may be found between French law as applied in France, and local Guinean law').

[24] P. Koschaker, *Europa und das römische Recht* (1946, 2nd ed. 1953), discussed by K. Zweigert and H. Kötz, *An Introduction to Comparative Law* (trs, Tony Weir, 3rd ed., 1998), at 100. But see R. Sacco, 'Legal Formants: A Dynamic Approach to Comparative Law', *American Journal of Comparative Law* 39 (1991), 1–34, 2 (deeming the spread of Roman law due to its own inherent worth, quality and prestige).

[25] P.G. Monateri, 'Black Gaius – A Quest for the Multicultural Origins of the "Western Legal Tradition"', *Hastings Law Journal* 51 (1999–2000), 479, 484 (highlighting that Roman law is a multicultural product due to the interaction of different civilizations and that Western law is derived not only from Roman law, but from other laws as well).

[26] R. Banakar, 'Review Essay – Power, Culture and Method in Comparative Law', *International Journal of Law in Context* 5 (2009), 69–85, 82.

[27] M. Chiba (ed.), *Asian Indigenous Law in Interaction with Received Law* (London and New York: Kegan Paul International, 1986), p. 7

[28] N. Kasirer, 'Legal Education as Métissage', *Tulane Law Review* 78 (2003–2004), 481.

[29] J. Ellis, 'General Principles and Comparative Law', *European Journal of International Law* 22 (2011), 949–971, 966.

families 'are fading or spreading into other systems'.[30] At present, 'all legal systems are to different degrees hybrids, *i.e.*, cultural and legal mixtures consisting of various elements borrowed from different legal traditions and customs'.[31] In this context, the migration of legal concepts has become an increasingly common phenomenon,[32] highlighting the cosmopolitan, if not 'nomadic', character of law.[33] Finally, there is a growing awareness that given the diversity of the world's legal systems, polycentric approaches should be preferred.[34]

In parallel, non-state law, both within and across state borders, which used to be excluded from the purview of comparative studies and international law, has come to the fore.[35] Both comparative legal studies and international law have increasingly recognised the pluralism and polycentricism of law.[36] The idea that comparative studies should focus merely on the positive laws of nation-states has been overcome by a more pluralistic understanding of the law. Moreover, comparative studies can 'illuminate the marginalized, the excluded and silenced voices in the other – and one's own – legal . . . regime'.[37] Analogously, bottom-up approaches to the making of international law have gradually emerged.[38]

---

[30] Picker, 'International Law's Mixed Heritage: A Common/Civil Law Jurisdiction', 1094. But see V. Grosswald Curran, 'Romantic Common Law, Enlightened Civil Law: Legal Uniformity and the Homogenization of the European Union', *Columbia Journal of European Law* 7 (2001), 63 (stressing the enduring difference between civil law and common law systems).

[31] Banakar, 'Review Essay – Power, Culture and Method in Comparative Law', 74.

[32] S. Choudry, 'Migration as a New Metaphor in Comparative Constitutional Law', in S. Choudry (ed.), *The Migration of Constitutional Ideas* (Cambridge: Cambridge University Press, 2006), p. 1.

[33] A. Watson, *Legal Transplants: An Approach to Comparative Law* (Edinburgh: Scottish Academic Press, 1974), p. 108; Kasirer, 'Legal Education as Métissage', 481.

[34] U. Baxi, 'The Colonialist Heritage', in P. Legrand and R. Munday (eds.), *Comparative Legal Studies: Traditions and Transitions* (Cambridge: Cambridge University Press, 2003), 46 ff.

[35] Twining famously called the assumption that domestic law consists of the state law and that public international law consists of the law of sovereign states as the 'Westphalian duo'. See W. Twining, *General Jurisprudence: Understanding Law from a Global Perspective* (Cambridge: Cambridge University Press, 2008), p. 362.

[36] Banakar, 'Review Essay – Power, Culture and Method in Comparative Law', 82.

[37] P. Zumbansen, 'Comparative Law's Coming of Age? Twenty Years after *Critical Comparisons*', *German Law Journal* 6 (2005), 1073–1084, 1078.

[38] See A.-M. Slaughter, 'A Liberal Theory of International Law', *American Society International Law Proceedings* 94 (2000), 240, 241 (arguing that a liberal theory of international law includes bottom-up approaches). See also B. de Sousa Santos and C.A. Rodríguez-Garavito (eds.), *Law and Globalization from Below. Towards a*

It is a matter of time, but it is likely that the role of comparative reasoning in international law will receive increasing attention. This chapter contributes to this emerging area of study by examining the traditional entry points of comparative reasoning in international law. This phenomenon deserves close scrutiny because investment treaty tribunals make constant use of analogies in their reasoning. Arbitral tribunals refer to the jurisprudence of other international courts and tribunals, the awards of other investment tribunals or even to national 'precedents'.[39] Reference to scholarly analysis is not uncommon. Yet, arbitrators do not explain *why* they refer to a given legal system rather than another; they do not mention the legal basis of such analogical reasoning. This chapter explores the way international law itself empowers arbitral tribunals to adopt comparative reasoning.

Comparative reasoning may play an important role in 'legitimising' investment treaty arbitration. By furthering the judicial dialogue among international courts and tribunals, horizontal judicial borrowing from one international legal subsystem to another may facilitate the insertion of human rights considerations and other non-economic values into investment treaty arbitration, and have the potential for ultimately promoting the humanisation of international law. In turn, vertical judicial borrowing, that is, borrowing from regional and national cases, may be appropriate following the relevant rules of international law which govern treaty interpretation and the sources of international law. Comparative reasoning can help detect both customary international law and general principles of law.[40]

However, analogical reasoning may act as a legitimising force only if it complies with the fundamental rules of international law. If such rules are neglected, paradoxically, rather than being a legitimising factor, analogical reasoning may contribute to the 'legitimacy crisis' of investment treaty arbitration. While comparative reasoning has the potential to promote a more pluralist, universal conception of international

---

Cosmopolitan Legality (Cambridge: Cambridge University Press, 2005); B. Rajagopal, *International Law from Below – Development, Social Movements and Third World Resistance* (Cambridge: Cambridge University Press, 2003).

[39] There is no such rule as binding precedent in international law. *See* Statute of the International Court of Justice Article 59, 26 June 1945, 59 Stat. 1055 (stating that a 'decision of the Court has no binding force except between the parties and in respect of that particular case') [hereinafter ICJ Statute].

[40] G.A. Bermann, P. Glenn, K. Lane Scheppele, A. Shalakany, D.V. Snyder and E. Zoller, 'Comparative Law: Problems and Prospects', *American University International Law Review* 26 (2010–2011), 935–968, 938.

investment law,[41] it can also have an undermining effect if its methodological underpinnings are not harnessed. In fact, narrow inquiries can be plausible from a comparative law perspective, but may not necessarily be acceptable at the international law level.[42]

Comparative reasoning plays multiple roles in international law. First, comparative reasoning helps identify general principles of law, which are a source of international law according to Article 38(1)(c) of the Statute of the International Court of Justice (ICJ)[43] and its predecessor Article 38(3) of the Statute of the Permanent Court of Justice. Comparative reasoning can lead to the identification of general principles of law that are part of the applicable law in investment arbitration.[44] Although this source has long been 'highly controversial and largely neglected',[45] recent cases have demonstrated its growing importance.[46] While comparative lawyers claim that the identification and application of general principles of law is impossible without comparative analysis,[47] in fact international law scholars rarely rely on thorough comparative surveys.[48]

Second, in drafting relevant international investment treaties, treaty-makers often rely on comparative legal studies to find optimal alternatives or 'at least facilitate consensus'.[49] Third, systemic interpretation also relies on comparative tools. Courts interpreting a given treaty provision often consider how other courts and tribunals have applied it. Pursuant to Article 31(3)(b) of the Vienna Convention on the Law of Treaties, treaty interpretation should take into account 'any subsequent practice in the application of the treaty'. Moreover, pursuant to Article 31(3)(c) of the same convention, 'There shall be taken into account, together with

---

[41] See M. Delmas-Marty, 'The Contribution of Comparative Law to a Pluralist Conception of International Criminal Law', *Journal of International Criminal Justice* 1 (2003), 13–25, 13.

[42] See, for instance, the Separate and Dissenting Opinion of Judge Cassese to the case *Prosecutor v. Drazen Erdemovic*, Judgment of 7 October 1997, paras. 1–2 (arguing that the reference to national law was not necessary, as the notion of guilty plea could be determined on the basis of the Statute of the Court and pinpointing that 'legal constructs and terms of art upheld in national law should not be automatically applied at the international level').

[43] Statute of the International Court of Justice, 26 June 1945, 33 UNTS 993.

[44] E. De Brabandere and T. Gazzini (eds.), *International Investment Law: The Sources of Rights and Obligations* (Leiden: Martinus Nijhoff, 2012).

[45] Ellis, 'General Principles and Comparative Law', 949.

[46] See generally De Brabandere and Gazzini (eds.), *International Investment Law: The Sources of Rights and Obligations*.

[47] R. David and C. Jauffret-Spinosi, *Les grands systems de droit contemporains* (Paris: Dalloz, 2002), p. 7.

[48] Reimann, 'Comparative Law and Neighbouring Disciplines', 19.   [49] *Ibid.*

the context: ... any relevant rules of international law applicable in the relations between the parties.'[50]

Fourth, comparative reasoning plays an important role in the increasing cross-fertilisation between different international tribunals pursuant to Article 38(d) of the ICJ Statute, which considers judicial decisions as 'subsidiary means for the determination of rules of law'. The practice of international judicial borrowing, that is, borrowing decisions from other international *fora*, in the interpretation of public international law promotes the unity and coherence of the same. The decisions of international courts and tribunals can be taken into consideration 'because their reasoning and conclusions may provide guidance to [arbitral tribunals and Annulment Committees] in settling similar issues ... and help to ensure consistency and legal certainty ..., thereby contributing to ensuring trust in the ... dispute settlement system and predictability for governments and investors'.[51] This form of judicial borrowing, which is particularly useful in coping with systemic lacunae of a given legal system,[52] creates path coherence, a dynamic process which may lead to a sort of judicial globalisation.[53]

Finally, in scrutinising international investment law and arbitration, scholars, arbitrators and practitioners have made extensive use of analogies. Reference to national, regional and international case law is a constant feature in publications concerning international investment law and is based on both *macro-comparisons* (concerned with entire legal systems) and *micro-comparisons* (dealing with specific institutions or specific problems). With regard to macro-comparison, authors have compared international investment law and arbitration to different legal systems. For instance, investment treaty law has been compared to administrative law,[54] commercial law and different fields of international law, including international trade law and human rights law. With regard to micro-comparison, specific investment treaty standards have been compared to

---

[50] Vienna Convention on the Law of Treaties, adopted 23 May 1969, in force 27 January 1980) 1155 UNTS 331 (VCLT). See R. Gardiner, *Treaty Interpretation* (Oxford: Oxford University Press, 2008), pp. 225–249.

[51] *M.C.I. Power Group L.C. and New Turbine Inc.* v. *Republic of Ecuador*, ICSID Case No. ARB/03/6, Decision on Annulment, 19 October 2009, para. 25.

[52] A. Watson, *Legal Transplants An Approach to Comparative Law*, 2nd ed. (Athens/ London: University of Georgia Press, 1994), p. 95.

[53] A.-M. Slaughter, 'Judicial Globalization', *Virginia Journal of International Law* 40 (1999– 2000), 1103–1124.

[54] G. Van Harten and M. Loughlin, 'Investment Treaty Arbitration as a Species of Global Administrative Law', *European Journal of International Law* 17 (2006), 121–150.

rules belonging to other legal orders.[55] For instance, the procedural features of investment treaty arbitration have been investigated through comparative lenses (e.g. standards of review, transparency and representation of the public interest in investment treaty arbitration).

More explicitly, some authors have advocated a proactive use of comparative reasoning in the course of arbitral proceedings. For instance, Montt has proposed the adoption of the comparative method pursuant to Articles 31(3)(c) of the Vienna Convention on the Law of Treaties and 38(1)(c) of the ICJ Statute to restrain arbitrators' discretion in reviewing state action, and enhance the perceived legitimacy of the system. As like issues have arisen before a number of other courts and tribunals, Montt states that useful lessons can be learned from this experience. According to Montt, as international law lacks experience in controlling the regulatory state, comparative reasoning can provide general guidance, bringing objectivity into legal reasoning.[56]

Analogously, acknowledging the imperfections and growth pains of international investment law and arbitration, Schill has proposed the use of a comparative public law methodology to develop international investment law and arbitration and strengthen its legitimacy. According to Schill, adopting a comparative approach to international investment law and arbitration helps to (1) concretise and clarify the interpretation of investment treaty provisions; (2) balance investment provisions with non-investment concerns; (3) improve consistency within investment treaty arbitration; (4) promote cross-regime consistency; (5) legitimise the existing arbitral jurisprudence; (6) suggest legal reform; and (7) develop general principles of law.[57]

With regard to the choice of legal orders to identify general principles of law, Schill refers to the principal legal orders of the world, including, *inter alia*, those of Germany, France and the United States.[58] Schill claims that 'the reason for this choice is not one of legal hegemony, but rather the fact that these legal orders are easily accessible and above all, have

---

[55] See, for example, T. Wälde and A. Kolo, 'Environmental Regulation, Investment Protection and "Regulatory Taking" in International Law', *International and Comparative Law Quarterly* 50 (2001), 811–848, at 821.

[56] S. Montt, *State Liability in Investment Treaty Arbitration – Global Constitutional and Administrative Law in the BIT Generation* (Oxford and Portland, Oregon, US: Hart Publishing, 2009), pp. 371–372.

[57] S. Schill, 'International Investment Law and Comparative Public Law: An Introduction', in S. Schill (ed.), *International Investment Law and Comparative Public Law* (Oxford: Oxford University Press, 2010), pp. 25–27.

[58] *Ibid.* pp. 29–30.

influenced the public law system of many other countries'.[59] He concludes that 'comparative law analysis can restrict itself to a qualitative study'.[60]

One wonders whether a more critical approach to the use of comparative reasoning should be adopted. Most of the available literature adopts a functionalist approach (understanding legal norms as responses to analogous problems) and considers comparative reasoning as a tool to settle the alleged legitimacy crisis of international investment law and arbitration. Little, if any, analysis has been devoted to methodology issues. Yet, legal systems express a certain political position as they are the outcome of a certain historical and cultural evolution. If the adjudicators drew on the particular constitutional experience of a foreign country, this could repoliticise investment disputes against more neutral international canons,[61] would be incompatible with the principle of sovereign equality and could not prevent adjudicators 'from referring only to the legal systems they kn[ew] best'.[62] Finally, one may question the legitimacy of establishing comparators by reference only to some constitutional traditions. Insofar as the selected comparators reflect general principles of law, however, they matter in the interpretative process.

This chapter will now examine the four different, albeit related, areas in which comparative reasoning plays a distinct role in the governance of foreign direct investments: (1) comparative investment law, (2) comparative arbitration law, (3) legal doctrine and (4) treaty interpretation.

Comparative investment law

Comparative investment law can be defined as a branch of comparative law[63] aimed at studying and comparing different legal frameworks regulating foreign investment at the national levels.[64] As foreign direct investment and economic integration increase in importance, knowledge about foreign legal systems increases in value. On the one hand, 'even in

---

[59] Ibid.   [60] Ibid.   [61] Kennedy, 'New Approaches to Comparative Law', 545, 606–608.

[62] Ellis, 'General Principles and Comparative Law', 953.

[63] A. Roberts, 'Comparative International Law? The Role of National Courts in Creating and Enforcing International Law', International and Comparative Law Quarterly 60 (2011), 57–92, 57 (defining comparative international law as the way courts, lawyers and academics seek to identify and interpret international law by comparing various domestic laws and court decisions).

[64] J.P. Trachtman, 'The International Economic Law Revolution', University of Pennsylvania Journal of International Economic Law 17 (1996), 44.

transboundary issues, national laws continue to matter, and, very often, they are still what really counts'.[65] On the other hand, different states approach, conceptualise and interpret international law differently.[66] Even when domestic courts 'may be purporting to apply international law, [their] view of international law may be heavily influenced by domestic rules and practices'.[67] Therefore, comparative investment law has developed in parallel to the expansion of international investment law.

Comparative investment law does not differ from general comparative law: rather, it applies existing comparative methods to study the diverse national approaches to the regulation of foreign direct investments. The national legal frameworks regulating foreign investment can be and have been studied through comparative lenses. For instance, a number of authors have questioned whether recent top-down harmonisation efforts as spurred by international organisations are the best way to reform legal systems in order to attract and support foreign direct investment.[68] The idea that law is a form of social engineering was endorsed by the law and development movement, which aimed to use law to foster the economic growth of developing countries. These ideas, out of fashion for some time,[69] have been revived due to economic globalisation.[70] Legal changes on a massive scale have been induced by the adhesion of states to a range of international regimes. For instance, international financial institutions – the International Monetary Fund and the World Bank – have launched ambitious programmes of legal reform, with the purported aim of promoting the rule of law and economic development. At the same time, adhesion and membership to the WTO has often required substantive changes in the domestic legal frameworks of the member states. As noted by a comparative lawyer, 'during most of

---

[65] Reimann, 'Beyond National Systems', 1112.

[66] B.N. Mamlyuk and U. Mattei, 'Comparative International Law', *Brooklyn Journal of International Law* 36 (2010–2011), 385–452, 426.

[67] J.S. Martinez, 'Towards an International Judicial System', *Stanford Law Review* 56 (2003), 429, 528.

[68] See, for example, J.-Y.P. Steyt, *Comparative Foreign Investment Law: Determinants of the Legal Framework and the Level of Openness and Attractiveness of Host Economies* (May 2006) Cornell Law School, LLM Graduate Research Papers, Paper No. 1 *available at* http://scholarship.law.cornell.edu/lps_LLMGRP/1/; A. Perry-Kessaris, 'Finding and Facing Facts about Legal Systems and FDI in South Asia', *Legal Studies* 23 (2003), 649.

[69] D.M. Trubek, 'Towards a Social Theory of Law: An Essay on the Study of Law and Development', *Yale Law Journal* 82 (1982), 1–50.

[70] See generally D. Trubek and A. Santos (eds.), *The New Law and Economic Development* (Cambridge: Cambridge University Press, 2006).

the twentieth century, economic policy in pursuit of economic growth was designed without paying much attention to institutional settings . . . The assumption was that once the choice of a market economy was made, the market itself would create the conditions necessary for its own success'.[71]

Yet, top-down institutional change aimed at improving economic performance may not necessarily promote good governance. On the one hand, '[W]hen external forces, such as international institutions, assume institutional, cultural, or political realities that are not present in the target country, these transplanted laws are often rejected and fail because they are not appropriate for the country . . . '[72] On the other hand, good governance is a vague notion, and it can be instrumental in furthering the interests of capital-exporting states.[73] Moreover, World Bank and IMF programmes have been criticised for determining some instances of social and economic disruptions as well as for affecting democratic choices.[74] Only recently have international financial institutions attempted to recalibrate their policies and infuse them with human rights considerations with varying results.

Comparative investment law can facilitate a keener understanding of the reasons for the failures or successes of vertically imposed reforms and can shed light on the different ways states implement their international commitments. National courts play an important role in creating and enforcing international (investment) law.[75] Furthermore, the quality of local institutions matters for promoting economic development.[76] Therefore, while the top-down imposition of models adopted in indus-trialised countries for less developed regions 'is now widely regarded

---

[71] M. Graziadei, 'Comparative Law as the Study of Transplants and Receptions', in M. Reimann and R. Zimmermann (eds.), *The Oxford Handbook of Comparative Law* (Oxford: Oxford University Press, 2006), pp. 442, 459.

[72] J. Brown, A. Kudat and K. McGeeney, 'Improving Legislation through Social Analysis: A Case Study in Methodology from the Water Sector in Uzbekistan', *Sustainable Development Law and Policy* 5 (2005), 49–57, 49.

[73] K. Miles, *The Origins of International Investment Law* (Cambridge: Cambridge University Press, 2013), p. 275; Y. Dezalay and B.G. Garth (eds.), *Global Prescriptions: The Production, Exportation and Importation of a New Legal Orthodoxy* (Ann Arbor, MI: Michigan University Press, 2002).

[74] C. Thomas, 'Does the "Good Governance Policy" of the International Financial Institutions Privilege Markets at the Expense of Democracy?', *Connecticut Journal of International Law* 14 (1999), 551–562.

[75] Roberts, 'Comparative International Law?', 57.

[76] Graziadei, 'Comparative Law as the Study of Transplants and Receptions', 459.

as unsuitable and discredited',[77] some scholars argue that country-specific approaches are better suited to address developmental challenges.[78] Certainly, comparative investment law studies can influence national parliamentary law,[79] driving regulatory changes towards good governance.

Comparative investment law focuses on national investment codes. While these national codes often reflect and implement international law norms, they maintain a national character as national lawmakers and local courts have elaborated and adjudicated them, respectively. On the other hand, however, examining state practice matters for international businesses, for the determination of customs[80] and general principles of law,[81] and as a subsidiary means of determining international law.[82]

Comparative arbitration law

Not many fields of law use comparative reasoning as extensively as international arbitration. International arbitration is a method for settling transnational disputes and is often perceived as a more neutral forum than a national court.[83] International arbitration is an intercultural field,[84] as it involves parties and adjudicators of different nationalities and requires the application of different sets of procedural and substantive norms. As an eminent arbitrator, the late Professor Pierre Lalive, put it, 'an international arbitration should be decided by a truly "international" arbitrator, *i.e.*, someone who is *more* than a national lawyer, someone who is internationally-minded, trained in comparative

[77] *Ibid.* 460.
[78] A.J. Perry, *Legal Systems as Determinant of Foreign Direct Investment: Lessons from Sri Lanka* (London: Kluwer Law, 2001); A.J. Perry, 'Effective Legal Systems and Foreign Direct Investment: In Search of the Evidence', *International and Comparative Law Quarterly* 49 (2000), 779.
[79] See D. Barak-Erez, 'An International Community of Legislatures?', in R.W. Bauman and T. Kahana (eds.), *The Least Examined Branch: The Role of Legislatures in the Constitutional State* (Cambridge: Cambridge University Press, 2006), p. 532.
[80] D.J. Bederman, *Custom as a Source of Law* (Cambridge: Cambridge University Press, 2010).
[81] Mamlyuk and Mattei, 'Comparative International Law', 427.
[82] Roberts, 'Comparative International Law?', 59.
[83] P. Esposito and J. Martire, 'Arbitrating in a World of Communicative Reason', *Arbitration International* 28 (2012), 325–341, 331.
[84] P. Lalive, 'Sur des dimensions culturelles de l'arbitrage international', in J. Makarczyk and K. Skubiszewski (eds.), *Theory of International Law at the Threshold of the 21st Century – Essays in Honour of Krzystof Skubiszewski* (The Hague: Kluwer Law International, 1996), p. 772.

law and inclined to adopt a *comparative and truly "international outlook"*.[85] Accordingly, 'the main duty of the international arbitrator is to be open to other cultures'.[86]

Paradoxically, despite the perceived need for an international arbitral culture that is detached from national practices, procedures and bias, there is a risk that the parties view such culture as alien. The idea that international arbitration is a dispute settlement mechanism that reflects a cosmopolitan culture and yet may stand apart from the cultural context of the given dispute demands further analysis. The parties to international arbitration expect the dispute to be handled in a way that respects their cultural background 'and does not impose on them a different alien cultural model'.[87] To be perceived as legitimate, the arbitral process should rely on deliberative dynamics 'respectful of the diverse legal, social and cultural backgrounds of the members of the international community'.[88] To express a 'cosmopolitan legal culture',[89] international arbitration 'must respect and reflect all cultures emerging within the system'.[90]

While many comparative lawyers have analysed international arbitration,[91] until recently investment treaty arbitration has received little attention. This neglect is due to two interlinked reasons. First, investment treaty arbitration is often associated with international arbitration. Second, the boom in investment disputes has only a recent pedigree. Consequently, only in the past several decades have authors analysed the phenomenon of investment treaty arbitration.

However, investment treaty arbitration differs from international commercial arbitration.[92] While international arbitration generally

---

[85] P. Lalive, 'On the Neutrality of the Arbitrator and of the Place of Arbitration', in C. Reymond and E. Bucher (eds.), *Recueil de Travaux Suisses sur l'arbitrage international* (Zürich: Schulthess, 1984), pp. 23–33, 27 (emphasis added).

[86] S. Dookhun, 'Q&A with Professor Pierre Lalive', *Global Arbitration Review* 3 (2008), 5 (emphasis added).

[87] Esposito and Martire, 'Arbitrating in a World of Communicative Reason', 329 and 331.

[88] *Ibid.*, at 334.

[89] Y. Dezalay and B. Garth, *Dealing in Virtue* (Chicago: University of Chicago Press, 1996), p. 97.

[90] Esposito and Martire, 'Arbitrating in a World of Communicative Reason', 337.

[91] J.D.M. Lew, L.A. Mistelis and S.M. Kröll (eds.), *Comparative International Commercial Arbitration* (The Hague: Kluwer Law International, 2003), pp. 2–3.

[92] See N. Blackaby, 'Investment Arbitration and Commercial Arbitration (or the Tale of the Dolphin and the Shark)', in L.A. Mistelis and J.D.M. Lew (eds.), *Pervasive Problems in International Arbitration* (The Hague/Boston/London: Kluwer, 2006), pp. 217–219; J. Paulsson, 'International Arbitration is Not Arbitration', *Stockholm Int'l Arbitration*

involves private parties and concerns disputes of a commercial nature, investment treaty arbitration involves states and private actors.[93] This 'diagonal' dispute settlement mechanism is a major novelty in international law since international disputes have traditionally involved states only.[94] In light of the recent proliferation of investment disputes,[95] the peculiar character of investment treaty arbitration and persistent concerns about the system's deficiencies, the debate about the pros and cons of the mechanism has gained momentum, and the role of comparative reasoning in investment treaty arbitration requires an independent analysis. This scrutiny is not only theoretically interesting but also concretely useful: investment treaty disputes may have a deep impact on public welfare. Some authors have pointed out the inadequacies of arbitration, which is historically rooted in private law, for dealing with disputes involving public law.[96] As Lalive puts it, 'the importance and complexity of the questions raised in investor–state settlement of disputes, and the fact that public interest and the development of the country concerned are involved, are all dynamics that militate in favour of a very carefully and fully reasoned award, much more so than in what may be considered normal in cases of commercial transactions'.[97]

Both investment treaty arbitration and international arbitration are paradigmatic melting pots of legal cultures,[98] constituting 'place[s] of convergence and interchange wherein practitioners from different backgrounds create new practices'.[99] The emerging arbitration culture fuses together

---

Review 2 (2008), 1–20, 1; G. Cordero Moss, 'Commercial Arbitration and Investment Arbitration: Fertile Soil for False Friends?', in C. Binder, U. Kriebaum, A. Reinisch and S. Wittich (eds.), *International Investment Law for the 21st Century: Essays in Honour of Christoph Schreuer* (Oxford: Oxford University Press, 2009), pp. 782, 782–784.

[93] Moss, 'Commercial Arbitration and Investment Arbitration', at pp. 784–793.

[94] Paulsson, 'International Arbitration is Not Arbitration', at 5–6.

[95] Reportedly, in 2013, the total number of known investor-state arbitrations was 514 and the total number of countries that responded to one or more arbitration was 95. United Nations Conference on Trade and Development (UNCTAD), *World Investment Report 2013 - Global Value Chains: Investment and Trade for Development* (New York and Geneva: United Nations, 2013), p. XXI. The number of arbitrations, however, is only approximate because disputes might be unknown due to confidentiality requirements.

[96] See generally G. Van Harten, *Investment Treaty Arbitration and Public Law* (Oxford: Oxford University Press, 2007).

[97] P. Lalive, 'On the Reasoning of International Arbitral Awards', *Journal of International Dispute Settlement* 1 (2010), 55–65, at 57 (internal citations omitted).

[98] See G. Kaufmann-Kohler, 'Globalization of Arbitral Procedure', *Vanderbilt Journal of Transnational Law* 36 (2003), 1313.

[99] See T. Ginsburg, 'The Culture of Arbitration', *Vanderbilt Journal of Transnational Law* 36 (2003), 1335.

elements of the common law and civil law tradition. Therefore, comparative studies provide international law scholars with important theoretical and logical tools for their profession.

Legal doctrine

In scrutinising investment law and arbitration, scholars have made use of comparative reasoning, albeit in an implicit manner. In their writings on international law, scholars necessarily resort to concepts and approaches with which they are familiar.[100] Reference to national and regional case law is a constant feature in academic writings concerning international investment law, but this does not necessarily reflect a form of nationalism, as reference is often made to the case law of other countries as well.[101]

The use of comparative reasoning by investment law scholars matters because, in international law, the opinion of legal scholars is deemed to have a certain, albeit subsidiary, legal value. The Statute of the ICJ expressly enumerates 'the teachings of the most highly qualified publicists of the various nations' as 'subsidiary means for the determination of the sources of law'.[102] In other words, doctrine 'do[es] not create law' but assists in determining and elucidating the existing law.[103] As Oppenheim clarified more than a century ago, 'the writers on international law ... have to pronounce whether there is an established custom or not, whether there is a usage only in contradistinction to a custom, whether a recognized usage has now ripened into a custom, and the like'.[104]

Scholarly analysis can influence the development of international investment law and arbitration.[105] International investment scholars

---

[100] Picker, 'International Law's Mixed Heritage: A Common/Civil Law Jurisdiction', 1093.

[101] For instance, while the *Tecmed* Tribunal relied on ECtHR cases, none of the members of the Tribunal were Europeans. See W. Ben Hamida, 'Investment Arbitration and Human Rights', *Transnational Dispute Management* 5 (2007), 14.

[102] ICJ Statute, Article 38(1)(d). The ICJ Statute is annexed to the Charter of the United Nations of which it forms an integral part. UN Charter, 26 June 1945, 1 UNTS XVI.

[103] PCIJ, *Proces Verbaux of the Proceedings of the Committee* (1920) Advisory Committee of Jurists, 16 June–24 July 1920, at 336 (with reference to the precursor of Article 38(1)(d) of the ICJ Statute). But see R.J. Jennings, 'The Judiciary, International and National and the Development of International Law', *International and Comparative Law Quarterly* 45 (1996), 1, 3–4 (seeing 'no great difficulty in seeing a subsidiary means for the determination of rules of law as being a source of law, not merely by analogy but directly').

[104] L. Oppenheim, 'The Science of International Law: Its Task and Method', *American Journal of International Law* 2 (1908), 313, 315.

[105] See Ginsburg, 'The Culture of Arbitration', at 1341–1342 (stating that '[l]ike the grand civil law tradition, it is scholarly commentary that produces the law and technique of

have a distinct responsibility to clarify international investment law, to improve its internal consistency and contribute to shaping its future. On the one hand, scholars and professors of international law are often selected as arbitrators in investment treaty disputes. Therefore, their academic background and experience are relied upon in the settlement of such disputes. On the other hand, both advocates and arbitrators make reference to the works of scholars in their pleadings and awards, respectively. The teachings of publicists are regularly cited in arbitral awards.[106] While the ICJ Statute refers to 'the most highly qualified publicists in the field of international law', there is no clear-cut rule on how to identify these publicists,[107] and arbitral tribunals have referred to a variety of scholarly writings.[108] This reference can complement legal analysis or can avoid a *non liquet* in the event that the applicable law is inconclusive.

Academics have contributed to the development of international investment law through both *macro-comparisons* and *micro-comparisons*. While micro-comparison 'has to do with specific legal institutions or problems', macro-comparison aims to 'compare the spirit and style of different legal systems, the methods of thought and procedures ... for resolving and deciding disputes, or the roles of those engaged in the law'.[109] With regard to macro-comparison, authors have compared

arbitration'). By contrast, in the common law tradition, a different approach has prevailed; 'Until recently English judgments were characterised by a dearth of references to academic legal writing' due to the existence of a 'professional convention preventing judges and counsel from citing living authors'. See A. Braun, 'Burying the Living? The Citation of Legal Writings in English Courts', *American Journal of Comparative Law* 58 (2010), 27–52.

[106] For instance, in his separate opinion to the *Thunderbird* case, Professor Wälde made reference to Professor Gaillard's work. *Int'l Thunderbird Gaming Corp.* v. *United Mexican States*, 255 Fed. Appx. 531 (2007) (Separate Opinion of arbitrator Thomas Walde), at 13, n. 7. In *Malaysian Historical Salvors SDN BHD* v. *the Government of Malaysia*, the ad hoc Annulment Committee cited the work of Professor Christoph Schreuer and Yulia Andreeva. *Malaysian Historical Salvors SDN BHD* v. *Government of Malaysia*, ICSID Case No. ARB/05/10, Decision on the Application for Annulment, 28 February 2009, paras. 67, 76.

[107] See, for example, Schwarzenberger, 'The Inductive Approach to International Law', *Harvard Law Review* 60 (1947), 539, 559–562.

[108] On the one hand, like other international courts, arbitral tribunals have referred to studies on specific aspects of general international law such as state responsibility and diplomatic relations. On the other hand, and more interestingly, they have also referred to more specific emerging literature on various aspects of international investment law. This latter development shows once more the vitality of the field.

[109] K. Zweigert and H. Kotz, *Introduction to Comparative Law*, Tony Weir, transl., 3rd ed. (Oxford: Oxford University Press, 1998), p. 4–5.

international investment law and arbitration to different legal systems. For instance, investment treaty law has been compared to administrative law, human rights law and other subsystems of international law.[110]

With regard to micro-comparison, authors have compared specific investment treaty standards to rules belonging to other legal orders.[111] For instance, reference has been made to WTO cases to critically assess the application of the most favoured nation (MFN) treatment to investor–state arbitration.[112] Some scholars have contended that only by comparing the fair and equitable treatment (FET) standard with the national articulations of the rule of law can the meaning of the standard become concrete.[113] Another key area of international investment law in which the use of analogy has been expansively adopted is that regarding the concept of investment and the related notion of expropriation.[114] For instance, on the theme of regulatory expropriation, scholars have referred, *inter alia*, to the jurisprudence of the US Supreme Court.[115]

While these functionalist approaches seem to offer concrete solutions to emerging conceptual dilemmas, one wonders whether a more critical approach to the use of comparative reasoning should be adopted. While scholarly analysis has made extensive use of comparative reasoning and has deemed it a panacea for solving interpretative dilemmas, methodology issues have been neglected. Scholarly writings should be resorted to 'not for the speculations of their authors concerning what the law ought to be but for trustworthy evidence of what the law really was'.[116] In fact, the function of the arbitrators is to settle disputes 'in accordance with international law'.[117]

---

[110] See Chapter 5 below.   [111] See Chapter 4 below.

[112] See, for example, N. Di Mascio and J. Pauwelyn, 'Non Discrimination in Trade and Investment Treaties: Two Worlds Apart or Two Sides of the Same Coin?', *American Journal of International Law* 102 (2008), 48.

[113] S.W. Schill, 'Fair and Equitable Treatment under Investment Treaties as an Embodiment of the Rule of Law', New York University Law School, International Law & Justice Working Paper No. 6, 2006, 26.

[114] See, for example, C. Schreuer and U. Kriebaum, 'The Concept of Property in Human Rights Law and International Investment Law', in S. Breitenmoser, B. Ehrenzeller and M. Sassoli (eds.), *Human Rights, Democracy and the Rule of Law: Liber Amicorum Luzius Wildhaber* (Baden/Baden: Dike, 2007), p. 743.

[115] Wälde and Kolo, 'Environmental Regulation, Investment Protection and "Regulatory Taking" in International Law', 821.

[116] M. Lachs, 'Teachings and Teaching of International Law', *Recueil des Cours de l'Académie de Droit International de la Haye* 151 (1976/III), 161, at 169.

[117] ICJ Statute, Article 38(1).

For instance, many arbitral awards relating to the Argentinian financial crisis referred to the International Law Commission's (ILC's) Articles on State Responsibility,[118] which are deemed to reflect customary international law. When Argentina adopted the Emergency Law in the aftermath of its financial crisis, dozens of investors brought disputes against Argentina, alleging breach of the relevant investment treaty provisions. Several arbitral tribunals mainly relied on Article 25 of the ILC's Articles, which requires very strict conditions for the application of necessity, rather than considering it together with the relevant treaty provision, Article XI of the US–Argentina BIT. This had the effect of restricting the applicability of the exceptions.[119] For instance, in *CMS* v. *Argentina*, the claimant relied on expert opinion and contended that Article XI should be read in the light of Article 25 of the ILC's Articles on State Responsibility.[120] On the other hand, the expert appointed by Argentina argued that 'Article XI was "self-judging" and that as a consequence the Tribunal had to limit itself to considering whether it acted in good faith in invoking this Article.'[121] The Tribunal 'assum[ed] that Article XI and Article 25 [we]re on the same footing'.[122]

The Annulment Committee noted that 'there is some analogy in the language used in Article XI of the BIT and in Article 25 of the ILC's Articles on State Responsibility' as '[t]he first text mentions "necessary" measures and the second relates to the "state of necessity"'.[123] However, the two provisions have 'a different operation and content',[124] and 'the excuse based on customary international law could only be subsidiary to the exclusion based on Article XI'.[125] In other words, 'if the Tribunal was satisfied by the arguments based on Article XI, it should have held that there had been "no breach" of the BIT'.[126] However, the Annulment Committee considered that there was no manifest excess of power to annul the award on this matter.[127] The case is interesting because it shows that scholarly opinion of the most qualified publicists may diverge on treaty interpretation and that scholarly writings are subsidiary or evidentiary sources of law.

---

[118] Articles on Responsibility of States for Internationally Wrongful Acts, annexed to UNGA Resolution 56/83, 14 December 2001.
[119] See *CMS Gas Transmission Company* v. *the Argentine Republic*, Case No. ARB/01/8, Award, 12 May 2005, para. 318.
[120] *CMS Gas Transmission Company* v. *the Argentine Republic*, Case No. ARB/01/8, Decision on Annulment, 25 September 2007, para. 123.
[121] *Ibid.*   [122] *Ibid.*, para. 131.   [123] *Ibid.*, para. 129.   [124] *Ibid.*, para. 131.
[125] *Ibid.*, para. 132.   [126] *Ibid.*, para. 133.   [127] *Ibid.*, para. 136.

In conclusion, investment law scholars have made use of comparative reasoning in their writings to map the ground of international investment law. Far from being an 'invisible college of international lawyers',[128] they are contributing to the development of international investment law. Their writings are subsidiary means for the determination of the sources of law. Not only do some scholars wear multiple hats, serving as academics, arbitrators and counsels, but arbitral tribunals rely upon scholarly writings for interpreting treaty provisions.

Judicial borrowing

Arbitral tribunals are increasingly involved in dialogues with other courts and tribunals across the traditional jurisdictional divides. Investment treaty arbitration has become a laboratory of confrontation characterised by growing patterns of judicial borrowing. Judicial borrowing – meant as the 'reference to' or 'transplanting' or 'acquisition' of legal reasoning developed in one jurisdiction by another – is essentially a comparative process based on 'similarity, analogy and differentiation'.[129] In fact, the essence of judicial borrowing is analogical reasoning: analogous issues urge adjudicators to find similar solutions and to learn from one another. Although there is no doctrine of precedent in international law,[130] in most cases 'conversations across cases' take place,[131] and a systematic study of the jurisprudence of international tribunals suggests the 'tendency to chart a coherent course within international law'.[132]

Arbitral authority to engage in judicial borrowing derives from the fluid nature of international law. Under Article 38(d) of the ICJ Statute, judicial decisions are 'subsidiary means for the determination of rules of law'[133] and can constitute evidence of state practice. In theory, the

---

[128] O. Schachter, 'The Invisible College of International Lawyers', *Northwestern University Law Review* 72 (1977), 217.

[129] V.V. Palmer, 'From Lerotholi to Lando: Some Examples of Comparative Law Methodology', *American Journal of Comparative Law* 53 (2005), 261–290, 261.

[130] See, for instance, Article 59 of the ICJ Statute (affirming that 'The decision of the Court has no binding force except between the parties and in respect of that particular case').

[131] C. Schreuer and M. Weiniger, 'Conversations Across Cases – Is There a Doctrine of Precedent in Investment Arbitration?', *Transnational Dispute Management* 5 (2008), 3; C. Schreuer, 'A Doctrine of Precedent?', in P. Muchlinski, F. Ortino and C. Schreuer (eds.), *The Oxford Handbook of International Investment Law* (Oxford: Oxford University Press, 2008), p. 1190.

[132] C. McLachlan, 'The Principle of Systemic Integration and Article 31(3)(c) of the Vienna Convention', *International and Comparative Law Quarterly* 54 (2005), 279, 289.

[133] ICJ Statute, Article 38(1)(d).

subsidiary nature of judicial decisions vis-à-vis other sources of international law – such as treaties, custom and general principles – expresses the concept that only states are subjects under international law and entitled, as such, to make international law.[134] Judicial decisions are considered to provide evidence of international law rather than constituting sources of the same. In practice, however, 'judicial decisions play an extremely important role in the identification and formation of international law'.[135]

Judicial borrowing is particularly useful when adjudicators are facing (1) a legal gap; (2) hard cases whose outcomes are uncertain due to diverging interpretations; and (3) vague provisions.[136] Investment law provisions are particularly open to arbitral interpretation through comparative reasoning because of the brevity of international investment treaties (which make them predisposed to possible gaps); the vague formulation of investment treaty standards; and the existence of diverging lines of arguments in the arbitral jurisprudence. As Lauterpacht put it, 'a court, otherwise endowed with jurisdiction, must not refuse to give a decision on the ground that the law is non-existent or controversial, or uncertain and lacking in clarity'.[137] In fact, *non liquet* relates to the fundamental structure of international law and aims to ensure the 'completeness' of international law through hermeneutics.

Judicial borrowing can be a fertile source of development.[138] Comparing cases and cross-referencing them is a dynamic process that can lead to the development of a 'common law of international adjudication'[139] or

---

[134] C. Cutler, *Private Power and Global Authority – Transnational Merchant Law in the Global Political Economy* (New York, NY: Cambridge University Press, 2003), p. 37.

[135] Roberts, 'Comparative International Law?', 63.

[136] S. Montt, *State Liability in Investment Treaty Arbitration – Global Constitutional and Administrative Law in the BIT Generation* (Oxford: Hart Publishing, 2009), p. 166 (noting that judicial borrowing can be particularly useful in coping with legal gaps, interpreting concepts and adjudicating hard cases by way of analogy to other cases).

[137] H. Lauterpacht, 'Some Observations on the Prohibition of Non Liquet and the Completeness of the Legal Order', in *Symbolae Verzijl présentées au Professeur J.H.W. Verzijl à l'occasion de son VXXième anniversaire* (The Hague: Martinus Nijhoff, 1958), p.196, 199.

[138] A. Watson, *Legal Transplants – An Approach to Comparative Law*, 2nd ed. (Athens; London: University of Georgia Press, 1994), p. 95.

[139] C. Brown, *A Common Law of International Adjudication* (Oxford: Oxford University Press, 2007), p. 53.

'judicial globalization'.[140] Professor Slaughter, who first identified the twin issues of global community of courts and global jurisprudence, defines judicial globalisation as 'the ... conceptual shift ... from two systems – international and domestic – to one; from international and national judges to judges applying international law, national law or a mixture of both'.[141] Cross-fertilisation and judicial dialogue between different tribunals have created an important body of 'global comparative jurisprudence'.[142] As Slaughter highlights, 'increasing cross fertilization of ideas and precedents among constitutional judges around the world is gradually giving rise to an increasingly visible international consensus on various issues – a consensus that, in turn, carries its own compelling weight'.[143]

Critics contend that judicial recourse to comparative reasoning 'is but a covert means of maximising judicial power and advancing subjective preferences of judges'.[144] According to such argument, arbitrators – unlike legislators – are expected to interpret and apply the law rather than create norms. Yet, critics contend, when tribunals refer to cases, they retain significant latitude regarding decisions on when to borrow and from which source. This can lead to 'the adoption of legal solutions which are either undesirable on their merits or in tension with the fundamental principles of the importing system'.[145] This criticism highlights the fact that there is an untold element of creativity in analogical reasoning and the possibilities for meaningful comparisons remain countless. Accordingly, the boundaries between interpretation of existing law and the making of new law are inevitably fluid.

[140] Slaughter, 'Judicial Globalization', 1103; C. Baudenbacher, 'Judicial Globalization: New Development or Old Wine in New Bottles?', *Texas International Law Journal* 38 (2003), 505.

[141] A.-M. Slaughter, 'A Global Community of Courts', *Harvard Journal of International Law* 44 (2003), 193.

[142] See C. McCrudden, 'Judicial Comparativism and Human Rights', in E. Örükü and D. Nelken (eds.), *Comparative Law: A Handbook* (Oxford: Hart Publishing, 2007), pp. 371–398.

[143] A.-M. Slaughter, *A New World Order* (Princeton and Oxford: Princeton University Press, 2004), p. 78.

[144] D. Barak-Erez, 'The Institutional Aspects of Comparative Law', *Columbia Journal of European Law* 15 (2008–2009), 490 (countering this criticism by examining the institutional aspects of comparative law). On this controversy, see also V. Jackson, 'Constitutional Comparisons: Convergence, Resistance, Engagement', *Harvard Law Review* 119 (2005), 109; R.A. Posner, 'Forward: A Political Court', *Harvard Law Review* 119 (2005), 84–91.

[145] Barak-Erez, 'The Institutional Aspects of Comparative Law', 492 (dismissing this risk as 'relatively negligible').

Yet, vague provisions, diverging scholarly opinions and legal gaps are factors which compel some form of analogical reasoning in investment treaty arbitration. Certain ideas are not represented in international investment law. Consider, for instance, indigenous peoples' rights or state police powers to adopt measures to protect public health. Rarely do these interests receive specific mention in the text of international investment treaties. At the same time, international investment law includes concepts which cannot be comprehended in full without referring to other systems, such as national law. Consider, for instance, the crucial issue of the nationality of the investor. In order to invoke the protection of the relevant BIT, the investor's nationality must be ascertained on the basis of the relevant domestic law.[146] Furthermore, diverging lines of interpretation are not uncommon in international investment law. All these features support reference to the decisions of other tribunals.

Should the use of comparative reasoning 'result from a relatively free choice', that is, when the adjudicators consider the analogue decision as 'desirable on its merits'?[147] In order to address this question, one should first address other fundamental issues including the questions as to whether there is only one right answer to any problem in international investment law, as well as whether international investment law is a complete system, or if, on the other hand, it is included in the broader system of public international law and partially overlaps with other systems of law as well.

Whatever the answer one gives to these questions, it seems that reason-giving would improve the perception of transparency, preventing arbitrariness and legitimising judicial borrowing. Like most contemporary legal systems,[148] international investment law requires that arbitrators provide reasons for their decisions.[149] Both the award and the process by which the decision was reached are more likely to be accepted if the parties are able to judge the soundness of the decision. More discussion and disclosure of the criteria used by arbitrators for judicial borrowing

---

[146] *Champion Trading Company, Ameritrade International Inc., James T. Wahba, John B. Wahba and Timothy T. Wahba* v. *Arab Republic of Egypt*, ICSID Case No. ARB/02/9, Decision on Jurisdiction, 21 October 2003.

[147] Barak-Erez, 'The Institutional Aspects of Comparative Law', 492.

[148] M. Cohen, 'Reason-Giving in Court Practice: Decision-Makers at the Crossroads', *Columbia Journal of European Law* 14 (2007–2008), 257, 259.

[149] A party may request the annulment of the award, *inter alia*, on the ground that 'the award has failed to state the reasons on which it is based'. ICSID Convention, Article 52(1)(e).

would lessen, if not remove, the risk of free decision-making by adjudicators.

Arbitral tribunals have made extensive use of judicial borrowing, referring to the jurisprudence of local courts, on the one hand, and to the cases of previous arbitral tribunals and other international courts and tribunals, on the other. Yet, while the phenomenon of judicial borrowing has been investigated in relation to human rights adjudication[150] and constitutional law,[151] it has never been the object of a specific study in relation to international investment law and arbitration. Therefore, it seems crucial to map the current dimension of the phenomenon and to propose a more conscious use of the comparative method.

Looking at the arbitral awards, there is not only a sort of *endogenous* or *internal path coherence* by which arbitrators look at previous arbitral awards, but also an increasingly *exogeneous* or *external path coherence* or exchange between legal orders by which arbitrators look at the jurisprudence of other courts. In particular, one may identify three main streams of comparative reasoning. First, arbitrators often refer to previous arbitral awards. Second, they refer to other international or regional cases. Third, they refer to national cases. The following subsections will scrutinise these three streams of comparative reasoning.

Reference to previous arbitral awards

Although the rule of *stare decisis*, or binding precedent, does not apply to international arbitration and awards are binding *inter partes* only,[152] previous arbitral awards have influenced, if not shaped, much of contemporary investment law.[153] Investment treaties generally tend to converge and often present similar if not identical wording. Most countries have predisposed Model BITs to streamline and simplify the negotiating process. This phenomenon facilitates

---

[150] See, for example, McCrudden, 'Judicial Comparativism and Human Rights', p. 371.

[151] S. Choudhry, *The Migration of Constitutional Ideas* (Cambridge: Cambridge University Press, 2011).

[152] See, for example, ICSID Convention, Article 53 (stating that 'The award shall be binding on the parties ... '); NAFTA Article 1136(1) (providing that 'an award made by a Tribunal shall have no binding force except between the disputing parties and in respect of the particular case').

[153] G. Kaufmann-Kohler, 'Arbitral Precedent: Dream, Necessity or Excuse?', *Arbitration International* 23 (2007), 357.

borrowing.[154] When interpreting and applying investment treaty provisions, arbitral tribunals, albeit selected on an *ad hoc* basis, apply a sort of common law of investment protection.[155]

Arbitral tribunals acknowledge that previous cases are not binding precedents[156] and may adopt a different solution for resolving the same problem.[157] They are aware that 'the actual specificities' featured in each case must be carefully considered[158] 'in the context of the particular bilateral investment treaty in which they appear'.[159] They have affirmed that 'Even presuming that relevant principles could be distilled from prior arbitral awards . . ., [such awards] cannot be deemed to constitute the expression of a general consensus of the international community, and much less a formal source of international law.'[160]

Yet, arbitral tribunals rely on previous cases on a variety of grounds. First, legal interpretative canons dictate the reference to earlier rulings. As the *Suez–Vivendi* Tribunal stated, 'prior decisions . . . do constitute a "subsidiary means for the determination of the rules of [international]

---

[154] *See* A.F. Lowenfeld, 'Investment Agreements and International Law', *Columbia Journal of Transnational Law* 42 (2003), 123, 128–130 (noting that similar treaty provisions can gradually coalesce and become part of customary law).

[155] S.W. Schill, *The Multilateralization of International Investment Law* (Cambridge: Cambridge University Press, 2009).

[156] *Suez, Sociedad General de Aguas de Barcelona S.A., and Vivendi Universal S.A. v. the Argentine Republic*, ICSID Case No. ARB/03/19 and *AWG Group v. Argentine Republic*, UNCITRAL (joint cases), Decision on Liability, 30 July 2010, para. 189 (holding that 'Although this tribunal is not bound by such prior decisions, they do constitute "a subsidiary means for the determination of the rules of [international] law"'); *Bayindir Insaat Turizm Tecaret Ve Sanayi AS v. Pakistan*, Decision on Jurisdiction, ICSID Case No. ARB/03/29, 14 November 2005, para. 76 (stating that 'The Tribunal agrees that it is not bound by earlier decisions, but will certainly carefully consider such decisions whenever appropriate'); *RosInvestCo UK Ltd v. Russian Federation*, Jurisdiction Award, SCC Case No. V079/2005, para. 49 (holding that 'It is at all events plain that the decisions of other tribunals are not binding on this Tribunal . . . This does not however preclude the Tribunal from considering other arbitral decisions and the arguments of the Parties based upon them, to the extent that it may find that they throw any useful light on the issues that arise for decision in this case'); *Chevron Corp. v. Republic of Ecuador*, UNCITRAL, PCA Case No. 34877, Interim Award, 1 December 2008, at para. 122 (holding that 'the decisions of other tribunals are not binding on this Tribunal . . .')

[157] *AES Corporation v. Argentina*, ICSID Case No. ARB/02/17, Decision on Jurisdiction, 26 April 2005, para. 30 (reaffirming that 'Each tribunal remains sovereign').

[158] *Ibid.*, para. 32.

[159] *RosInvestCo UK Ltd v. Russian Federation*, Jurisdiction Award, para. 49.

[160] *Romak S.A. v. Republic of Uzbekistan*, UNCITRAL, PCA Case No. AA280, Award of 26 November 2009, para. 170.

law"'.[161] In *Chevron* v. *Ecuador*, the Arbitral Tribunal held that tribunals may have recourse, as a supplementary means of treaty interpretation, not only to a treaty's preparatory works, but also to other supplementary means of treaty interpretation including previous awards.[162] Furthermore, earlier decisions can help the interpreter to clarify the ordinary meaning of treaty provisions under Article 31 of the Vienna Convention.[163]

Second, functional approaches compel the reference to earlier rulings. Comparisons are perceived as useful for shedding light on the relevant issues.[164] As stated by the *AES* Tribunal, 'decisions on jurisdiction dealing with the same or very similar issues may at least indicate some lines of reasoning of real interest; this Tribunal may consider them in order to compare its own position with those already adopted by its predecessors and, if it shares the views already expressed by one or more of these tribunals on a specific point of law, it is free to adopt the same solution'.[165] As another tribunal acknowledged, 'In interpreting … vague, flexible, basic, and widely used treaty term[s], [it] ha[d] the benefit of decisions by prior tribunals'.[166] Previous cases have been considered 'at least as a matter of comparison and, if so considered by the Tribunal, of inspiration'.[167] Analogously, the *Romak* Tribunal held that it might and would consider 'awards rendered by distinguished arbitrators … as a means to provide context to the Parties' allegations and arguments, and … to explain succinctly the Arbitral Tribunal's own reasoning'.[168]

---

[161] *Suez, Sociedad General de Aguas de Barcelona S.A., and Vivendi Universal S.A.* v. *the Argentine Republic*, and *AWG Group* v. *Argentine Republic*, Decision on Liability, para. 189.

[162] *Chevron Corp.* v. *Republic of Ecuador*, Interim Award, at para. 121.

[163] *Azurix Corp.* v. *the Argentine Republic*, ICSID Case No. ARB/01/12, Award, 14 July 2006, para. 391.

[164] *Chevron-Texaco* v. *Ecuador*, Partial Award on the Merits, 30 March 2010, para. 164 ('considering arbitral decisions and the arguments of the Parties based upon them, to the extent that [the Tribunal] may find that they shed any useful light on the issues that arise for decision in this case').

[165] *AES Corporation* v. *Argentina*, Decision on Jurisdiction, para. 30.

[166] *Suez, Sociedad General de Aguas de Barcelona S.A., and Vivendi Universal S.A.* v. *the Argentine Republic*, and *AWG Group* v. *Argentine Republic*, Decision on Liability, para. 189 (with reference to the interpretation of the fair and equitable treatment standard).

[167] *AES Corp.* v. *Argentine Republic*, Decision on Jurisdiction, para. 31. See also *Romak S.A.* v. *Republic of Uzbekistan*, Award, para. 170 (considering previous awards 'mere sources of inspiration, comfort or reference to arbitrators').

[168] *Romak S.A.* v. *Republic of Uzbekistan*, Award, para. 171.

Third, like other international courts and tribunals,[169] arbitrators have highlighted the importance of treating like cases alike. The principle 'treat like cases alike' – often seen as key to the concept of fairness, justice and equality – requires tribunals to be consistent. As the *Suez–Vivendi* Tribunal stated, 'considerations of basic justice would lead tribunals to be guided by the basic judicial principle that "like cases should be decided alike", unless a strong reason exists to distinguish the current case from previous ones'.[170] Analogously, the *Saipem* Tribunal held that 'subject to compelling contrary grounds, [it] ha[d] a duty to adopt solutions established in a series of consistent cases'.[171]

Fourth, if one adopts a teleological interpretation of investment treaties, 'a recognized goal of international investment law is to establish a predictable, stable legal framework for investments, a factor that justifies tribunals in giving due regard to previous decisions on similar issues'.[172] Another tribunal observed that '[the] responsibility for ensuring consistency in the jurisprudence and for building a coherent body of law rests

---

[169] See, for example, PCIJ, *Readaptation of the Mavrommatis Jerusalem Concessions (Greece v. Britain)*, Jurisdiction, 1927 PCIJ (ser. A) No. 11, at 18, 10 October 1927 (finding that it had 'no reason to depart from a construction which clearly flows from the previous judgments the reasoning of which it still regards as sound'). The Appellate Body in *US–Stainless Steel* analogously required panels to advance 'cogent reasons' to justify departure from its previous decisions. See Appellate Body Report, *United States–Final Anti-Dumping Measures on Stainless Steel from Mexico*, WT/DS344/AB/R, 30 April 2008, para. 160. In *US–Oil Country Tubular Goods Sunset Reviews*, the AB stated that 'to rely on the Appellate Body's conclusions in earlier disputes is not only appropriate, but is what would be expected from panels, especially where the issues are the same'. AB Report, *US–Oil Country Tubular Goods Sunset Reviews*, WT/DS268/AB/R, 29 November 2004, para. 188. In *Japan–Alcoholic Beverages II*, the AB held that 'Adopted panel reports are an important part of the GATT *acquis*. They are often considered by subsequent panels. They create legitimate expectations among WTO Members, and, therefore, should be taken into account where they are relevant to any dispute.' Even with regard to unadopted panel reports, the AB confirmed that 'a panel could nevertheless find useful guidance in the reasoning of an unadopted panel report that it considered to be relevant'. *Japan–Taxes on Alcoholic Beverages*, AB Report, WT/DS8/AB/R, WT/DS10/AB/R and WT/DS11/AB/R, 4 October 1996, at pp. 14–15.
[170] *Suez, Sociedad General de Aguas de Barcelona S.A., and Vivendi Universal S.A. v. the Argentine Republic and AWG Group v. Argentine Republic*, Decision on Liability, para. 189.
[171] *Saipem S.p.A. v. People's Republic of Bangladesh*, ICSID Case No. ARB/05/7, Award, 30 June 2009, para. 90.
[172] *Suez, Sociedad General de Aguas de Barcelona S.A., and Vivendi Universal S.A. v. the Argentine Republic and AWG Group v. Argentine Republic*, Decision on Liability, para. 189.

primarily with the investment tribunals'.[173] Analogously, the *Saipem* Tribunal considered that 'subject to the specifics of a given treaty and of the circumstances of the actual case, it has a duty to seek to contribute to the harmonious development of investment law and thereby to meet the legitimate expectations of the community of States and investors towards certainty of the rule of law'.[174]

Finally, arbitral tribunals are aware that consistent awards can contribute to the development of a *jurisprudence constante*.[175] Reference to previous arbitral awards 'contributes to the making of international law',[176] enhances the persuasive authority of past and present awards and responds to the expectations of the parties,[177] which heavily rely on precedents in their written pleadings.[178] This creates a sort of endogenous coherence (i.e. a coherence which is internal to international investment law).

---

[173] *M.C.I. Power Group L.C. and New Turbine Inc.* v. *Republic of Ecuador*, ICSID Case No. Arb/03/6, Decision on Annulment, 19 October 2009, para. 24.

[174] *Saipem S.p.A.* v. *People's Republic of Bangladesh*, Award, para. 90.

[175] *AES Corp.* v. *Argentine Republic*, Decision on Jurisdiction, para. 33. But see *Romak S.A.* v. *Republic of Uzbekistan*, Award, at para. 171 (holding that 'the Arbitral Tribunal has not been entrusted, by the Parties or otherwise, with a mission to ensure the coherence or development of "arbitral jurisprudence." The Arbitral Tribunal's mission is more mundane, but no less important: to resolve the present dispute between the Parties in a reasoned and persuasive manner, irrespective of the unintended consequences that this Arbitral Tribunal's analysis might have on future disputes in general. It is for the legal doctrine as reflected in articles and books, and not for arbitrators in their awards, to set forth, promote or criticize general views regarding trends in, and the desired evolution of, investment law').

[176] I. Venzke, 'The Role of International Courts as Interpreters and Developers of the Law: Working Out the Jurisgenerative Practice of Interpretation', *Loyola of Los Angeles International and Comparative Law Review* 34 (2011), 99–131, 125.

[177] S. Schill, 'System Building in Investment Arbitration and Lawmaking', *German Law Journal* 12 (2011), 1083.

[178] *El Paso Energy International Company* v. *The Argentine Republic*, ICSID Case No. ARB/03/15, Decision on Jurisdiction, 27 April 2006, para. 39 (stating that the Tribunal will take into account earlier decisions, 'especially since both parties, in their written pleadings and oral arguments, have heavily relied on precedent'); *Chevron Texaco* v. *Ecuador*, Partial Award on the Merits, para. 163 (referring to the 'many references by the Parties to certain arbitral decisions in their pleadings'). *See also Marvin Feldman* v. *United Mexican States*, ICSID Case No. ARB(AF)/9901, Award on Merits, 16 December 2002, para. 107 (reaffirming that a tribunal award has no binding force except between the parties and in respect of a particular case; however, 'in view of the fact that both of the parties in this proceeding have extensively cited and relied upon some of the earlier decisions, the Tribunal believe[d] it appropriate to discuss briefly relevant aspects of earlier decisions...').

Reference to the jurisprudence of other international courts and tribunals

More and more arbitral tribunals have considered the judgments of other international courts and tribunals,[179] taking into account the approaches that have been adopted with regard to similar legal problems elsewhere. This form of judicial borrowing creates hetero-geneous path coherence, contributing to cross-fertilisation, judicial dialogue and judicial globalisation,[180] or the development of a 'common law of international adjudication'.[181]

The inclination to borrow precedents decided in other jurisdictions takes place more often in newly established legal systems, as they lack a jurisprudence of their own.[182] In early arbitral awards, arbitrators con-sistently referred to the jurisprudence of other international courts and tribunals as well as regional and national courts.[183] More recently, the 'internal references' to other arbitral awards have become more and more common.[184] This is not to say that arbitral tribunals fall short of referring to a range of other sources, but it seems that both parties and arbitral tribunals first look at the available arbitral jurisprudence and then look for other sources if the arbitral jurisprudence does not provide satisfactory reference.

In certain cases, however, landmark cases belonging to other courts and tribunals are referred to in the very first instance, especially when they epitomise a given legal concept. For instance, in case of reparation, the *Chorzow Factory* case[185] is the standard point of reference, despite the

---

[179] *El Paso Energy* v. *The Argentine Republic*, Decision on Jurisdiction, para. 39 (holding that 'It is ... a reasonable assumption that international arbitral tribunals, notably those established within the ICSID system, will generally take account of the precedents established by other arbitration organs, *especially those set by other international tribu-nals*' (emphasis added)). *Azurix Corp.* v. *the Argentine Republic*, Award, para. 391 (mentioning that 'The findings of other tribunals, and in particular of the ICJ, should be helpful to the Tribunal in its interpretative task').

[180] Slaughter, 'Judicial Globalization', 1103.

[181] See Brown, *A Common Law of International Adjudication*, pp. 4–5.

[182] Barak-Erez, 'The Institutional Aspects of Comparative Law', 477, 487.

[183] *Ibid.*, at 486 (noting that 'the inclination to borrow precedents decided by other tribunals becomes stronger when "the basic principles of both the borrowing and the lending systems are similar"').

[184] J. Commission, 'Precedent in Investment Treaty Arbitration: A Citation Analysis of a Developing Jurisprudence', *Journal of International Arbitration* 24 (2007), 149 (noting a 'marked increase of citations to ICSID decisions by ICSID tribunals').

[185] *Case Concerning Chorzow Factory (Germany v. Poland)*, Merits, Judgment of 13 September 1928, 1928 P.C.I.J. (ser. A) No. 17, p. 47 (holding that 'reparation must, as

fact that many decades have passed since it was decided.[186] Not only is this leading case still relevant, but it also serves a sort of legitimising function: since the parties would expect arbitral tribunals to mention this case with regard to reparation, these tribunals cannot but refer to the case.

Arbitral tribunals have referred to the jurisprudence of a number of international courts and tribunals. The Iran–US Claims Tribunal has been a useful source of reference for arbitral tribunals with regard to some key issues such as regulatory expropriation.[187] For instance, in *Saipem* v. *Bangladesh*, the Tribunal made reference to a case of the Iran–US Claims Tribunal to hold that a state can expropriate immaterial rights.[188] In his separate opinion in the *Thunderbird* case, Professor Wälde made reference to the Iran–US Tribunal's practice with regard to the award of attorney costs.[189]

ICSID tribunals have extensively referred to decisions of the ICJ[190] and its predecessor, the Permanent Court of International Justice (PCIJ).[191] Arbitral tribunals refer to the jurisprudence of the ICJ and PCIJ because of their perceived authority and persuasiveness. Moreover, several investment disputes have been adjudicated by both courts. In fact, before the

---

far as possible, wipe out all the consequences of the illegal act and re-establish the situation which would, in all probability, have existed if that act had not been committed').

[186] See, for example, *Metalclad Corporation* v. *Mexico*, ICSID Case No. ARB(AF)/97/1, Award, 30 August 2000, para. 122; *CMS Gas Transmission Company* v. *The Argentine Republic*, ICSID Case No. ARB/01/8, Award, 12 May 2005, para. 400; and *MTD Equity Sdn Bhd and MTD Chile SA* v. *Chile*, ICSID Case No. ARB/01/7, Award, 25 May 2004, para. 238.

[187] The tribunal was established in 1979 to resolve a number of disputes arising out of political crisis between Iran and the United States. See, for example, C.R. Drahozal and C.S. Gibson, *The Iran–U.S. Claims Tribunal at 25: The Cases Everyone Needs to Know for Investor-State and International Arbitration* (Oxford: Oxford University Press, 2009).

[188] *Saipem S.p.A.* v. *People's Republic of Bangladesh*, ICSID Case No. ARB/05/7, Decision on Jurisdiction and Recommendation on Provisional Measures, 21 March 2007, para. 130 (citing *Phillips Petroleum Company Iran* v. *Islamic Republic of Iran*, 21 Iran–US CTR 79 (1989).

[189] *International Thunderbird Gaming Corp.* v. *United Mexican States*, 255 Fed. Appx. 531 (2007), Separate Opinion of Arbitrator Thomas Wälde, at para. 140 (quoting *Sylvania* v. *Iran*, 8 Iran–US CTR 298, 324 (1985)).

[190] For instance, in *Maffezini* v. *Spain*, the Tribunal referred to the ICJ decision *Rights of Nationals of America in Morocco* (*France* v. *United States*) when deciding on the scope of protection of the MFN clause. *Maffezini* v. *Spain*, ICSID Case No. ARB/97/7, Award on Jurisdiction, 25 January 2000, paras. 43–50.

[191] See, for example, *LG&E Energy Corp.* v. *Argentine Republic*, ICSID Case No. ARB/02/1, Award, 25 July 2007, para. 11.

inception of investment treaty arbitration, customary international law and earlier treaties provided for an interstate process only; governments therefore had to 'sponsor' private claims before international tribunals such as the PCIJ and the ICJ. Currently, recourse to diplomatic protection has become 'residual',[192] and primarily international investment treaties, rather than customary international law alone, now protect foreign investors. Yet, arbitral tribunals still take into account the jurisprudence of the ICJ and PCIJ relating to interstate disputes to clarify the meaning of legal concepts. Notable examples relate to the determination of the nationality of the claimant.[193] For instance, in *Soufraki v. United Arab Emirates*, the Arbitral Tribunal referred to the *Nottebohm* case (*Liechtenstein v. Guatemala*) when discussing the question of the nationality of the claimant.[194]

More recently, arbitral tribunals have referred to the *dicta* of international tribunals as a starting point for further enquiry. For instance, in the *Europe Cement* case,[195] when the respondent alleged that the claimant had abused the process and requested declaratory relief (i.e. a declaration that there had been such abuse), the Arbitral Tribunal stated: 'Declaratory relief is a common form of relief in international tribunals in state-to-state cases, but no cases were cited to us of tribunals established under the ICSID Convention ... or under international investment treaties more generally where declarations were granted as a form of relief.'[196] In conclusion, the Tribunal acknowledged that declaratory relief had been used in the *Corfu Channel Case*[197] but it also questioned

---

[192] While in the 1970s, the ICJ in the *Barcelona Traction* case found it 'surprising' that the evolution of international investment law had not gone further in the light of the expansion of economic activities in the preceding half century, in the more recent *Diallo* case, the Court recognised the residual nature of the exercise of diplomatic protection and recourse to the Court in case of investment disputes. These different *obiter dicta* reflect the recent flourishing of investment treaties and investment treaty arbitration. *Barcelona Traction, Light & Power Company, Limited (Belgium v. Spain)*, Judgment of 5 February 1970, 1970 ICJ 3, at para. 89; *Case Concerning* Ahmadou Sadio Diallo *(Guinea v. Democratic Republic Congo)*, *(Preliminary Objections)*, Judgment of 24 May 2007, at paras. 88–91.

[193] ICSID Convention, Article 25.

[194] *Hussein Nuaman Soufraki v. U.A.E.*, ICSID Case No. ARB/02/7, Decision on Jurisdiction, 7 July 2004, para. 45.

[195] *Europe Cement Investment & Trade S.A. v. Republic of Turkey*, ICSID Case No. ARB(AF)/07/2, Award, 7 August 2009.

[196] *Id.*, para. 148.

[197] *The Corfu Channel Case (United Kingdom of Great Britain and Northern Ireland v. Albania)*, Judgment of 9 April 1949, *ICJ Reports* 4 [1949].

whether previous arbitral tribunals had adopted such declarations.[198] In other words, notwithstanding the persuasiveness of the ICJ decision, the Arbitral Tribunal was enquiring into further developments of the investment jurisprudence.

Arbitral tribunals have cursorily relied on WTO jurisprudence for interpreting investment treaty provisions. For instance, in *ADF* v. *United States of America*,[199] the Arbitral Tribunal referred to the *Shrimp Turtle* and *Hormones* AB reports when applying customary rules of treaty interpretation.[200] In his separate opinion in the *Thunderbird* case,[201] Thomas Wälde argued that 'gambling services, in particular if not typically accompanied by criminal by-products, have to be treated as a fully legitimate investment', relying *inter alia* on a WTO case.[202]

The case for referring to the WTO jurisprudence is evident. International economic courts 'essentially do share the same functions' by settling international disputes in accordance with international economic law and ensuring the proper administration of justice.[203] In parallel, certain international treaties present an articulated regime that the investment treaties presuppose. For instance, while investment treaties protect intellectual property as a form of investment, the WTO Trade Related Aspects of Intellectual Property Rights (TRIPS) Agreement[204] requires member states to ensure a minimum level of protection and enforcement of intellectual property rights in their territories. Given the almost universal membership of the WTO, the TRIPS Agreement has had a harmonising effect on intellectual property (IP) regulation at the global level. When IP-related investment disputes have arisen, the parties

---

[198] *Id.*, para. 148, n. 32.

[199] *ADF Group Inc.* v. *U.S.*, ICSID Case No. ARB/AF/00/1, Award, 9 January 2003.

[200] *Id.*, at para. 147 (citing AB report, *United States–Import Prohibition of Certain Shrimp and Shrimp Products*, 12 October 1998, WT/DS58/AB/R, para. 114; AB report, *EC–Measures Concerning Meat and Meat Products (Hormones)*, 16 January 1998, WT/DS26/AB/R, WT/DS48/AB/R, paras. 165, 181).

[201] *International Thunderbird Gaming Corp.* v. *United Mexican States*, 255 Fed. Appx. 531 (2007), Separate Opinion of Arbitrator Thomas Wälde.

[202] *Id.*, at para. 18 (citing the WTO Appellate Body report, *United States–Measures Affecting the Cross-Border Supply of Gambling and Betting Services (US–Gambling)*, 7 April 2005, WT/DS285/AB/R).

[203] C. Brown, 'The Use of Precedents of Other International Courts and Tribunals in Investment Treaty Arbitration', *Transnational Dispute Management* 5 (2008), 1, 2.

[204] Agreement on Trade-Related Aspects of Intellectual Property Rights (TRIPS Agreement), 15 April 1994, Marrakesh Agreement Establishing the World Trade Organization, Annex 1C, Legal Instruments – Results of the Uruguay Round, 33 ILM 1994.

have referred to the TRIPS standards, contending that the alleged violations of the TRIPS Agreement also constitute a breach of the relevant investment treaty provisions, including the FET standard.[205] Reference to the WTO jurisprudence by arbitral tribunals would impede the dilution of multilateral norms while providing predictability.[206] Such borrowing can offer direction in the substantive interpretation of treaty language as arbitral panels could 'draw upon the expertise of WTO dispute panels and the Appellate Body in the development of legal concepts and principles' albeit maintaining the possibility to contract away such jurisprudence by setting their own interpretation.[207]

In parallel, arbitral tribunals have referred to and relied on human rights jurisprudence, to varying degrees, to determine the content of investment law.[208] For instance, in *Lauder v. Czech Republic*, the UNCITRAL Tribunal made reference to the European Court of Human Rights (ECtHR) case *Mellachr v. Austria* to derive the distinction between a *formal* and a *de facto* expropriation.[209] The *Tecmed* Tribunal referred to an Inter-American Court of Human Rights case, *Ivcher Bronstein v. Peru*, to determine the content of indirect expropriation.[210] In *Saipem S.p.A v. Bangladesh*, the Tribunal cited several cases from the ECtHR for affirming that arbitral awards confer on parties a right to the sums awarded.[211] Finally, human rights obligations have also been

---

[205] See, for example, *Philip Morris Asia Limited* v. *the Commonwealth of Australia*, Notification of Claim, 22 June 2011, para. 10(b).

[206] L. Hsu, 'Applicability of WTO Law in Regional Trade Agreements: Identifying the Links', in L. Bartels and F. Ortino (eds.), *Regional Trade Agreements and the WTO Legal System* (Oxford: Oxford University Press, 2006), p. 449.

[207] *Id.*, at pp. 551–552.

[208] J.D. Fry, 'International Human Rights Law in Investment Arbitration: Evidence of International Law's Unity', *Duke Journal of Comparative and International Law* 18 (2007), 83.

[209] *Lauder v. Czech Republic*, Final Award, 3 September 2001, para. 200, 9 *ICSID Reports* 66 (2001) (quoting *Mellacher v. Austria*, 169 Eur. Ct. H.R. (ser. A) (1989)).

[210] *Técnicas Medioambientales S.A.* v. *United Mexican States*, ICSID Case No. ARB/(AF)/00/2, Award, 29 May 2003, para. 116, n. 36, 43 ILM 133 (2004) (quoting *Baruch Ivcher Bronstein v. Peru*, 2001 Inter-Am. Ct. H.R. (ser. C) No. 74, at paras. 120–124).

[211] *Saipem S.p.A.* v. *People's Republic of Bangladesh*, ICSID Case No. ARB/05/7, Decision on Jurisdiction and Recommendation on Provisional Measures, 21 March 2007, para. 130 (citing *Stran Greek Refineries and Stratis Andreadis v. Greece*, App. No. 13427/87, Eur. Ct. H.R., paras. 59–62 (1994), and *Brumarescu v. Romania*, App. No. 28342/95, Eur. Ct. H.R., 10 Hum. Rts. Case Dig. 237–241 (1999).

invoked in the determination of the remedies phase.[212] Other cases have made indirect reference to human rights cases. For instance, in *Azurix Corp.* v. *Argentine Republic*, the Tribunal indirectly cited human rights jurisprudence by relying on the relevant aspects of the *Tecmed* decision.[213] Similarly, the *EnCana* Tribunal cited a domestic arbitration case that quoted a human rights case.[214] Arbitral tribunals increasingly rely on human rights cases 'in their decisions, not merely in their *obiter dicta*'.[215]

Arbitral tribunals have generally clarified that they are tribunals of limited jurisdiction. For instance, the Arbitral Tribunal in *Biloune* held that its jurisdiction was limited to disputes in respect of foreign investment and that it lacked 'jurisdiction to address, as an independent cause of action, a claim of violation of human rights'.[216] Similarly, the *Siemens* Tribunal rejected the application of the margin of appreciation doctrine in investment arbitration, holding that 'Article I of the First Protocol to the European Convention on Human Rights permits a margin of appreciation not found in customary international law or the Treaty.'[217] In the *Euro-tunnel* case, the Tribunal defined its jurisdiction as arising only from the Canterbury Treaty and the related concessionary contract.[218] Therefore, the Tribunal deemed that its jurisdiction was limited only to claims concerning the alleged violation of the concession contract and/or the Treaty. Accordingly, it held that any violation of other international rules of the European Convention on Human Rights or EU law was beyond its jurisdiction. However, the Arbitral Tribunal did not exclude the possibility that violations of the Treaty and the contract could be

---

[212] See, for example, *Compañía del Desarollo de Santa Elena* v. *Republic of Costa Rica*, ICSID Case No. ARB/96/1, Final Award, 17 February 2000, paras. 64–68.

[213] *Azurix Corp.* v. *Argentine Republic*, ICSID Case No. ARB/01/12, Award, 23 June 2006, paras. 311–312.

[214] *EnCana* v. *Ecuador*, LCIA Award, 3 February 2006, para. 176, n. 124.

[215] Fry, 'International Human Rights Law in Investment Arbitration', 81, n. 15 (noting that '[a]rbitral tribunals are not throwing in references to human rights cases merely for the sake of appearances').

[216] *Biloune and Marine Drive Complex Ltd.* v. *Ghana Investments. Ctr. and Government of Ghana*, Award on Jurisdiction and Liability, UNCITRAL, 27 October 1989, 95 ILR 183, 203.

[217] *Siemens A.G.* v. *Argentine Republic*, ICSID No. ARB/02/08, Award, 6 February 2007, para. 354.

[218] *Channel Tunnel Group Ltd. and France Manche S.A.* v. *Governments of U.K. and France*, Partial Award on Jurisdiction, 30 January 2007 paras. 124, 135, 152 (referencing the jurisprudence of the Permanent Court of International Justice, the ICJ, and the International Tribunal for the Law of the Sea).

examined in light of rules of general public international law. As some authors have pointed out, 'even if the direct violation of such rules was beyond its jurisdiction, the evaluation of a violation of the concession contract *in comparison* with these provisions was not excluded'.[219]

Borrowing decisions from other international *fora* in the interpretation of international law promotes the coherence of international law. Informal linkages already exist as some arbitrators have been professors of public international law or judges in other international fora.[220]

However, on a cautionary note, textual differences need to be taken into account, as interpretation cannot be used to transpose obligations from one field to another or to create new obligations. For instance, in *Victor Pey Casado* v. *Chile*, the Arbitral Tribunal made reference to the ICJ *LaGrand* judgment,[221] which found that the provisional measures under Article 41 of the ICJ Statute were binding.[222] The Tribunal held that the judgment could be applied by way of analogy to Article 47 of the ICSID Convention.[223] However, Article 47 of the ICSID Convention contains different wording, as it states that arbitral tribunals shall have the power to 'recommend' and not to 'indicate' provisional measures.[224] While one may agree that such an interpretation favours the effectiveness

---

[219] M. Audit, 'The Channel Tunnel Group Ltd and France-Manche SA v. United Kingdom and France', *International and Comparative Law Quarterly* 57 (2008), 724, 728 (emphasis added).

[220] For instance, arbitrators have served as former presidents or judges of the ICJ, members of the WTO panels or AB, former judges of the Inter-American Court of Human Rights, former presidents of the UN Security Council, or may be academics. See, for example, D. Kapeliuk, 'The Repeat Appointment Factor: Exploring Decision Patterns of Elite Investment Arbitrators', *Cornell Law Review* 96 (2010–2011), 47; J.A. Fontoura Costa, 'Comparing WTO Panelists and ICSID Arbitrators: The Creation of International Legal Fields', *Oñati Socio-Legal Series* 1 (2011), 19 (noting the high number of AB members who are nominated as ICSID arbitrators); S. Puig, 'Social Capital in the Arbitration Market', *European Journal of International Law* 25 (2014), 387–424.

[221] ICJ, *LaGrand (Germany v. United States of America)*, Judgment, 27 June 2001, *ICJ Reports* (2001), p. 466.

[222] *Victor Pey Casado and President Allende Foundation* v. *Republic of Chile*, ICSID Case No. ARB/98/2, Decision on Provisional Measures, 25 September 2001, para. 17, *ICSID Reports* 16 (2001), 603.

[223] *Ibid.*, para. 20 (stating that 'La conclusion de l'arrêt, particulièrement nette, mérite d'être citée, et ce d'autant plus qu'elle paraît manifestement pouvoir s'appliquer par analogie à l'article 47 de la Convention CIRDI ... ').

[224] Brown, 'The Use of Precedents of Other International Courts and Tribunals in Investment Treaty Arbitration', at 4 (criticizing this approach as inappropriate use of precedent).

of the ICSID Convention,[225] and can be justified by the inherent powers of international courts to grant provisional measures, certainly such a line of reasoning expands the treaty terms beyond the purpose of the treaty-makers,[226] contributing to the development of law, but creating margins of uncertainty.[227] In the *Methanex* case, when the claimant sought to show that it was a producer 'in like circumstances' with respect to US domestic producers by arguing that Methanex produced 'like products' and relying on related WTO jurisprudence, the Tribunal declined to rely on such jurisprudence, because NAFTA Chapter 11 did not contain the term of art 'like product', which is relevant to the interpretation of GATT Article III.[228]

Judicial borrowing is a very powerful instrument which can create problems if not done appropriately. Major risks consist of adopting an ideology of free decision-making[229] and creating unpredictable outcomes. In the selection of cases to be used as persuasive precedents, there may be a certain bias as relying on human rights case law rather than WTO jurisprudence can make a difference in the context of a specific case.[230] Some have pointed out that 'the dissimilar architecture of treaties, including objectives, obligations, defenses, and remedies advises against attempts of outright transposition of rules, methodologies, or solutions'.[231]

Reference to the jurisprudence of national courts

Article 38(1)(d) of the Statute of the ICJ considers judicial decisions 'as subsidiary means for the determination of rules of law'. This provision

---

[225] *Victor Pey Casado and President Allende Foundation* v. *Republic of Chile*, Decision on Provisional Measures, para. 26.

[226] Schreuer, *The ICSID Convention: A Commentary*, p. 758 (highlighting that the 'Convention's legislative history shows clearly that a conscious decision was made *not* to grant the Tribunal the power to order binding provisional measures' (emphasis added)).

[227] F. Latty, 'Les techniques interprétative du CIRDI', *Revue Générale de Droit International Public* 115 (2011), 459, 475.

[228] *Methanex Corp.* v. *U.S.*, NAFTA, Final Award, 15 January 2001, Part IV, ch. B, paras. 23–35.

[229] See, for example, R. Siltala, *A Theory of Precedent – From Analytical Positivism to a Post-Analytical Philosophy of Law* (Oxford: Hart Publishing, 2000), p. 4 (analysing free judicial decision-making).

[230] See R. Hischl, 'The Question of Case Selection in Comparative Constitutional Law', *American Journal of Comparative Law* 53 (2005), 125.

[231] M.A. Orellana, 'Science, Risk and Uncertainty: Public Health Measures and Investment Disciplines', in P. Kahn and T.W. Wälde (eds.), *New Aspects of International Investment Law* (Leiden: Martinus Nijhoff, 2007), pp. 671, 788.

does not distinguish between 'international' and 'national' decisions.[232] Therefore, arguably, arbitral tribunals can refer to both national and international decisions. However, several sets of critical distinctions emerge from scholarship. On the one hand, some scholars distinguish international decisions from national decisions on the basis of the character of the adjudicative body. Accordingly, these authors stress that reference to national decisions should be made carefully as decisions of national courts 'are primarily required to apply national law', whereas judicial decisions of international courts 'are required to apply international law'.[233] Other scholars distinguish between international and national decisions on the basis of the type of law being applied.[234] According to these scholars, if a tribunal applies international law, then its decision is considered as an international judicial decision.

This study follows the former approach, that is, it distinguishes between national and international decisions on the basis of the type of court or tribunal. This distinction is chosen over the other because it provides more formal and objective criteria for distinguishing national and international decisions. In fact, while certain subjects can be considered of national import in some countries and of international relevance in others, it is relatively straightforward to ascertain the national or international character of a given tribunal. Moreover, this distinction has the merit of classifying as international those decisions which have a truly international character because of their object, applicable law and relevant court.

In addition to the distinction between national and international decisions, other scholars distinguish decisions based on whether the sources are internal or external.[235] As McCrudden puts it, 'Internal sources are those that relate to those jurisdictions to which the relevant court has direct relevance and those jurisdictions that are considered part of the same legal system'.[236] For instance, the Court of Justice of the European Union (CJEU) uses 'internal sources', when it relies on the constitutional practice of some or all of its member states.[237] In contrast,

---

[232] A. Zammit Borda, 'A Formal Approach to Article 38(1)(d) of the ICJ Statute from the Perspective of the International Criminal Courts and Tribunals', *European Journal of International Law* 24 (2013), 649, 652.

[233] *Ibid.*, 658.   [234] *Ibid.*

[235] C. McCrudden, 'Using Comparative Reasoning in Human Rights Adjudication: The Court of Justice of the European Union and the European Court of Human Rights Compared', *Cambridge Yearbook of European Legal Studies* 15 (2012–2013), 383–415, 385.

[236] *Ibid.*   [237] *Ibid.*

'external sources are those that do not relate to those jurisdictions to which the respective courts have direct relevance'.[238] For instance, the CJEU uses 'external sources', when it relies on the jurisprudence of the US Supreme Court.[239] In light of this additional categorisation, the various distinctions can be combined so that, with regard to international investment arbitration, any judicial borrowing can fit in one of these four categories: internal/domestic, internal/international, external/domestic and external/international.

For instance, in a hypothetical scenario, if an arbitral tribunal refers to a decision by a Ruritanian tribunal applying Ruritanian law in an arbitration brought against Ruritania, this would be a case of internal/domestic judicial borrowing. If an arbitral tribunal refers to an arbitral tribunal's decision applying international investment law, this would be a case of internal/international judicial borrowing. If an arbitral tribunal refers to the jurisprudence of the Supreme Court of Oglasa applying Oglasan law in arbitration against Ruritania, this would be a case of external/domestic judicial borrowing. Finally, if an arbitral tribunal refers to the jurisprudence of another international court or tribunal applying other branches of international law, this would be a case of external/international judicial borrowing.

While the previous sections examined various aspects of internal and external types of international judicial borrowing, this section examines the internal and external types of domestic judicial borrowing. On the one hand, domestic judicial borrowing is sometimes considered of lesser importance than international judicial borrowing. While 'national law-oriented scholars tend to advocate the transplantation of national solutions to international legal settings',[240] international law is considered to 'offe[r] more open, ... more diverse and possibly more appropriate solutions for the global context ...'[241] On the other, while internal/domestic judicial borrowing seems appropriate in most cases, questions arise with regard to the appropriateness of external/domestic judicial borrowing, as only in the case of the existence of general principles of law or customary law would such reference seem appropriate.

---

[238] *Ibid.*   [239] *Ibid*, at 404.
[240] See E. Hey and E. Mak, 'Introduction: The Possibilities of Comparative Law Method for Research on the Rule of Law in a Global Context', *Erasmus Law Review* 2 (2009), 287–288, 287.
[241] *Ibid.*

Arbitral tribunals often refer to judicial decisions of national courts.[242] If the applicable law is that of the host state, reference to its jurisprudence in order to clarify relevant provisions can be made.[243] For instance, in the *Trail Smelter* arbitration between the United States and Canada, the parties instructed the Tribunal to 'apply the law and practice followed in dealing with cognate questions in the United States of America as well as international law and practice'.[244] In assessing the indemnity to be paid, the Arbitral Tribunal examined a number of American cases.[245]

Questions may arise regarding an arbitral tribunal's reliance on the jurisprudence of other national courts and tribunals. In earlier times, some scholars and practitioners sought to ascertain the existence of general principles of law by deducing them solely from given local systems. For instance, in the *Cayuga Indians Claim*, when the Tribunal considered the position of the tribe under international law, it referred to a number of decisions of the US Supreme Court to conclude that an Indian tribe 'is not a legal unit of international law'.[246]

In the *Abu Dhabi arbitration*,[247] the arbitrator, Lord Asquith of Bishopstone, decided that international law was applicable as the proper law of the contract. After pinpointing that the contract was 'made in Abu Dhabi and wholly to be performed in that country', he noted that, at the time, there was no settled body of law applicable to commercial instruments. Therefore, he applied 'principles rooted in the good sense and common practice of the generality of a civilized nation …' Although he acknowledged that 'English municipal law [wa]s inapplicable as such', he considered that 'some of its rules [we]re … so firmly grounded in reason' as to have 'ecumenical validity'. Only certain English maxims relied on by one of the parties

---

[242] See, for example, *Grand River Enterprises Six Nations, Ltd., et al. v. U.S.*, Decision on Objections to Jurisdiction, 20 July 2006, para. 77, n. 34 (referencing US national cases to validate the concept that 'a person may "incur" expenses before he or she actually disburses any funds').

[243] See A.F.M. Maniruzzaman, 'State Contracts in Contemporary International Law: Monist versus Dualist Controversies', *European Journal of International Law* 12 (2001), 309, 320.

[244] *Trail Smelter Arbitration, United States v. Canada*, U.N. *Reports of International Arbitral Awards* 3 (1938–1941), 1905, 1920.

[245] *Ibid.*, pp. 1925–1926.

[246] *Cayuga Indians (United Kingdom v. United States)*, *Reports of International Arbitral Awards* 6 (1926), 173.

[247] *Petroleum Development Ltd. v. Sheikh of Abu Dhabi*, *International Law Reports* 18 (1951), 144, 149–150 (no. 37) (Lord Asquith of Bishopstone, Umpire).

were not considered to be applicable to the facts of the case due to their origin, determined by 'incidents of English feudal polity and royal prerogative' which were of 'little relevance' to the Persian Gulf. However, such an approach, based on the arbitrator's national system, is no longer tenable; 'only comparative legal research ... can ascertain principles of law which can validly be termed "general"'.[248]

Adopting a functionalist approach, some emphasise that the issue of regulatory expropriation and other similar issues identified in investor–state dispute settlement initially emerged as 'constitutional issue[s] in national law'.[249] For instance, according to Wälde and Kolo, the jurisprudence of the US Supreme Court on regulatory taking would be 'particularly apposite to serve as a laboratory – but also as relative precedent' – for interpreting the relevant investment treaty provisions.[250] The functionalist approach is based on the *praesumptio similitudinis* and holds that '[c]omparative constitutional law seems to provide the most suitable analogy and precedent' to investor–state arbitration.[251]

However, such a functionalist approach reduces the law to a formal technique of conflict resolution denying its political underpinnings. The functionalists deprive legal provisions of their systemic context and 'integrat[e] them in an artificial universal typology of "solutions"'.[252] One of the main features of investment arbitration is its detachment or separation from national courts and their potential biases.

Judicial decisions are not a source of law under international law; rather, they can help with identifying and elucidating existing law. National judicial decisions are 'facts which express the will and constitute the activities of states'.[253] They 'can play a pivotal function as evidences of customary international law'[254] and of general principles of law. In order to ascertain general principles of law, 'it is necessary to apply comparative

---

[248] G. Winterton, 'Comparative Legal Teaching', *American Journal of Comparative Law* 23 (1975), 69–118, 105–106.

[249] Wälde and Kolo, 'Environmental Regulation, Investment Protection and "Regulatory Taking" in International Law', 821.

[250] *Id.*, at 847.   [251] *Id.*, at 822.

[252] G. Frankenberg, 'Critical Comparisons: Rethinking Comparative Law', *Harvard International Law Journal* 26 (1985), 411, at 411.

[253] *German Interests in Polish Upper Silesia (Germany v. Poland)*, Judgment of 25 May 1926, 1926 PCIJ (ser. A) No. 7, at 52.

[254] Zammit Borda, 'A Formal Approach to Article 38(1)(d) of the ICJ Statute', 658.

methodology'.[255] While it may be practically impossible to take the wide variety of national jurisprudence into account, ideally, an arbitral tribunal should make a thorough survey of comparative law, making use of the scholarly work that has been done on the issue. However, this does not happen in practice. Usually, only the laws of a small number of countries are cited.[256] The lack of both comparative research and/or reference to a large number of legal systems risks jeopardising the perceived legitimacy of the system.[257] For example, some authors have criticised reliance on the US jurisprudence because this would be tantamount to rewriting other countries' constitutional culture and experience.[258] Drawing on the particular constitutional experience of a country would repoliticise investment disputes against more neutral international canons.[259] Finally, one wonders whether this can amount to extraterritorial application of the law. Projecting concepts and values of certain countries on other peoples should be avoided. As Ellis points out,

> In a post-colonial setting, in a heterogeneous society marked by gross imbalances of wealth and power, in a legal system in which the legitimacy of courts and tribunals and the validity of their findings rests on a narrow consensus and can never be taken for granted, international jurists must take great care when they mine municipal systems for potential international legal norms.[260]

In conclusion, '[t]he conscious and limited use of national legal traditions is advantageous in that it enriches international law with useful source materials, analogies and techniques'.[261] National courts play a role in the creation, evolution and enforcement of international law.[262] First, they constitute evidence of state practice, which is relevant to the formation of

---

[255] Green, 'Comparative Law as a "Source" of International Law', 59.

[256] See Frankenberg, 'Critical Comparisons', 442.

[257] F. Raimondo, 'Les principes généraux de droit dans la jurisprudence des Tribunaux ad hoc: une approche functionelle', in M. Delmas-Marty and E. Fronza (eds.), *Les sources du droit international penal: L'expérience des tribunaux pénaux internationaux et le statut de la Cour pénale international* (Paris: Societé de législation comparée, 2004), p. 79.

[258] See, for example, D. Schneiderman, 'NAFTA's Takings Rule: American Constitutionalism Comes to Canada', *University of Toronto Law Journal* 46 (1996), 499.

[259] Kennedy, 'New Approaches to Comparative Law', at 606–608.

[260] Ellis, 'General Principles and Comparative Law', 956.

[261] L.V. Prott, *The Latent Power of Culture and the International Judge* (Abingdon: Professional Books Ltd., 1979), p. 230.

[262] Lauterpacht, 'Decisions of Municipal Courts as a Source of International Law'; R. Jennings, 'The Judiciary, International and National Law, and the Development of International Law', *International and Comparative Law Quarterly* 45 (1996), 1.

custom.[263] Second, they constitute 'subsidiary means for the determination of rules of law'.[264] Third, they can be relevant in establishing the existence of general principles of law.[265] Finally, domestic cases also play a role in the enforcement of arbitral awards.

However, the underlying methodology is rarely spelled out; there is a margin of discretion in the selection of the comparators, as those engaged in comparative analysis could elevate foreign decisions that they like and downgrade ones they dislike.[266] More than a century ago, Oppenheim warned that 'the science of international law must be careful in the appreciation of such municipal case-law'.[267] If the applicable law is the law of the host state, of course reference may be made to the jurisprudence of the host state. Where the applicable law is international law, whether reference to national cases is appropriate becomes a more sensitive issue. In any case, if national precedents as well as international ones may be taken into account for the persuasiveness of their *ratio decidendi*, they are not binding on international arbitrators unless they are deemed to reflect customary law and/or general principles of law.

Treaty interpretation

Comparative reasoning plays an important role in treaty interpretation. Customary rules of treaty interpretation, as restated by the Vienna Convention on the Law of Treaties (VCLT), offer adjudicators the conceptual and legal framework to settle disputes 'in conformity with the principles of justice and international law'.[268] While a number of investment treaties expressly refer to these rules,[269] they are generally applicable in investment arbitrations because they are considered to form part of customary law.[270]

---

[263] Article 38(1)(b) of the ICJ Statute.   [264] Article 38(1)(d) of the ICJ Statute.

[265] Article 38(1)(c) of the ICJ Statute.

[266] Roberts, 'Comparative International Law?', 61.

[267] L. Oppenheim, 'The Science of International Law: Its Tasks and Methods', *American Journal of International Law* 2 (1908), 313, at 338.

[268] VCLT, Preamble.

[269] For instance, NAFTA Article 1131(1) expressly requires NAFTA Tribunals to settle disputes in accordance with the Agreement and 'applicable rules of international law'.

[270] See, for example, *Canadian Cattlemen for Fair Trade* v. *United States*, Award on Jurisdiction, 28 January 2008, para. 46 (clarified that 'applicable rules of international law comprise the customary international rules of treaty interpretation which are reflected and codified in Articles 31 and 32 of the VCLT'). See also *Bureau Veritas,*

Customary rules of treaty interpretation are not meant to resolve all sorts of interpretive difficulties. While arbitrators often refer to customary rules of treaty interpretation to legitimise their rulings and frame them in a structured way, these rules are neither an algorithm for interpretation nor mathematical rules with exact outcomes. Literary interpretation constitutes a point of departure. If the meaning of a given treaty provision is clear, the other interpretative methods may not be used.[271] If it remains unclear, Articles 31 and 32 of the VCLT provide an 'interpretative framework'.[272] This interpretative matrix is rather flexible allowing arbiters to use different combinations of interpretative tools on a case-by-case basis.[273]

The flexibility of the interpretative matrix is also proven by the existence of conflicting trends in arbitral jurisprudence concerning a variety of provisions, including the very notion of investment,[274] the MFN treatment[275] and the non-precluded measures clause.[276] Arbitrators navigate between the Scylla of a too literal treaty interpretation and the Charybdis of a too liberal approach.[277] Not by chance, Lauterpacht

---

Inspection, Valuation, Assessment and Control, BIVAC BV v. The Republic of Paraguay, ICSID Case No. ARB/07/9, Decision of the Tribunal on Objections to Jurisdiction, 29 May 2009, para. 59; *Noble Ventures v. Romania,* ICSID Case No. ARB/01/11, Award, 12 October 2005, para. 50.

[271] See, for example, *Global Trading Resource Corp. and Globex International Inc. v. Ukraine,* ICSID Case No. ARB/09/11, Award, 1 December 2010, para. 50 ('the Tribunal does not find that it needs to go beyond the text itself of Article I(1)(a) of the BIT'); *Murphy Exploration and Production Company International v. Ecuador,* ICSID Case No. ARB/08/4, Award on Jurisdiction, 15 December 2010, para. 71 (the Tribunal held that 'Taking into account the general rule on the interpretation of treaties of Article 31(1) of the Vienna Convention on the Law of Treaties of 1969, . . . the language of Article 25(4) is clear and unambiguous').

[272] *Alpha Projektholding GmbH v. Ukraine,* ICSID Case No. ARB/07/16, Award, 8 November 2010, para. 221.

[273] See Latty, 'Les techniques interprétative du CIRDI', 462.

[274] See, for example, *Malaysian Historical Salvors SDN BHD v. The Government of Malaysia,* ICSID Case No. ARB/05/10, Decision on the Application for Annulment, 16 April 2009, para. 57.

[275] Compare *Emilio Agustin Maffezini v. Spain,* ICSID Case No. ARB/97/7, Decision of the Tribunal on Objections to Jurisdiction, 25 January 2000, paras. 56 ff., with *Salini Costruttori SpA and Italstrade SpA v. The Hashemite Kingdom of Jordan,* Case No. ARB/02/13, Decision on Jurisdiction, 9 November 2004, para. 118, and *Wintershall Aktiengesellschaft v. Argentine Republic,* ICSID case No. ARB/04/14, Award, 8 December 2008, para. 191.

[276] W.W. Burke-White and A. Von Staden, 'Investment Protection in Extraordinary Times: The Interpretation and Application of Non-Precluded Measures Provisions in Bilateral Investment Treaties', *Virginia Journal of International Law* 48 (2007), 307.

[277] Latty, 'Les techniques interprétative du CIRDI', 480.

contended that rules of treaty interpretation 'are not the determining cause of judicial decision, but the form in which the [adjudicator] cloaks a result arrived at by other means'.[278] More recently, others have pointed out that there is a risk of a cleavage between the formal reasoning as stated in awards and the concrete reasons which guided the majority of arbitrators. For instance, in the *Hrvatska Elektroprivreda DD. v. Slovenia* case,[279] one of the arbitrators criticised the way the majority of the Arbitral Tribunal interpreted the treaty, suggesting that more attention should be paid to the text of the treaty.[280] The Arbitral Tribunal, however, after carefully considering the opinion of the arbitrator, respectfully disagreed.[281]

Given the fact that arbitral tribunals often adjudicate issues related to the public interest, an equilibrated approach to interpretation seems demanded by the need to balance the interests of the state and those of the investor. In this regard, some scholars have argued that 'preference for one interpretation over another should be based on a comparison of the consequences that would be likely to follow from each interpretation'.[282] Among these consequences, the authors include both the flows of foreign direct investment and the realisation of human rights and environmental conservation into host states.[283]

In *Bureau Veritas v. Paraguay*, the Tribunal pointed out that 'The principles set forth by Articles 31–32 of the VCLT point to a balanced approach to interpretation, one that, in the case of investment treaties . . . recognises the equally legitimate interests of the State and of the investor.'[284] Analogously, in *Renta 4 SVSA et al. v. The Russian Federation*, the Arbitral Tribunal cautioned that

[278] H. Lauterpacht, 'Restrictive Interpretation and the Principle of Effectiveness in the Interpretation of Treaties', *British Yearbook of International Law* 26 (1949), 48 at 53.

[279] See, for example, the Individual Opinion of Judge Jan Paulsson pursuant to Article 48(4), ICSID Convention, appended to *Hrvatska Elektroprivreda DD v. The Republic of Slovenia*, ICSID Case No. ARB/05/24, Decision on the Treaty Interpretation Issue, 12 June 2009, para. 47.

[280] Individual Opinion of Judge Jan Paulsson, para. 47.

[281] *Hrvatska Elektroprivreda DD v. The Republic of Slovenia*, Decision on the Treaty Interpretation Issue, footnote 171.

[282] J. Bonnitcha, 'Outline of a Normative Framework for Evaluating Interpretations of Investment Treaty Protections', in C. Brown and K. Miles (eds.), *Evolution in Investment Treaty Arbitration* (Cambridge: Cambridge University Press, 2011), pp. 117, 118.

[283] *Ibid.*

[284] *Bureau Veritas, Inspection, Valuation, Assessment and Control, BIVAC B.V. v. The Republic of Paraguay*, Decision of the Tribunal on Objections to Jurisdiction, para. 59.

Article 31 must be considered with caution and discipline lest it become a palimpsest constantly altered by the projections of subjective suppositions. It does not for example compel the result that all textual doubts should be resolved in favour of the investor. The long-term promotion of investment is likely to be better ensured by a well-balanced regime rather than by one which goes so far that it provokes a swing of the pendulum in the other direction.[285]

Customary rules of treaty interpretation 'leave considerable scope for analogical reasoning'[286] and, potentially, for arbitral politics. A myriad of analogies is concretely possible; rules of interpretation empower arbitrators and practitioners to undertake analogical thinking but they do not delimit this capability, which in turn needs to be scrutinised and critically assessed.[287]

This section illustrates the way in which customary rules of treaty interpretation allow analogical thinking. Although there is no hierarchical order among the canons of treaty interpretations, as a matter of convenience, the following analysis will follow the order in which these norms generally appear. According to the *general rule of interpretation*, which comprises several subnorms, 'a treaty shall be interpreted in good faith in accordance with the ordinary meaning to be given to the terms of the treaty in their context and in the light of its object and purpose'.[288] Text, context, object and purpose are to be considered in a holistic fashion to identify the exact meaning of a treaty provision.

Textual interpretation

According to the principle of textuality, treaties are to be interpreted on the basis of their actual text. Treaty terms may be inherently vague or general. In determining the ordinary meaning of investment provisions, dictionary definitions 'are unlikely to provide much assistance'.[289] Therefore, arbitral tribunals – like other international courts and

---

[285] Arbitration Institute of the Stockholm Chamber of Commerce, *Renta 4 SVSA et al.* v. *The Russian Federation*, Award on Preliminary Objections, 20 March 2009, para. 55.

[286] A. Roberts, 'Clash of Paradigms: Actors and Analogies Shaping the Investment Treaty System', *American Journal of International Law* 107 (2013), 45, 50.

[287] The process of convergence on a single set of accepted analogies is not necessarily a desirable outcome; yet some methodological insights will be offered in the second part of the book.

[288] VCLT, Article 31.1.

[289] Roberts, 'Clash of Paradigms: Actors and Analogies Shaping the Investment Treaty System', 50.

tribunals[290] – have made frequent use of analogies in interpreting the text of the relevant treaty provisions.[291] In fact, the ordinary meaning of a term in a treaty may be derived from the meaning attributed to analogous expressions in similar treaties.[292] The determination of similarity of terms and instruments proceeds by way of analogical reasoning. As Elihu Lauterpacht put it,

> There have been a number of cases in which the Permanent Court of International Justice and the International Court of Justice have, for the purpose of ascertaining the meaning of expressions employed in one treaty, used the device of ascertaining the meaning of similar expressions employed in other treaties. The Court has then proceeded on the basis that the Parties must have had in contemplation at the time when they concluded the second instrument the meaning which had been attributed to like expressions in the earlier instrument.[293]

Certain treaty rules repeat or closely follow earlier treaty rules on the same or analogous subject matter; therefore, 'the meaning attributed to the latter can inform the ordinary meaning of the former'.[294] For example, the Canada 2004 Model Foreign Investment Promotion and Protection Agreement (FIPA) states:

> subject to the requirement that such measures are not applied in a manner that would constitute arbitrary or unjustifiable discrimination between investments or between investors, or a disguised restriction on international trade or investment, nothing in this agreement shall be construed to prevent a Party from adopting or enforcing measures necessary (a) to protect human, animal or plant life of health . . . or (c) for the conservation of living or non-living exhaustible resources.[295]

---

[290] See, for example, *Demir and Baykara* v. *Turkey*, App. No. 34503/97, ECHR (2008) 85 (stating that '[t]he Court in defining the meaning of terms and notions in the text of the Convention, can and must take into account elements of international law other than the Convention, the interpretation of such elements by competent organs, and the practice of European States reflecting their common values').

[291] Roberts, 'Clash of Paradigms: Actors and Analogies Shaping the Investment Treaty System', 52.

[292] F. Berman, 'Treaty Interpretation in a Judicial Context', *Yale Journal International Law* 29 (2004), 315, at 318.

[293] E. Lauterpacht, 'The Development of the Law of International Organizations by the Decision of Arbitral Tribunals', *Recueil des Courses* 152 (1976), 396.

[294] M. Paparinskis, 'Analogies and Other Regimes of International Law', in Z. Douglas, J. Pauwelyn and J.E. Viñuales (eds.), *The Foundations of International Investment Law: Bringing Theory into Practice* (Oxford: Oxford University Press, 2014), p. 5.

[295] Canada Model Foreign Investment Promotion and Protection Agreement (FIPA), Article 11.

This wording recalls Article XX of the GATT 1994, which includes measures necessary to protect human, animal or plant life or health, conservation of exhaustible natural resources and the like. If an arbitral tribunal hypothetically established under a Canada BIT had to interpret the term 'exhaustible natural resources', it could refer to the text of Article XX(g) of the GATT and the interpretation of this term provided by the relevant jurisprudence.[296] In defining the requirement to treat foreign investors no less favourably than nationals 'in like circumstances', the *S.D. Myers* tribunal drew comparisons with trade law jurisprudence on 'like products'.[297]

In a more complicated scenario, previous treaties use different terms and deal with different subject matters; yet, if the earlier rules are sufficiently similar, 'they may *mutatis mutandis* illuminate the ordinary meaning'.[298] A number of international courts and tribunals have used such a technique,[299] including arbitral tribunals. For instance, the *Mondev* Tribunal determined the scope of the minimum standard of treatment under the North American Free Trade Agreement (NAFTA), referring to cases of the ECtHR concerning the 'right to a court' as providing possible 'guidance by analogy'.[300] The *Total* Tribunal interpreted the concept of 'legitimate expectations' conducting a comparative analysis of domestic public law, European human rights law, European Union law and public international law.[301]

---

[296] *US–Tuna/Dolphin II*, Panel Report, para. 5.13; *US–Shrimp*, AB Report, para. 132.

[297] Compare *S.D. Myers, Inc.* v. *Canada*, First Partial Award, 13 November 2000, paras. 243–251 (drawing on GATT and WTO jurisprudence in conceptualizing 'likeness'), with *Methanex Corp.* v. *United States*, NAFTA Ch. 11/UNCITRAL Arbitration, Final Award on Jurisdiction and Merits, 3 August 2005, pt. IV, ch. B, paras. 29–35 (rejecting the relevance of trade law jurisprudence).

[298] Paparinskis, 'Analogies and Other Regimes of International Law', 5.

[299] For instance, the WTO AB has interpreted the term 'exhaustible natural resources' in Article XX(g) of the GATT 1994 and the need to safeguard endangered species in accordance with a Multilateral Environmental Agreement. WTO Appellate Body Report, *US–Shrimp*, para. 130. Analogously, when the ICJ interpreted the term 'freedom of commerce' in a 1955 Treaty of Amity, Economic Relations and Consular Rights, it referred to the concept 'freedom of trade' from the 1919 Convention of St Germain and its interpretation by the PCIJ in the *Oscar Chinn* case. *Oil Platforms* (*Iran* v. *United States*) (Preliminary Objections), [1996] *ICJ Reports* 803, para. 48.

[300] *Mondev International Ltd.* v. *United States*, ICSID Case No. ARB(AF)/99/2, NAFTA Ch. 11 Arbitral Tribunal, Award, 11 October 2002, para. 144, 42 ILM 85 (2003).

[301] *Total S.A.* v. *Argentine Republic*, ICSID Case No. ARB/04/1, Decision on Liability, 27 December 2010, paras. 128–134.

Context

The context of a treaty comprises, *inter alia*, its preamble.[302] While preambles do not contain binding obligations *per se*,[303] they are influential in the interpretation of treaties, as they explain the underlying philosophy of such instruments. Besides 'setting a tone for interpreting the obligations in the agreement',[304] preambles establish a dialogue between the treaty drafters and the adjudicators.[305]

Preambles contextualise investment obligations in the broader framework of public international law. They legitimise the use of analogies in the interpretation of the relevant provisions of a given BIT in the light of public international law. More precisely, not only does the wording of preambles allow the reference to other branches of international law but it may also require it for interpretive purposes. For instance, the preamble of the NAFTA commits the parties to attain investment goals in a manner consistent with environmental protection, preserving the flexibility to safeguard the public welfare and promote sustainable development.[306] The preamble of the Energy Charter Treaty 'recogniz[es] the increasingly urgent need for measures to protect the environment'.[307] The preamble of the 2012 US Model BIT expresses the parties' desire to achieve the stated objectives 'in a manner consistent with the protection of health, safety and the environment, and the promotion of internationally recognized labor rights'.[308] Certainly, when considering the meaning of terms such as the protection of health or 'internationally recognized labor rights', arbitrators can take into account the relevant international law instruments adopted under the aegis of the World Health Organization and the International Labour Organization, respectively.

---

[302] VCLT, Article 31.2.

[303] *Victor Pey Casado et Foundation 'President Allende' contre Republique du Chili*, ICSID Case No ARB/98/2, Arbitral Award, 8 May 2008, at para. 348.

[304] See H. Mann, *International Investment Agreements, Business and Human Rights: Key Issues and Opportunities* (Winnipeg: IISD, 2008), p. 10.

[305] K. Roach, 'The Uses and Audiences of Preambles in Legislation', *McGill Law Journal* 47 (2001), 129.

[306] NAFTA, preamble.

[307] Energy Charter Treaty (ECT), 17 December 1994, 2080 UNTS 95, 34 ILM 360 (1995), preamble.

[308] 2012 US Model Bilateral Investment Treaty, available at http://www.ustr.gov/sites/default/files/BIT%20text%20for%20ACIEP%20Meeting.pdf.

Teleological interpretation

The method of teleological interpretation searches for the purpose of a norm to identify its exact content. In general terms, investment treaties aim at promoting the economic development of the host state and establishing a level playing field for foreign investors. As foreigners have been amongst the most vulnerable sectors of societies, easy objects of reprisals, without vote or voice in local political affairs,[309] investment treaties establish a shield against discrimination and mistreatment by the host state. Being based on the assumed vulnerability of the foreign investor, such treaties rarely refer to responsibilities of multinational corporations. Have investment treaties become 'a charter of rights for foreign investors, with no concomitant responsibilities or liabilities'[310] or a 'corporate bill of rights'?[311]

Even assuming that the protection of foreign investments is one of the fundamental purposes of international investment treaties, it is not the only aim of such treaties, as the economic development of the host state can leverage but also counterbalance such rationale. Recent BITs explicitly include multiple objectives in their preambles clarifying that the promotion of foreign direct investment should not be considered an end in itself but should be conducive to economic and/or sustainable development.

Moreover, if one conceives foreign investments as forms of property, limits and boundaries must be duly acknowledged.[312] Comparative legal studies show that property is not absolute; rather, property systems are 'a major battleground' on which the conflict 'between individual liberty and privacy on the one hand and community and equality on the other' is resolved.[313] Most constitutional systems and even human rights systems which protect property as a human right recognise the intrinsic limits of

---

[309] See J. Paulsson, *Denial of Justice in International Law* (Cambridge: Cambridge University Press, 2005); F. Francioni, 'Access to Justice, Denial of Justice, and International Investment Law', *European Journal of international Law* 20 (2009), 729–747.

[310] H. Mann, 'The Right of States to Regulate and International Investment Law: A Comment', in UNCTAD *The Development Dimension of FDI: Policy and Rule-Making Perspectives* (New York: UN, 2003), pp. 211–223, at p. 212.

[311] T. Weiler, 'Balancing Human Rights and Investor Protection: A New Approach for a Different Legal Order', *Transnational Dispute Management* 1 (2004), 1–15, at 2.

[312] V. Bean and J.C. Beauvais, 'The Global Fifth Amendment? NAFTA's Investment Protection and the Misguided Quest for an International Regulatory Takings Doctrine', *New York University Law Review* 78 (2003), 30.

[313] R.C. Ellickson, 'Property in Land', *Yale Law Journal* 102 (1993), 1315, 1345.

property rights.[314] While the owner has the power to use what she owns, she must use it lawfully.[315]

Not only have these comparative surveys analytical merits but they also have practical implications. In fact, if we accept an absolutist conception of property, interference with the use of property becomes *ipso facto* expropriation. However, this absolutist view is a misconception of property, as most constitutional systems and even human rights systems, which protect property as a human right, also recognise the intrinsic limits of property rights. Comparative studies concretise the idea that property rights 'can be allocated in a variety of ways, with the balance between community and individual struck differently depending on societal needs and preferences'.[316]

In conclusion, when interpreting and applying international investment treaties, arbitrators should be mindful that the purpose of investment treaties, as often stated in their preambles, is not unilateral; rather, it encompasses a mixture of private and public interests, whose balance must be found on a case-by-case basis.

Systemic interpretation

Article 31(3) of the Vienna Convention requires interpreters to take into account the subsequent agreements and practice of the treaty parties on interpretation[317] along with 'any relevant rules of international law applicable in the relations between the parties'.[318] As noted by Anthea Roberts, the two provisions embodied in Article 31(3) of the VCLT express a 'battle over interpretative power': 'the claim that the treaty parties have interpretative authority over their treaties exists in tension with the claim to interpretive authority by international courts and

---

[314] First Protocol to the Convention for the Protection of Human Rights and Fundamental Freedoms (the European Convention on Human Rights [ECHR]), 4 November 1950, in force 3 September 1953, 213 UNTS 222, Article 1.2 (recognising 'the right of the state to enforce such laws as it deems necessary to control the use of property in accordance with the general interest or to secure the payment of taxes or other contributions or penalties'); American Convention on Human Rights, 22 November 1969, 9 ILM 673 (1970), Article 21.1 (stating that 'the law may subordinate [the] use and enjoyment [of property] to the interest of society').

[315] S. Van Erp, 'Comparative Property Law', in M. Reimann and R. Zimmermann (eds.), *The Oxford Handbook of Comparative Law* (Oxford: Oxford University Press, 2006).

[316] J.L. Anderson, 'Comparative Perspectives on Property Rights', *Journal of Legal Education* 56 (2006), 1–12, 3.

[317] VCLT, Article 31(3)(a) and (b).   [318] VCLT, Article 31(3)(c).

tribunals'.[319] Pursuant to Article 31(3)(c), '[e]very treaty provision must be read not only in its own context, but in the wider context of general international law, whether conventional or customary'.[320] Therefore, this provision properly expresses the principle of *systemic* integration within the international legal system, indicating that treaty regimes are themselves creatures of international law.[321]

Article 31(3)(c) also allows space for dynamic or *evolutionary* treaty interpretation. Evolutionary interpretation means that the sense of certain terms of investment treaties might change over time reflecting changes in societies. A comparative assessment is thus inherent in this kind of treaty interpretation. As the ICJ recognised in its advisory opinion on *Legal Consequences for States of the Continued Presence of South Africa in Namibia*, an adjudicator's interpretation cannot remain unaffected by subsequent developments of law and 'an international instrument has to be interpreted and applied within the framework of the entire legal system prevailing at the time of interpretation'.[322] An evolutionary approach can help interpreters to take into account evolving standards and emerging norms of customary international law. Investment treaties have been interpreted as living treaties, whose interpretation may evolve over time. For instance, the *Glamis* Tribunal found 'apparent agreement that the fair and equitable treatment standard is subject to ... evolution'.[323]

The Emergence of general principles of law

Defined as 'a core of legal ideas which are common to all legal systems',[324] general principles of law are a primary source of international

---

[319] A. Roberts, 'Subsequent Agreements and Practice: The Battle over Interpretive Power', in G. Nolte (ed.), *Treaties and Subsequent Practice* (Oxford: Oxford University Press, 2013), chapter 8, 1–2.

[320] I. Sinclair, *The Vienna Convention on the Law of Treaties* (Manchester: Manchester University Press, 1984), p. 139.

[321] C. McLachlan, 'The Principles of Systematic Integration and Article 31(3)(c) of the Vienna Convention', *International and Comparative Law Quarterly* 54 (2005), 279–320, at 280.

[322] ICJ, *Legal Consequences for States of the Continued Presence of South Africa in Namibia (South-West Africa) Notwithstanding Security Council Resolution 276 (1970)*, Advisory Opinion, 21 June 1971, *ICJ Reports 1971*, 31

[323] *Glamis Gold, Ltd* v. *The United States of America*, UNCITRAL, Award, 8 June 2009, para. 613 ('the *Neer* standard, when applied with current sentiments and to modern situations, may find shocking and egregious events not considered to reach this level in the past').

[324] R.B. Schlesinger, 'Research on the General Principles of Law Recognized by Civilized Nations', *American Journal of International Law* 51 (1957), 734–753, at 739.

law.[325] Article 38(3) of the Statute of the PCIJ empowered the court, if occasion should arise, to apply the 'general principles of law recognised by civilised nations'.[326] The same formulation has been transposed *verbatim* in the Statute of the ICJ.[327] Although both statutes applied to the respective courts, Article 38 has been deemed to reflect customary international law.[328] Therefore, other international law courts and tribunals consider general principles of law as a source of international law.

Often considered as a dormant source of international law, general principles of law can revive and govern a certain issue if such issue is not regulated by treaty law and customary law.[329] General principles of law have a flexible, subsidiary and dynamic nature. They help adjudicators to settle a given dispute, filling in the gaps in the applicable law, and allow international law to evolve and respond to new challenges.[330]

General principles of law can also play a prominent role in the legal reasoning of international courts and tribunals to reinforce certain legal arguments. As Cassese put it, general principles 'constitute both the backbone of the body of law governing international dealings and the potent cement that binds together the various and often disparate cogs and wheels of the normative framework of the international community'.[331]

General principles of law can contribute to the doctrinaire construction of international law as a unitary legal system.[332] Some authors

---

[325] B. Cheng, *General Principles of Law as Applied by International Courts and Tribunals* (Cambridge: Cambridge University Press, 1953).

[326] Article 38(3) of the Statute of the Permanent Court of International Justice. League of Nations, *Statute of the Permanent Court of International Justice*, Geneva, 16 December 1920. 17 AJIL Supp. 115 (1923).

[327] Article 38 Statute of the ICJ. The Statute of the International Court of Justice is annexed to the Charter of the United Nations. Charter of the United Nations, 26 June 1945, in force 24 October 1946, 1 UNTS XVI.

[328] J.L. Brierly, *The Law of Nations: An Introduction to the International Law of Peace*, 6th ed., H. Waldock ed. (New York: Oxford University Press, 1963), p. 56.

[329] Admittedly, the difference between customary law and general principles of law is often not clear. Custom refers to what is a general practice among states and accepted by them as law. General principles are recognised by states but they do not require general practice by the same.

[330] C. Voigt, 'The Role of General Principles in International Law and Their Relationship to Treaty Law', *Retfærd Årgang* 31 (2008), 3–25, 5.

[331] A. Cassese, *International Law*, 2nd ed. (Oxford: Oxford University Press, 2005), p. 188.

[332] See M. Rotondi, 'Technique du droit, dogmatique et droit comparé', *Revue internationale de droit comparé* 20 (1968), 5–18, 12.

contend that 'it is largely due to general principles that international law can be defined as a system'.[333] Some principles such as *pacta sunt servanda* provide the foundations of the international legal system.[334] Other principles can be a source of higher law, that is, *jus cogens*.[335] General principles 'form the irreducible essence of all legal systems'[336] and express a 'belief in a "common heritage" of international law',[337] or common law of mankind.[338]

As international courts and tribunals can refer to general principles of law even in the absence of general practice (which is an element of customary law)[339] or an express consent of the parties in the form of treaty law, arguments have been made that general principles of law amount to an external constraint on state behaviour and in fact 'go beyond legal positivism, according to which states are bound by their will only'.[340] Yet, if one conceives general principles as expressing a common juridical heritage of mankind, then, rather than representing a delimitation of state autonomy, general principles of law constitute its highest expression.[341] Certainly, the identification and application of general principles of law give significant discretion to international adjudicators.[342]

---

[333] Voigt, 'The Role of General Principles in International Law and Their Relationship to Treaty Law', 5.

[334] *Ibid.*, 12.

[335] M. Cherif Bassiouni, 'A Functional Approach to General Principles of International Law', *Michigan Journal of International Law* 11 (1990), 768, 780.

[336] F.T. Freeman Jalet, 'The Quest for the General Principles of Law Recognized by Civilized Nations', *University of California Los Angeles Law Review* 10 (1963), 1041, 1044.

[337] G. Del Vecchio, *Sui principi generali del diritto* (Milano: Giuffré, 1958), p. 11.

[338] J. Waldron, 'Foreign Law and the Modern *Jus Gentium*', *Harvard Law Review* 119 (2005), 129, 132.

[339] Cheng, *General Principles of Law as Applied by International Courts and Tribunals*, p. 24.

[340] *South West African Cases* (Second Phase), Dissenting Opinion, Judge Tanaka, ICJ Reports 1966, 298.

[341] Del Vecchio, *Sui principi generali del diritto*, p. 69.

[342] One could argue that in certain cases, the determination of legal principles of law has amounted to judicial law-making, giving rise to a sort of Praetorian law. But see Ellis, 'General Principles and Comparative Law', 949 (arguing that recourse to general principles does not amount to judicial law-making). See also ICTY, *Prosecutor v. Zoran Kupreskic*, Case No.: IT-95-16-T, Judgment, 14 January 2000, para. 669 (noting that 'In this search for and examination of the relevant legal standards, and the consequent enunciation of the principles applicable at the international level, the Trial Chamber might be deemed to set out a sort of *ius praetorium*. However, its powers in finding the law are of course far more limited than those belonging to the Roman *praetor*: under the

What is the *gestalt* of general principles of law? As Schlesinger questioned half a century ago, 'Are these principles conceived as having their roots in a local or national *Volkgeist*, or do they transcend national territories?'[343] General principles of law can indicate (1) principles which are common to diverse legal systems (from which they can be induced) or (2) principles recognised by the international community (from which they can be deduced).[344] An example of a general principle of municipal origin is that of requiring reparation as a consequence of a wrongful act. Examples of general principles of international foundation include, for instance, the principle of non-intervention in national affairs.[345] Both types of principles – irrespective of their legal origin – are acknowledged as binding by the international community,[346] as they enable international adjudicators to gain 'insights generated by decades, even centuries, of collected experience' at the municipal and international level.[347]

How do arbitral tribunals identify general principles of law? Methods for determining general principles of law may differ from one jurisdiction to another and can change with time.[348] For instance, regional economic courts will refer to the traditions which are common to the member states. Arbitral tribunals refer to the decisions and awards rendered by other international, regional and national courts as well as scholarly writings. The identification of general principles of law entails two processes: (1) the abstraction of the norm from national constitutions, legislations and judicial decisions – a vertical process; (2) the comparison of the national legal systems – a horizontal process – to distil the essence of the legal concept.[349]

In ascertaining general principles of law, what legal systems should be considered and how? Comparative methods require no minimum number of jurisdictions to be compared; even two systems can be compared meaningfully provided that they are comparable and share a common

International Tribunal's Statute, the Trial Chamber must apply *lex lata i.e.* existing law, although it has broad powers in determining such law').
[343] Schlesinger, 'Research on the General Principles of Law Recognized by Civilized Nations', 742.
[344] Voigt, 'The Role of General Principles in International Law and Their Relationship to Treaty Law', 3 and 7.
[345] *Id.*, at 8.   [346] *Ibid.*   [347] Ellis, 'General Principles and Comparative Law', 970.
[348] Bassiouni, 'A Functional Approach to General Principles of International Law', 773.
[349] F. Raimondo, *General Principles of Law in the Decisions of International Criminal Courts and Tribunals* (Oxford: Oxford University Press, 2008), p. 1.

ideological foundation.[350] In harvesting general principles of international law, however, the criteria of such a survey are necessarily different. As Raimondo put it, 'if a legal principle derived from national legal systems is going to be part of international law, then that legal principle should arguably be more universally recognized'.[351] By its name, international law indicates law among nations: reference to a couple of countries can be sufficient to detect the existence of common principles between those two countries; reference to a given region can be sufficient to identify the existence of regional principles of law.[352] However, reference to a couple of or a few jurisdictions is not sufficient for ascertaining the content of general principles of international law.[353] The ICJ Statute requires the court, *inter alia*, to consider *general* practice as one of the constitutive elements of a custom and to apply the *general* principles of law.[354] The comparative legal analysis to detect general state practice and general principles of law must be extensive and representative, albeit not necessarily uniform or universal.[355] As the ICTY stated,

> reference should not be made to one national legal system only, say that of common-law or that of civil-law States. Rather, international courts must draw upon the general concepts and legal institutions common to all the major legal systems of the world. This pre-supposes a process of identification of the common denominators in these legal systems so as to pinpoint the basic notions they share.[356]

The criterion of representativeness helps to ensure a level of abstraction and objectivity in the process of elucidating general principles of law. The idea of representativeness is based on three different but related grounds.[357] First, the presence of a concept in many legal systems shows its legal objectivity. Second, the presence of a concept in many legal systems is evidence of state consent. Third, the fact that democratic processes have adopted a given concept in their legal systems indirectly legitimises the use of the concept in international law.

---

[350] A. Zammit Borda, 'Comparative Law and Ad Hoc Tribunals: The Dangers of a Narrow Inquiry', *International Journal of Legal Information* 40 (2012), 22–38, 28.

[351] Raimondo, *General Principles of Law*, p. 4.

[352] *Odièvre* v. *France*, ECHR 13 February 2003, ECHR 2003–III.

[353] Bassiouni, 'A Functional Approach to "General Principles of International Law"', 789.

[354] Article 38(1)(c) of the ICJ Statute.

[355] Zammit Borda, 'Comparative Law and Ad Hoc Tribunals', 28.

[356] ICTY, *Furundzija*, Judgment of 10 December 1998, para. 178.

[357] Ellis, 'General Principles and Comparative Law', 970–971 (criticising the concept of representativeness in favour of the concept of persuasiveness of legal argumentation).

With regard to the modality of the analysis, while pure comparative analysis requires comparability and analogous ideological foundation, the review of evidence for elucidating general principles of international law does not have the same prerequisites. Rather, the international adjudicator should be guided by the generality requirement.[358] The international adjudicator is expected to refer to more than a single country for determining the existence of general principles of law. 'The mere fact that a principle is to be found in several systems of . . . law does not, of course, invest that principle with the attributes of universality and entitle it to be translated into the international sphere.'[359] As Gutteridge put it, 'a judge sitting in an international tribunal must not forget that he is an international judge and before making use of a principle . . . on which to base his decision must test it by ascertaining whether it is one which finds acceptance in the main systems . . . '[360] In order to be considered as a general principle, a principle does not necessarily have to be unanimously accepted in the legal systems of the world, nor represent the lowest common denominator of the world's laws.[361] A given principle must be part of most national legal systems to be considered a general principle of law, and the conclusion reached in practice must 'be founded on a balanced and thoroughly researched basis'.[362]

While 'the international judge is not expected to enter into the same level of critical analysis of legislation and case law as a comparatist',[363] she should avoid a mechanical importation or transposition of concepts from national law into international proceedings.[364] For instance, in *Klöckner* v. *Cameroon*, although the applicable law was Cameroonian, the Arbitral Tribunal based its decision on the 'basic principle' of 'frankness and loyalty', borrowing it from French civil law and noting (without reference) that it also belonged to both English law and international law.[365] The Annulment Committee annulled the award, holding that the

---

[358] Zammit Borda, 'Comparative Law and Ad Hoc Tribunals', 29.

[359] H.C. Gutteridge, 'Comparative Law and the Law of Nations', *British Yearbook of International Law* 21 (1944), 1–10, 1.

[360] *Ibid.*, 9.

[361] See Ellis, 'General Principles and Comparative Law', 968 (pinpointing that international judges seek to avoid a lowest common denominator approach).

[362] M. Bohlander and M. Findlay, 'The Use of Domestic Sources as a Basis for International Criminal Law Principles', in G.Z. Capaldo (ed.), *The Global Community – Yearbook of International Law and Jurisprudence* (New York: Oceana Publications, 2002), pp. 3–26, pp. 16–17.

[363] *Ibid.*   [364] ICTY, *Furundzija*, Judgment of 10 December 1998, para. 178.

[365] *Klöckner* v. *Cameroon*, Award, 21 October 1983, 2 *ICSID Reports*, 59–61.

Arbitral Tribunal had failed to apply the proper law and had based its decision 'more on a sort of general equity than on positive law'.[366]

Yet, it may not be feasible to consider all of the existing jurisdictions. A comprehensive survey of all of the national legal systems on a given issue is beyond the capacity of international courts and tribunals. In practice, as English has become the lingua franca of international law, the use and reliance on cases, commentaries and texts in English has increased steadily. International adjudicators are often multilingual, but they are not (nor should they be) expected to master the rich diversity of languages in which legal systems are formulated. In this regard, comparative surveys of the various systems published in different languages are useful to cope with these unavoidable linguistic hurdles.[367]

Which legal families should be considered? Should a qualitative search be preferred to a quantitative one? By definition, general principles of law are those principles which are common to the generality of nations and should not be conceived as the principles of only a handful of countries. The adoption of 'a narrow inquiry, which at best attaches special weight and at worst confines the scope of the review to a single, specific legal system'[368] for the determination of general principles of law can lead to the perception that international adjudicators 'interpret legal norms through the lexicons of their respective traditions, rather than through a truly sui generis prism',[369] elevating municipal concepts with which they are familiar to the level of 'universal truths'.[370] Although Article 38(1)(c) of the ICJ Statute still formally refers to general principles of law recognised by *civilised nations*, this qualification is now commonly understood as indicating the community of nations.[371]

Law scholars have developed several taxonomies of legal systems based on diverse criteria such as substance, style, method and ideology among

---

[366] *Klöckner v. Cameroon*, Decision on Annulment, 16 May 1986, 1 *ICSID Reports* 515 (noting that '[The Tribunal's] reasoning [is] limited to postulating and not demonstrating the existence of a principle ... ').

[367] For a seminal study, see P. Allott, 'Language, Method and the Nature of International Law', *British Yearbook of International Law* 45 (1971), 79–135, 120.

[368] Zammit Borda, 'Comparative Law and Ad Hoc Tribunals', 36.

[369] *Ibid.* (internal citation omitted).

[370] Ellis, 'General Principles and Comparative Law', 965.

[371] Alvarez, 'Contemporary Foreign Investment Law', 943–975 at 950 (noting that 'Those once seen as uncivilized are today full members of the polity that makes and enforces international law. All states, large or small, enjoy sovereign equality under the UN Charter').

others. Some classifications include, for instance, common law, Romano-Germanic law and Islamic law;[372] others adopt a broader spectrum, including civil law, common law, Asian law, chthonic law,[373] Talmudic law, Islamic law and Hindu law.[374] Zweigert and Kötz classified legal systems into eight families: Romanistic law, Germanic law, Nordic law, Common law, socialist law, Far Eastern law, Islamic law and Hindu law.[375] René David classified the major legal systems of the world as (1) the Romanist/Germanic; (2) the socialist; (3) the common law; (4) Islamic law; and (5) Asian legal systems.[376] The classification in legal families is inadequate under many respects – most notably as it fails to reflect the complexities and overlapping of the various systems – but it is still relied upon as it is deemed 'necessary for comparative analysis to proceed'.[377] Different classifications therefore coexist for different purposes, and 'any new taxonomy should be evaluated on the basis of whether it serves a given aim better than the previous ones . . . '[378]

The common/civil law divide maintains 'some value in framing the scope of our study'.[379] Although the various categorisations used for any scrutiny of this sort can be challenged, and legal systems evolve and are subject to variations, reportedly,

> Common Law . . . whether in 'pure' or 'mixed' form, is utilized by some fifty-one nations, or 26.7 percent of all nations of the world. These nations account for 34.81 percent of the world's population. On the other hand, Civil Law . . ., whether in 'pure' or 'mixed' form, is utilized by some 115 nations, or 60.21 percent of all nations of the world. These nations account for 59.01 percent of the world's population.[380]

---

[372] See, for example, S. McLaughlin Mitchell and E.J. Powell, *Domestic Law Goes Global* (Cambridge: Cambridge University Press, 2011), p. 22.

[373] Chthonic law indicates oral legal traditions, including those found in Africa, parts of North and Latin America and the South Pacific. H.P. Glenn, *Legal Traditions of the World*, 3rd ed. (Oxford: Oxford University Press, 2007).

[374] *Ibid.*, p. 136.

[375] Zweigert and Kötz, *Introduction to Comparative Law*, vol. 1, pp. 69–75.

[376] R. David, *Les Grands Systèmes de Droit Contemporaines*, 5th ed. (Paris: Dalloz, 1973), pp. 22–32.

[377] Picker, 'International Law's Mixed Heritage', 1094.

[378] U. Mattei, 'Three Patterns of Law: Taxonomy and Change in the World's Legal Systems', *American Journal of Comparative Law* 45 (1997), 5–45, 8.

[379] P. Giliker, 'Book Review – *The Enigma of Comparative Law: Variations on a Theme for the Twenty-first Century and Methodology of Comparative Law*' by E. Örücü (Leiden: Martinus Nijhoff Publishers, 2004), *International and Comparative Law Quarterly* 55 (2006), 243–246, 245.

[380] W.R. Barnes, 'Contemplating a Civil Law Paradigm for a Future International Commercial Code', *Louisiana Law Review* 65 (2004–2005), 769.

Therefore, a discrete and representative number of common law, civil law and mixed systems will have to be taken into account to determine general principles of law. The outcome of the research may not change but comparative reasoning 'is not a mechanical process; rather, it is a tool which assists the adjudicator in applying (and developing) rules of international law'.[381]

Conclusions

This chapter has focused on the use of comparative reasoning in international investment law and arbitration. Arbitrators make extensive use of analogic reasoning and borrow concepts from other legal systems. Legal comparison is a form of inquiry for coming closer to the meaning of legal texts. It also helps to ascertain the content of general principles of law. However, while comparisons are made, they are often done implicitly without spelling out their rationale and/or considering their systemic implications. Therefore, this chapter submitted that a more conscious use of comparative reasoning can benefit investment treaty arbitration.

The use of comparative reasoning in investment treaty law and arbitration is multilayered. *First*, under the label 'comparative investment law', scholars have compared the different legal frameworks which regulate foreign investments at the national level. *Second*, under the label 'comparative arbitration law', scholars have investigated the emergence of a mixed procedural culture in international arbitration. *Third*, investment law scholars have compared specific investment treaty provisions to analogous provisions in international and national regimes, thus contributing to the emergence of a legal culture composed of consistent patterns, attitudes and opinions which characterise investment treaty arbitration.[382] This legal culture constitutes a melting pot of different legal traditions and presents mixed features.

Fourth, arbitrators make analogies and resort to judicial borrowing in the light of customary rules of treaty interpretation. National case law becomes relevant where the applicable law is the domestic law (*lex loci*) or where the arbitral tribunal is identifying the emergence of general principles of law or customary law. Reference to foreign law may be

---

[381] Gutteridge, 'Comparative Law and the Law of Nations', 10.
[382] See, for example, R. Cotterell, 'The Concept of Legal Culture', in D. Nelken (ed.), *Comparing Legal Cultures* (Aldershot: Dartmouth, 1997), pp. 13–14.

problematic in consideration of the extraterritorial character of such application and of the risk of repoliticising investment treaty disputes. Specific features of national law can get lost in translation, as the legal formants of national systems are often not approached holistically but in a scattered fashion. Moreover, there is a risk of cherry-picking as adjudicators rely on their prior knowledge comparing the systems with those with which they are familiar.[383] Furthermore, some legal systems predominate in the citation race due to a number of factors such as accessibility, language, culture, geographical proximity and other variables.

Reliance on persuasive precedents of previous arbitral tribunals may lead to an increased coherence of the system. As Lauterpacht pointed out, '[i]nternational arbitral law has produced a body of precedent which is full of instruction and authority. Numerous arbitral awards have made a distinct contribution to international law by reason of their scope, their elaboration, and the accuracy with which they have examined the issue before them'.[384]

In parallel, the increasing reliance on cases of other international courts and tribunals may increase the perceived legitimacy of the system. This robust dialogue between arbitral tribunals and other international courts contributes to the unity of international law and can improve the quality of arbitral jurisprudence. The comparative attitude of arbitral tribunals should not be read as arbitral activism but as an interpretative tool allowed for in customary rules of treaty interpretation[385] or as a matter of arbitral craft. As the parties also refer to previous awards and/or other cases of other courts and tribunals, this is also a matter of legal advocacy and persuasion. Of course, there is a margin of variance in the process: certain arbitral tribunals are more self-referential in that they refer to previous arbitral awards only; others are open to other systems of law. Rather than having binding force, such precedents do have persuasive authority.

---

[383] An argument can (and has) been made that cherry-picking is not bad *per se*; one is supposed to pick the best developments among different legal systems. However, this utilitarian approach is based on a value judgment on which criteria can and should be used to identify the best model. Unless such criteria are spelled out, cherry-picking risks ending up being an arbitrary exercise of judicial authority, thus delegitimising any comparative analysis.

[384] H. Lauterpacht, *The Development of International Law by the International Court* (London: Stevens & Sons, Ltd, 1958), pp. 17–18.

[385] C. McLachlan, 'Investment Treaties and General International Law', *International and Comparative Law Quarterly* 57 (2008), 361.

Finally, arbitrators may detect international principles of law through the analysis of relevant jurisprudence of other courts and tribunals, in order to clarify the existing law or to avoid lacunae or *non liquet*. While there is no common transnational canon to detect general principles of law, certainly, the fact that such principles are general requires a cosmopolitan orientation.[386] Insofar as certain legal principles have become norms of customary law or general principles of law, they may be applied to disputes as applicable law.

In conclusion, arbitral tribunals borrow from the experience of other courts and tribunals, look beyond the boundaries of international investment law and are engaged in a dialogue with the world community. While awards are binding only on the parties to the given dispute, they also address other audiences including subsequent arbitral tribunals, other courts and tribunals and the international community as a whole.[387] Arbitral awards reverberate beyond the boundaries of the single dispute as they are cited by (and cross-pollinate the jurisprudence of) subsequent arbitral tribunals and other international, regional and national *fora*.[388] Awards can also shape and influence subsequent governmental policies. Arbitral tribunals review legislative, executive and even jurisprudential measures adopted by states, contributing to the increasing erosion of the autonomy of the state and the pervasiveness of international law.

Certainly the migration of ideas from different legal systems to international investment law and arbitration – and, arguably, from the latter to the former – contributes to building a distinct identity of

---

[386] One could contend that, by adopting a pluralist approach, cutting-edge adjudicative experiences risk being neglected as they might not be attuned with most jurisdictions. Yet, one can counterargue that such cutting-edge experiences can be referred to as a matter of treaty interpretation rather than as a part of the applicable law. In fact, general principles of law indicate principles belonging to the generality of nations. They are sources of international law and matter as a part of the applicable law.

[387] J.E. Alvarez, 'What Are International Judges for? The Main Functions of International Adjudication', in K. Alter, C. Romano and Y. Shany (eds.), *The Oxford Handbook on International Adjudication* (Oxford: Oxford University Press, 2014), pp. 158–176, 171.

[388] See WTO Appellate Body, *United States – Final Antidumping Measures on Stainless Steel from Mexico*, at para. 160 (referring to *Saipem S.p.A.* v. *The People Republic of Bangladesh*, ICSID Case No. ARB/05/7, Award, 30 June 2009, ICSID IIC 280 (2007), para. 67, for the proposition that '[t]he Tribunal considers that it is not bound by previous decisions. At the same time, it is of the opinion that it must pay due consideration to earlier decisions of international tribunals').

investment treaty tribunals as transnational dispute settlement mechanisms, akin to other international courts and tribunals. By participating in judicial borrowing, arbitral tribunals position themselves within the cosmopolitan network of international courts and tribunals.

However, the use of comparative reasoning in international investment law and arbitration cannot be an uncritical exercise. Legal norms express a certain political position, being the outcome of historical evolution.[389] Analogously, courts and tribunals have different epistemological agendas. The outcome of a selected case may be affected by the selection of the comparator (*tertium comparationis*). In fact, comparative research is determined, on the one hand, by the choice of elements compared and, on the other, by the choice of the comparative question. While the argument goes that common problems may be addressed by adopting common approaches, the risk of exporting systemic failures is high. Moreover, given approaches may be successful in one system but not necessarily in another. There is a risk of repoliticising investment disputes by referring to given legal systems instead of others due to their different political and social contexts. By citing a given case, arbitral tribunals also import the associated cultural baggage.

Therefore, a more conscious use of the comparative methods would improve the overall process. There is no single comparative method. Rather, there are different ways of conducting proper comparative research; the method depends on the research question one aims to answer. Yet, methodological choices must be made and discussed concerning the acquisition and use of the research material.[390] Certainly, comparisons should not be implicit. Rather, the reasons for undertaking a comparison should be unpacked, for fostering the enforceability and acceptability of the award. This is particularly the case when tribunals apply general principles of law and/or customary law. Comparisons are not a neutral phenomenon: '[T]he comparativist has to regard herself as being involved: involved in an ongoing social practice constituted and pervaded by law; involved in a given legal tradition . . .; and involved in

---

[389] R. Rodière, *Introduction au droit comparé* (Paris: Dalloz, 1979), p. 4.
[390] J. Husa, 'Research Designs of Comparative Law – Methodology or Heuristics?', in M. Adams and D. Heirbaut (eds.), *The Method and Culture of Comparative Law* (Oxford and Portland: Hart Publishing, 2014), pp. 53–68, p. 55.

a specific mode of thinking and talking about law.'[391] Once aware of perspective, arbitral tribunals and interpreters can make sound use of analogies. Not only would such awareness limit potential abuses of the comparative method, but it would also favour the coherence of the international legal order as a whole.

[391] Frankenberg, 'Critical Comparisons', 443.

PART II

Analogies in investment treaty arbitration

Introductory note

This book addresses three vital questions: why, what and how to compare in international investment law and arbitration. First, it identifies the aim of analogies. This question – *why to compare* – was addressed in Chapters 1 and 3, which illustrated the functioning of comparative reasoning in different areas of international investment law and arbitration – such as treaty interpretation and the identification of the applicable law – respectively. Second, the book aims at investigating what kind of analogies are made. The question *what to compare* requires the identification of the sources of comparison and the level of abstraction of the comparative process.[1] Chapters 4 and 5 examine what kind of analogies are drawn (micro-comparisons) and which legal systems are compared (macro-comparisons), respectively. Third, the book addresses the question of *how to compare*. Chapter 6 examines the ways in which comparisons are (and/or should be) carried out, illustrating the merit and risks of analogical thinking and highlighting some of the best practices in the use of comparisons in international investment law and arbitration. The analysis is conducted from within international investment law, to identify how comparisons have been (and/or should be) made within this area of law.

Analogical thinking has traditionally played a very important role in the making of international (investment) law, not only as a matter of treaty interpretation but also as a matter of law creation. As a matter of treaty interpretation, analogies reflect 'the gradual interpenetration and cross-fertilisation of previously somewhat compartmentalised areas of international law'[2] and 'between the national and international legal

---

[1] R. Cotterell, 'Seeking Similarity, Appreciating Difference: Comparative Law and Communities', in A. Harding and E. Örücü (eds.), *Comparative Law in the 21st Century* (The Hague: Kluwer Law International, 2002), p. 36.

[2] A. Cassese, *International Law* (Oxford: Oxford University Press, 2001), p. 45.

spaces'.[3] As a matter of law creation, comparative surveys are needed for ascertaining no less than two sources of international law, that is, state practice, which is an element of customary law, and general principles of law.[4] Finally, comparative reasoning also plays a role in the implementing process of international (investment) law when international investment law becomes part of the law of the land.

After addressing the question *why to compare* in Part I, Part II of the book examines the use of analogies in international investment law and arbitration and proceeds as follows. First, Chapter 4 shows what kind of micro-comparisons are drawn; then Chapter 5 reflects on which systems are better suited for macro-comparisons, and then, in turn, might constitute better sources for micro-comparisons. Chapter 5 goes beyond the traditional horizontal comparisons,[5] which focus on national systems – to include vertical comparisons across national, regional and international regimes. This pluralistic perspective – already advocated by some comparativists[6] – captures the multilayered complexity of the law allowing for dialogue among different legal regimes and at different levels. The conclusions will then sum up the key findings of the chapter.

---

[3] M. Delmas-Marty, 'The Contribution of Comparative Law to a Pluralist Conception of International Criminal Law', *Journal of International Criminal Justice* 1 (2003), 13–25, 15.

[4] See, for example, F. Davis, 'Comparative Law Contributions to the International Legal Order: Common Core Research', *George Washington Law Review* 37 (1969), 615–633; L. Amede Obiora, 'Toward an Auspicious Reconciliation of International and Comparative Analyses', *American Journal of Comparative Law* 46 (1998), 669–682; B.N. Mamlyuk and U. Mattei, 'Comparative International Law', *Brooklyn Journal of International Law* 36 (2010–2011), 385–452.

[5] J. Husa, 'Classification of Legal Families Today – Is it Time for Memorial Hymn?' *Revue International de Droit Comparé* 56 (2004), 11–38.

[6] F. Reyntjens, 'Note sur l'utilité d'introduire un system juridique "pluraliste" dans la macro-comparaison des droits', *Revue de droit international et droit comparé* 68 (1991), 41–50.

4

Micro-comparisons in investment treaty arbitration

> Undoubtedly, philosophers are in the right when they tell us that nothing is great or little otherwise than by comparison.[7]

Introduction

Analogies play an important role in international investment law and arbitration. To map their use in this field, different levels of abstraction are possible. Like different maps are used for different purposes, different levels of abstraction allow us to address different analytical goals. In fact, 'an atlas may be useful to plan a journey, but is likely to be of little use to navigate an unknown city'.[8] Vice versa, an A–Z street map may be useful to navigate an unknown city, but it is likely to be of little use to plan a journey. Like maps, all theoretical discussions of the use of comparative reasoning in international investment law and arbitration suppress some information to highlight others and, in that sense, they are incomplete in one way or another because of their selected level of abstraction. Like cartographers, scholars and practitioners select the information relevant to their analysis on the basis of the purpose of the study.

While macro-comparisons are concerned with entire legal systems, micro-comparisons deal with specific institutions or specific problems. Macro-comparisons relate different legal systems, allowing the comparatist to 'situate herself' and mapping the most appropriate systems which can constitute the sources of micro-analogies.[9] Micro-comparisons focus

---

[7] J. Swift, *Travels into Several Remote Nations of the World. In Four Parts. By Lemuel Gulliver, First a Surgeon, and then a Captain of Several Ships* [*Gulliver's Travels*] (London: Benjamin Motte, 1726).

[8] I. Scobbie, 'Wicked Heresies or Legitimate Perspectives? Theory and International Law', in M. Evans (ed.), *International Law* (Oxford: Oxford University Press, 2010), pp. 58–92, p. 59.

[9] B. Jaluzot, 'Méthodologie du droit comparé – Bilan et prospective', *Revue Internationale du Droit Comparé* 1 (2005), 29–48, 46.

on specific legal issues. Therefore, the two approaches of macro-comparing and micro-comparing are complementary; macro-comparisons are often a preliminary step before proceeding to micro-comparisons and vice versa.[10]

This chapter examines the use of micro-comparisons in international investment law and arbitration, that is, how this system has borrowed specific 'legal formants' – statutory rules, scholarly writings and judicial decisions – from other legal systems.[11] The importance of legal formants 'varies enormously from one system to another'.[12] In fact, while civil law scholars and practitioners tend to emphasise scholarly writings, their common law counterparts stress case law. Furthermore, the legal formants of a given system can give rise to several interpretations.[13] Different legal systems have different assumptions – for example, the common law pragmatism and the more conceptual approach of the civil law system.[14] Finally, in the process of borrowing elements from other systems, '[o]ne must avoid the optical illusion caused by magnifying the more general statements of law, the large definitions, and neglecting the specific operational rules that courts actually follow. By the same token, one must avoid the error of perspective that makes the more abstract legal conclusions invisible.'[15]

This chapter explores the use of analogies in arbitral awards and doctrinal writings as subsidiary means for the determination of rules of law. It then examines the use of comparative surveys as a legitimating factor of policy measures and as evidence of state practice. A critical assessment and some conclusions will sum up the key findings of the chapter.

Analogies in arbitral awards as subsidiary means for the determination of rules of law

Like other international courts and tribunals, arbitral tribunals are not bound by previous awards or cases adjudicated by other international,

---

[10] *Ibid.*, at 46.
[11] On the notion of legal formants, see R. Sacco, 'Legal Formants: A Dynamic Approach to Comparative Law', *American Journal of Comparative Law* 39 (1991), 1–34, 22.
[12] *Ibid.*, at 32.   [13] *Ibid.*, at 22.
[14] R. Sacco, 'Mute Law', *American Journal of Comparative Law* 43 (1995), 455.
[15] Sacco, 'Legal Formants', 27.

regional and national courts and tribunals.[16] Their task is to interpret and
apply the applicable law rather than to 'make' the law.[17] This is clarified
by a number of provisions at the international law level. For instance, the
Convention on the Settlement of Investment Disputes between States
and Nationals of Other States (ICSID Convention)[18] states that 'The
award shall be binding on the parties . . . '.[19]

Yet, like other international courts and tribunals, arbitral tribunals
discuss previous decisions and use them extensively to elucidate and
give meaning to treaty provisions and justify their decisions.[20] Judicial
decisions, arbitral awards and reports adopted by international, regional and national courts and tribunals contribute to the development of
international law.[21] As Lauterpacht highlighted, judicial decisions are
'a repository of legal experience to which it is convenient to adhere; . . .
because respect for decisions given in the past makes for certainty
and stability, which are the essence of an orderly administration of
justice . . . '.[22] Furthermore, investment treaties are characterised by
'elastic legal concepts' or general clauses such as fair and equitable
treatment, indirect expropriation and full protection and security.[23]
These core concepts 'only assume a more concretized meaning over
time because of the interpretations investment treaty tribunals give to
them in their decisions'.[24]

---

[16] See *SGS Societé Générale de Surveillance SA* v. *Republic of the Philippines*, ICSID Case No. ARB/02/6, Decision on Jurisdiction, 29 January 2004, para. 97 (holding that '[T]here is no doctrine of precedent in international law ... There is no hierarchy of international tribunals, and even if there were, there is no good reason for allowing the first tribunal in time to resolve issues for all later tribunals').

[17] R. Higgins, 'Policy Considerations and the International Judicial Process', *International and Comparative Law Quarterly* 17 (1968), 58, 58.

[18] Convention on the Settlement of Investment Disputes between States and Nationals of Other States (ICSID Convention or Washington Convention), Washington, 18 March 1965, in force 14 October 1966, 575 UNTS 159.

[19] ICSID Convention, Article 53(1).

[20] A. Pellet, 'The Case Law of the ICJ in Investment Arbitration', *ICSID Review –Foreign Investment Law Journal* 28 (2013), 223–240, 229.

[21] See H. Lauterpacht, 'Decisions of Municipal Courts as a Source of International Law', *British Yearbook of International Law* 10 (1929), 65, 85; H. Lauterpacht, *The Development of International Law by the International Court* (London: Stevens & Sons, 1958).

[22] Lauterpacht, *The Development of International Law by the International Court*, p. 14.

[23] L. Reed, 'The *De Facto* Precedent Regime in Investment Arbitration: A Case for Proactive Case Management', *ICSID Review –Foreign Investment Law Journal* 25 (2010), 95, 96–97.

[24] S.W. Schill, 'System Building in Investment Treaty Arbitration and Lawmaking', *German Law Journal* 12 (2011), 1083, 1092.

Like other international courts and tribunals, arbitral tribunals rely on previous cases, not because such cases have any binding authority, but because they constitute 'a subsidiary means for the determination of the rules of [international] law'.[25] Judicial decisions help determine the existing law. As arbitral tribunals are international in nature and apply mainly international law, they rely upon the sources of the latter and, within this framework, upon judicial decisions. Although ICSID tribunals have expressly referred to judicial decisions as 'a source of international law', according to Article 38(1) of the Statute of the ICJ,[26] judicial decisions are not formal sources of law; rather, they are 'subsidiary means for the determination of rules of law'.

Past cases constitute not only the stock from which analogies are retrieved, but also the categories or *topoi* in terms of which cases are characterised. Adjudicators often explain the driving force of analogy on the basis of the ideas of treating like cases alike (fairness or justice) and/or building systemic coherence, that is, 'attempting to see the law as a fairly consistent whole'.[27] For instance, both arguments of justice and coherence figure prominently in *AWG* v. *Argentina*, where the tribunal held:

> [C]onsiderations of basic justice would lead tribunals to be guided by the basic judicial principle that 'like cases should be decided alike', unless a strong reason exists to distinguish the current case from previous ones. In addition, a recognized goal of international investment law is to establish a predictable, stable legal framework for investments, a factor that justifies tribunals in giving due regard to previous decisions on similar issues.[28]

The various categories of decisions, however, are valued differently for the purpose of identifying an international rule or principle.[29] Generally speaking, 'decisions of national courts ... delivered on the

---

[25] Article 38(1)(d) of the Statute of the International Court of Justice.

[26] See, among others, *AWG Group Ltd* v. *The Argentine Republic*, UNCITRAL, Decision on Liability, 30 July 2010, para. 189; *Camuzzi International SA* v. *Argentine Republic*, ICSID Case No. ARB/03/2, Decision on Jurisdiction, 11 May 2005, para. 135; *Sempra Energy International* v. *Argentine Republic*, ICSID Case No. ARB/02/16, Decision on Jurisdiction, 11 May 2005, para. 147.

[27] E.H. Levi, *An Introduction to Legal Reasoning* (Chicago, IL: University of Chicago Press, 1949), p. 131.

[28] *AWG Group Ltd* v. *The Argentine Republic*, UNCITRAL, Decision on Liability, 30 July 2010, para. 189.

[29] ICTY, *Prosecutor* v. *Zoran Kupreskic*, Case No.: IT-95–16-T, Judgment, 14 January 2000, para. 541.

basis of national legislation would carry relatively less weight' than national decisions delivered on the basis of international law.[30] In parallel, international tribunals 'should apply a stricter level of scrutiny to national decisions than to international judgments, as the latter are at least based on the same *corpus* of law as that applied by international courts, whereas the former tend to apply national law, or primarily that law, or else interpret international rules through the prism of national legislation'.[31]

Precedents may 'constitute evidence of a customary rule in that they are indicative of the existence of *opinio juris sive necessitatis* and widespread international practice on a certain matter, or else they may be indicative of the emergence of a general principle of international law'.[32] They can also persuade a tribunal 'that the decision taken on a prior occasion propounded the correct interpretation of existing law'.[33]

Reference to previous arbitral awards

In investment arbitration, each arbitral tribunal is constituted *ad hoc* for settling the particular case. Arbitral tribunals are not standing bodies, they do not have general jurisdiction over states and their awards are case specific. Even institutionalised arbitral tribunals, like those organised under the auspices of ICSID, the London Court of International Arbitration (LCIA) and other arbitral institutions, derive their authority from the consent of the parties.[34] Therefore, awards are binding only on the parties to the given dispute. Different tribunals apply differently worded treaties and may reach different, if not conflicting, conclusions on analogous issues.[35] Finally, there is no appeals mechanism to bring about coherence and consistency. In fact, arbitral tribunals have acknowledged that 'the [ICSID] annulment mechanism is not designed

---

[30] *Ibid.*   [31] *Ibid.*, para. 542.

[32] *Ibid.*, para. 540 (referring to international criminal courts specifically).   [33] *Ibid.*

[34] L. Hsu, 'International Investment Disputes: Ideological Fault Lines and an Evolving Zeitgeist', *Journal of World Investment and Trade* 12 (2011), 827–853, 831.

[35] See *SGS Societé Générale de Surveillance SA* v. *Republic of the Philippines*, ICSID Case No. ARB/02/6, Decision on Jurisdiction, 29 January 2004, para. 97 (stating that '[A]lthough different tribunals constituted under the ICSID system should in general seek to act consistently with each other, in the end it must be for each tribunal to exercise its competence in accordance with the applicable law, which will by definition be different for each BIT and each Respondent state'). See also *Wintershall Aktiengesellschaft* v. *Argentina*, ICSID Case No. ARB/04/14, Award, 8 November 2008, para. 177.

to bring about consistency in the interpretation and application of international investment law'.[36]

Yet, arbitral tribunals and the parties do consider the reasoning of previous awards; such awards are often cited by the parties in their pleadings and written submissions and by the arbitral tribunals for supporting their legal arguments, respectively.[37] The vagueness of many substantive investment treaty provisions, such as national treatment, most-favoured nation treatment and fair and equitable treatment, drives arbitrators to consider previous interpretations of analogous provisions for clarification.[38] As Pellet points out, 'In general, ICSID tribunals give priority to the case law of their peers or other investment tribunals', because they 'have dealt most with identical issues'.[39]

The interpretations and *ratio decidendi* of previous awards become part of the *acquis* of international investment law and arbitration, potentially contributing to its consistency, coherence and predictability.[40] Eminent scholars have noted that, despite the lack of formal precedent, a *de facto* system of precedent has emerged, as arbitral tribunals follow the paths of reasoning of previous tribunals.[41] The corpus of international arbitration cases is coalescing in a *jurisprudence*

---

[36] *MCI Power Group LV and New Turbine, Inc.* v. *Republic of Ecuador*, ICSID Case No. ARB/03/6, Decision on Annulment, 19 October 2009, para. 24; *Continental Casualty Company* v. *Argentine Republic*, ICSID Case No. ARB/03/9, Decision on Annulment, 16 September 2011, para. 83.

[37] See, for instance, *El Paso Energy International Company* v. *Argentina*, ICSID Case No. ARB/03/15, Decision on Jurisdiction, 27 April 2006, para. 39 (holding that it was reasonable to consider the awards of other international tribunals, 'especially since both parties, in their written pleadings and oral arguments, have relied on precedent').

[38] S.W. Schill, *The Multilateralization of International Investment Law* (Cambridge: Cambridge University Press, 2014), p. 332.

[39] Pellet, 'The Case Law of the ICJ in Investment Arbitration', 230.

[40] A.K. Bjorklund, 'Investment Treaty Arbitral Decisions as Jurisprudence Constante', in C. Picker, I. Bunn and D. Arner (eds.), *International Economic Law: The State and Future of the Discipline* (Oxford: Hart Publishing, 2008), p. 265; C. Schreuer, 'Conversations Across Cases: Is There a Doctrine of Precedent in Investment Arbitration?', *Transnational Dispute Management* 5 (2008), 1–15; G. Kaufmann-Kohler 'Arbitral Precedent: Dream, Necessity or Excuse?', *Arbitration International* 23 (2007), 357–378; Z. Douglas, 'Can a Doctrine of Precedent be Justified in Investment Treaty Arbitration?', *ICSID Review–Foreign Law Investment Journal* 25 (2010), 104.

[41] C. Schreuer and M. Weiniger, 'A Doctrine of Precedent?', in P. Muchlinski, F. Ortino and C. Schreuer (eds.), *The Oxford Handbook of International Investment Law* (Oxford: Oxford University Press, 2008), pp. 1191–1196.

constante.[42] While there exists 'an unfortunate jurisprudential mess on many [points] – eg with regard to the definition of an "investment", . . . there exists "some" jurisprudences constantes on a limited number of points . . . '.[43]

As noted by Paulsson, while 'the corpus of decided cases in the field of international investment arbitration is of recent vintage . . . [i]ts legal status as a source of law is in theory equal to that of other types of international courts and tribunals'.[44] Furthermore, arbitral tribunals 'include numerous scholars and practitioners of international renown', and 'among the authors of these awards are those who must surely qualify for consideration as "the most highly qualified publicists of various nations"'.[45]

Cross-treaty interpretation, that is, 'interpret[ing] the governing treaty in light of other international investment treaties and prior arbitral [awards] interpreting those treaties', can foster the multi-lateralisation,[46] consistency and coherence of international invest-ment law.[47] The perceived legitimacy of arbitral tribunals can be heightened by the coalescence of a well-developed jurisprudence. Tribunals can refer to the jurisprudence of arbitral tribunals for clarifying the meaning of treaty text[48] or detecting emerging general principles of law.[49]

Yet, cross-treaty interpretation can be 'problematic in view of the *inter partes* effects of international treaties, since using a third-party treaty as an interpretative aid can amount to either creating additional obligations,

---

[42] Bjorklund, 'Investment Treaty Arbitral Decisions as Jurisprudence Constante', p. 265.

[43] Pellet, 'The Case Law of the ICJ in Investment Arbitration', 224.

[44] J. Paulsson, 'International Arbitration and the Generation of Legal Norms: Treaty Arbitration and International Law', in A.J. Van den Berg (ed.), *International Arbitration 2006: Back to Basics? ICCA Congress Series No. 13* (Kluwer Law International, 2007), pp. 879–889, at pp. 881–882.

[45] *Ibid.*   [46] Schill, *The Multilateralization of International Investment Law*, p. 305.

[47] A.M. Johnston and M.J. Trebilcock, 'Fragmentation in International Trade Law: Insights from the Global Investment Regime', *World Trade Review* 12 (2013), 621, 622.

[48] M. Paparinskis, 'Sources of Law and Arbitral Interpretations of *Pari Materia* Investment Protection Rules', in O.K. Fauchald and A. Nollkamper (eds.), *The Practice of International and National Courts and (De-) Fragmentation of International Law* (Portland, OR: Hart Publishing, 2012), p. 97.

[49] *Duke Energy International Peru Investment No. 1, Ltd. v. Peru*, ICSID Case No. ARB/03/28, Annulment Proceeding, Decision of the *Ad Hoc* Committee, 1 March 2012, para. 88 (stating that 'reference to wider sources of jurisprudence may help to determine the existence of a general principle of law . . . ').

or conversely diminishing a right of one of the parties'.[50] Moreover, not only does a certain level of inconsistency in the arbitral jurisprudence appear natural, given the relative young age of the field, but it may also be desirable. As Paulsson points out, there are awards and awards. Good awards will be referred to; 'the unfit will perish', 'be[ing] subject to the same Darwinian imperative'.[51]

In conclusion, arbitral tribunals do refer to the earlier rulings of other arbitral tribunals. The interaction among arbitral tribunals suggests the gradual multilateralisation of the investment law regime. This does not necessarily mean that the 'system' as it stands is the best one possible or that good reasons cannot be found to improve it. Certainly, however, the ultimate quality of arbitral awards and the perceived legitimacy of international investment law can be heightened by the coalescence of a well-developed jurisprudence.

Reference to the jurisprudence of other international courts

When facing complex issues, arbitrators have also referred to analogous cases presented before other international *fora*, including the International Court of Justice (ICJ), the Permanent Court of International Justice (PCIJ) and those acting in international subsystems such as the World Trade Organization (WTO) dispute settlement mechanism,[52] the International Tribunal for the Law of the Sea (ITLOS)[53] and international criminal courts and tribunals.[54] Arbitral tribunals use 'judicial decisions' as 'subsidiary means for the determination of rules of law' in accordance with Article 38(1)(d) of the Statute of the ICJ to which Article 42(1) of the ICSID Convention implicitly refers.

Although this jurisprudence may seem to be 'external' case law, that is, outside the realm of international investment law and arbitration, in fact,

---

[50] Schill, *The Multilateralization of International Investment Law*, p. 295.

[51] Paulsson, 'International Arbitration and the Generation of Legal Norms', pp. 881–882.

[52] See E. Voeten, 'Borrowing and Nonborrowing among International Courts', *The Journal of Legal Studies* 39 (2010), 547, 571 (noting that about one quarter of NAFTA tribunals 'make at least a passing reference to WTO decisions').

[53] *CME Czech Republic BV* v. *The Czech Republic*, Final Award, 14 March 2002, para. 433, referring to the *Mox Plant Case, Ireland* v. *United Kingdom*, Request for Provisional Measures, Order, 3 December 2001, ITLOS Case No. 10, para. 51.

[54] See, for example, *Hrvatska Elektroprivreda, dd* v. *Republic of Slovenia*, ICSID Case No. ARB/05/24, Decision on Participation of Counsel, 6 May 2008, para. 33, footnote 17 (referring to the ICTY).

it is only 'semi-external' as the international investment system is 'rooted in international law and internationally oriented'.[55] Arbitral tribunals apply general principles of international law, 'the scope of which goes far beyond investment law alone'.[56] They position themselves at the same level as other international courts and tribunals, perceiving themselves as part of the international bench and rejecting any notion of hierarchy.[57] The cross-fertilisation between the jurisprudence of arbitral tribunals and that of other international courts and tribunals suggests that 'international investment law has its roots in general international law, despite its undeniable specificities'[58] and that '[it] is not a self-contained closed legal system ..., but it has to be envisaged within a wider juridical context in which rules from other sources are integrated through implied incorporation methods, or by direct reference to certain supplementary rules, whether of international law character or of domestic law nature'.[59]

The jurisprudence of the ICJ

Like most international courts and tribunals,[60] arbitral tribunals have shown a particular deference to the jurisprudence of the International Court of Justice,[61] finding it useful in the interpretation of the relevant investment treaty provisions.[62]

While the ICJ has rarely dealt with investment disputes – and when it has done so, some have found its positions 'unattractive'[63] – it has adjudicated on a number of key issues that can (and have) be(en) relevant for investment disputes. For instance, arbitral tribunals have referred to the jurisprudence of the ICJ with regard to treaty

---

[55] Pellet, 'The Case Law of the ICJ in Investment Arbitration', 230.   [56] *Ibid.*, 225.

[57] See, for example, *Saipem SpA* v. *Bangladesh*, ICSID Case No. ARB/05/07, Award, 30 June 2009, para. 90.

[58] Pellet, 'The Case Law of the ICJ in Investment Arbitration', 240.

[59] *Asian Agricultural Products Ltd* v. *Democratic Socialist Republic of Sri Lanka*, ICSID Case No. ARB/87/3, Award, 27 June 1990, para. 21.

[60] See N. Miller, 'An International Jurisprudence? The Operation of "Precedent" Across International Tribunals', *Leiden Journal of International Law* 15 (2002), 483, at 488 (finding the over a half of all references by international courts and tribunals were to ICJ jurisprudence).

[61] Pellet, 'The Case Law of the ICJ in Investment Arbitration', 230.

[62] See, for example, *Azurix Corp.* v. *Argentine Republic*, ICSID Case No. ARB/01/12, Award, 14 July 2006, para. 391 (acknowledging that 'The findings of other tribunals, and in particular of the ICJ, should be helpful to the Tribunal in its interpretative task').

[63] Pellet, 'The Case Law of the ICJ in Investment Arbitration', 231.

interpretation,[64] the jurisdiction of international courts and tribunals,[65] other procedural issues[66] and the notion of necessity.[67]

Arbitral tribunals have not followed a consistent methodology in
referring to ICJ decisions; rather, 'ICSID tribunals refer to the ICJ
case law in a pragmatic manner, without resorting to predetermined
methods'.[68] While arbitral tribunals tend to refer to the ICJ jurisprudence
for matters of procedure rather than substance,[69] the World Court
retains 'a significant influence on investment tribunals'.[70]

Yet, the frequency and the intensity with which arbitral tribunals
borrow the jurisprudence of the ICJ vary.[71] Arbitral tribunals have
reaffirmed the lack of either binding precedent or 'precedential order
in regard to previous decisions on the construction of bilateral

---

[64] See *Asian Agricultural Products Ltd* v. *Democratic Socialist Republic of Sri Lanka*,
ICSID Case No. ARB/87/3, Award, 27 June 1990, para. 40; *Methanex Corporation*
v. *United States of America*, Final Award, 3 August 2005, paras. 19–20; *Wintershall
Aktiengesellschaft* v. *Argentine Republic*, ICSID Case No. ARB/04/14, Award,
8 December 2008, paras. 68–69; *ICS Inspection and Control Services Limited* v.
The Republic of Argentina, PCA Case No. 2010-9, Award on Jurisdiction, 10
February 2012, paras. 252–262; *Kilic Insaat Ithalat Ihracat Sanayi ve Ticaret
Anonim Sirketi* v. *Turkmenistan*, ICSID Case No. ARB/10/1, Decision on Article
VII.2 of the Turkey-Turkmenistan Bilateral Investment Treaty, 7 May 2012, para.
6.4 footnote 34; *Ambiente Ufficio SpA and Others* v. *Argentine Republic*, ICSID Case
No. ARB/08/9, Decision on Jurisdiction and Admissibility, 8 February 2013,
para. 600, footnote 317.

[65] See, for example, *Southern Pacific Properties (Middle East) Limited* v. *Arab Republic of
Egypt*, ICSID Case No. ARB/84/3, Decision on Jurisdiction, 27 November 1985, para. 63;
Ceskoslovenska Obchodni Banka AS v. *Slovak Republic*, ICSID Case No. ARB/97/4,
Decision on Jurisdiction, 1 December 2000, para. 31; *Hochtief Aktiengesellshaft* v.
Argentine Republic, ICSID Case No. ARB/07/31, Decision on Jurisdiction, 24 October
2011, paras. 90–96; *Chevron Corporation and Texaco Petroleum Corporation* v. *The
Republic of Ecuador*, PCA Case No. 2009-23, Third Decision on Jurisdiction, 27
February 2012, paras. 4.60–4.71.

[66] See, for example, *Salini Costruttori SpA and Italstrade SpA* v. *Hashemite Kingdom of
Jordan*, ICSID Case No. ARB/02/13, Award, 31 January 2006, paras. 72 and 74 (the
burden of proof); *Antoine Goetz and Others* v. *Republic of Burundi*, ICSID Case No.
ARB/95/3, Award, 10 February 1999, paras. 53–57 (*in absentia* proceedings); *Victor Pey
Casado and President Allende Foundation* v. *Republic of Chile*, ICSID Case No. ARB/98/2,
Decision on Provisional Measures, 25 September 2001, para. 10 (provisional measures).

[67] See, for example, *ATA Construction, Industrial and Trading Company* v. *Hashemite
Kingdom of Jordan*, ICSID Case No. ARB/08/2, Award, 18 May 2010, para. 129; *Joseph
Charles Lemire* v. *Ukraine*, ICSID Case No. ARB/06/18, Award, 28 March 2011, para. 149;
Franck Charles Arif v. *Republic of Moldavia*, ICSID Case No. ARB/11/23, Award, 8 April
2013, para. 559 (all referring to the *Chorzow Factory* case).

[68] Pellet, 'The Case Law of the ICJ in Investment Arbitration', 239.   [69] *Ibid.*, at 239–240.
[70] *Ibid.*, at 240.   [71] *Ibid.*, at 233.

investment treaties'.[72] In other words, 'the relevant enquiry remains for the Tribunal to interpret and apply the terms of the BIT itself'.[73] Some awards pay only formal deference to the jurisprudence of the ICJ, while informally dismissing its holdings.[74] For instance, with regard to the protection of shareholders, the *Barcelona Traction* case[75] has been 'eclipsed' by later arbitral jurisprudence:[76] 'whatever may have been the merits of *Barcelona Traction*, that case was concerned solely with the diplomatic protection of nationals by their State, while the case here disputed concerns the contemporary concept of direct access for investors to dispute resolution by means of arbitration between investors and the state'.[77] Analogously, with regard to the state of necessity, the *Gabcikovo-Nagymaros* case[78] has been eclipsed by increasing reference to Article 25 of the 2001 ILC Articles.[79] In other cases, the jurisprudence of the ICJ has been used inconsistently by arbitral tribunals.[80] Finally, in some instances, reference to the jurisprudence of the ICJ, and subsequent cross-pollination, has expanded the authority of arbitral tribunals. For instance, arbitral tribunals have followed the ICJ in holding that the provisional measures they provide for have binding force,[81] despite the text of the ICSID Convention.[82]

---

[72] *Tulip Real Estate and Development Netherlands BV* v. *Republic of Turkey*, ICSID Case No. ARB/11/28, Decision on Bifurcation, 5 March 2013, para. 45.

[73] *Ibid.*   [74] Pellet, 'The Case Law of the ICJ in Investment Arbitration', 233.

[75] ICJ, *Case Concerning the Barcelona Traction, Light and Power Company, Limited* (*Belgium* v. *Spain*), Second Phase, Judgment of 5 February 1970, *ICJ Reports* 1970, p. 3.

[76] Pellet, 'The Case Law of the ICJ in Investment Arbitration', 235.

[77] *Camuzzi International SA* v. *Argentine Republic*, ICSID Case No. ARB/03/2, Decision on Jurisdiction, 11 May 2005, paras. 141–142.

[78] ICJ, *Case Concerning the Gabčíkovo Nagymaros Project* (*Hungary* v. *Slovakia*), Judgment, 25 September 1997, *ICJ Reports* 1997, p. 7.

[79] *CMS Gas Transmission Company* v. *Argentine Republic*, ICSID Case No. ARB/01/8, Award, 12 May 2005, para. 330.

[80] *Compare Emilio Augustin Maffezini* v. *Kingdom of Spain*, ICSID Case No. ARB/97/7, Decision on Jurisdiction, 25 January 2000, para. 51 (referring to the *Anglo-Iranian* Case, the *Case concerning the Rights of Nationals of the United States of America in Morocco* and *Ambatielos* for interpreting the MFN clause) with *Plama Consortium Limited* v. *Republic of Bulgaria*, ICSID Case No. ARB/03/24, Decision on Jurisdiction, 8 February 2005, paras. 210 and 217 (holding that 'the foregoing review of those decisions shows that they do not provide a conclusive answer to the question').

[81] *Victor Pey Casado and President Allende Foundation* v. *Republic of Chile*, ICSID Case No. ARB/98/2, Decision on Provisional Measures, 25 September 2001, para. 10, para. 17 (referring to *LaGrand* (*Germany* v. *United States of America*), Judgment, 27 June 2001, *ICJ Reports* 502–503, para. 102).

[82] ICSID Convention, Article 47.

The WTO jurisprudence

Dozens of investment awards refer to the WTO jurisprudence.[83] While it is not possible to draw sound or definitive conclusions on the substantive impact of WTO cases on the findings of investment treaty tribunals,[84] procedurally, it is important to investigate the parameters and criteria for such borrowing. Two types of convergences can be identified. The first type of convergence naturally occurs when given investment and trade disputes draw on the same underlying range of facts. In this case, arbitral tribunals may refer to relevant trade disputes, although they are not bound by these decisions. The second type of reference occurs when arbitrators refer to WTO cases dealing with different facts and legal issues. In the latter case, the analogy is text driven: for instance, analogies are drawn for the interpretation of the non-discrimination provision, the scope for exceptions and the application of general principles of law.

Several investment and trade disputes draw on the same underlying range of facts. For instance, Australia's *Plain Packaging Act* 2011 – requiring the removal of all colours, imagery and trademarks from cigarette packaging and permitting manufacturers to print only the brand name in a mandated size, font and place on the pack, in addition to health warnings – has become the object of a number of international disputes pending before the WTO dispute settlement mechanism[85] and

---

[83] See, for example, *SD Myers, Inc.* v. *Government of Canada*, Partial Award, 13 November 2000, paras. 244 and 291–293; *Pope & Talbot Inc.* v. *The Government of Canada*, Award on the Merits of Phase 2, 10 April 2001, paras. 46–63 and 68; *Marvin Roy Feldman Karpa* v. *United Mexican States*, ICSID Case No. ARB(AF)/99/1, Award, 16 December 2002, para. 177; *United Parcel Service of America Inc.* v. *Canada*, Award on Jurisdiction, 22 November 2002, para. 40; *Continental Casualty Company* v. *Argentine Republic*, ICSID Case No. ARB/03/9, Award, 5 September 2008, para. 195.

[84] See G. Marceau, V. Lanovoy and A. Izaguerri Vila, 'A Lighthouse in the Storm of Fragmentation', *Journal of World Trade* 47 (2013), 481.

[85] See, for example, *Australia – Certain Measures Concerning Trademarks and Other Plain Packaging Requirements Applicable to Tobacco Products and Packaging*, complaint by Ukraine, dispute DS434. On 28 May 2015, Ukraine requested the panel to suspend its proceedings in accordance with Article 12.12 of the DSU. On 2 June 2015, the panel informed the DSB of its decision of 29 May 2015 to grant Ukraine's request and suspend its work. Reportedly, the suspension will be with a view to finding a mutually agreed solution. At the time of this writing, Cuba, the Dominican Republic, Honduras and Indonesia have also filed complaints against Australia.

before arbitral tribunals, respectively.[86] The claimants allege that the measure violates Australia's commitments under the WTO agreements and the relevant bilateral investment treaties, respectively.

Another interesting set of pending cases includes those concerning the *Ontario Green Energy Act* 2009 creating the Feed-In Tariff Program.[87] In order to increase the production of clean energy, Ontario adopted a number of incentives to attract investments in the renewable energy sector.[88] Among these incentives was a 'feed-in tariff' (FIT), that is, a guaranteed electricity purchase price set higher than market rates.[89] Japan and the European Union (EU) brought claims against Canada before the WTO dispute settlement mechanism regarding Canada's measures relating to domestic content requirements in the FIT Program.[90] Japan and the EU claimed, among other things, that the measures were inconsistent with (1) the national treatment obligation under Article III:4 and III:5 of the General Agreement on Tariffs and Trade (GATT) 1994 because they appeared to accord less favourable treatment to imported equipment than that accorded to like domestic products;[91] and (2) the prohibition on the application of any trade-related investment measures that are inconsistent with Article III of the GATT 1994.[92] The Panel and the Appellate Body (AB) upheld both claims.[93] In a pending arbitration, a US company contends that the FIT Program amounts to a violation of the relevant investment treaty obligations, including the principle of fair and equitable treatment, non-discrimination and the prohibition of performance requirements.[94] As this arbitration is pending at the time of this writing, it is not possible to foresee how it will be

---

[86] *Philip Morris Asia Ltd* v. *The Commonwealth of Australia*, Notice of Claim, 15 July 2011; *Philip Morris Asia Ltd* v. *The Commonwealth of Australia*, Notice of Arbitration, 21 November 2011.

[87] See *Mesa Power Group LLC* v. *Government of Canada*, Notice of Intent to Submit a Claim to Arbitration, 6 July 2011, and *Canada – Certain Measures Affecting the Renewable Energy Generation Sector, Canada – Measures Relating to the Feed-In Tariff Program*, Reports of the Appellate Body, WT/DS412/AB/R; WT/DS426/AB/R, 6 May 2013.

[88] *Mesa Power Group LLC* v. *Government of Canada*, Notice of Intent to Submit a Claim to Arbitration, para. 5.

[89] *Ibid.*

[90] *Canada – Certain Measures Affecting the Renewable Energy Generation Sector, Canada – Measures Relating to the Feed-In Tariff Program*, Reports of the Appellate Body, para. 1.1.

[91] *Ibid.*, para. 1.6.b. (Japan) and para. 1.7.c (EU).

[92] *Ibid.*, para. 1.6.c. (Japan) and para. 1.7.b (EU).   [93] *Ibid.*, para. 1.15.

[94] *Mesa Power Group LLC* v. *Government of Canada*, Notice of Intent to Submit a Claim to Arbitration, para. 33.

adjudicated by the relevant arbitral tribunal and what impact, if any, WTO law will have in the same.

It would be difficult to neglect the WTO case, especially if state liability is found and the state agrees to comply with the relevant report. For instance, the *US–Mexico Sweetener* disputes before the WTO influenced the outcomes of the arbitrations initiated by US sweetener companies against Mexico. When Mexico imposed an extra 20% tax on soft drinks using sweeteners other than cane sugar, the Panel and the AB found the tax to be discriminatory in violation of the GATT 1994.[95] When three US sweetener companies filed a notice of arbitration against Mexico under North American Free Trade Agreement (NAFTA) Chapter 11, claiming, *inter alia*, that the tax violated NAFTA Article 1102 regarding national treatment,[96] the Arbitral Tribunal unanimously held that the tax was discriminatory. It expressly referred to the WTO rulings and acknowledged that the dispute before the Panel and AB was factually similar to the arbitration, concerning the same tax measures.[97] After analysing both reports,[98] which held that 'the protective effect of the measure on Mexican domestic production of sugar' seemed 'an intentional objective',[99] the Tribunal concluded that the Mexican tax 'was the culmination of a series of measures adopted by the Respondent to protect the domestic cane sugar industry'.[100] The case shows that there may be convergence between the outcomes of trade disputes and investment disputes.

However, arbitral awards do not constitute *res judicata* for subsequent trade disputes and vice versa. *Res judicata* (i.e. 'a matter [already] judged') is a general principle of law indicating that a case in which there has been a final judgment is no longer subject to

---

[95] WTO Panel Report, *Mexico – Measures on Soft Drinks and Other Beverages*, WT/DS308/R, 7 October 2005; WTO Appellate Body Report, *Mexico – Tax Measures on Soft Drinks and Other Beverages*, WT/DS308/AB/R, 6 March 2006.

[96] *Archer Daniels Midland Company and Tate & Lyle Ingredients Americas, Inc. v. United Mexican States*, ICSID Case No. ARB(AF)/04/5, Award, 26 September 2007; *Corn Products International, Inc. v. United Mexican States*, ICSID Case No. ARB (AF)/04/1, Award, 18 August 2009 (not public).

[97] *Archer Daniels Midland Company and Tate & Lyle Ingredients Americas, Inc. v. United Mexican States*, Award, para. 87.

[98] *Ibid.*, paras. 85–95.

[99] WTO Panel Report, *Mexico– Measures on Soft Drinks and Other Beverages*, para. 8.91.

[100] *Archer Daniels Midland Company and Tate & Lyle Ingredients Americas, Inc. v. United Mexican States*, Award, para. 142.

litigation.[101] The aim of *res judicata* is to prevent continued litigation of identical disputes. To have identical disputes, three elements are needed: *personae* (same parties), *petitum* (same object) and *causa petendi* (same legal grounds).[102] Even when they concern similar matters, investment treaty disputes and trade disputes are not identical disputes. Not only do investment disputes and trade disputes have different parties, but they also present different subject matter and legal claims.

With regard to the parties, while trade disputes are international disputes, investment disputes typically involve a state and a private actor.[103] With regard to the object of the dispute, while WTO cases deal with international trade, investment disputes deal with foreign investments in the host state. There may be a partial overlap in the object of given disputes where the concept of investment is interpreted in a broad fashion, but the remedies are different. With regard to the *causa petendi* or legal grounds of the disputes, the legal instruments to be interpreted and applied to the disputes are different. In the case of investment disputes, depending on the choice of the parties, relevant investment treaties and/or customary law or domestic law will constitute the applicable law. In the case of trade disputes, the Dispute Settlement Understanding[104] empowers the Dispute Settlement Body to clarify the provisions of the covered agreements.[105] The fact that the non-discrimination provisions or the prohibition of performance requirement included in investment treaties partially overlap with

[101] ICJ, *Effect of Awards of Compensation Made by the United Nations Administrative Tribunal*, Advisory Opinion, 13 July 1953, *ICJ Reports* (1954), 47; B. Chen, *General Principles of Law as Applied by International Courts and Tribunals* (Cambridge: Cambridge University Press, 1953), pp. 25–26. See also *Amco Asia Corp. v. Republic of Indonesia*, ICSID Case No. ARB/81/1, Resubmitted Case, Decision on Jurisdiction, 10 May 1988, 27 ILM 1281 (1988), para. 30; *Apotex Holdings Inc., Apotex Inc. v. United States of America*, ICSID Case No. ARB(AF)/12/1, Award, 25 August 2014, para. 7.11 (holding that 'the doctrine of *res judicata* is a general principle of law and is thus an applicable rule of international law ... ').
[102] The 'triple identity test' was identified by Judge Anzilotti in his Separate Opinion in the *Chórzow Factory* Case. PCIJ, Ser. A. No. 13, at 23–27. See also *Apotex Holdings Inc., Apotex Inc. v. United States of America*, Award, para. 7.13.
[103] But see A. Roberts, 'State-to-State Investment Treaty Arbitration: A Hybrid Theory of Interdependent Rights and Shared Interpretive Authority', *Harvard International Law Journal* 55 (2014) 1.
[104] Understanding on Rules and Procedures Governing the Settlement of Disputes (DSU), Marrakesh Agreement Establishing the World Trade Organization, Annex 2 33 ILM 1226 (1994).
[105] DSU, Articles 3.2 and 19.2.

the General Agreement on Tariffs and Trade 1994 (GATT 1994)[106] or the Agreement on Trade-Related Investment Measures (TRIMS Agreement)[107] provisions does not change the different institutional and normative settings.

While arbitral tribunals have referred to the WTO jurisprudence to settle complex issues, they have not felt bound by its interpretation. As an Arbitral Tribunal put it, '[t]he findings of WTO Panels and its Appellate Body have no binding effect upon this Tribunal ...'[108] There is no hierarchy between different international courts and tribunals. Moreover, there is no binding precedent in international law. The two dispute settlement mechanisms run in parallel but are conceptually distinct.[109] Therefore, the existence of a pending trade dispute does not impede the foreign investor from having recourse to arbitration. Nor does the existence of a pending investment dispute impede the home state from submitting to the WTO dispute settlement mechanism provided that it does not espouse the investor's claim.[110]

This is particularly evident in another interesting set of cases: the *UPS* arbitration and the *Canada–Periodicals* case. In the *UPS* case,[111] United Parcel Service of America (UPS), a US company providing package delivery services both throughout Canada and worldwide,[112] claimed

[106] General Agreement on Tariffs and Trade 1994 (GATT 1994), 15 April 1994, Marrakesh Agreement Establishing the World Trade Organization, Annex 1A, 33 ILM 1153 (1994).

[107] Agreement on Trade-Related Investment Measures (TRIMS Agreement), 15 April 1994, Annex 1A to the Marrakesh Agreement Establishing the World Trade Organization (WTO Agreement), 1868 UNTS 186.

[108] *Canfor Corporation v. United States of America, and Terminal Forest Products Ltd. v. United States of America*, Decision on Preliminary Question, 6 June 2006, para. 327.

[109] *Corn Products International, Inc. v. United Mexican States*, ICSID Case No. ARB (AF)/04/1, Award, Separate Opinion of Andreas F. Lowenfeld, 18 August 2009, para. 2 (noting that '[t]he host state cannot take out against the investor its disputes with the state of the investor's nationality, and that the investor cannot be held responsible for the actions of its host state. Nor can the state of the investor's nationality prevent an investor from bringing a claim, or oblige the investor to reach a settlement. The fact that two controversies – investor–host state and state-to-state – may concern the same economic sector or activity cannot alter this fundamental principle').

[110] *Ibid.*, para. 1 (noting that 'In return for agreeing to independent international arbitration, the host state is assured that the state of the investor's nationality ... will not espouse the investor's claim or otherwise intervene in the controversy between an investor and a host state ... Correspondingly, the state of the investor's nationality is relieved of the pressure of having its relations with the host state disturbed or distorted by a controversy between its national and the host state').

[111] *United Parcel Service of America Inc. v. Government of Canada*, Award on the Merits, 24 May 2007, 46 ILM 922 (2007).

[112] *Ibid.*, para. 8.

that Canada's Publications Assistance Program (PAP) – a policy designed to promote the wider distribution of Canadian periodicals – was discriminatory to foreign investors.[113] Such a policy 'provide[d] financial assistance to the Canadian magazine industry but only on the condition that any magazines benefitting from the financial assistance [we]re distributed through Canada Post [an institution of the Government of Canada], and not through companies such as UPS Canada'.[114] The investor did not challenge the cultural policy measure *per se* (i.e. the financial assistance to the Canadian magazine industry) because such measure arguably fell within the cultural exception clause as set out in the NAFTA.[115] Rather, the investor challenged the design and implementation of the cultural policy.[116] According to UPS, the preferential treatment received by Canada Post 'ha[d] nothing to do with protecting cultural industries and so f[ell] outside the scope of the cultural industries exception . . .'[117] UPS maintained that the cultural industries exception 'applie[d] only to cultural industries themselves, not to their delivery mechanism, and that there [wa]s no connection between the program's objective and Canada Post's involvement'.[118]

The Arbitral Tribunal upheld Canada's argument that PAP was exempted from review under NAFTA by virtue of the cultural industries exception, which removed from the scope of the NAFTA any measure adopted or maintained *'with respect to* cultural industries'.[119] After noting that the language of the cultural exception is intentionally broad,[120] the Tribunal held that the involvement of Canada Post was 'rationally and intrinsically connected to assisting the Canadian publishing industry'[121] and 'strengthening Canada's cultural identity', as delivery through Canada Post was 'the best and most effective way' to meet such policy objective.[122]

Finally, the Tribunal concluded that the PAP did not breach the national treatment provision of NAFTA Chapter 11 because it deemed that UPS Canada and Canada Post were not 'in like circumstances'.[123] As the Canadian market for publications was characterised by a high

---

[113] *Ibid.*, paras. 156–160.   [114] *Ibid.*, para. 80.
[115] North American Free Trade Agreement (NAFTA), 17 December 1992, in force 1 January 1994 (1993) 32 ILM 289.
[116] *United Parcel Service of America Inc.* v. *Government of Canada*, Award on the Merits, para. 151.
[117] *Ibid.*, para. 157.   [118] *Ibid.*, para. 159.   [119] *Ibid.*, para. 167.   [120] *Ibid.*, para. 162.
[121] *Ibid.*, para. 168.   [122] *Ibid.*, para. 166.   [123] *Ibid.*, para. 173.

percentage of home-delivered subscription sales as opposed to news stand sales, the PAP aimed to achieve the widest possible distribution of Canadian publications at affordable prices throughout the country. While Canada Post was capable of delivering to individual readers across the country, UPS Canada had a different delivery capacity.[124] In a separate statement, however, one arbitrator dissented with the majority and deemed that the implementation of the programme amounted to a subsidy of Canadian mail and package delivery services and should not fall within the cultural industries exception.[125]

The approach adopted by the Arbitral Tribunal sensibly differs from the approach adopted by the WTO panels and Appellate Body in an analogous dispute, *Canada–Periodicals*,[126] which concerned the restriction of the commercialisation and the imposition of high taxes on split-run magazines marketed in Canada, that is, magazines having substantially the same content as a foreign publication, but containing advertisements aimed at the Canadian market. The Canadian government prohibited the import of split-run periodicals that contained advertisement directed at the Canadian market that did not appear in the home country edition of that periodical, arguing that such publications threatened to supplant Canadian culture. The Parliament also imposed a tax on split-run periodicals equal to 80% of the value of all the advertising revenue earned by the edition. The United States challenged the Canadian measure before a WTO panel, arguing that the Canadian ban violated the prohibition on import ban under Article XI of the GATT and the national treatment provision under Article III of the GATT. The United States also argued that the application of favourable postage rates to certain Canadian periodicals was inconsistent with GATT Article III.

The panel found that both GATT and the General Agreement on Trade in Services (GATS)[127] were applicable and accepted the US view that split-run periodicals were like Canadian magazines, and thus held that the Canadian measures were inconsistent with the GATT. The panel highlighted that 'despite the Canadian claim that the purpose of

[124] *Ibid.*, paras. 175–176.
[125] *UPS* v. *Canada*, Separate Statement of Dean Ronald A. Cass, para. 147.
[126] WTO Panel Report, *Canada–Certain Measures Concerning Periodicals*, WT/DS31/R, 15 March 1997; WTO Appellate Body Report, *Canada–Certain Measures Concerning Periodicals*, WT/DS31/AB/R, 30 June 1997.
[127] General Agreement on Trade in Services (GATS), 15 April 1994, Marrakesh Agreement Establishing the World Trade Organization, Annex 1B, 33 ILM 1167 (1994).

the legislation is to promote publications of original Canadian content, this definition essentially relies on factors external to the Canadian market – whether the same editorial content is included in a foreign edition and whether the periodical carries different advertisements in foreign editions'.[128] In an *obiter dictum* the panel concluded that 'the ability of a Member to take measures to protect its cultural identity was not an issue in the present case'.[129] The Appellate Body voided the panel's finding that split-run periodicals and domestic periodicals were like products; rather, it deemed them to be directly competitive or substitutable products. In conclusion, however, the AB concurred with the panel that – in violation of GATT Article III – the tax afforded protection to domestic products. Finally, the application of favourable postage rates to certain Canadian periodicals was found to be inconsistent with GATT Article III.

In the *UPS* arbitration, the investor made reference to the panel report, mentioning *inter alia* its finding that the application of higher rates to foreign products 'clearly affected the sale, transportation and distribution of imported periodicals' violating the national treatment provision under GATT Article III:4.[130] The Arbitral Tribunal, however, held that the analysis of the WTO panel report in the *Canada Periodicals* case was not on point. The approaches adopted by the different international economic tribunals diverged in two respects. First, the NAFTA expressly provides for a cultural exemption, while the GATT for historical reasons only has an exception concerning 'the protection of national treasures of artistic, historic or archaeological value'[131] and a provision on movies.[132] Second, the non-discrimination provisions in investment agreements are less defined than the analogous trade law provisions.[133] UPS called for a 'least restrictive means test – one that would require any government program to be tailored so that it discriminates as little as possible between national investors or investments and other parties' investors or investments'.[134] It argued that there was no need to have the PAP benefits go to a single firm and that two or more firms together could achieve nationwide coverage.[135] However,

---

[128] WTO Panel Report, *Canada–Certain Measures Concerning Periodicals*, para. 5.24.
[129] *Ibid.*, para. 5.45. [130] *UPS* v. *Canada*, Awards on the Merits, para. 52.
[131] GATT Article XX. [132] GATT Article IV.
[133] For instance, with regard to national treatment, compare GATT Article III with NAFTA Article 1102.
[134] See *UPS* v. *Canada*, Separate Statement of Dean Ronald A. Cass, para. 113.
[135] *Ibid.*, para. 99.

arbitral tribunals have been reluctant to adopt an overly critical examination of governmental policy choices.[136]

Yet, the lack of *res judicata* does not mean that arbitral tribunals
should (or do) ignore the WTO jurisprudence. The existence of conflicting decisions in different legal orders can jeopardise the situation of
the parties 'with each of them in danger of being deprived in one place
of what it has been awarded in another'.[137] As an arbitral tribunal put it,
'While ... the findings of WTO Panels and its Appellate Body have no
binding effect upon this Tribunal, they constitute relevant factual
evidence which the Tribunal can and should appropriately take into
account ... '.[138]

For instance, in an investment arbitration brought by Canadian
Lumber companies against the United States, the Tribunal expressly
referred to the *US–Canada softwood lumber* disputes before the WTO.
In 2004, a WTO panel held that the anti-dumping and countervailing
measures imposed by the United States' International Trade
Commission (ITC) on imports of softwood lumber from Canada
were inconsistent with the United States' obligations under the
Anti-Dumping Agreement[139] and Agreement on Subsidies and
Countervailing Measures (SCM Agreement),[140] and recommended
that those measures be brought into conformity with the obligations.[141] The Appellate Body, however, reversed, in part, the WTO
panel's findings,[142] expressing deference to the exercise of discretion
by the ILC and upholding some of its findings.

Two Canadian lumber companies initiated investment treaty arbitrations against the United States under NAFTA Chapter 11, claiming

---

[136] *Ibid.*, para. 125.
[137] G. Cuniberti, 'Parallel Litigation and Foreign Investment Dispute Settlement', *ICSID Review–Foreign Investment Law Journal* 21 (2006), 381, 421.
[138] *Canfor Corporation* v. *United States of America, and Terminal Forest Products Ltd.* v. *United States of America*, Decision on Preliminary Question, 6 June 2006, para. 327.
[139] Agreement on Implementation of Article VI of the General Agreement on Tariffs and Trade 1994, 15 April 1994, Final Act Embodying the Results of the Uruguay Round of Multilateral Trade Negotiations, Annex 1A, 33 ILM 1197(1994).
[140] Agreement on Subsidies and Countervailing Measures, 15 April 1994, Final Act Embodying the Results of the Uruguay Round of Multilateral Trade Negotiations, Annex 1A, 33 ILM 1197 (1994).
[141] WTO Panel Report, *United States –Investigation of the International Trade Commission in Softwood Lumber from Canada*, WT/DS277/R, 22 March 2004.
[142] *United States – Investigation of the International Trade Commission in Softwood Lumber from Canada – Recourse to Article 21.5 of the DSU by Canada*, WT/DS277/AB/RW, 13 April 2006.

that US treatment of Canadian lumber imports amounted to an indirect expropriation and violated the non-discrimination provision and the fair and equitable treatment standard.[143] The Arbitral Tribunal examined the WTO proceedings at length[144] and stated that 'general principles are to be found in the NAFTA' and that 'these include ... [the] compatibility of NAFTA with GATT/WTO law; and the priority of NAFTA over the GATT/WTO in case of direct conflict'.[145] Yet, stating that 'the antidumping and countervailing duty determinations by the United States authorities are not reviewable under Chapter Eleven',[146] it declined jurisdiction on the matter, while it affirmed its jurisdiction on other aspects of the case.

The second type of reference is functional: arbitrators refer to WTO cases for interpreting the non-discrimination provision,[147] the scope for exceptions[148] and other treaty terms.[149] In some cases, there is convergence between the interpretations of analogous treaty provisions. For instance, in the *Myers* arbitration, concerning Canada's imposition of a temporary export ban on a type of hazardous waste, the Tribunal referred to the GATT Article III jurisprudence, taking into account the textual differences between the two regimes, that is, the lack of general exceptions in Chapter 11 of the NAFTA.[150] Analogously, in *Pope & Talbot v. Canada*, the Tribunal affirmed competition as a condition of likeness referring to WTO law.[151] In *Canfor*, the Tribunal 'subscribe[d] to the view expressed by the GATT Panel in *Canada – Import Restrictions on Ice Cream and Yoghurt*' that 'exceptions were to be interpreted narrowly'.[152] In *Phoenix*, the Arbitral

---

[143] *Canfor Corporation v. United States of America, and Terminal Forest Products Ltd.* v. *United States of America*, Decision on Preliminary Question, 6 June 2006, para. 142.

[144] *Ibid.*, para. 85.   [145] *Ibid.*, para. 183.   [146] *Ibid.*, para. 153.

[147] J. Kurtz, 'The Merits and Limits of Comparativism: National Treatment in International Investment Law and the WTO', in S. Schill (ed.), *International Investment Law and Comparative Public Law* (Oxford: Oxford University Press, 2010).

[148] *Canfor Corporation v. United States of America, and Terminal Forest Products Ltd.* v. *United States of America*, Decision on Preliminary Question, 6 June 2006, para. 187.

[149] See generally J. Kurtz, 'The Use and Abuse of WTO Law in Investor–State Arbitration: Competition and Its Discontents', *European Journal of International Law* 20 (2009), 749–771.

[150] *SD Myers Inc.* v. *Canada*, Partial Award, 13 November 2000, at paras. 244–246.

[151] *Pope & Talbot Inc.* v. *Canada*, Award on the Merits of Phase 2, 10 April 2001, at para. 78.

[152] *Canfor Corporation v. United States of America, and Terminal Forest Products Ltd.* v. *United States of America*, Decision on Preliminary Question, para. 187.

Tribunal referred to the jurisprudence of the WTO for noting that specific branches of international law should not be conceived in a clinical isolation from public international law.[153] Therefore, according to the Tribunal, the ICSID Convention should be 'analyzed with due regard to the requirements of the general principles of law, such as the principles of non-retroactivity or the principle of good faith'.[154]

In other cases, however, there is a significant divergence between the interpretations of analogous treaty provisions. For instance, in *Occidental v. Ecuador*, the Arbitral Tribunal rejected the competition criterion in the interpretation of national treatment. The oil exporting company filed an investor–state arbitration against Ecuador for breach of the national treatment provision, alleging that it was discriminated against, as national companies involved in the export of flowers and seafood products received VAT refunds. The Tribunal referred to the WTO, but upheld the claimant's arguments. WTO scholars have criticised this reasoning as 'offering inutile and misleading comparison with selective parts of WTO law'[155] and cautioned against 'impressionistic methods' of interpretation.[156]

In conclusion, arbitral tribunals often refer to previous rulings of the WTO panels and Appellate Body for clarifying treaty provisions. Moreover, certain investment and trade law cases arise from the same set of facts. In the latter scenario, to have several *fora* available can 'guarantee that all elements of a multi-faceted dispute are actually resolved'.[157] Moreover, some mutual reference and indirect control between different *fora* can enhance their legitimacy.[158] This is not to say, however, that consistency between international investment and trade jurisprudence should be considered a desideratum at all costs. Arbitral tribunals and WTO panels and AB decide different aspects of the same dispute, operating from 'a distinct legal angle'.[159]

---

[153] *Phoenix Action, Ltd v. the Czech Republic*, ICSID Case no. ARB/06/5, Award, 15 April 2009, paras. 77–78 (referring to Appellate Body Report, *United States – Standards for Reformulated and Conventional Gasoline*, WT/DS2/AB/R, 29 April 1996, p. 18).

[154] *Ibid.*, para. 77.

[155] Kurtz, 'The Use and Abuse of WTO Law in Investor–State Arbitration', 765.

[156] *Ibid.*, at 770.

[157] J. Pauwelyn and L.E. Salle, 'Forum Shopping Before International Tribunals: (Real) Concerns, (Im)possible Solutions', *Cornell International Law Journal* 42 (2009), 80.

[158] *Ibid.*   [159] *Ibid.*, 84.

Reference to the jurisprudence of regional courts

Arbitral tribunals have also referred to the jurisprudence of regional human rights courts[160] and that of the EU.[161] While reference to regional law is driven by functional reasons, namely by the need of clarifying vague investment treaty provisions, some arbitral tribunals have referred to human rights cases because the relevant investment arbitrations and human rights disputes arose from the same set of facts. This section examines both types of reference.

With regard to functional references, that is, references to clarify vague investment treaty provisions, the selection of the comparators (*elementa comparationis*) is crucial; the outcome of a given case may differ depending upon which material is selected for comparison. For instance, the *Lauder* case[162] and the *CME* case[163] – which were parallel proceedings over the same underlying dispute – had different outcomes because different BITs governed the relative substantive law and the arbitral

---

[160] See, for example, *Ronald Lauder v. The Czech Republic*, Final Award, 3 September 2001, para. 200 (referring to the ECHR); *Mondev International Ltd v. United States of America*, ICSID Case No. ARB(AF)/99/2, Award, 11 October 2002, paras. 137–138 and 143–144 (referring to the ECHR); *Tecnicas Medioambientales Tecmed SA v. United Mexican States*, ICSID Case No. ARB(AF)/00/2, Award, 29 May 2003, para. 116 (referring to the ECHR and the IAHR); *The Lowen Group, Inc. and Raymond L Lowen v. United States of America*, ICSID Case No. ARB(AF)/98/3, Award, 26 June 2003 para. 165 (referring to the ECHR); *Azurix Corp. v. Argentine Republic*, ICSID Case No. ARB/01/12, Award, 14 July 2006 paras. 311–312 (ECHR); *ADC Affiliate Limited and ADC & ADMC Management Limited v. Republic of Hungary*, ICSID Case No. ARB/03/16, Award, 2 October 2006, para. 497 (ECHR); *Saipem SpA v. People's Republic of Bangladesh*, ICSID Case No. ARB/05/07, Decision on Jurisdiction and Recommendation on Provisional Measures, 21 March 2007, para. 130 (ECHR); *Fraport AG Frankfurt Airport Services Worldwide v. Republic of the Philippines*, ICSID Case No. ARB/03/25, Decision on Annulment, 23 December 2010, (ECHR); *Total SA v. Argentine Republic*, ICSID Case No. ARB/04/1, Decision on Liability, 27 December 2010, para. 129 (ECHR); and *El Paso Energy International Company v. Argentine Republic*, ICSID Case No. ARB/03/15, Award, 31 October 2011, para. 598, footnote 554 (ECHR).
[161] See, for example, *Eastern Sugar BV (Netherlands) v. The Czech Republic*, SCC Case No. 088/2004, Partial Award, 27 March 2007, paras. 133–135; *Eureko BV v. Slovakia*, PCA Case No. 2008-13, Award on Jurisdiction, Arbitrability and Suspension, 26 October 2010, paras. 274, 276 and 282; *Swisslion DOO Skopje v. Former Yugoslav Republic of Macedonia*, ICSID Case No. ARB/09/16, Award, 6 July 2012, para. 261; *Electrabel SA v. Hungary*, ICSID Case ARB/07/19, Decision on Jurisdiction, Applicable Law and Liability, 30 November 2012, para. 4.12.
[162] *Lauder v. Czech Rep.*, Final Award, 3 September 2001, 9 *ICSID Reports* 66 (2001).
[163] *CME Czech Rep. B.V. v. Czech Republic*, Partial Award, 13 September 2001, *available at* http://ita.law.uvic.ca/documents/CME-2001PartialAward.pdf; *CME Czech Rep. B.V. v. Czech Republic*, Final Award, 14 March 2003, 9 *ICSID Reports* 121 (2003).

tribunals gave different weight to the comparative method. While the *Lauder* Tribunal referred to a human rights case for establishing the expropriation standards,[164] the other tribunal did not. As one author put it, 'one is left to wonder, therefore, whether this would explain how the two tribunals came to ... opposite decisions'.[165]

Another example may clarify the issues at stake. The ICSID Convention and other arbitral rules leave arbitral tribunals wide discretion with regard to costs.[166] In the *Thunderbird* case, in deciding how to allocate the costs for legal representation, Professor Wälde opined that '[t]he judicial practice *most comparable* to treaty-based investor–state arbitration is the judicial recourse available to individuals against states under the European Convention on Human Rights; again, states have to defray their own legal representation expenditures, even if they prevail'.[167] By contrast, in the *Europe Cement* case, the Arbitral Tribunal awarded the respondent full costs to 'compensat[e] the Respondent for having to defend a claim that had no jurisdictional basis and discourage others from pursuing such unmeritorious claims'.[168] The latter approach reflects 'the principle that the successful party should have its costs paid by the unsuccessful party, *as adopted in commercial arbitration*'.[169] This example clearly shows that depending on which material is selected for comparison, the outcome may be different.

More generally, regional jurisprudence on the right to property can (and has) provided useful guidance to arbitrators facing expropriation claims, especially with regard to the amount of compensation that should be paid or not paid in case of regulatory measures.[170]

In some arbitrations, however, arbitral tribunals have shown a more careful approach, declining to borrow *dicta* from the jurisprudence of

---

[164] *Lauder v. Czech Republic*, at para. 200 (quoting *Mellacher v. Austria*, 169 Eur. Ct. H.R. (ser. A) (1989)).

[165] J.D. Fry, 'International Human Rights Law in Investment Arbitration: Evidence of International Law's Unity', *Duke Journal of Comparative & International Law* 18 (2007), 77, 84.

[166] ICSID Convention, Article 61(2).

[167] *Int'l Thunderbird Gaming Corp. v. United Mexican States*, 255 Fed. Appx. 531, (2007) para. 141, Separate Opinion of arbitrator Thomas Wälde, at 13 (emphasis added).

[168] *Europe Cement Investment & Trade S.A. v. Republic of Turkey*, ICSID Case No. ARB(AF)/07/2, Award, 7 August 2009, para. 185 and 182.

[169] *ADC Affiliate Ltd. and ADC & ADMC Mgmt. Ltd. v. Republic of Hungary*, ICSID Case No. ARB/03/16, Award, 27 September 2006, para. 532.

[170] E. Freeman, 'Regulatory Expropriation Under NAFTA Chapter 11: Some Lessons From the European Court of Human Rights', *Columbia Journal of Transnational Law* 42 (2003–2004), 177–215.

human rights courts and noting the textual differences of the applicable treaties. For instance, in *Azurix* v. *Argentina*, the Annulment Committee noted that 'As the extent of the protections afforded by an investment protection treaty depends in each case on the specific terms of the treaty in question, the Committee regards comparisons with differently worded treaties as of limited utility, especially treaties outside the field of investment protection.'[171] In particular, the Committee noted that the European Court of Human Rights has held that 'a shareholder in a company does not have standing to bring a claim for a violation of the company's right's under Article 1 of Protocol No. 1 of the European Convention on Human Rights'.[172] However, it held that 'such an approach does not inform the situation where a law or treaty might confer certain rights directly on a shareholder ...'[173]

As mentioned, some investment arbitrations and human rights disputes may arise from the same set of facts. In fact, state misbehaviour affecting a given investment may give rise to an alleged violation of both an investment treaty and a human rights treaty. This may be the case when an investor alleges an indirect or otherwise unlawful expropriation under the relevant BIT and a breach to her right to property under a human rights treaty. International investment law and human rights law also present other overlapping provisions, including non-discrimination.

As the *SPP* Tribunal pointed out, '[w]hen the jurisdiction of two unrelated and independent tribunals extends to the same dispute, there is no rule of international law which prevents either tribunal from exercising its jurisdiction'.[174] In fact, investment and human rights disputes arising from the same set of facts are not identical disputes. To ascertain the identity of given disputes and therefore declining their jurisdiction on the basis of principles such as *lis pendens* or *res judicata*,[175] international tribunals apply the triple identity test preventing the (re-)litigation of claims (1) between the same parties, (2) regarding

---

[171] *Azurix Corp. v. The Argentine Republic*, ICSID Case No. ARB/01/12, Decision on the Application for Annulment of the Argentine Republic, 1 September 2009, para. 128.

[172] *Ibid.* [173] *Ibid.*

[174] *Southern Pacific Properties (Middle East) Ltd. v. Arab Republic of Egypt*, ICSID Case No. ARB/84/3, Decision on Jurisdiction (1985), 3 *ICSID Reports* 112, 129 (1995).

[175] P.J. Martinez-Fraga and H.J. Samra, 'The Role of Precedent in Defining Res Judicata in Investor–State Arbitration', *Northwestern Journal of International Law & Business* 32 (2011–2012), 435 (explaining that while '*lis pendens* applies when the parallel proceedings are ongoing', '*res judicata* relates to the binding and preclusive effects of completed proceedings').

the same subject matter and (3) on the same legal grounds.[176] The claimants may be different; the legal grounds of a given investment dispute will typically be the alleged violation of the relevant investment treaty provisions, whereas the legal grounds of a given human rights dispute will relate to the alleged violation of the applicable human rights treaty provisions. Therefore, investors can (and in some cases have) file(d) parallel claims before human rights courts and arbitral tribunals. Usually in these cases, arbitral tribunals have referred to the parallel proceedings, applied the triple identity test and affirmed their jurisdiction.[177]

Reference to the jurisprudence of national courts

Arbitral tribunals sometimes look at the jurisprudence of national courts when interpreting investment treaty provisions.[178] There are several entry points for the consideration of national decisions in investment treaty arbitration. Decisions of national courts – as subsequent practice in the application of a given treaty – may provide evidence of an 'agreement on interpretation'.[179] However, such practice must be 'concordant, common and consistent' and 'sufficient to establish a discernible pattern implying the agreement of the parties regarding its implementation'.[180]

---

[176] *Ibid.*, at 421. See also *OAO Neftyanaya Kompaniya Yukos* v. *Russia*, ECtHR, Appl. No. 14902/04, Judgment, 20 September 2011, para. 521 (highlighting that 'the assessment of similarity of the cases would usually involve the comparison of the parties in the respective proceedings, the relevant legal provisions relied on by them, the scope of their claims and the types of redress sought').

[177] *Hulley Enterprises Ltd (Cyprus) and Others* v. *Russia*, Interim Award on Jurisdiction and Admissibility, 30 November 2009, paras. 586 to 593; Final Award, 18 July 2014, paras. 1256 to 1272; *Yukos Universal Limited (Isle of Man)* v. *The Russian Federation*, Interim Award, 30 November 2009, paras. 598–600, Final Award, 18 July 2014, para. 76; *Veteran Petroleum Limited (Cyprus)* v. *The Russian Federation*, Interim Award, 30 November 2009, paras. 609–611, Final Award, 18 July 2014, para. 1257. See also *OAO Neftyanaya Kompaniya Yukos* v. *Russia*, ECtHR, Appl. No. 14902/04, Judgment, 20 September 2011, para. 521. See also *Limited Liability Company Amto* v. *Ukraine*, Arbitration Institute of the Stockholm Chamber of Commerce, Arbitration No. 080/2005, p. 44.

[178] For example, *International Thunderbird Gaming Corporation* v. *Mexico*, UNCITRAL Arbitration, Final Award, 26 January 2006, Separate Opinion of Arbitrator Waelde, paras. 27–28; *Total S.A.* v. *Argentina*, ICSID Case No. ARB/04/1, Decision on Liability, 21 December 2010, paras. 128–130.

[179] VCLT, Article 31(3)(b).

[180] Appellate Body report, *Japan–Taxes on Alcoholic Beverages*, 1 November 1996, WT/DS8/AB/R, WT/DS10/AB/R, WT/DS11/AB/R, at 12–13.

National decisions may constitute evidence of state practice which is an element of customary international law.[181] Such state practice should be consistent, widespread and representative in character. Yet, it is often unclear when the required density of practice is reached.[182] Accurate comparative assessments are rarely undertaken, and ascertaining state practice is extremely complicated due to the large number of states composing the international community, the different languages in which both primary and secondary sources are available and the theoretical difficulties in articulating a clear divide between the objective element, or state practice, and the subjective element of customary law, or *opinio juris*.[183] It is generally accepted that state practice takes many forms including national decisions.[184] Accurate comparative assessments are rarely undertaken; as a result, 'international courts routinely assert the existence of custom based on a handful of examples of state practice . . . '[185]

National decisions may indicate the emergence of a general principle of international law.[186] With regard to the choice of legal orders to identify general principles of law, some refer to German, French, English and US law as classical comparative canons, adding that 'comparative law analysis can restrict itself to a qualitative study'.[187] However, international tribunals 'cannot rely on a set of cases, let alone on a single precedent, as sufficient to establish a principle of law'.[188] Reference to a few national experiences may be problematic, in consideration of the risk of repoliticising investment treaty disputes. Legal norms are the outcome

---

[181] See, for example, *Case Concerning the Continental Shelf* (*Libya* v. *Malta*), Judgment, 3 June 1985, 1985 *ICJ Reports* 13, 29 (stating that 'it is of course axiomatic that the material of customary international law is to be looked for primarily in the actual practice and *opinio juris* of States').

[182] M.H. Mendelson, 'The Formation of Customary International Law', *Recueil des Cours* 272 (1998), 155, 174.

[183] A. Roberts, 'Comparative International Law? The Role of National Courts in Creating and Enforcing International Law', *International & Comparative Law Quarterly* 60 (2011), 90.

[184] I. Brownlie, *Principles of Public International Law*, 6th ed. (Oxford: Oxford University Press, 2003), p. 6.

[185] Roberts, 'Comparative International Law?', 90.

[186] ICTY, *Prosecutor* v. *Zoran Kupreskic*, Case No.: IT-95–16-T, Judgment, 14 January, para. 540.

[187] S.W. Schill, 'International Investment Law and Comparative Public Law – An Introduction', in S.W. Schill (ed.), *International Investment Law and Comparative Public Law* (New York: Oxford University Press, 2010), p. 30.

[188] ICTY, *Prosecutor* v. *Zoran Kupreskic*, para. 540.

of specific historical evolution, and the selection of the comparative canon may affect the outcome of the case.

In addition, arbitrators may not be given comprehensive evidence of national law, and this, in turn, may leave them likely to rely randomly on readily available cases. Even if inclusive evidence is presented, arbitrators are susceptible to cherry-picking, citing cases they are more familiar with and overlooking others. In this manner, arbitral discretion as to whether and how to rely upon national cases may lead to arbitral 'fig-leafing' as arbitrators might use such national cases to cover their own reasoning.[189] As Roberts highlights, most comparative reasoning 'draw[s] on a limited range of countries with familiar language or legal systems, meaning that such references are usually not truly representative of the full range of systems and approaches'.[190] Even polyglots may not have the sufficient time, skills and willingness to undertake comprehensive surveys.[191] Finally, the complete understanding of cases originating in other jurisdictions may be elusive.[192]

However, arbitrators should not elevate legal concepts and rules with which they are familiar to the rank of general principles of law or state practice. Comparative reasoning provides the adjudicator with a way to identify general principles of law. As Gutteridge put it, '[For] if any real meaning is to be given to the wor[d] "general" ..., the correct test would seem to be that an international judge ... must satisfy himself that [a given principle] is recognized in substance by all the main systems of law.'[193]

Analogies in doctrinal writings as subsidiary means for the determination of rules of law

Doctrinal writing can take two main forms. First, doctrinal writing can be essayistic, seeking to persuade the reader of the validity of a given thesis. Second, it may be didactic, providing an ostensibly neutral scrutiny of a given topic. Both types of scholarly writing include descriptive and argumentative elements[194] and can (and have) influence(d) the development of international investment law. The growing number of investment arbitrations, and their wide distribution through online

---

[189] R.A. Posner, 'Foreword: A Political Court', *Harvard Law Review* 119 (2005), 32, 88–89.
[190] Roberts, 'Comparative International Law?', 88.   [191] *Ibid.*   [192] *Ibid.*, at 89.
[193] H. Gutteridge, *Comparative Law*, 2nd ed. (Cambridge: Cambridge University Press, 1949), p. 65.
[194] Sacco, 'Legal Formants', 34.

publication, has spurred scholarly debate on issues of international investment law. In turn, scholarly debate has contributed to the development of international investment law.

Under international law, doctrinal writings constitute a subsidiary source of the law. There is no rule governing the citation of doctrinal writings analogous to the ancient *Law of Citations*.[195] If some scholars tend to be cited more often than others, this is due to the topical nature of their work, their reputation and their contribution to the field rather than specific rules on citation. Doctrinal sources have traditionally played a role in investment arbitration as a mechanism to support given arguments. Usually, the parties to an investment arbitration prefer referring to previous arbitral awards or other international law cases, but reference to doctrinal writings is not uncommon.

The role of doctrinal sources in investment arbitration recently came to the fore in *Urbaser SA and Consorcio de Aguas Bilbao Bizkaia, Bilbao Bizkaia ur Partzuergoa v. Argentina*,[196] where the selection of one arbitrator was challenged on the grounds of certain opinions expressed in his scholarly writings. In a scholarly work, the arbitrator had expressed specific views on the interpretation of the MFN clause. One of the parties contended that these views, as expressed in his previous academic work, might influence the consideration of the same or similar issues.[197] The remaining two members of the Tribunal dismissed the objections to the impartiality and independence of the third arbitrator based on his academic opinions. The members held that 'a legal scholar who becomes an ICSID arbitrator does not lose his/her capacity of being a scholar that conveys academic opinions, which might become relevant to the legal analysis undertaken in the resolution of a particular dispute'.[198] According to the members of the Tribunal,

[195] A Roman emperor, Theodosius II, enacted the *Law of Citations* (*lex citationum*) in 426 CE establishing that the opinions of five important jurists of the classical period of Roman law – Gaius, Modestinus, Papinian, Paul and Ulpian – should prevail over the opinions of other scholars. In the event of a disagreement among the five jurists as to a particular question of law, the majority of their opinions ruled on the matter. See A. Watson, *The Law of the Ancient Romans* (Dallas: Southern Methodist University, 1970), pp. 90–91.

[196] *Urbaser SA and Consorcio de Aguas Bilbao Bizkaia, Bilbao Bizkaia ur Partzuergoa v. Argentine Republic*, ICSID Case No. ARB/07/26, Decision on Claimant's Request to Disqualify an Arbitrator, 12 August 2010.

[197] *Ibid.*, para. 52.   [198] *Ibid.*

[the dense exchange of views throughout the world on matters of international investment law] is very largely considered as a positive contribution to the development of the law and policies in this segment of the
world's economy ... [S]uch debate would be fruitless if it did not include
an exchange of opinions given by those who are actually involved in the
ICSID arbitration process, whether they are writing and speaking as
scholars, arbitrators or counsel. Such activity is part of the 'system' and
well known to all concerned.[199]

The members of the Tribunal also added that a contrary approach 'would
lead to the disqualification of as many arbitrators, including in particular
those who have acquired the greatest experience, thus leading to the
paralysis of the ICSID arbitral process'.[200]

In conclusion, arbitral tribunals 'may be reluctant to find a lack of
independence or impartiality based merely on views stated by an appoin-
tee in prior academic writings' due to 'pragmatic considerations since
experienced and knowledgeable investment arbitrators form a limited
pool of persons who need to be called upon to deal with various
disputes'.[201] In the absence of an Appeals Court for international investment law, 'a free and fair battle of ideas is the only way to achieve
coherency in the law and the sustainability of the system'.[202]

Comparative surveys as a legitimating factor of policy measures and as evidence of state practice

Comparative reasoning can constitute a tool for preventing arbitral
law-making. Many of the recent arbitral awards have concerned the
determination of the appropriate boundary between two conflicting
values: the legitimate sphere for state regulation in the pursuit of public
goods, on the one hand, and the protection of foreign investments from
state interference, on the other. The adoption of comparative legal
benchmarks can help adjudicators in interpreting and applying broad-
and open-ended investment treaty provisions,[203] while restraining their
discretion in reviewing state action. The adoption of comparative legal
benchmarks pursuant to Articles 31(3)(c) of the Vienna Convention on

---

[199] *Ibid.*, para. 48.   [200] *Ibid.*, para. 54.
[201] Hsu, 'International Investment Disputes', 852.
[202] Z. Douglas, *The International Law of Investment Claims* (Cambridge: Cambridge
University Press, 2009), p. xxiv.
[203] S. Montt, *State Liability in Investment Treaty Arbitration – Global Constitutional and
Administrative Law in the BIT Generation* (Oxford and Portland, Oregon: Hart
Publishing, 2009), p. 166.

the Law of Treaties and 38(1)(c) of the Statute of the International Court of Justice puts limits to arbitrary exercise of power.[204]

For instance, in *Maffezini v. Spain*,[205] an Argentine investor brought a claim for denial of fair and equitable treatment with regard to an environmental impact assessment (EIA) that had blocked his chemical plant in Spain. In 1992, the construction of the chemical plant had to be discontinued because of the investor's financial crisis. In the subsequent ICSID arbitration, Maffezini *inter alia* complained that the Spanish authorities had misinformed it about the costs of the project and pressured the company to make the investment before the EIA process was finalised and before its implications were known. Therefore, according to the claimant, the Spanish authorities should have been responsible for the additional costs resulting from the EIA. The Arbitral Tribunal dismissed these claims holding that 'the environmental impact assessment procedure is basic for adequate protection of the environment and the application of appropriate environmental measures'.[206] The Tribunal acknowledged that this was true 'not only under Spanish[207] and [the then European Economic Community] EEC Law,[208] but also increasingly so under international law'.[209] The Tribunal pointed out that both national law and European law required chemical industries to undertake an EIA[210] and that Spain had required compliance with its environmental laws in a manner consistent with its investment treaty commitments.[211] In sum, the Tribunal had the perception that 'the investor, as happens so often, tried to minimize this requirement so as to avoid additional costs or technical difficulties'.[212]

More recently, the *Chemtura* case concerned the question of whether the government of Canada should pay compensation to a US agricultural pesticide manufacturer for its ban of an agro-chemical. As Canada's Pest Management Regulatory Agency (PMRA) banned the chemical on the basis of its health and environmental effects,[213] Chemtura – formerly known as Crompton – initiated arbitral proceedings, requesting by way

---

[204] F.F. Stone, 'The End to be Served by Comparative Law', *Tulane Law Review* 25 (1950–1951), 335.

[205] *Emilio Augusto Maffezini v. The Kingdom of Spain*, ICSID Case No ARB/97/7, Award of the Tribunal, 13 November 2000, 5 *ICSID Reports* 419.

[206] *Ibid.*, para. 67.   [207] *Ibid.*, para. 68.   [208] *Ibid.*, para. 69.   [209] *Ibid.*, para. 67.

[210] *Ibid.*, para. 69.   [211] *Ibid.*, para. 71.   [212] *Ibid.*, para. 70.

[213] *Chemtura Corporation (formerly Crompton Corporation) v. Government of Canada*, Award, August 2010, para. 29.

of restitution, the reinstatement of all registrations relating to its product and/or the damages resulting from Canada's alleged breaches. According to Chemtura, the regulation was not based on a rigorous scientific risk assessment.[214] According to the claimant, the ban of the product also provoked a discriminatory effect requiring the use of substitute Canadian products in lieu of the chemical, thus amounting to an indirect expropriation. Therefore, according to the firm, Canada was, *inter alia*, in violation of NAFTA Articles 1105 (minimum standard of treatment) and 1110 (expropriation).

The Tribunal held that Canada did not violate its obligations under NAFTA. As Article 1105 of NAFTA seeks to ensure that investors from NAFTA State Parties benefit from regulatory fairness, the Tribunal investigated whether the review of the chemical product was conducted in good faith and whether it breached the due process rights of the claimant.[215] In the Tribunal's view, 'the evidence of the record [di]d not show bad faith or disingenuous conduct on the part of Canada' but it showed that the agency acted 'in pursuance of its mandate and as a result of Canada's international obligations'.[216] Although the Tribunal noted at the outset that 'the rule of a Chapter 11 Tribunal is not to second-guess the correctness of the science-based decision-making of highly specialized national regulatory agencies',[217] the Tribunal could not ignore the 'number of countries banning or restricting the use of lindane and international legal instruments further signalling international concern about the human health and environmental effects of the chemical'.[218]

With regard to the propriety of the assessment process, the Tribunal found that the special review was not conducted in a manner that reached the threshold to violate the FET standard: '[A]s a sophisticated registrant experienced in a highly regulated industry, the Claimant could not reasonably ignore the PMRA's practices and the importance of the evaluation of exposure risks within such practices.'[219] More importantly, the Tribunal affirmed that 'scientific divergence ... cannot in and of itself serve as a basis for a finding of breach of Article 1105 of NAFTA'.[220]

With regard to the allegation of expropriation, the Tribunal held that, since the sales from lindane products were a relatively small part of the overall sales of Chemtura, 'the interference of the Respondent with the

---

[214] *Ibid.*, paras. 35 and 41.   [215] *Ibid.*, para. 145.   [216] *Ibid.*, para. 138.
[217] *Ibid.*, para. 134.   [218] *Ibid.*   [219] *Ibid.*, para. 149.   [220] *Ibid.*, para. 154.

Claimant's investment c[ould] not be deemed "substantial"'[221] and that, in any event, '[a] measure adopted under such circumstances is a valid exercise of the State's police powers and, as a result, does not constitute an expropriation'.[222] Thus, the Tribunal found that no expropriation had occurred.[223]

By placing some weight on the fact that many countries had taken steps to ban and restrict the use of lindane and by referring to multilateral environmental agreements (MEAs), the Arbitral Tribunal implicitly confirmed the view that international investment law does not constitute a self-contained regime; rather, it must be interpreted and applied in the light of public international law. While the existence of MEAs and the comparative survey did not shield the regulatory action of the host state from review, they constituted evidence of the government's good faith vis-à-vis Chemtura and its products.[224]

In *Lemire v. Ukraine*, the Ukrainian *Law on Television and Radio Broadcasting* required that at least 50% of the general broadcasting of each radio company be comprised of music produced in Ukraine including any music where the author, the composer and/or the performer was Ukrainian.[225] The claimant argued that the 50% local music requirement implied a violation of Article II.6 of the US–Ukraine BIT, namely, of the prohibition to 'impose performance requirements ... which specify that goods and services must be purchased locally, or which impose any other similar requirements'.[226] In the claimant's opinion, the abnormally high level of the requirement caused significant damages, because its programme concept was based 100% on hits.[227] As there were too few music hits in Ukrainian music, the radio company had to continuously replay the same few Ukrainian songs.[228] Thus, the claimant claimed to have suffered loss of advertising revenue.[229]

In the opinion of the respondent, however, local music requirements were justified on 'public policy grounds'[230] due to 'the State's legitimate right to organize broadcasting'.[231] In this regard, Ukraine claimed that

---

[221] *Ibid.*, para. 263.   [222] *Ibid.*, para. 266.   [223] *Ibid.*, para. 267.
[224] On the need for comparative surveys of best regulatory practices, see P. Eeckhout, 'The Scales of Trade – Reflections on the Growth and Functions of the WTO Adjudicative Branch', *Journal of International Economic Law* 13 (2010), 3–26.
[225] *Joseph Charles Lemire v. Ukraine*, ICSID Case No. ARB/06/18, Decision on Jurisdiction and Liability, 14 January 2010, para. 227.
[226] US–Ukraine BIT, Article II.6.
[227] *Lemire v. Ukraine*, Decision on Jurisdiction and Liability, para. 499.
[228] *Ibid.*, para. 503.   [229] *Ibid.*, para. 499.   [230] *Ibid.*, para. 218.   [231] *Ibid.*, para. 227.

> In all jurisdictions, radio and TV are special sectors subject to specific regulations ... [W]hen regulating private activity in the media sector, states can, and frequently do, take into consideration a number of legitimate policy issues: thus media companies can be subject to specific regulation and supervision in order to guarantee transparency, political and linguistic pluralism, protection of children or minorities and other similar factors.[232]

The Arbitral Tribunal upheld Ukraine's line of argument. After considering that the local music requirement applied to all broadcasters in Ukraine,[233] it affirmed that 'As a sovereign state, Ukraine has the inherent right to regulate its affairs and adopt laws in order to protect the common good of its people, as defined by its Parliament and Government. The prerogative extends to promulgating regulations which define the State's own cultural policy.'[234] Therefore, the Tribunal reaffirmed full respect for Ukraine's cultural sovereignty, stating that 'It certainly is not the task of this Arbitral Tribunal, constituted under the ICSID Convention, to review or second-guess the rules which the representatives of the Ukrainian people have promulgated.'[235] According to the Lemire Tribunal, 'The "high measure of deference that international law generally extends to the right of domestic authorities to regulate matters within their own borders" is reinforced in cases when the purpose of the legislation affects deeply felt cultural or linguistic traits of the community.'[236]

To ascertain whether Ukraine had violated certain guarantees offered to foreign investors under the relevant BITs in adopting the domestic content requirement rule, the Arbitral Tribunal adopted a comparative approach holding that 'a rule cannot be said to be unfair, inadequate, inequitable or discriminatory when it has been adopted by many countries around the world'.[237] The Arbitral Tribunal inquired about international society's prevailing ideas about ways to protect national culture, acknowledging that 'the desire to protect national culture is not unique to Ukraine' and taking into account the fact that 'a number of other countries impose similar requirements'.[238] For instance, France requires that radio stations broadcast a minimum of 40% of French music, and Portugal has a 25–40% Portuguese music quota.[239] Therefore, the Tribunal held that the domestic content requirement rule could not be deemed to be 'unfair' or 'inequitable'.[240]

---

[232] Ibid., para. 241.   [233] Ibid., para. 501.   [234] Ibid., para. 505.   [235] Ibid., para. 240.
[236] Ibid., para. 505 [internal citation omitted].   [237] Ibid., para. 506.
[238] Ibid., para. 506 [internal citations omitted].   [239] Ibid.   [240] Ibid., para. 507.

This comparative approach may clearly play a positive role in building coherence at the international law level. Comparative surveys may help adjudicators to reach results in harmony with what may have achieved the status of general principles of international law or even customary law. More importantly, the Tribunal was interested in the 'normality' of such measure – that is, assessing whether the regulatory choice diverged from the canons commonly accepted by the international community. Analogously, in an investment arbitration under the International Chamber of Commerce, the Arbitral Tribunal 'accepted a later change of a telecommunication law which introduced a mandatory majority of nationals of that state in telecommunication companies depriving the investor of its majority, because the law affected all such companies and other states have similar laws for reasons of national security'.[241]

Finally, in determining the meaning of treaty provisions and the scope of a right or obligation, arbitral tribunals have used international or comparative standards as a benchmark.[242] For instance, in *Noble Ventures, Inc.* v. *Romania*,[243] the Arbitral Tribunal stated that a legal proceeding that exists in virtually all legal systems, such as bankruptcy proceedings, cannot be regarded as arbitrary.[244] In *Total* v. *Argentina*,[245] the Tribunal held that 'a comparative analysis of what is considered generally fair or unfair conduct by domestic public authorities in respect of private firms and investors in domestic law may also be relevant to identify the legal standards under BITs'.[246] The Tribunal held that this approach is justified for two principal reasons: first, 'because, factually, the situations and conduct to be evaluated under a BIT occur within the legal system and social, economic and business environment of the host State';[247] second, 'legally, the fair and equitable treatment standard is derived from the requirement of good faith which is undoubtedly a general principle of law under Article 38(1) of the Statute of the International Court of Justice'.[248]

---

[241] See K.-H. Böckstiegel, 'Commercial and Investment Arbitration: How Different Are They Today?', *Arbitration International* 28 (2012), 577–590, 580.

[242] See, for example, *Total* v. *Argentina*, ICSID Case No. ARB/04/1, Decision on Liability, 27 December 2010, para. 111. See also *S.D. Myers, Inc.* v. *Canada*, UNCITRAL, First Partial Award, 13 November 2000, paras. 263–264 and *Genin and Others* v. *Estonia*, Award, 25 June 2001, para. 367 ff.

[243] *Noble Ventures, Inc.* v. *Romania*, ICSID Case No. ARB/01/11, Award, 12 October 2005.

[244] *Ibid.*, paras. 177–178.

[245] *Total* v. *Argentina*, ICSID Case No. ARB/04/1, Decision on Liability, 27 December 2010.

[246] *Ibid.*, para. 111 (internal reference omitted).   [247] *Ibid.*   [248] *Ibid.*

Critical assessment

Our understanding of the nature of international investment law – of what it is and what it can and should do – ultimately depends on theoretical assumptions. Framing plays a vital, albeit not often acknowledged, role in the development of international investment law. Paradigms – a term which comes from Greek παράδειγμα (*paradeigma*) and indicates a 'pattern' or 'examplar' – are perspectives that provide a structure for the organisation of data, facilitate the understanding of the international investment system and guide practitioners. These theoretical frameworks or theories about investment law are tools for ordering the vital chaos which pervades the field. In fact, international investment law has entered its post-ontological era. The literature on various aspects of international investment law is thriving. Its lawyers need no longer defend the very existence of international investment law; rather, they can now undertake a critical assessment of its content. Active engagement with theory is required as theoretical assumptions influence legal practice. Theoretical models of international investment law bring to light portions of reality and obscure others, reflecting specific views of the world and of relations between states. Different paradigms endorse particular views, have distinct normative implications and compete for hegemony. If it is true that 'law is like art in that typically it is made to be interpreted',[249] the same interpretative process 'is to some extent an art, not an exact science'.[250]

Is international investment law completely separate from politics? As acknowledged by Judge Alvarez in the *Corfu Channel* Case, 'pure law does not exists: law is the result of social life and evolves with it; in other words, it is to a large extent, the effect of politics ... as practiced by the States'.[251] Some scholars posit that international investment law is not separate from politics; rather, according to these scholars, it is a mechanism for legitimating configurations of economic and political power, containing structural biases and epitomising historical struggles between the North and the South, the East and the West for economic

---

[249] J. Raz, 'Why Interpret?', *Ratio Juris* 9 (1996), 349–363, 357.
[250] A. Szpak, 'A Few Reflections on the Interpretation of Treaties in Public International Law', *Hague Yearbook of International Law* 18 (2005), 59–70, 59.
[251] *Corfu Channel Case (United Kingdom of Great Britain and Northern Ireland* v. *People's Republic of Albania)*, Judgment, 9 April 1949, *ICJ Rep.*, at 41–42 (Individual Opinion Judge Alvarez).

hegemony.[252] Even if one assumes that the system has been recalibrated recently, because of the emergence of new powerful economies, including China, India, Brazil and others, and that the text of investment treaties has become more comprehensive, holistic and balanced,[253] international investment law remains value laden, as it ultimately aims at promoting foreign direct investment, assuming that it can promote economic development and human well-being.

Furthermore, the indeterminacy of investment treaty provisions is both empowering and threatening. It is empowering because it allows arbitrators, in applying rules, to fit the law to given circumstances. This power enables justice to be done in particular cases. At the same time, however, indeterminacy is threatening because it allows arbitrators much discretion. For instance, more than fifty claims have been filed against Argentina in the aftermath of its economic crisis, and while inconsistent lines of interpretation have emerged regarding the defence of necessity as a circumstance precluding wrongfulness, Argentina has been held liable to pay billions of dollars. Not surprisingly, several states decided to quit the ICSID system in the fear of an avalanche of expensive investor claims.[254] Others have omitted investor–state arbitration from the provisions of their treaties.[255]

Paradigms are not neutral as adopting a commercial law paradigm implicitly adheres to a neo-liberal vision of the world as a free market. The public law paradigm counteracts this liberal vision, but it risks becoming parochial and impeding the free flow of capital, which can promote the economic development of the host state. Even worse, the public law paradigm can camouflage extremely liberal approaches, that is, those adopted by industrialised countries, if no meaningful comparison between different legal systems is conducted. On the other

---

[252] See generally K. Miles, *The Origins of International Investment Law – Empire, Environment and the Safeguarding of Capital* (Cambridge: Cambridge University Press, 2013).

[253] J.E. Alvarez, 'The Return of the State', *Minnesota Journal of International Law* 20 (2011), 223, 237.

[254] For instance, Bolivia, Ecuador and Venezuela have withdrawn from the ICSID Convention. See S. Ripinsky, 'Venezuela's Withdrawal from ICSID: What It Does and Does Not Achieve', *Investment Treaty News*, 13 April 2012.

[255] For instance, the 2005 Australia–US FTA does not include investor–state arbitration and Australia announced it will no longer include investor–state arbitration in its treaties with developing countries. See L.E. Peterson, 'In Policy Switch, Australia Disavows Need for Investor–State Arbitration Provisions in Trade and Investment Agreements', *Investment Arbitration Reporter*, 14 April 2011.

hand, adopting an international law paradigm enables the lawyer to acknowledge the specificities of international investment law, its positive role for promoting development and the autonomy of states to protect fundamental values, including public health, security and others.

Conclusions

This chapter examined the use of micro-comparisons in international investment law and arbitration, that is, how this system has borrowed specific 'legal formants' – statutory rules, scholarly writings and judicial decisions – from other legal systems. It explored the use of analogies in arbitral awards and doctrinal writings, respectively, as subsidiary means for the determination of rules of law. It then examined the use of comparative surveys as a legitimating factor of policy measures and as evidence of state practice.

Analogic reasoning is one of the oldest modes of legal reasoning and plays an important role in investment treaty arbitration as a tool to fill gaps in treaty provisions and to identify sources of international law. In determining the meaning of treaty provisions and the scope of a right or obligation, arbitral tribunals also use international or comparative standards as a benchmark. While the existence of MEAs and comparative surveys does not shield the regulatory action of the host state from review, it can constitute evidence of the government's good faith.

Comparative reasoning can constitute a tool for preventing arbitral law-making. Many of the recent arbitral awards have concerned the determination of the appropriate boundary between the legitimate sphere for state regulation in the pursuit of public goods, on the one hand, and the protection of foreign investments from state interference, on the other. The adoption of comparative benchmarks can help adjudicators in interpreting and applying broad and open-ended investment treaty provisions, while restraining their discretion in reviewing state action. The adoption of comparative benchmarks pursuant to Articles 31(3)(c) of the Vienna Convention on the Law of Treaties and 38(1)(c) of the Statute of the International Court of Justice puts limits to arbitrary exercise of power.

5

Macro-comparisons in investment treaty arbitration

We do not see things as they are, we see them as we are.[1]

Introduction

The scale at which comparative analysis should be done is a fundamental methodological issue in law.[2] There are 'infinite levels of possible inquiry':[3] 'The more closely you look, the more detailed things are bound to become. Increase in one dimension (focus) increases the other (detail of data).'[4] Micro-level comparative questions garner information, data and facts and help to address specific legal issues. Yet, they may fragment the study in a range of subsidiary questions thus forming a house of mirrors where the same different fragments of glass combine again and again in new designs, in a sort of kaleidoscope.[5] Micro-comparative analysis has a labyrinthine quality as it can leave lawyers with more questions than answers in a never-ending search for the ultimate micro-level of analysis: the more accurately you measure a given phenomenon, the less accurately you are able to identify where it is going.[6]

The same research questions, however, can be addressed at a more general level to gain insight, knowledge and perspective. Globalisation

---

[1] A. Nin, *Solar Barque* (Ann Arbour: MI, Edwards Brothers, 1958), p. 124.
[2] A. Riles, 'Wigmore's Treasure Box: Comparative Law in the Era of Information', *Harvard International Law Journal* 40 (1999), 221–464, 231.
[3] *Ibid.*, at 252.
[4] *Ibid.*, citing M. Strathern, *Partial Connections* (California: Alta Mira Press, 1991), pp. xiii–xiv.
[5] *Ibid.*, at 272 citing J.H. Wigmore, *A Kaleidoscope of Justice* (Washington, DC: Washington Law Books Co., 1941).
[6] L.H. Tribe, 'The Curvature of Constitutional Space: What Lawyers Can Learn from Modern Physics', *Harvard Law Review* 103 (1989), 1, 17 (highlighting that in quantum mechanics the more precisely the position of some particle is determined, the less precisely its momentum can be known, and vice versa).

has altered the way scholars approach their field of study and engage with comparative reasoning. States have integrated themselves into networks, national borders have become increasingly permeable and law has become increasingly deterritorialised or 'post-territorial'.[7] At a time of 'tectonic shifts',[8] there is 'an urge to rise above the micro-level complexities' and move beyond insular technicalities to explore the broader horizon of 'law as a global phenomenon'.[9] Therefore 'the field of comparison of laws is expanding its ambit'.[10] Like cartographers, legal scholars aim to chart the features of their legal field and are aware that comparative aims would risk collapsing into infinite factual details unless they remained anchored at a selected macro-level of inquiry. In fact, any account that becomes too specific risks merely depicting a given legal system, rather than mapping it analytically.[11] As lawyers study transnational legal phenomena, economic globalisation promotes a 'renaissance in comparative legal studies' around the world[12] by shifting the scale of the comparative inquiry.

This is not to say that micro-comparisons are useless. Rather, micro- and macro-comparisons are different, yet complementary, like a set of Matryoshka dolls.[13] Macro-comparisons do not supersede micro-comparisons; rather they complement their microscopic vision with an aerial one in order to grasp the 'big picture' or obtain a bird's-eye view of international investment law and arbitration. In this manner, while through micro-comparisons, one obtains a kaleidoscope of fragmented, albeit interesting, forms, through macro- comparisons, one obtain a useful analytical map. The two are distinct yet matching tools to explore a single 'castle of crossed destinies' where multilayered interpretations are possible.[14]

---

[7] H.P. Glenn, 'Against Method?', in P.G. Monateri (ed.), *Methods of Comparative Law* (Cheltenham, UK: Edward Elgar, 2012), pp. 177–188, p. 186.

[8] Riles, 'Wigmore's Treasure Box', 251.

[9] J. Husa, 'Legal Families', in J. Smit (ed.), *Elgar Encyclopaedia of Comparative Law* (Cheltenham: Edward Elgar, 2010), p. 492.

[10] Glenn, 'Against Method?', p. 186.

[11] Riles, 'Wigmore's Treasure Box', 239 (reminding 'Baudrillard's account of the cartographers who sought to make a map of the Empire so accurate that in the end it covered the territory exactly, and then simply disintegrated into dust').

[12] *Ibid.*, at 251.

[13] Matryoshkas consist of a set of red wooden dolls of decreasing size placed one inside the other. Each doll can separate, top from bottom, to reveal a smaller figure of the same sort inside, which has, in turn, another figure inside of it, and so on. What is interesting is not the number of nested figures, which varies, but the fact that each of the figures or level of analysis can reflect fine craftsmanship.

[14] I. Calvino, *Il Castello dei destini incrociati* (Torino: Einaudi, 1971).

If 'the better vision of science' is that of 'a journey',[15] the voyage from one scale of analysis to the next is well worth undertaking. One should keep in mind 'the importance of the interaction between background and foreground'.[16] In fact, the study of micro-comparisons would be incomplete without the parallel study of macro-comparisons. The thread which connects one level of analysis to the next is given by the constant patterns of analogic reasoning which characterise international investment law and arbitration. Like the repetitive features depicted on the Matryoshkas, the arbitral themes which are encompassed in the field recur again and again.

If one wishes to understand investment treaty arbitration, what is the proper analogue or context for interpretation? Is it the parallel realm of decision-making at the World Trade Organization (WTO)? Is it the human rights regime or the domestic legal framework governing the economic sector involved? Is investment treaty arbitration to be conceived as a *sui generis* legal system or as a creature of international law? Which paradigm best explains the available data?

Micro-comparisons help investment lawyers address these questions by focusing on specific legal issues. For instance, the issue of damages is approached differently in human rights law, commercial arbitration and other legal fields. Macro-comparisons help investment law scholars and practitioners address these questions by identifying the best analogue first at a general level and then investigating more specific issues at a later stage. Macro-comparisons focus on large-scale themes and questions, analogising entire legal systems. While the two scales of analysis are theoretically separate, they are concretely intertwined.

Is anything to be gained or lost from adopting this dialogic model? The joint study of both micro- and macro-comparisons holds the promise to promote an increased awareness among investment lawyers of the specificities of the field thus fostering the coherence of international investment law and arbitration. On the other hand, the use of comparisons is tied to concerns about arbitral activism or arbitral law-making.[17] The multiplication of sources, options and possibilities can lead to fragmenting the core and generating inconsistency in the law thus eventually leading to a crisis of legitimacy. Yet, persuasion comes with

---

[15] Tribe, 'The Curvature of Constitutional Space', 2.   [16] *Ibid.*, at 20.

[17] See C. Titi, 'The Arbitrator as a Lawmaker: Jurisgenerative Processes in Investment Arbitration', *Journal of World Investment and Trade* 14 (2013), 829–851 (pinpointing various forms of creative interpretation.)

dialogue.[18] Comparisons can be a tool for legitimising both arbitral tribunals and their awards to the international community, the business world and the local population because of their persuasiveness and reliance on communal knowledge.

Macro-comparative law has traditionally focused on the horizontal comparison of legal systems belonging to the same – mainly national – level and their systematisation in groupings or families.[19] Only recently have macro-comparisons extended beyond their traditional horizontal focus and started investigating vertical horizons, that is, vertical processes of interaction between international, regional and domestic law. Vertical comparisons occur among legal systems belonging to different levels, that is, cross-echelon.[20] Vertical comparisons can assist lawyers to interpret and apply given concepts such as reasonableness, proportionality and non-discrimination at the national, regional and international levels. Vertical comparisons overcome the traditional boundaries between national, regional and international levels of analysis and are particularly suited to address transnational phenomena. Vertical bottom-up analogies indicate the transposition of concepts from national to international level. For instance, general principles of law such as good faith, *pacta sunt servanda* and *res judicata* derive from national law.[21] Vertical top-down analogies typically occur in the contexts of the internationalisation of specific areas of the law, such as intellectual property, requiring the reception of international rules into the domestic systems.[22]

This chapter considers the way international investment law and arbitration has been compared to other legal systems, at the national, regional and international law levels.[23] Given its hybrid

---

[18] H.P. Glenn, 'Persuasive Authority', *McGill Law Journal* 32 (1987), 261–298, 297.

[19] Husa, 'Legal Families', 491.

[20] A. Momirov and A. Naudé Fourie, 'Vertical Comparative Methods: Tools for Conceptualising the International Rule of Law', *Erasmus Law Review* 2 (2009), 291–308, 295.

[21] M. Bothe and G. Ress, 'The Comparative Method and Public International Law', in W.E. Butler (ed.), *International Law in Comparative Perspective* (Alphen aan den Rijn: Sijthoff & Noordhoff, 1980), at p. 51.

[22] See Momirov and Naudé Fourie, 'Vertical Comparative Methods', 296.

[23] Although interdisciplinary analogies are possible – and, in fact, authors have proposed to consider law through the lenses of economics, sociology and even physics – this book focuses on intradisciplinary analogies only, that is, analogies within the legal systems. For an excellent example of interdisciplinary analysis, see, for example, Tribe, 'The Curvature of Constitutional Space', 2 (stating that 'the metaphors and intuitions that guide physicists can enrich our comprehension of social and legal issues').

features,[24] international investment law and arbitration has been considered to be a *sui generis* system[25] or 'a new legal order of international law'.[26] Scholars have analogised it to different legal systems.[27] These paradigms – meant as theories, the entire worldviews which they express and all of the implications which come with them[28] – are not normative; rather, they are descriptive in nature and reflect and emphasise some aspects of investment treaty arbitration rather than others. As enough significant anomalies have accrued against each of these paradigms, a battle of ideas takes place between the followers of each paradigm and the hold-outs of the other paradigms. Three main paradigms can be identified.

First, given the fact that arbitrators have comprehensive jurisdiction over what are essentially regulatory disputes, such review has been compared to a sort of administrative review.[29] For instance, Van Harten and Loughlin claim that investment arbitration can be analogised to domestic administrative review since investment disputes arise from the exercise of public authority by the state and arbitral tribunals are given the power to review such an exercise of public

---

[24] Z. Douglas, 'The Hybrid Foundations of Investment Treaty Arbitration', *British Yearbook of International Law* 74 (2003), 151 at 152–153 (characterising the investment treaty regime as having a 'hybrid or *sui generis* character'); A. Roberts, 'Clash of Paradigms: Actors and Analogies Shaping the Investment Treaty System', *American Journal of International Law* 107 (2013), 45–94, 94 (also characterising investment arbitration as *sui generis*). But see M. Paparinskis, 'Analogies and Other Regimes of International Law', in Z. Douglas, J. Pauwelyn and J.E. Viñuales (eds.), *The Foundations of International Investment Law: Bringing Theory into Practice* (Oxford: Oxford University Press, 2014), p. 1 (arguing that 'there is nothing conceptually different, innovatory or sui generis about investment protection law').

[25] J. Paulsson, 'Arbitration Without Privity', *ICSID Review – Foreign Investment Law Journal* 10 (1995), 232, at 256.

[26] A. Pellet, 'The Case Law of the ICJ in Investment Arbitration', *ICSID Review – Foreign Investment Law Journal* 28 (2013), 223–240, 240.

[27] Roberts, 'Clash of Paradigms', 45–94.

[28] On the notion of paradigm, see T. Kuhn, *La structure des révolutions scientifiques* (Paris: Flammarion, 1972), p. 216.

[29] G. Van Harten and M. Loughlin, 'Investment Treaty Arbitration as a Species of Global Administrative Law', *European Journal of International Law* 17 (2006), 121; G. Van Harten, *Investment Treaty Arbitration and Public Law* (Oxford: Oxford University Press, 2007); S. Montt, *State Liability in Investment Treaty Arbitration: Global Constitutional Law and Administrative Law in the BIT Generation* (Oxford: Hart Publishing, 2009); D. Schneiderman, *Constitutionalizing Economic Globalization: Investment Rules and Democracy's Premise* (Oxford: Oxford University Press, 2008).

authority.[30] According to these authors, while arbitration structurally constitutes a private model of adjudication, investment treaty arbitration can be viewed as public law adjudication.[31] Arbitral awards ultimately shape the relationship between the state, on the one hand, and private individuals, on the other.[32] Arbitrators determine matters such as the legality of governmental activity, the degree to which individuals should be protected from regulation and the appropriate role of the state.[33]

Second, because of the procedural rules which govern it, investor–state arbitration has been analogised to commercial arbitration. Arbitrators are selected by the parties and/or an appointing institution, and the hearings are held *in camera*. However, the distinction between investment treaty arbitration and international commercial arbitration is clear:[34] while international arbitration generally involves private parties and concerns disputes of a commercial nature, investment treaty arbitration involves states and private actors. This 'diagonal' dispute settlement mechanism is a major novelty in international law since, traditionally, international disputes have only involved states.[35]

Third, arbitral tribunals have been analogised to other public international law tribunals. For instance, it has been argued that access to investor–state arbitration shares many characteristics of the direct right of action before human rights courts.[36] However, arbitral tribunals constitute not only an additional forum with respect to state courts, but also an alternative to the same. Thus, not only can foreign investors seek

---

[30] Van Harten and Loughlin, 'Investment Treaty Arbitration as a Species of Global Administrative Law', 121.

[31] Van Harten, 'The Public-Private Distinction in the International Arbitration of Individual Claims Against the State', *International and Comparative Law Quarterly* 56 (2007), 372.

[32] Van Harten, *Investment Treaty Arbitration and Public Law*, 70.

[33] M. Sornarajah, 'The Clash of Globalizations and the International Law on Foreign Investment', *Canadian Foreign Policy* 12 (2003), 17.

[34] See N. Blackaby, 'Investment Arbitration and Commercial Arbitration (or the Tale of the Dolphin and the Shark)', in J. Lew and L. Mistelis (eds), *Pervasive Problems in International Arbitration* (Aalphen aan den Rijn: Kluwer Law International 2006), pp. 217-233; J. Paulsson, 'International Arbitration is not Arbitration', *Stockholm International Arbitration Review* 2 (2008), 1–20.

[35] ICJ, *Judgment No. 2867 of the Administrative Tribunal of the International Labour Organization*, Advisory Opinion, 1 February 2012 (noting the diagonal structure of the proceeding brought in the ILOAT by the staff member against the agency and comparing it to investment treaty arbitration).

[36] See G. Burdeau, 'Nouvelles perspectives pour l'arbitrage dans le contentieux economique intéressant l'Etat', *Revue de l'Arbitrage* 1 (1995), 16.

another decision after an eventual recourse to the national courts, but in most cases they are not required to exhaust local remedies prior to pursuing an international legal claim.

At the same time, arbitral tribunals have been analogised to the WTO panels and the Appellate Body.[37] Arbitral tribunals and WTO dispute settlement panels essentially do share the same functions by settling international disputes in accordance with international economic law and ensuring the proper administration of justice.[38] Like WTO panels and the Appellate Body, arbitral tribunals are asked to strike a balance between economic and non-economic concerns. In parallel, certain international trade treaties present an articulated regime that the investment treaties presuppose. For instance, the Agreement on Trade-Related Investment Measures (TRIMS Agreement) governs trade-related investment measures.[39] Some authors support such an approach, as it would impede the dilution of multilateral norms while providing predictability.[40] However, while only states can file claims before the WTO panels and the Appellate Body, investor–state arbitration can be pursued by foreign investors directly without any intervention of the home state. Furthermore, arbitral tribunals can authorise damages, while remedies at the WTO have a prospective character only.

Compelling arguments stand in favour of assimilating arbitrators to international judges. From a historical perspective, arbitration is entrenched in public international law. As Crawford puts it, '[i]nvestment law ... is about the way in which we bring the state under some measure of control, which is the main aspiration of general international law'.[41] As international judges, arbitrators are asked to

---

[37] See generally T. Weiler (ed.), *Intersections: Dissemblance or Convergence between International Trade and Investment Law, Transnational Dispute Management* Special 3 (2011).

[38] C. Brown, 'The Use of Precedents of Other International Courts and Tribunals in Investment Treaty Arbitration', *Transnational Dispute Management* 5 (2008), 1–4.

[39] Agreement on Trade-Related Investment Measures (TRIMS Agreement), 15 April 1994, Marrakesh Agreement Establishing the World Trade Organization, Annex 1A, 1868 UNTS 186.

[40] L. Hsu, 'Applicability of WTO Law in Regional Trade Agreements: Identifying the Links', in L. Bartels and F. Ortino (eds), *Regional Trade Agreements and the WTO Legal System* (Oxford: Oxford University Press, 2006), p. 551.

[41] J. Crawford, 'International Protection of Foreign Direct Investment: Between Clinical Isolation and Systematic Integration', in R. Hofmann and C.J. Tams (eds.), *International Investment Law and General International Law – from Clinical Isolation to Systemic Integration?* (Baden/Baden: Nomos, 2011), pp. 17–28, at p. 22.

safeguard vital community interests as well as to settle disputes in conformity with 'principles of justice and international law'.[42]

These conceptualisations of investment treaty arbitration all have merits and weaknesses and may diverge and converge on specific aspects. Most notably, none of them – except perhaps the international law and public law paradigms due to their comprehensive nature – fully encapsulates the complexity of investor–state arbitration. Awareness of the existence of different paradigms promotes a better understanding and functioning of the same and helps in identifying the appropriate micro-comparisons. At the same time, as stressed in earlier chapters, comparisons are not neutral and the selection of a given analogue may have implications for cases. The development of international investment law is a never-ending battle for the control of analogy.[43]

The commercial law paradigm

Is investment treaty arbitration analogous to international commercial arbitration? Practitioners and scholars of international commercial arbitration analogise international investment law to transnational commercial law,[44] regarding it as an additional structure for the efficient regulation of foreign capital flows. In parallel, they analogise investment treaty arbitration to commercial arbitration.[45] While this approach remains undertheorised,[46] it 'dominates much of the investor–state arbitral jurisprudence'.[47] The section discusses the international commercial arbitration analogy and proceeds as follows. After briefly discussing the similarities and divergences between investment arbitration and commercial arbitration, it concludes that they are distinct dispute settlement mechanisms, albeit some overlappings are inevitable as the systems are not self-contained.

---

[42] VCLT, Preamble.

[43] A.V. Lowe, 'The Politics of Law Making', in M. Byers (ed.), *The Role of Law in International Politics* (Oxford: Oxford University Press, 2000), at p. 201, footnote 5.

[44] For critical discussion, see J.A. Maupin, 'Public and Private in International Investment Law: An Integrated Systems Approach', *Virginia Journal of International Law* 54 (2013–2014), 394.

[45] See, for example, C.N. Brower, 'W(h)ither International Commercial Arbitration?', *Arbitration International* 24 (2008), 181, 190.

[46] But see E. Gaillard, *Aspects philosophiques du droit de l'arbitrage international* (Leiden: Martinus Nijhoff Publishers, 2008).

[47] Maupin, 'Public and Private in International Investment Law', 394 (noting that about two-thirds of known investment arbitrators have a commercial law background).

Most similarities between investment arbitration and commercial arbitration relate to their procedural and historical features. First, the procedural rules which govern investment treaty arbitration patently borrow from international commercial arbitration. The traditional architecture of commercial arbitration is plain: the parties to a dispute select an uneven number of arbitrators to settle their disputes. In addition, the parties can shape the procedural and substantive aspects of the proceedings selecting the *lex arbitri* (the rules applying to the procedure) and the substantive law (the law applying to the dispute). The courts at the seat of the arbitration have jurisdiction to annul an arbitral award under the municipal law. The courts at the place of enforcement of that award have jurisdiction to rule on the enforcement most often under the New York Convention.[48] Commercial arbitration is regarded as cheaper, faster and more attuned to business needs than domestic courts.

Analogously, in investment treaty arbitration, arbitrators are selected by the parties and/or an appointing institution and the hearings are held behind closed doors (*in camera*). The ICSID Convention imposes to all states parties to the ICSID Convention to enforce an ICSID award 'as if it were a final judgment of a court in that state' with no review possibilities by the domestic courts of the state in which enforcement is sought.[49] However, if the investor submits its claims before other arbitral institutions such as the Arbitration Institute of the Stockholm Chamber of Commerce or an *ad hoc* arbitration established under the UNCITRAL Arbitration Rules, enforcement of investment treaty awards is analogous to that of commercial awards as it falls under the New York Convention. Like commercial arbitration, investment treaty arbitration often leads to faster decisions than those which can be obtained in domestic courts.

Furthermore, 'in the latter half of the twentieth century, the vast majority of investor–state disputes involved claims for breach of contract ...'.[50] Even today, investment claims based on *acta jure gestionis* (i.e. contracts with the host government of a private law nature, comparable to contracts between private entities) may not substantially differ from ordinary contract claims under commercial law, for they are rooted in a functionally *more privatorum* relationship

---

[48] Convention on Recognition and Enforcement of Foreign Arbitral Awards, 10 June 1958, 330 UNTS 3.
[49] ICSID Convention, Article 54(1).
[50] Maupin, 'Public and Private in International Investment Law', 394.

in which the state acts as a private person. Contract-based investment claims often strive for monetary compensation, rather than amending or overhauling elements of national law.

However, investment treaty arbitration and international commercial arbitration also differ in many respects, including the parties, the subject matter of the dispute and the applicable law.[51] First, while international commercial arbitration generally involves a horizontal relationship between private parties, investment arbitration invariably involves a state as one of the litigants and often implies a diagonal relationship between states and private actors. This 'diagonal' dispute settlement mechanism is a relatively new development in international law as international disputes have traditionally involved states only. Private actors no longer depend on the eventual exercise of diplomatic protection by their home state, but can file claims against the host state directly.[52] Thus, investment arbitration facilitates access to justice to foreign investors at the international level.[53]

Second, while commercial arbitration concerns disputes of a commercial nature, investment arbitration often entails regulatory issues of wide public interest. In the absence of an umbrella clause, a mechanism which elevates contractual obligations directly to the level of international treaty obligations,[54] some arbitral tribunals have interpreted investment treaty obligations as applicable only to the 'public' governmental activities of the state. Under a well-established rule of public international law, a

---

[51] See Blackaby, 'Investment Arbitration and Commercial Arbitration (or the Tale of the Dolphin and the Shark)', pp. 217–233; Paulsson, 'International Arbitration is not Arbitration', 1.

[52] International investment arbitration has increasingly side-lined diplomatic protection – a tool used by states to protect their nationals overseas. See, ex multis, Barcelona Traction, Light and Power Company, Limited (Belgium v. Spain), ICJ, Judgment of 5 February 1970, 1970 ICJ Reports 3; Nottebohm Case (second Phase) Judgment of 6 April 1955, 1955 ICJ Rep. 4. In the Diallo case, the ICJ recognised the residual nature of the exercise of diplomatic protection and recourse to the Court in case of investment disputes. Case Concerning Ahmadou Sadio Diallo (Guinea v. Democratic Republic Congo), (Preliminary Objections), Judgment of 24 May 2007, at paras. 88–91.

[53] See, for example, F. Francioni, 'Access to Justice, Denial of Justice and International Investment Law', European Journal of International Law 20 (2009), 729.

[54] Private law claims by the investor against the host state may be elevated to public international law claims where there is an umbrella clause. Private law claims by the investor against third parties may be elevated to public international law claims for denial of justice. See generally J. Paulsson, Denial of Justice in International Law (Cambridge: Cambridge University Press, 2005). See also M. Sattorova, 'Denial of Justice Disguised?: Investment Arbitration and the Protection of Investors from Judicial Misconduct', International & Comparative Law Quarterly 61 (2012), 223–246.

breach of a contract by the state does not in itself give rise to international responsibility on the part of the state. The assumption is that '[o]nly the State in the exercise of its sovereign authority (*"puissance publique"*), and not as a contracting party, may breach the obligations assumed under the BIT'.[55] For instance, if the state acts in its capacity as a public entity exercising public authority, that is, seizing the other side's assets, or enacting regulation affecting the rights enshrined in the contract, in this case the relationship is hierarchical and such dispute is of a public law character.

Third, investment disputes and commercial disputes are governed by different legal frameworks. In investment arbitration, the consent of the state is generally expressed in a public international law treaty, such as the ICSID Convention and the relevant bilateral investment treaty, and has a general character because the option to arbitrate is available to any legal and natural person that meets the terms and conditions to file a claim. By contrast, in commercial disputes, such consent is expressed in a contractual arbitration clause and is based on the parties' autonomy.[56]

Investment disputes are governed by a framework of public international law,[57] while the principal public international law treaty relevant for commercial disputes is the New York Convention. Unlike commercial arbitrators who apply different laws depending on the subject matter of the disputes, investment treaty arbitrators generally apply a limited number of concepts under public international law. Therefore, in investment disputes, 'the typical expertise required [of] arbitrators is one of public international law',[58] whereas in commercial disputes, the parties usually select arbitrators well acquainted with the relevant field of commerce such as trade, manufacturing and construction. Moreover, in investment disputes, customary rules of treaty interpretation will be relevant,[59] and the involvement of states 'tends to make the proceeding more formal' and lengthy.[60]

As investment arbitration concerns state interests, many recent arbitration rules have provided for greater transparency.[61] For instance,

---

[55] *Impregilo* v. *Pakistan*, ICSID Case No. ARB/03/3, Decision on Jurisdiction, 22 April 2005, at para. 260.
[56] K.-H. Böckstiegel, 'Commercial and Investment Arbitration: How Different Are They Today?', *Arbitration International* 28 (2012), 577–590, 583.
[57] *Ibid.*, at 578.   [58] *Ibid.*, at 582.   [59] *Ibid.*, at 583.   [60] *Ibid.*, at 584.
[61] See G.B. Born and E.G. Shenkman, 'Confidentiality and Transparency in Commercial and Investor–State International Arbitration', in C.A. Rogers and R.P. Alford (eds.), *The Future of Investment Arbitration* (Oxford: Oxford University Press, 2009), pp. 5–42.

while the publication of commercial arbitration awards is rare, in investment arbitration, a larger body of jurisprudence is available. The disclosure of arbitral awards can foster the development of a coherent jurisprudence, contributing to legal certainty and predictability as well as enhancing the confidence of the relevant actors in the dispute settlement mechanism.[62] As commercial arbitration awards usually remain confidential, 'guidance from commercial arbitration awards and practice is rare'.[63] By contrast, investment treaty arbitral tribunals consider previous awards, while acknowledging their lack of binding force. Analogously, although third parties do not usually participate in commercial arbitration, they have participated in investment arbitrations as friends of the court (*amici curiae*), to contribute their specific perspective in relation to the given dispute.[64]

In conclusion, investment arbitration and commercial arbitration are distinct dispute settlement mechanisms. This does not mean that they should be considered as self-contained regimes. For instance, commercial arbitrators have referred to the widely available jurisprudence of investment arbitration awards in commercial arbitration cases.[65] Moreover, recent 'crossover cases' have emerged where parties seek remedies before investment tribunals and human rights courts against decisions of national courts annulling awards or refusing enforcement.[66] The argument contends that a given arbitral award,

---

[62] J.D.M. Lew, 'The Case for the Publication of Arbitration Awards', in J.C. Schultsz, A.J. van den Berg (eds.), *The Art of Arbitration, Essays on International Arbitration, Liber Amicorum Pieter Sanders* (The Hague: Kluwer Law, 1982), p. 227.

[63] N. Kaplan, 'Investment Arbitration's Influence on Practice and Procedure in Commercial Arbitration', *Asian Dispute Review* (2013), 122–125, 122.

[64] See E. Levine, 'Amicus Curiae' in International Investment Arbitration: The Implication of an Increase in Third-Party Participation', *Berkeley Journal of International Law* 29 (2011), 200–224, 207.

[65] Kaplan, 'Investment Arbitration's Influence on Practice and Procedure in Commercial Arbitration', 122.

[66] See, for example, *Saipem S.p.A. v. The People's Republic of Bangladesh*, ICSID Case No. ARB/05/07 (finding that a Bangladeshi court's failure to recognise an ICC award amounted to an expropriation under the Italy–Bangladesh BIT); *Romak S.A. v. The Republic of Uzbekistan*, PCA Case No. AA280, Award, 26 November 2009 (finding that the arbitral award did not constitute an investment because the underlying contract could not be considered an investment under the BIT and therefore declining jurisdiction); *GEA Group Aktiengesellschaft v. Ukraine*, ICSID Case No. ARB/08/16, Award, 31 March 2011 (dismissing the claim that an ICC award itself was a protected investment under the BIT); *ATA Construction, Industrial and Trading Company v. The Hashemite Kingdom of Jordan*, ICSID Case No. ARB/08/02, Award, 18 May 2010, para. 121 (considering the judicial extinguishment of the claimant's right to arbitrate to be a violation of the fair and

rendered via commercial arbitration 'crystallises' the parties' original contract rights and subjects them to the standards of protection of international investment law.[67] While arbitral tribunals have diverged on the question as to whether refusing enforcement of an award can constitute a breach of the relevant BIT, certainly they have declined to consider the actual enforcement of an award under the New York Convention as a breach of a BIT.[68] These cases confirm that the public/private divide is 'permeable'.[69] Moreover, as both scholars and practitioners of international investment law are trained in either public international law or international commercial arbitration, investment arbitration can be seen as 'situated in the disputed territory at the boundary of the two communities of public international law and ... commercial arbitration'.[70]

equitable treatment standard); *Frontier Petroleum Services Ltd.* v. *Czech Republic*, Award, UNCITRAL Arbitration Rules, PCA, 12 November 2010 (holding that the Czech courts' refusal to recognise and enforce an award on grounds of public policy under the New York Convention did not amount to a breach of the applicable BIT); *White Industries Australia Limited* v. *The Republic of India*, Award, UNCITRAL Arbitration Rules, 30 November 2011 (deeming that an ICC award was part of the investment and that the local court's delays in dealing with the award breached the BIT provision requiring effective means of asserting claims and enforcing rights). For commentary, see W.M. Reisman, 'Investment and Human Rights Tribunals as Courts of Last Appeal in International Commercial Arbitration', in L. Levy and Y. Derains (eds.), *Liber Amicorum en honneur de Serge Lazareff* (Paris: Pedone, 2011), p. 521 (criticising these developments); C. Priem, 'International Investment Treaty Arbitration as a Potential Check for Domestic Courts Refusing Enforcement of Foreign Arbitration Awards', *New York University Journal of Law & Business* 10 (2013), 189–221, 221 (praising the 'supervisory jurisdiction' of arbitral tribunals on domestic courts' conduct when enforcing arbitral awards); J.E. Alvarez, 'Crossing the Public/Private Divide: Saipem v. Bangladesh and Other "Crossover" Cases', ICCA Congress Series No. 16, Singapore 2012, pp. 2–28 (arguing that 'the judicial/arbitral interactions produced by these cases could, counter-intuitively, provide opportunities for on-going dialogues between investor–state arbitrators and national judges').

[67] *White Industries Australia Limited* v. *The Republic of India*, Award, para. 7.6.10.

[68] *Kaliningrad Region* v. *Lithuania*, ICC, Final Award (not public), 28 January 2009. As the Region of Kaliningrad, part of the Russian Federation, applied to the Paris Court of Appeal to have the ICC award set aside, some information about the underlying award is available. See Cour d'Appel de Paris, Arrêt du 18 Novembre 2010, RG No. 09/19535, p. 3–6.

[69] Alvarez, 'Crossing the Public/Private Divide', 27–28.

[70] A. Mills, 'Antinomies of Public and Private at the Foundations of International Investment Law and Arbitration', *Journal of International Economic Law* 14 (2011), 469–503, 486.

The rise of the public law paradigm

Can international investment law be read through the lenses of public law? Can public law benchmarks help arbitrators in interpreting and applying broad and open-ended investment treaty provisions? Can these constitutional ideas help facilitate the consideration of the commonweal in investment treaty arbitration and/or contribute to the humanisation of international (investment) law? What are the merits and limits of public law approaches to investment treaty law and arbitration? This section addresses these questions and proceeds as follows. First, it illustrates the meaning of public law. Second, it highlights the progressive overcoming of the public/private divide. Third, it sheds light on the hybrid nature of international investment law. Fourth, it discusses the role of public law in shaping investment law and the migration of constitutional ideas to investment treaty arbitration. Finally, it examines the merits and pitfalls of the public law paradigm focusing on methodological issues.

International investment law and arbitration is often compared to a public law system. Public law can be defined as 'an assemblage of rules, principles, canons, maxims, customs, usages, and manners that condition and sustain the activity of governing'.[71] Public law governs the relationship between the state organs and private individuals, and – at least in democratic countries – provides a system of checks and balances on the exercise of public authority to protect individual entitlements. Public law is articulated in various fields including constitutional law and administrative law. While constitutional law concerns 'the highest norms of the state', administrative law 'governs sub-legislative action, somewhat lower in the hierarchy of sources and hence in importance'.[72]

Yet, 'there is no consensus on what constitutes public law', as the distinction between private and public law has faded in the past decades,[73] remaining ambiguous and meaning different things in different jurisdictions.[74] The distinction between public and private law presupposes a division of spheres of activities between the state and non-state actors which characterised the *laissez-faire* philosophy as it

---

[71] M. Loughlin, *The Idea of Public Law* (Oxford: Oxford University Press, 2003), p. 30.

[72] T. Ginsburg, 'Written Constitutions and the Administrative State: On the Constitutional Character of Administrative Law', in S. Rose-Ackerman and P.L. Lindseth (eds.), *Comparative Administrative Law* (Cheltenham: Edward Elgar, 2011), p. 117.

[73] M.J. Horwitz, 'The History of the Public/Private Distinction', *University of Pennsylvania Law Review* 130 (1982), 1423, at 1426.

[74] J. Boughey, 'Administrative Law: The Next Frontier for Comparative Law', *International & Comparative Law Quarterly* 62 (2013), 55–95, 57.

prospered particularly in the earlier part of the nineteenth century.[75] This theory assumes that the sphere of government is confined to certain limited functions such as the administration of justice, policing and defence, while economic activities are carried out between private actors.[76]

However, both states and the international community as a whole have assumed a number of additional 'welfare' functions concerning public health and the conservation of natural resources among others.[77] Furthermore, 'global governance flattens the difference between public and private phenomena':[78] 'The emergence of new spheres of normativity distinct from the nation state [and] the appearance of powerful private . . . transnational actors in the public international arena . . . blur distinctions between the public and private spheres . . . '[79]

The hybrid nature of international investment law and arbitration may itself be viewed as 'evidence of the breakdown of the distinction in practice'.[80] International investment law deals with both public and private concerns, involves both states and non-state actors and 'crosses over traditional divides' using a blend of public and private concepts.[81] For instance, concession contracts are regarded as having a mixed character, containing public law elements[82] and being made by public authorities and private actors. At the heart of most investment arbitrations lies the conflict between the state's regulatory autonomy and the protection of foreign investments.[83] Arbitral tribunals are given the

[75] W. Friedmann, 'The Uses of "General Principles" in the Development of International Law', *American Journal of International Law* 57 (1963), 279, 282.
[76] *Ibid.* [77] *Ibid.*
[78] A. von Bogdandy, P. Dann and M. Goldmann, 'Developing the Publicness of Public International Law: Towards a Legal Framework for Global Governance Activities', in A. von Bogdandy, R. Wolfrum, J. von Bernstorff, P. Dann, M. Goldmann (eds.), *The Exercise of Public Authority by International Institutions* (Heidelberg: Springer, 2009), pp. 3–32, p. 10.
[79] H. Muir Watt, 'Globalization and Comparative Law', in M. Reimann and R. Zimmermann (eds.), *The Oxford Handbook of Comparative Law* (Oxford: Oxford University Press, 2006), pp. 583–606, p. 583.
[80] Mills, 'Antinomies of Public and Private at the Foundations of International Investment Law and Arbitration', 477.
[81] Maupin, 'Public and Private in International Investment Law', 267.
[82] For instance, in the *Lighthouse* case between France and Greece, the PCIJ held that 'a contract granting a public utility concession does not fall within the category of ordinary instruments of private law'. PCIJ, *France v. Greece*, Judgment, 17 March 1934, Ser. A/B, No. 62, p. 20.
[83] Friedmann, 'The Uses of "General Principles" in the Development of International Law', 291.

power to review state conduct in the light of the relevant treaty provisions. Adjudication over a state's *acta jure imperii* implies a significant departure from the conventional use of international arbitration in the commercial sphere.[84] Arbitrators determine matters such as the legality of governmental activity, the degree to which individuals should be protected from regulation and the appropriate role of the state.[85] Therefore, such an investment review has been conceptualised as Public law review.[86]

Certainly, public law has played a pivotal role in the making of international (investment) law. For instance, the provisions against indirect expropriation in a number of international investment treaties derive from the *Penn Central* test, articulated by the US Supreme Court.[87] In parallel, as the US Model BIT is often used as a template by a number of countries for treaty negotiations, the *lex Americana* has become the gold standard in the area.[88] This process has not been uncontroversial or uncontested. Some commentators have argued that the extensive protection granted to investors' rights amount to an extraterritorial application of the Fifth Amendment of the US Constitution[89] or an expression of the 'Americanisation' of international law.

At the adjudicative level, constitutional ideas have migrated across boundaries,[90] contributing to the phenomenon of 'judicial

---

[84] Douglas, 'The Hybrid Foundations of Investment Treaty Arbitration', at 221–222.

[85] Sornarajah, 'The Clash of Globalizations and the International Law on Foreign Investment', 17.

[86] S. Schill, 'Enhancing International Investment Law's Legitimacy: Conceptual and Methodological Foundations of a New Public Law Approach', *Virginia Journal of International Law* 52 (2011), 57; Douglas, 'The Hybrid Foundations of Investment Treaty Arbitration', 221; Van Harten, 'The Public-Private Distinction in the International Arbitration of Individual Claims Against the State', 372; Van Harten and Loughlin, 'Investment Treaty Arbitration as a Species of Global Administrative Law', 121; Van Harten, *Investment Treaty Arbitration and Public Law*; D. Schneiderman, *Constitutionalizing Economic Globalization: Investment Rules and Democracy's Premise* (Cambridge: Cambridge University Press, 2008); Montt, *State Liability in Investment Treaty Arbitration: Global Constitutional Law and Administrative Law in the BIT Generation*.

[87] *Penn Central Transportation Co. v. New York City*, 438 U.S. 104, 124 (1978).

[88] J. Alvarez, 'The Evolving BIT', in I.A. Laird and T. Weiler (eds), *Investment Treaty Arbitration and International Law* (New York: Juris, 2010), pp. 12–13.

[89] G.M. Starner, 'Taking a Constitutional Look: NAFTA Chapter 11 as an Extension of Member States' Constitutional Protection of Property', *Law & Policy in International Business* 33 (2002), 405.

[90] S. Choudry, 'Migration as the New Metaphor in Comparative Constitutional Law', in S. Choudry (ed.), *The Migration of Constitutional Ideas* (Cambridge: Cambridge University Press, 2006), pp. 1–25.

globalization'.[91] The migration of constitutional ideas reflects the spirit of the time due to globalisation, the polycentric nature of law and the coexistence of different, at times overlapping and at times diverging, legal systems.[92] Once the exclusive domain of states, law has now become the terrain of competition among multiple regulatory entities at national, regional and international levels. International courts and tribunals as well as constitutional courts around the world have increasingly 'cross-judged', that is, cited and/or relied upon each other's opinions. The migration of constitutional ideas from constitutional law to the international sphere allows a dialogue between national constitutional courts, on the one hand, and international courts and tribunals, on the other. This judicial dialogue can foster the circular migration of constitutional ideas from constitutional courts to international *fora* and then back to constitutional courts.[93] Moreover, the migration of constitutional ideas can allow international courts and tribunals to defragment fragmentation across the various regimes of international law.[94] Arbitral tribunals resort to domestic cases to reinforce their perceived legitimacy, especially when they face difficult cases.[95] The influence of borrowing goes beyond the specific case, influencing the culture of the importing system[96] and determining gravitation towards certain models which exert dominant influence.

However, the migration of constitutional ideas to international law is not without limits; the duty to bring national law into conformity with international law is a well-settled part of customary law[97] and this is

---

[91] See generally A.M. Slaughter, 'Judicial Globalization', *Virginia Journal of International Law* 40 (2000), 1103–1124.

[92] See, for example, G. Teubner, '"Global Bukovina": Legal Pluralism in the World Society', in G. Teubner (ed.), *Global Law Without a State* (Dartmouth: Aldershot, 1997).

[93] E. Benvenisti, 'Reclaiming Democracy: The Strategic Uses of Foreign and International Law by National Courts', *American Journal of International Law* 102 (2008), 241.

[94] R. Teitel, 'Comparative Constitutional Law in a Global Age', *Harvard Law Review* 117 (2004), 2570–2596.

[95] L.R. Helfer, 'Constitutional Analogies in the International Legal System', *Loyola Los Angeles Law Review* 37 (2003–2004), 193–237, at 237 (pointing out that 'although the analogies between domestic constitutions and treaty regimes are inexact, they may nevertheless help to generate insights for international law scholars ...').

[96] See C. Picker, 'International Investment Law: Some Legal Cultural Insights', in L. Trakman and N. Ranieri (eds.), *Regionalism in International Investment Law* (New York: Oxford University Press, 2013), pp. 27–58.

[97] I. Brownlie, *Principles of Public International Law* (Oxford: Oxford University Press, 2008), p. 35.

confirmed by consistent jurisprudence.[98] A number of ICSID awards applying Article 42 of the ICSID Convention have recognised that where the parties have not agreed to the applicable law, and there is a conflict between public international law and domestic law, then it is international law which should prevail.[99]

Against this background, eminent scholars have argued in favour of reading international investment law and arbitration through the lenses of public law, albeit for different reasons.[100] For instance, some argue that investment treaty law constitutes a creature of global administrative law (GAL),[101] which impels states to conform to GAL principles and to adopt principles of good governance.[102] In parallel, Montt suggests that public law analogies may contribute to the legitimisation of the international investment law system, constituting useful benchmarks for interpreting investment treaty provisions.[103] Therefore, he urges arbitral tribunals to develop their jurisprudence by anchoring their awards in comparative public reasoning. Analogously, in *Thunderbird Gaming Corp. v. United Mexican States*, the late Professor Wälde, acting as an arbitrator, stated that the proper

[98] See, for example, *Treatment of Polish Nationals and Other Persons of Polish Origin or Speech in the Danzig Territory*, Advisory Opinion, 4 February 1932, PCIJ Ser. A/B, no. 44 p. 24 (holding that reliance on national constitutional provisions does not justify a violation of public international law).

[99] See, for example, *EDF International S.A., SAUR International S.A. and Léon Participationes Argentinas S.A. v. The Argentine Republic*, ICSID Case No. ARB/03/23, Award, 11 June 2012, para. 907 (stating that '[T]he legality of Respondent's acts under national law does not determine their lawfulness under international legal principles'); *LG&E Energy Corporation, LG&E Capital Corp., and LG&E International, Inc. v. Argentine Republic*, Decision on Liability, 3 October 2006, ICSID Case No. ARB 02/1, para. 94 (holding that 'International law overrides domestic law when there is a contradiction since a state cannot justify non-compliance of its international obligations by asserting the provisions of its domestic law').

[100] See, for example, Van Harten, *Investment Treaty Arbitration and Public Law*; S. Schill (ed.), *International Investment Law and Comparative Public Law* (Oxford: Oxford University Press, 2010); A. Kulick, *Global Public Interest in International Investment Law* (Cambridge: Cambridge University Press, 2013).

[101] Van Harten and Loughlin, 'Investment Treaty Arbitration as a Species of Global Administrative Law', at 121.

[102] For a critical assessment of this theory, see C. Harlow, 'Global Administrative Law: The Quest for Principles and Values', *European Journal of International Law* 17 (2006), 187–214; B.S. Chimni, 'Co-option and Resistance: Two Faces of Global Administrative Law', *New York University Journal of International Law and Politics* 37 (2005), 799–827.

[103] Montt, *State Liability in Investment Treaty Arbitration: Global Constitutional and Administrative Law in the BIT Generation*.

analogy in interpreting investment treaties is not to international commercial arbitration or public international law, both of which involve disputants who are seen as equals, but rather to judicial review relating to governmental conduct. In particular, he referred to both 'international judicial review (as carried out by the WTO dispute panels and Appellate Body, by the European- or Inter-American Human Rights Courts or the European Court of Justice)' and 'national administrative courts judging disputes of individual citizens over alleged abuse by public bodies of their governmental powers'.[104] By contrast, Van Harten contends that the public law features of investment treaty law make the use of the arbitration mechanism inapposite to settle the relevant disputes.[105] Therefore, he proposes the creation of a standing body.

The public law paradigm has the merit of bringing to light the role of individuals (and their entitlements) in international investment law and arbitration. The public law framing also takes into account the interests of third parties standing outside the immediate investor–state relationship.[106] The public law approach 'takes a holistic view of a state's obligations by placing the state's duties to foreign investors under international investment law alongside its duties to its own citizens under domestic law and to other national and transnational constituencies under other bodies of international law'.[107] Furthermore, within given limits, it can complement public international law approaches by helping in the identification of general principles of law and/or state practice, which represents an important element of customary law.

Yet, further reflection on the methodology of public law analogies in international investment law and arbitration is needed. Can constitutional theory be generalised and transposed from the national terrain to the international sphere? Can constitutional ideas be 'conceived in near to complete isolation' of the cultural contexts 'in which the very concepts ... ha[d] their origin'?[108] Historical, political and economic

---

[104] *Int'l Thunderbird Gaming Corp.* v. *United Mexican States*, NAFTA Chapter 11, Separate Opinion of Arbitrator Thomas Wälde, 255 Fed. Appx. 531 (2007), at 13.

[105] Van Harten, *Investment Treaty Arbitration and Public Law*.

[106] Maupin, 'Public and Private in International Investment Law: An Integrated Systems Approach', 399.

[107] *Ibid.*, at 399–400.

[108] P. Zumbansen, 'Transnational Comparisons: Theory and Practice of Comparative Law as a Critique of Global Governance', Osgoode Hall Law School, Comparative Research in Law & Political Economy Research Paper No. 1/2012, 16.

forces shape public law.[109] Each national system is characterised by a particular distribution of power among different legislative, executive and judiciary institutions.[110] Not by chance, the traditional neglect of public law in comparative legal studies[111] was due to the perception of public law as an inherently political and 'nationally-specific' system,[112] being based on a particular understanding of the relationship between citizen and state.

Given the international law setting of investment treaty arbitration, it would be problematic to automatically transpose the experience of any particular jurisdiction to the international level. Arbitrators should not impose the 'foreign moods, fads, or fashions' of a given country on other domestic audiences, as this would infringe their mandate, undermining their very legitimacy. Rather, comparativists and international law scholars should acknowledge the array of country-specific factors characterising public law to conduct informed comparative studies and distil general principles of law, respectively.[113] Only insofar as a discrete number of constitutional experiences constitute evidence of state practice or general principles of law can they assume relevance in the context of international law adjudication. Another instance in which a given constitutional practice may be relevant is when the applicable law is national law.

Rethinking international investment law as a type of public law might repoliticise disputes. The rise of investment treaties with binding arbitration marks a departure from the Calvo doctrine, according to which a foreign investor would be entitled only to a national standard of treatment and could file claims only before the domestic courts of the host state. Therefore, the importation of domestic law into the interpretation of investment treaties can 'com[e] perilously close to violating the object and purpose of such treaties by returning to the age of Calvo'.[114]

---

[109] Boughey, 'Administrative Law', 57–58.

[110] Zumbansen, 'Transnational Comparisons', 16.

[111] See, for example, R. Hirschl, 'The Rise of Comparative Constitutional Law: Thoughts on Substance and Method', *Indian Journal of Constitutional Law* 2 (2008), 11 (highlighting that only recently have comparative legal studies started focusing on public law, while for most of the twentieth century they focused on private law issues). See also M. Cappelletti and W. Cohen, *Comparative Constitutional Law* (Indianapolis: Bobbs Merrill Co., 1979).

[112] Boughey, 'Administrative Law', 57–58.

[113] Hirschl, 'The Rise of Comparative Constitutional Law', 26–37.

[114] J.E. Alvarez, 'Beware: Boundary Crossings' in Tsvi Kahana and Anat Scolnicov (eds.) *Boundaries of Rights, Boundaries of State (forthcoming* 2015), 47.

In conclusion, the use of public law ideas in international investment law and arbitration can offer concrete solutions to emerging conceptual dilemmas. However, by importing public law conceptual frameworks into the fabric of international investment law, one risks harming international investment law rather than fixing it. Only insofar as the public law approach is conceived as wholly consistent with as well as complementary to the public international law framework in which international investment law is embedded can public law thinking contribute to the hermeneutical process of interpreting investment treaties and the identification of general principles of law under article 38(1)(c) of the ICJ Statute. Public law analogies can be legitimate and legitimising, but 'need to be undertaken with caution to prevent damage to the general law in the course of importation'.[115] Moreover, the 'relevant differences between the different regimes should not be forgotten'.[116]

The migration of constitutional ideas: proportionality as a case study

The advocated migration of the concept of proportionality from constitutional law into international investment law and arbitration exemplifies well how the use of constitutional ideas can be a mixed blessing. In a number of legal systems, the concept of proportionality is understood as a methodological framework for balancing conflicting values. While some scholars contend that arbitral tribunals should adopt proportionality analysis,[117] the section shows that while the concept of proportionality has analytical merits, it also presents a number of flaws when applied to the context of investment disputes. Transplanting proportionality into international investment law and arbitration would be legitimate if proportionality was part of the applicable law as a general principle of law, or reflected state practice, which is an element of customary international law, or as a matter of treaty interpretation. Despite that some authors contend that proportionality is a general principle of law – at least in some jurisdictions, including the European

---

[115] Ibid.

[116] S. Schill, 'International Investment Law and Comparative Public Law: An Introduction', in S. Schill (ed.), International Investment Law and Comparative Public Law (Oxford: Oxford University Press, 2010), p. 35.

[117] See A. Stone Sweet, 'Investor–State Arbitration: Proportionality's New Frontier', Law and Ethics of Human Rights 4 (2010), 46–76.

Union[118] – no consensus seems to have arisen with regard to the legal status of proportionality in international law. Certainly, if the applicable law is the law of the host state and this law includes the proportionality principle, such principle becomes relevant in the context of investment treaty arbitration.[119] Beyond this specific case, however, this section concludes that more studies are needed to ascertain the legal status of proportionality in international law.

The proportionality test is usually articulated in three main phases: suitability, necessity and proportionality.[120] First, the suitability test requires that the adopted measure be suitable to achieve the stated objectives. There must be a rational, logical and causal relationship between the measure and its objectives. Second, the necessity test aims at verifying that the measure was the least restrictive (reasonably) available alternative or that no less drastic means were available. The given objective cannot be achieved by means that are more restrictive than other available options, provided that they are suitable to achieve the same objective. Third, the proportionality test in the narrow sense requires adjudicators to ascertain that the benefit gained from realising the objective exceeds the harm caused by the adopted measure.

Conceived as a tool for reviewing state conduct (and thus closely connected with the aim of ensuring good governance), proportionality can restrain the exercise of public authority, shape judicial review and manage private actors' expectations. Proportionality is based on 'a culture of justification' which 'requires that governments should provide substantive justification for all their actions ... '[121] Proportionality is a 'deliberative methodology',[122] which requires that all of the relevant factors be considered and, then, that an equilibrium be struck according to their relative importance depending on the contextual circumstances.

---

[118] E. Ellis (ed), *The Principle of Proportionality in the Laws of Europe* (Oxford: Hart Publishing, 1999).

[119] See, for example, *Aucoven v. Venezuela*, ICSID Case No. ARB/00/5, Award, 23 September 2003, para. 338.

[120] See J.H. Jans, 'Proportionality Revisited', *Legal Issues of Economic Integration* 27 (2000), 240–241. A number of scholars include a preliminary phase, that of legitimacy, 'in which the judge confirms that the government is constitutionally-authorized to take such a measure'. W.W. Burke White and A. von Staden, 'Private Litigation in a Public Private Sphere: The Standard of Review in Investor–state Arbitrations', *Yale Journal of International Law* 35 (2010), 283, 334.

[121] M. Cohen-Eliya and I. Porat, 'Proportionality and the Culture of Justification', *American Journal of Comparative Law* 59 (2011), 463–490, 467.

[122] I. Porat, 'Some Critical Thoughts on Proportionality', in G. Bongiovanni, G. Sartor and C. Valentini (eds), *Reasonableness and Law* (Heidelberg: Springer, 2009), pp. 243, 244.

Proportionality also limits the subjectivity of the adjudicator, empowering courts and tribunals to review state conduct in a significant fashion and providing a structured, formalised and seemingly objective test. All awards and decisions must state the reasons on which the award is based;[123] failure to state such reasons is a ground for annulment of the same awards.[124] Proportionality can provide 'a common language that transcends national borders and that allows for dialogue and exchange of information' between courts and tribunals.[125] Proportionality allows adjudicators to adopt nuanced decisions rather than 'all-or-nothing' approaches[126] and to structure their analysis in a framework which 'may produce better and more convincing reasoning ... '[127] In addition, 'proportionality analysis can constitute a gateway for non-investment law principles to enter into the argumentative framework of investment treaty arbitration and thereby help to overcome the fragmentation of international law ... '.[128] In turn, proportionality can also delimit the legitimate expectations of private actors vis-à-vis state action.

Given the pervasiveness of the concept of proportionality in a few constitutional traditions[129] and in various areas of international law, some authors contend that proportionality is an emerging general principle of international law[130] or even an already established one.[131] If one admits that such a proposition is true, then such a contention would constitute a formidable entry point for proportionality analysis in

---

[123] See generally P. Lalive, 'On the Reasoning of International Arbitral Awards', *Journal of International Dispute Settlement* 1 (2010), 55, 55; G. Aguilar Alvarez and W.M. Reisman, 'How Well are Investment Awards Reasoned?', in G. Aguilar Alvarez and W.M. Reisman (eds), *The Reasons Requirement in International Investment Arbitration* (Leiden: Martinus Nijhoff Publishers, 2008), p. 2; T. Landau, 'Reasons for Reasons: The Tribunal's Duty in Investor–State Arbitration', in A.J. Van den Berg (ed.), *50 Years of the New York Convention – ICCA International Arbitration Conference ICCA Congress Series No. 14, Dublin Conference, 2008* (2009), pp. 187–205.

[124] Article 52(1) of the ICSID Convention.

[125] Cohen-Eliya and Porat, 'Proportionality and the Culture of Justification', 472.

[126] B. Kingsbury and S. Schill, 'Public Law Concepts to Balance Investors' Rights with State Regulatory Actions in the Public Interest – The Concept of Proportionality', in S. Schill (ed.), *International Investment Law and Comparative Public Law* (Oxford: Oxford University Press, 2010), p. 75, 79.

[127] *Ibid.*, p. 103.   [128] *Ibid.*, p. 104.

[129] See A. Stone Sweet and D. Mathews, 'Proportionality Balancing and Global Constitutionalism', *Columbia Journal of Transnational Law* 47 (2008), 73, 98–111.

[130] Kulick, *Global Public Interest in International Investment Law*, p. 169.

[131] See, for example, E. Cannizzaro, *Il principio della proporzionalitá nell'ordinamento internazionale* (Milano: Giuffré, 2000).

investment treaty arbitration, as arbitrators could refer to proportionality in their award as either part of the applicable law, under Article 42 of the ICSID Convention,[132] or as a rule of international law applicable in the relations between the parties under Article 31(3)(c) of the Vienna Convention on the Law of Treaties (VCLT).[133] Others contend that also good faith interpretation, as restated by Article 31(1) of the VCLT, may require some balancing between the public and the private interest.[134]

Proportionality in investment treaty arbitration

In the past decade, arbitral tribunals have increasingly relied on some form of proportionality analysis[135] to clarify the contours and content of substantive investment provisions such as expropriation, fair and equitable treatment, full protection and security, and non-discrimination. Proportionality has also been used to define the ambit of application of given exceptions or with regard to procedural matters.

With regard to the notion of expropriation, in *Tecmed*, which concerned the replacement of an unlimited licence by a licence of limited duration for the operation of a landfill, the Arbitral Tribunal used the concept of proportionality to ascertain whether given measures could be characterised as expropriatory. The Tribunal considered whether such actions or measures were 'proportional to the public interest presumably protected thereby, and to the protection legally granted to investments,

---

[132] Convention on the Settlement of Investment Disputes between States and Nationals of Other States (ICSID Convention or Washington Convention), Washington, 18 March 1965, in force 14 October 1966, 575 UNTS 159.

[133] Vienna Convention on the Law of Treaties of 23 May 1969, in force 27 January 1980, UN Treaty Series vol. 1155, p. 331.

[134] B. Kingsbury and S. Schill, 'Investor–State Arbitration as Governance: Fair and Equitable Treatment, Proportionality and the Emerging Global Administrative Law', New York University School of Law, Public Law & Legal Research Theory Research Paper Series, Working Paper No. 09–46 (2009), 23.

[135] This section does not purport to be exhaustive, as some arbitral tribunals may not be disclosed to the public and other awards may have referred to proportionality only implicitly. This section acknowledges only a number of awards which have used the concept of proportionality *expressis verbis*. The argument is that the use of some elements of proportionality, like suitability, is a common judicial endeavour and therefore should not be reconnected to proportionality as such, while the implicit use of all of the various elements of proportionality without naming it would give rise to a number of distinct hermeneutical concerns.

taking into account that the significance of such impact has a key role upon deciding proportionality'.[136]

In *Azurix*, which involved a water concession contract, Argentina had enacted measures for the protection of public health after an algae outbreak contaminated water supply after privatisation.[137] Warnings not to drink water were enacted and customers were dissuaded from paying their water bills.[138] In order to ascertain whether there was a (compensable) expropriation or a (non-compensable) legitimate exercise of police powers, the Tribunal relied on *Tecmed*, and its analysis of the European Court of Human Rights (ECtHR)'s jurisprudence, stating that an expropriatory measure must pursue a 'legitimate aim in the public interest' and the means employed must be (reasonably) proportional to the stated objective.[139] The Tribunal dismissed the claim of expropriation.

In *Burlington Resources Inc.* v. *Ecuador*, which related to the exploitation of oil reserves, Ecuador contended that its intervention in the exploration areas (or 'Blocks') awarded to the investor did not constitute an expropriation of Burlington's investment; rather, it 'aimed at preventing significant harm' to the same areas and, in Ecuador's view, it 'was necessary, adequate, proportionate under the circumstances'.[140] The Arbitral Tribunal confirmed that Ecuador's intervention in the areas 'was necessary to avoid significant economic loss and the risk of permanent damage to the Blocks. It was also appropriate because Ecuador entered the Blocks without using force. It was equally proportionate as the means employed were suited to the ends of protecting the Blocks.'[141]

In *Servier* v. *Poland*, a case concerning the denial of marketing authorisations preventing the sale of given medicines, the Tribunal stated that 'the Respondent's denial of marketing authorisations would divest the Claimants of their property, giving rise to a requirement of compensation under the BIT, if Poland exercised its administrative and regulatory powers in bad faith, for some non-public purpose, or in a fashion that was either discriminatory or lacking in proportionality between the

[136] *Tecnicas Medioambientales Tecmed S.A.* v. *the United Mexican States*, Case No. ARB (AF)/00/, Award, 29 May 2003, para. 122.
[137] *Azurix* v. *Argentine Republic*, ICSID Case No. ARB/01/12, Award, 23 June 2006.
[138] *Ibid.*, para. 283.   [139] *Ibid.*, para. 311.
[140] *Burlington Resources Inc.* v. *Ecuador*, ICSID Case No. ARB/08/5, Decision on Liability, 14 December 2012, para. 164.
[141] *Ibid.*, para. 504.

public purpose and the actions taken'.[142] The Tribunal then found a divestment, holding that 'Not only was the refusal of authorisation discriminatory, but the regulatory measures were disproportionate in nature and thus not a matter of public necessity.'[143]

With regard to the fair and equitable treatment standard, in *MTD v. Republic of Chile*, which concerned the failure of a construction project deemed to be inconsistent with zoning regulations, the Arbitral Tribunal held that fair and equitable treatment is 'a broad and widely-accepted standard encompassing such fundamental standards as good faith, due process, nondiscrimination and proportionality'.[144] In *Occidental Petroleum Corporation and Occidental Exploration and Production Company v. Republic of Ecuador*, concerning a contract for the exploration and exploitation of hydrocarbons in the Ecuadorian Amazon region, the Arbitral Tribunal stated that 'numerous investment treaty tribunals have found that the principle of proportionality is part and parcel of the overarching duty to accord fair and equitable treatment to investors'.[145] The claimant contended that a given sanction imposed by Ecuador was disproportionate and therefore violated legitimate expectations under the relevant BIT.[146] The Tribunal concluded that the measure 'was not a proportionate response by Ecuador in the particular circumstances of this case'.[147]

Yet, in *Glamis Gold v. United States of America*, concerning a gold mining project in California, the claimant's attempt to impose upon respondent the burden of justifying the appropriateness of the regulatory measures and proving that they are 'necessary, suitable and proportionate' failed.[148] The Tribunal noted that 'it is not for an international tribunal to delve into the details of and justifications of domestic law'.[149] It also stated that 'It is not the role of this Tribunal, or any international tribunal, to supplant its own judgment of underlying factual material and support for that of a qualified domestic agency.'[150]

---

[142] *Les Laboratoires Servier, S.A.A., Biofarma, S.A.S., Arts et Techniques du Progrès S.A.S. v. Republic of Poland*, UNCITRAL, PCA Award, 14 February 2012, para. 570.

[143] *Ibid.*, paras. 574–575.

[144] *MTD Equity SDN BHD and MTD Chile S.A. v. Republic of Chile*, Case No. ARB/01/7, Award, 25 May 2004, para. 109.

[145] *Occidental Petroleum Corporation and Occidental Exploration and Production Company v. Republic of Ecuador*, Case No. ARB/06/11, Award, 5 October 2012, footnote 7.

[146] *Ibid.*, para. 277.   [147] *Ibid.*, para. 338.

[148] *Glamis Gold, Ltd. v. United States of America*, Award, 8 June 2009, para. 590.

[149] *Ibid.*, para. 762.   [150] *Ibid.*, para. 779.

With regard to non-discrimination, in *Parkerings* v. *Lithuania*,[151] which concerned the planned construction of a parking area, the Arbitral Tribunal stated that 'to violate international law, discrimination must be unreasonable or lacking proportionality, for instance, it must be inapposite or excessive to achieve an otherwise legitimate objective of the State'.[152] Yet, in *Pope & Talbot* v. *Canada*, concerning the manufacturing and trade of softwood lumber, the Tribunal dismissed Canada's argument that the foreign investor should prove that it was 'disproportionately disadvantaged' by the measure.[153] The Tribunal considered that the disproportionate advantage test would weaken NAFTA's Chapter 11 ability to protect foreign investors.[154]

Other cases referred to proportionality as it was a requirement under the applicable national law. In *Aucoven* v. *Venezuela*, relating to a highway concession, Venezuela argued that Aucoven's claims did not meet the criteria of definiteness and proportionality required by Venezuelan law.[155] In *Spyridon Roussalis* v. *Romania*,[156] the claimant argued that 'instead of freezing only the cash equivalent to the claimed tax amount, Romania chose, through its fiscal authorities, to sequester all [Claimant's] assets, ... and bank accounts'. According to the claimant, 'this decision impaired Claimant's right to dispose of its investment and was taken in breach of the principles of due process, proportionality and reasonableness'.[157] However, the Tribunal held that 'Claimant has not proved that this sequestration was discriminatory, disproportionate or otherwise improper under Romanian law.'[158] In *Occidental Petroleum Corporation and Occidental Exploration and Production Company* v. *Republic of Ecuador*, the claimant contended that a given decree was 'in breach of the Respondent's obligations under the Treaty and Ecuadorian law because it was unfair, arbitrary, discriminatory and disproportionate'.[159] The Tribunal noted that the proportionality review of the decree 'pervaded the submissions

---

[151] *Parkerings* v. *Lithuania*, ICSID Case No. ARB/05/8, Award, 11 September 2007.
[152] *Ibid.*, para. 368.
[153] *Pope & Talbot* v. *Canada*, NAFTA Chapter 11, Award on the Merits of Phase 2, 10 April 2001, paras. 43–45.
[154] *Ibid.*, para. 79.
[155] *Autopista Concesionada de Venezuela, C.A.* (*'Aucoven'*) v. *Bolivarian Republic of Venezuela*, ICSID Case No. ARB/00/5, Award, 23 September 2003, para. 338.
[156] *Spyridon Roussalis* v. *Romania*, ICSID Case No. ARB/06/1, Award, 7 December 2011, para. 358.
[157] *Ibid.*, at para. 394.   [158] *Ibid.*, at para. 515.
[159] *Occidental Petroleum Corporation and Occidental Exploration and Production Company* v. *Republic of Ecuador*, ICSID Case No. ARB/06/11, 16 December 2011, para. 206.

of both parties' as 'the Ecuadorian Constitution firmly establishes as a matter of Ecuadorian law the principle of proportionality'.[160]

In other cases, proportionality was used to define the ambit of application of given exceptions. For instance, in *Continental Casualty* v. *Argentine Republic*, concerning an insurance business, the Tribunal imported the 'weighting and balancing' formula from international trade law.[161] Both parties had referred to the concept of proportionality. The Arbitral Tribunal considered that

> the Government's efforts struck an appropriate balance between that aim and the responsibility of any government towards the country's population: it is self-evident that not every sacrifice can properly be imposed on a country's people in order to safeguard a certain policy that would ensure full respect towards international obligations in the financial sphere, before a breach of those obligations can be considered justified as being necessary under this BIT. The standard of reasonableness and proportionality do not require as much.[162]

Finally, proportionality has been used also with regard to matters of procedure. For instance, in *Libananco Holdings Co. Limited* v. *Republic of Turkey*,[163] concerning the seizure of two electric utility companies, the Tribunal stated that 'there needs to be some proportionality in the award (as opposed to the expenditure) of legal costs and expenses. A party with a deep pocket may have its own justification for heavy spending, but it cannot expect to be reimbursed for all its expenditure as a matter of course simply because it is ultimately the prevailing party.'[164] In *Servier* v. *Poland*, the claimants submitted that 'the Respondent ha[d] failed to establish that its legal costs [we]re reasonable and proportionate'.[165] The Tribunal, however, held that each party would bear its own legal costs.[166] In *Liman Caspian Oil BV and NCL Dutch Investment BV* v. *Republic of Kazakhstan*, concerning a licence to explore and extract hydrocarbons, the Tribunal acknowledged that 'on [the] one hand, ordering the production of documents can be helpful for a party to present its case and in the Tribunal's task of establishing the facts of the

---

[160] *Ibid.*, footnote 7, and paras. 396–401 (on the principle of proportionality in Ecuadorian law).

[161] *Continental Casualty* v. *Argentine Republic*, ICSID Case No. ARB/03/9, Award, 5 September 2008, para. 192.

[162] *Ibid.*, para. 227.

[163] *Libananco Holdings Co. Limited* v. *Republic of Turkey*, ICSID Case No. ARB/06/8, Award, 2 September 2011.

[164] *Ibid.*, para. 565(c).   [165] *Servier* v. *Poland*, Final Award, para. 492.

[166] *Ibid.*, para. 678.

case relevant for the issues to be decided, but, on the other hand, (1) the process of discovery and disclosure may be time consuming, excessively burdensome and even oppressive and that unless carefully limited, the burden may be disproportionate to the value of the result, and (2) Parties may have a legitimate interest of confidentiality'.[167]

These awards show an increasingly frequent pattern in the use of some form of proportionality analysis in investment treaty arbitration. Proportionality analysis is used for delimiting substantive standards of protection, clarifying procedural matters and even quantifying damages and legal fees. Yet, the proportionality analysis is not used consistently in investment treaty arbitration. No single unified notion of proportionality has been used; rather, arbitral tribunals seem to have elaborated *ad hoc* notions of proportionality depending on circumstances. In the context of investment arbitration, the proportionality analysis is depicted using broad strokes, without the articulated structure it has in other fields of law.[168]

In conclusion, while generic reference to proportionality has increased in the past decade, a critical mass of awards relying on this test is missing. Furthermore, proportionality is often mentioned in passing together with other concepts such as reasonableness or rationality, rather than separately. Arbitral tribunals seem to prefer grounding their analysis in multiple rationales to strengthen their reasoning and ultimately their legitimacy. In addition, at an analytical level, one may legitimately wonder whether proportionality can contribute to better awards or can raise more questions than answers.

The promises and pitfalls of proportionality analysis in investment treaty arbitration

Conceived as a logical method to assist adjudicators in determining the interaction between public and private interests, the concept of proportionality has spread over different national, regional and international adjudicative systems, due to a variety of reasons. Proportionality analysis empowers courts and tribunals to review state conduct in a significant

---

[167] *Liman Caspian Oil BV and NCL Dutch Investment BV* v. *Republic of Kazakhstan*, ICSID Case No. ARB/07/14, Award, 22 June 2010, para. 26.

[168] V. Vadi, 'The Migration of Constitutional Ideas to Regional and International Economic Law: The Case of Proportionality', *Northwestern Journal of International Law and Business* 35 (*forthcoming* 2015).

fashion, allowing adjudicators to adopt nuanced decisions[169] and to structure their analysis in a robust framework which 'may produce better and more convincing reasoning'.[170] Proportionality analysis 'is consensus-oriented because it acknowledges explicitly that there are valid constitutional arguments on both sides, and that the arguments outweighed by the opposing ones do not lose thereby their constitutional weight'.[171] Furthermore, the adoption of this type of analysis can bring order and coherence into legal systems, facilitate dialogue in the global community of judges,[172] and 'constitute a gateway for non-investment law principles to enter into the argumentative framework of investment treaty arbitration and thereby help to overcome the fragmentation of international law ... '[173]

Yet, the migration of the concept of proportionality from constitutional law to the international sphere has been challenged on five grounds: (1) institutional competences; (2) scale of values; (3) cultural arguments; (4) incommensurability; and (5) overprotection of property rights. *First*, democratic arguments run against using balancing to review the host state's decisions because arbitrators would second-guess the decisions of the host state by replicating the original decision-making process.[174] By considering different alternatives to given legislative or executive measures and by balancing competing interests under the proportionality test, the adjudicator interferes with the regulatory autonomy of states, supplanting the role of legitimately deputed decision-makers.[175] As Stone Sweet and Mathews put it, 'balancing can never be dissociated from lawmaking: it requires judges to behave as legislators'.[176]

Second, proportionality analysis tells us nothing about the scale of values that will determine the final outcome. The critical question is

---

[169] Kingsbury and Schill, 'Public Law Concepts to Balance Investors' Rights with State Regulatory Actions in the Public Interest – The Concept of Proportionality', p. 79.

[170] *Ibid.*, 103.

[171] W. Sadurski, 'Reasonableness and Value Pluralism in Law and Politics', in G. Bongiovanni, G. Sartor and C. Valentini (eds.), *Reasonableness and Law* (Heidelberg: Springer, 2009), pp. 129, 145.

[172] Cohen-Eliya and Porat, 'Proportionality and the Culture of Justification', 463, 472.

[173] Kingsbury and Schill, 'Public Law Concepts to Balance Investors' Rights with State Regulatory Actions in the Public Interest – The Concept of Proportionality', 104.

[174] I. Porat, 'Why All Attempts to Make Judicial Review Balancing Principled Fail?', paper presented at the VII World Congress of the International Association of Constitutional Law, Athens, 11–15 June 2007, at 7.

[175] Kulick, *Global Public Interest in International Investment Law*, p. 172.

[176] Stone Sweet and Mathews, 'Proportionality Balancing and Global Constitutionalism', 88.

'what must be proportionate to what'.[177] Must the justification relied on by the host state – be it public health, morals or others – be proportional to the goal of promoting foreign direct investment? Or should this assessment be limited to the tools selected by the state to achieve a selected level of protection of the given public policy objective? The fact that proportionality concerns quantity rather than quality leaves the adjudicator free to select his or her own value system and to explain why one value is considered more important than another.[178]

Third, because value systems vary from one country to another and arbitrators may not be familiar with the context of a given policy measure, proportionality analysis may not be suitable to investment arbitration. As Burke White and von Staden point out, 'prioritization of the values chosen by the polity requires both familiarity with those values and a degree of embeddedness within that polity'.[179] However, arbitrators are far removed from the polities over which they have jurisdiction. Critical legal theorists contend that 'hegemonic elites' might use balancing to entrench their values and shift power from the democratic process to the courts.[180] Accordingly, proportionality might have an 'imperialistic effect', in that it might set aside local constitutional values.[181]

Moreover, proportionality is accompanied by a certain historical background,[182] reflecting distrust of public administration in the aftermath of Second World War.[183] Since the end of the war and the democratic transitions that followed,[184] constitutional courts have played a key role in making the constitution an 'impenetrable bulwark against any infringement of the rights of the people'.[185] At the same time, lawyers elaborated the respective constitutions on the basis of

[177] Jans, 'Proportionality Revisited', 239.

[178] Stone Sweet and Mathews, 'Proportionality Balancing and Global Constitutionalism', 89.

[179] Burke White and von Staden, 'Private Litigation in a Public Private Sphere', 336.

[180] See generally R. Hirschl, *Towards Juristocracy: The Origins and Consequences of the New Constitutionalism* (Boston, MA: Harvard University Press, 2004).

[181] Cohen-Elya and Porat, *Proportionality and Constitutional Culture*, pp. 8–9.

[182] *Ibid.*, p. 8.

[183] M. Bobek, 'Reasonableness in Administrative Law: A Comparative Reflection on Functional Equivalence', in G. Bongiovanni, G. Sartor and C. Valentini (eds), *Reasonableness and Law* (Heidelberg: Springer, 2009), pp. 311, 323.

[184] M. Schor, 'Mapping Comparative Judicial Review', *Washington University Global Studies Law Review* 7 (2008), 257, 271.

[185] Piero Calamandrei, quoted by M. Cappelletti, 'Repudiating Montesquieu? The Expansion and Legitimacy of "Constitutional Justice"', *Catholic University Law Review* 35 (1985), 191.

'their understanding of state and society' with 'distinct starting points and trajectories'.[186]

Fourth, proportionality assumes measurability; to be balanced, two competing principles should be based on a common denominator.[187] However, some values are not necessarily commensurable with others.[188] *Fifth*, in the international trade law context, the concept of proportionality seems to have 'tipped the balance in favour of trade liberalization'.[189] Analogously, investment law scholars suggest that the application of proportionality in investment arbitration could lead to the overprotection of property rights.[190]

In conclusion, the question as to whether proportionality can be transplanted from constitutional law to the field of international investment law and arbitration remains open. Several arbitral tribunals have expressly referred to proportionality. Although some eminent authors forcefully suggest a broader use of proportionality in international investment law and arbitration, other commentators consider proportionality analysis inappropriate for arbitral tribunals. According to the latter authors, democratic arguments run against using balancing to review the host state's decisions, because this would permit arbitrators to second-guess the decisions of the host state by replicating the original decision-making process. Rather, they consider that a degree of deference should be paid to the sovereign choices of the host state. Proportionality – critics argue – is not a neutral process; rather, it is based on the primacy and priority of individual entitlements over the exercise of public powers.[191] Therefore, the adoption of this concept can determine a race to the top of investment treaty standards, as the cultural background of proportionality aims to delimit public power vis-à-vis private entitlements. Moreover, as most investment treaties do

---

[186] P. Zumbansen, 'Transnational Comparisons', 19.

[187] A. Barak, *Proportionality Constitutional Rights and Their Limitations* (Cambridge: Cambridge University Press, 2012), pp. 482–484 (arguing that a common denominator exists in the form of the marginal social importance of each value).

[188] C. Sunstein, 'Incommensurability and Valuation in Law', *Michigan Law Review* 92 (1994), 779–861.

[189] G. Kapterian, 'A Critique of the WTO Jurisprudence on Necessity', *International and Comparative Law Quarterly* 59 (2010), 89–127, 91.

[190] H. Xiuli, 'The Application of the Principle of Proportionality in *Tecmed* v. *Mexico*', *Chinese Journal of International Law* 6 (2007), 635–652.

[191] M. Sakellaridou, 'La Généalogie de la proportionalité', paper presented at the VII World Congress of the International Association of Constitutional Law, held in Athens, 11–15 June 2007, at 20.

not refer to proportionality,[192] a few investment law scholars have pointed out that 'there does not seem to be a strong legal basis for the application [of the proportionality analysis] in the cases where it has been applied'[193] and that the conceptual foundations for using proportionality analysis in investment arbitration are shaky.[194] Certainly, more comparative studies are needed to determine whether proportionality is a general principle of international law.

The international public law paradigm

International investment law and arbitration is seen as a component of international law, partly borrowing and partly diverging from other regimes of international law.[195] Compelling arguments stand in favour of assimilating international investment law to international law. International investment law 'consists of layers of general international law, of general standards of international economic law and of distinct rules peculiar to its domain'.[196] Investment treaty arbitrations are conducted on the basis of international treaties; their specific function is to settle disputes in conformity with international law.[197] From a functional perspective, 'to some extent, arbitrators are expected to behave like judges in their concern for the public interest'.[198] Arbitral tribunals review state action in the light of international investment treaty provisions.[199] Like other international courts and tribunals, arbitral tribunals are asked to safeguard vital community interests as well as

---

[192] See, however, Annex 11-B(3)b of the Free Trade Agreement between the Republic of Korea and the United States of America.

[193] E. Leonhardsen, 'Looking for Legitimacy: Exploring Proportionality Analysis in Investment Treaty Arbitration', *Journal of International Dispute Settlement* 3 (2012), 95–136, 95.

[194] B. Pirker, *Proportionality Analysis and Models of Judicial Review* (Groningen: Europa Law Publishing, 2013).

[195] J. Alvarez, 'The Public International Law Regime Governing International Investment', *Recueil des Cours* 344 (Leiden: Martinus Nijhoff Publishers, 2011), pp. 193–542. Paparinskis, 'Analogies and Other Regimes of International Law', 3.

[196] R. Dolzer and C. Schreuer, *Principles of International Investment Law*, 2nd ed. (Oxford: Oxford University Press, 2012), p. 3.

[197] S.W. Schill, 'Crafting the International Economic Order: The Public Function of Investment Treaty Arbitration and Its Significance for the Role of the Arbitrator', *Leiden Journal of International Law* 23 (2010), 401–430, 406.

[198] W.W. Park, 'Private Disputes and the Public Good: Explaining Arbitration Law', *American University International Law Review* 20 (2004–2005), at 905.

[199] S. Schill, 'System-Building in Investment Treaty Arbitration and Lawmaking', *German Law Journal* 12 (2011), 1083, 1088.

to settle disputes in conformity with 'principles of justice and international law'.[200]

One could argue that investment treaty arbitration differs from
interstate arbitration because it constitutes a diagonal dispute settlement mechanism – generally involving private actors' claims against
the host state and a diversified range of epistemic communities,
including both public international lawyers and private commercial
lawyers.[201] These disparate epistemic communities have different
interpretative and argumentative styles which are reflected in arbitral
jurisprudence.[202] For instance, while public international lawyers
emphasise the importance of customary rules of treaty interpretation
for interpreting treaty provisions, commercial lawyers draw analogies
between treaty interpretation and the interpretation of contracts.[203]
Analogously, in their respective awards, public international lawyers
dedicate more attention to the analysis of the treaty text, while commercial lawyers put more emphasis on detailing the facts of the case.[204]
More substantively, public international lawyers and commercial
lawyers have a different understanding of investment arbitration.
While public international lawyers show more deference for the state's
performance of its public functions, commercial lawyers emphasise
procedural aspects such as equality of arms, party autonomy and the
confidentiality of proceedings.[205]

Yet, investment treaty arbitration has a significant international public
law dimension, as arbitrators review the conduct of the state in view of its
investment treaty obligations. International investment law and arbitration does not merely have the function of protecting investments; rather,
it aims at fostering public policy objectives such as economic growth and
peaceful relations among nations. Moreover, as mentioned, investment
treaty arbitration is a creature of international investment treaties
between sovereign states.[206]

---

[200] See Vienna Convention on the Law of Treaties (VCLT), 22 May 1969, in force 27 January
1980, 1155 UNTS 331, Preamble.

[201] Schill, 'Crafting the International Economic Order', 406.   [202] Ibid.

[203] Plama Consortium Ltd. v. Bulgaria, ICSID Case No. ARB/03/24, Decision on
Jurisdiction, 8 February 2005, para. 200.

[204] J. Paulsson, 'Avoiding Unintended Consequences', in K. Sauvant and M. Chiswick-
Patterson (eds.), Appeals Mechanism in International Investment Disputes (Oxford:
Oxford University Press, 2008), p. 241, pp. 262–263.

[205] Schill, 'Crafting the International Economic Order', 407.

[206] Glamis Gold, Ltd v. United States of America, Award, 8 June 2009, paras. 3–9 (stating that
investor–state arbitration is not only 'a creature of contract, tasked with resolving a

WTO law

Within the legal matrix of international law, several regimes may provide the default background against which the broader operation of investment law is read,[207] including international trade law and human rights law.[208] International trade law is sometimes chosen as an analogue,[209] due to perceived substantive, sociological and functional commonalities.

From a substantive perspective, international investment law and international trade law share the general objectives of providing security and predictability to economic actors, increasing world prosperity by reducing barriers to international flows of goods, services and investments and promoting (sustainable) development.[210] Foreign investments and international trade often interact in a globalised economy, and there is some partial overlapping in their respective legal frameworks, as some aspects of foreign direct investments are governed by relevant WTO agreements[211] and some trade elements surface in relevant investment arbitrations.[212] Both regimes prohibit unjustifiable discrimination.[213]

From a sociological perspective, more and more arbitrators, WTO panellists and Members of the Appellate Body have some legal

---

particular dispute arising under a particular contract' (para. 3) but a component of 'a significant public system of private investment protection' (para. 5)).

[207] Paparinskis, 'Analogies and Other Regimes of International Law', 7.

[208] *Ibid.*, (noting that other specific areas of international law may be of relevance, such as the law of treaties on third parties and diplomatic protection).

[209] See, for example, J. Kurtz, 'The Use and Abuse of WTO Law in Investor–State Arbitration: Competition and Its Discontents', *European Journal of International Law* 20 (2009), 749; M.E. Footer, 'International Investment Law and Trade: The Relationship that Never Went Away', in F. Baetens (ed.), *Investment Law within International Law: Integrationist Perspectives* (Cambridge: Cambridge University Press, 2013), ch. 12.

[210] While the preamble of the WTO Agreement expressly refers to sustainable development, preambles of investment treaties vary. Some refer to sustainable development, others to economic development. The NAFTA preamble and the Canadian Model BIT expressly list sustainable development among the objectives of the respective treaties. North American Free Trade Agreement, adopted 17 December 1992 and entered into force 1 January 1994, (1993), 32 ILM 289; 2004 Canadian Model BIT.

[211] See Chapter 2.

[212] On the issue of investors *qua* traders, see, for example, A. Gourgourinis 'Reviewing the Administration of Domestic Regulation in WTO and Investment Law: the International Minimum Standard as "One Standard to Rule them all?", in F. Baetens (ed.), *Investment Law within International Law Integrationist Perspectives* (Cambridge: Cambridge University Press, 2013), ch. 13.

[213] See, for example, N. DiMascio and J. Pauwelyn, 'Nondiscrimination in Trade and Investment Treaties: Worlds Apart or Two Sides of the Same Coin?', *American Journal of International Law* 102 (2008), 48–89, 88.

background.[214] Investment arbitration has been dominated by lawyers.[215] In parallel, although the GATT system used to be run by diplomats and economists, an increasing juridification of the system has taken place.[216] The background and expertise of the relevant epistemic communities constitutes an informal element that can contribute to mutual influence and possible convergence between international trade law and international investment law.[217] This is confirmed by the fact that several Appellate Body Members and – albeit to a lesser extent – panellists have served as ICSID arbitrators.[218]

From a functional perspective, investment treaty arbitration and the WTO dispute settlement mechanism do share the same function, settling international disputes in accordance with a specific set of international economic law rules and ensuring the proper administration of justice in this area. As noted by Alvarez, 'Investor–state dispute settlement was designed to avoid politicised espousal and the gunboat diplomacy by powerful states that often accompanied it, much as the WTO was intended to displace bilateral trade leverage ...'[219] Both foreign investments and international trade are domains where conflict is latent between market freedom and free flow of capitals, on the one hand, and the state regulatory autonomy to address public policy concerns, on the other.

These similarities explain why dozens of awards have referred to the WTO jurisprudence.[220] However, the substantive impact of the WTO case law on the findings of investment treaty tribunals remains unclear; it is not possible to draw sound or definitive conclusions as the

---

[214] J.A. Fontoura Costa, 'Comparing WTO Panelists and ICSID Arbitrators: The Creation of International Legal Fields', *Oñati Socio-Legal Series Working Paper* 1/4 (2011), 1–25, 16.

[215] On the judicialisation of investment arbitration, see, for example, A. Stone Sweet and F. Grisel, 'The Evolution of International Arbitration: Delegation, Judicialization, Governance', in W. Mattli and T. Dietz (eds), *International Arbitration and Global Governance: Contending Theories and Evidence* (Oxford: Oxford University Press, 2014), 22–46, 23.

[216] J.H.H. Weiler, 'The Rule of Lawyers and the Ethos of Diplomats: Reflections on the Internal and External Legitimacy of WTO Dispute Settlement', *Harvard Jean Monnet Working Paper* 9/00 (2000), 1–18, 2.

[217] The term 'epistemic community' is borrowed from international relations scholarship and indicates 'a network of professionals with recognized expertise and competence in a particular domain and an authoritative claim to policy-relevant knowledge within that domain or issue-area'. See P.M. Haas, 'Introduction: Epistemic Communities and International Policy Coordination', *International Organization* 46 (1992), 1–35, 3.

[218] Fontoura Costa, 'Comparing WTO Panelists and ICSID Arbitrators', 20.

[219] Alvarez, 'Beware: Boundary Crossings', p. 46.

[220] See G. Marceau, V. Lanovoy and A. Izaguerri Vila, 'A Lighthouse in the Storm of Fragmentation', *Journal of World Trade* 47 (2013), 481 (noting that more than 75 investment awards have referred to the WTO jurisprudence).

circumstances under which reference is made to the WTO cases are varied, and these relate to a range of different issues such as the concept of necessity, likeness and others.

Yet, international investment law and international trade law present a number of notable differences. Although the present investment treaty network has been characterised as multilateral in nature, due to the similarities among different treaties and dispute settlement mechanisms,[221] it is still structurally based on a myriad of international investment treaties. There is no world investment organisation charged with governing foreign investments, nor is there a 'World Investment Court'.[222] By contrast, since its inception in 1995, the WTO has emerged as the world forum for multilateral trade negotiations, and the Appellate Body has been frequently analogised to a World Trade Court.[223] The fact that the WTO 'as an organization possesses a separate legal personality under international law from WTO Member States . . . gives the organization the capacity to develop its own . . . "systemic interest" – that is independent from that of WTO Members'.[224]

At the procedural level, while *ad hoc* tribunals settle investment disputes without an appellate review by a permanent body, WTO panel reports can be appealed before the Appellate Body, which can review the relevant legal issues, thus ensuring consistency and predictability. Moreover, foreign investors can pursue investor–state arbitration directly without any intervention of the home state, and they can nominate one of the arbitrators. By contrast, access to the dispute settlement mechanism of the WTO is limited to members of the WTO. This is not to say that, at a substantive level, individuals do not play any role at the WTO; rather, many cases have been brought by states to protect the interests of given industrial sectors.[225] Yet, at a procedural level,

---

[221] See generally S.W. Schill, *The Multilateralization of International Investment Law* (Cambridge: Cambridge University Press, 2009); E. Chalamish, 'The Future of BITs: A De Facto Multilateral Agreement?', *Brooklyn Journal of International Law* 34 (2009), 303 (introducing the concept of multilateral bilateralism).

[222] On the idea of a standing 'World Investment Court' see M. Goldhaber, 'Wanted: A World Investment Court', *Transnational Dispute Management* 3 (2004), 1–5.

[223] C.D. Ehlermann, 'Six Years on the Bench of the World Trade Court – Some Personal Experiences as Member of the Appellate Body of the WTO', *Journal of World Trade* 36 (2002), 605–639.

[224] D. Sarooshi, 'Investment Treaty Arbitration and the World Trade Organization: What Role for Systemic Values in the Resolution of International Economic Disputes?', *Texas International Law Journal* 49 (2014), 445–467, 447.

[225] See, for example, Panel Report, *US–Section 301–310 of the Trade Act of 1974*, WT/DS152/R, adopted 27 January 2000, para. 7.73 (stating that 'it would be entirely wrong to consider that the position of individuals is of no relevance to the GATT/WTO legal matrix. Many of

companies 'depend on their state of nationality taking up a WTO case on their behalf'.[226] The various factors which influence the choice of a WTO member to bring a case against another member state include the magnitude of the impact of the measure in question, political considerations and the lobbying efforts of the relevant industry sectors.[227]

Furthermore, the trade and investment regimes offer different remedies to the aggrieved actors. In order to encourage trade liberalisation and prevent protectionism, the WTO dispute settlement mechanism enables the authorisation of trade retaliation by the injured state.[228] However, this is possible only after a state fails to withdraw or modify an offending measure within a 'reasonable period of time'.[229] The investment regime, on the other hand, provides a monetary remedy or, in some cases, even restoration (*restitutio in integrum*) to foreign investors whose investments have been affected because of government action.[230] Therefore, while remedies at the WTO only have prospective and state-centric character, arbitral tribunals can award damages to foreign investors.[231]

In conclusion, questions remain about the appropriateness and effects of the analogy between international investment law and WTO law. On the one hand, the borders between the legal systems are porous. As mentioned, there are several reasons for juxtaposing the two systems. First, international investment law and international trade law belong to the same branch of international law, namely international economic law. Second, the nature of problems that both systems encounter is similar – that is, arbitral tribunals and WTO adjudicative bodies are often required to review domestic regulation pursuing certain non-economic values against a set of obligations of an economic character (unlike, for instance, other international courts and tribunals). Third, a few WTO agreements touch upon

---

the benefits to Members which are meant to flow as a result of the acceptance of various disciplines under the GATT/WTO depend on the activity of individual economic operators in the national and global market places. The purpose of many of these disciplines, indeed one of the primary objects of the GATT/WTO as a whole, is to produce certain market conditions which would allow this individual activity to flourish').

[226] Sarooshi, 'Investment Treaty Arbitration and the World Trade Organization', 447.

[227] Kurtz, 'The Use and Abuse of WTO Law in Investor–State Arbitration', 757.

[228] Understanding on Rules and Procedures Governing the Settlement of Disputes (DSU), Marrakesh Agreement Establishing the World Trade Organization, Annex 2, 1869 UNTS 401, 33 ILM 1226 (1994), Article 22.

[229] DSU Articles 19–21.

[230] Arbitral tribunals usually refer to the *Chorzów Factory* case. *Case Concerning the Factory at Chorzów*, (Claim for Indemnity) (Jurisdiction), *Germany* v. *Poland*, Judgment, 26 July 1927, 1927 P.C.I.J. (ser. A) No. 9.

[231] Kurtz, 'The Use and Abuse of WTO Law in Investor–State Arbitration', 759.

various aspects of international investment law.[232] Finally, the WTO jurisprudence on a number of issues is well developed as compared to other sections of international law, thus providing rich practical material for comparison.

On the other hand, legal systems reflect the cultures within which they are located and thus have distinctive identities. There are reasons that may speak against comparing the two fields. Due to specific treaty language, actors and procedures, the two regimes require cognisance of their inherent differences. More importantly, analogies between international investment law and WTO law can affect aspects of judicial reasoning. Like other specialised international courts and tribunals, international economic *fora* may have a *Missionsbewusstsein* or 'in-built bias'.[233] They are aware that their mandate is to adjudicate on the eventual violation of relevant trade and investment treaty standards, respectively. While their review of domestic regulations can strengthen the rule of law and good governance, an overly intrusive review may undermine state regulatory autonomy and the pursuit of legitimate public policy goals. In turn, this may fuel the alleged 'legitimacy crisis' of the two international economic law regimes. By nurturing a dialogical interpretation – meaning a general willingness on the part of arbitrators to discuss, analyse and distinguish as well as borrow WTO jurisprudence – arbitrators are in danger of overemphasising economic values vis-à-vis other values. Moreover, there is a risk that arbitral tribunals will misunderstand the WTO acquis, eventually leading to incoherence and inconsistency. By contrast, international economic law should not be perceived as a self-contained system; rather, it should be conceived as a part of general international law.

The *Continental Casualty* case constitutes a paradigmatic example of the double-edged nature of the interplay between international trade law and international investment law.[234] The case arose from measures taken by Argentina in the wake of its economic crisis in 2001–2002. The arbitrators interpreted the US–Argentina BIT's non-precluded measures clause

---

[232] For example, Agreement on Trade-Related Aspects of Intellectual Property Rights, 15 April 1994, Marrakesh Agreement Establishing the World Trade Organization, Annex 1C, 1869 UNTS 299; Agreement on Trade Related Investment Measures, 15 April 1994, Marrakesh Agreement Establishing the World Trade Organization, Annex 1A, 1868 UNTS 186; General Agreement on Trade in Services, 15 April 1994, Marrakesh Agreement Establishing the World Trade Organization, Annex 1B, 1869 UNTS 183.

[233] Y. Shany, 'No Longer a Weak Department of Power? Reflections on the Emergence of a New International Judiciary', *European Journal of International Law* 20 (2009), 73, 81.

[234] *Continental Casualty Company* v. *Argentine Republic*, ICSID Case No. ARB/03/9, Award, 5 September 2008.

by drawing from WTO jurisprudence. 'Non-precluded measures' indicate 'measures necessary for the maintenance of public order' and international peace and security whose adoption is allowed under the relevant BIT.[235] Argentina contended that the term 'necessary' contained in the provision should be interpreted 'in line with the GATT–WTO case-law, under which "necessary" is not synonymous of "indispensable"'.[236] This line of interpretation would have exempted Argentina from liability.

The Tribunal endorsed this view noting that the non-precluded measures provision 'derive[d] from the parallel model clause of the U.S. [Friendship, Commerce and Navigation (FCN)] treaties and these treaties in turn reflect[ed] the formulation of Art. XX of GATT 1947'.[237] Article XX of GATT offers general exceptions from international trade obligations for unilateral trade measures in pursuit of specified purposes, including the protection of public health and the conservation of exhaustible natural resources. The Tribunal also considered that it was 'more appropriate to refer to the GATT and WTO case law which has extensively dealt with the concept and requirements of necessity in the context of economic measures derogating to the obligations contained in GATT, rather than to refer to the requirement of necessity under customary international law'.[238]

The Tribunal held that the non-precluded measures clause should be interpreted as absolving a state from liability and considered that

> the Government's efforts struck an appropriate balance between th[e aim of respecting its international obligations] and the responsibility of any government towards the country's population: it is self-evident that not every sacrifice can properly be imposed on a country's people in order to safeguard a certain policy that would ensure full respect towards international obligations in the financial sphere, before a breach of those obligations can be considered justified as being necessary under this BIT. The standard of reasonableness and proportionality do not require as much.[239]

The award has received mixed reactions. Some scholars criticised it fiercely,[240] contending that not only did the *Continental* Tribunal apply the wrong law, but it also 'g[o]t the borrowed law wrong'.[241] Critics

---

[235] Article XI of the US–Argentina BIT provides: 'This treaty shall not preclude the application by either Party of measures necessary for the maintenance of public order, the fulfilment of its obligations with respect to the maintenance or restoration of international peace or security, or the protection of its own essential security interests.'

[236] *Continental Casualty Company* v. *Argentine Republic*, Award, para. 85.

[237] *Ibid.*, para. 292.   [238] *Ibid.*   [239] *Ibid.*, para. 227.

[240] Alvarez, 'Beware: Boundary Crossings', pp. 23–31.   [241] *Ibid.*, p. 27.

highlight that the balancing test is not included in the text of BIT and does not constitute 'either a rule of customary law or ... a general principle of law'.[242] They also pinpoint that Article XI of the US–Argentina BIT and Article XX of the GATT 'cove[r] ... different subject matter[s]': accordingly, they contend that the proxy for the non-precluded measures is GATT's Article XXI on security exceptions.[243] Moreover, according to Alvarez, 'the WTO has developed its unique interpretation of what a necessary measure entails pursuant to a two-tier process', which includes (1) proving that a measure falls within one of the enumerated exceptions of Article XX (a–j) of the GATT; and (2) proving that the measure is consistent with the requirements of the introductory part or *chapeau* of the same provision.[244] The *chapeau* of Article XX prohibits arbitrary or unjustifiable discrimination in the application of the specific exceptions. Alvarez contends that the *Continental* Tribunal failed to apply the *chapeau* requirements to the balancing test.[245]

Yet, others praised the award because of its 'careful and sophisticated use of WTO exceptions jurisprudence'.[246] In addition to the general exceptions contained in Article XX of the GATT 1994, WTO law also provides for exceptions related to national and international security.[247] Although, at first sight, Article XXI of the GATT seems to provide a better analogue to the non-precluded measures clause, it strictly refers to the maintenance of peace and security. Given the fact that Argentina took measure to protect public order, rather than peace and security, reference to Article XX on general exceptions seems plausible, and even more so if one considers that 'Unlike Article XX, Article XXI has, to date, not played a significant role in the practice of dispute settlement under the GATT 1947 or the WTO.'[248] With regard to the alleged failure to consider the *chapeau* requirements in the interpretation of the non-precluded measures clause, while the word 'necessary' appears in both the non-precluded measures clause and Article XX of the GATT, the *chapeau* requirements qualify the latter provision only. Therefore, importing the *chapeau* requirements into the interpretation of the non-precluded measures clauses was not supported by the relevant BIT. Moreover, the application of the *chapeau* requirements would have favoured the economic interests of the foreign company against the public policy objectives of the host state. In fact, according to some

---

[242] *Ibid.*, p. 23.   [243] *Ibid.*, p. 24.   [244] *Ibid.*, p. 27.   [245] *Ibid.*

[246] Kurtz, 'The Use and Abuse of WTO Law in Investor–State Arbitration', 771.

[247] Article XXI of the GATT 1994.

[248] P. Van den Bossche and W. Zdouc, *The Law and Policy of the World Trade Organization*, 3rd ed., (Cambridge: Cambridge University Press, 2013), p. 595.

WTO law experts, the *chapeau* requirements can affect the line of equilibrium between conflicting economic and non-economic values.[249] Even if one admitted that the analogy between GATT Article XX and Article XI of the US–Argentina BIT is not a perfect match, arguably the process of legal development may be more important than the substance of the transplanted rule.[250] In fact, it might be a case of 'overfitting legal transplant',[251] that is, a transplant which works better in investment law than in international trade law.

The Annulment Committee refused to annul *Continental Casualty* on the ground that the Tribunal erred in its analysis of WTO law as Continental had argued.[252] The Annulment Committee stated that

> the Tribunal was clearly not purporting to apply that body of law, but merely took it into account as relevant to determining the correct interpretation and application of Article XI of the BIT. Even if it could be established by Continental that the Tribunal reached an erroneous interpretation of Article XI of the BIT based on an erroneous understanding of GATT-WTO law, that would amount only to an error of law, which is not a ground of annulment.[253]

The fact that the Annulment Committee did not annul the award on the ground of manifest excess of power does not necessarily mean that the award was perfect. Annulment committees have a level of discretion when deciding whether or not to annul an award.[254] Manifest excess of powers is a ground for annulment under Article 52(1)(b) of the ICSID Convention and 'may ... exist where the tribunal disregards the applicable law or bases the award on a law other than the applicable

---

[249] S. Gaines, 'The WTO's Reading of the GATT Article XX Chapeau: A Disguised Restriction on Environmental Measures', *University of Pennsylvania Journal of International Economic Law* 22 (2001), 739, 742.

[250] R. Peerenboom, 'Toward a Methodology for Successful Legal Transplant', *Chinese Journal of Comparative Law* (2013), 1–17, 16.

[251] M.M. Siems, 'The Curious Case of Overfitting Legal Transplants', in M. Adams and D. Heirbaut (eds.), *The Method and Culture of Comparative Law: Essays in Honour of Mark Van Hoecke* (Oxford: Hart Publishing, 2014), pp. 133–145.

[252] *Continental Casualty Company v. The Argentine Republic*, ICSID Case No. ARB/03/9, Decision on the Application for Partial Annulment of Continental Casualty Company and the Application for Partial Annulment of the Argentine Republic, 16 September 2011, para. 133.

[253] *Ibid.*

[254] *Compañia de Aguas del Aconquija S.A. and Vivendi Universal v. Argentine Republic*, Case No. ARB/97/3, Decision on Annulment, 3 July 2002, para. 66 ('it appears to be established that an *ad hoc* committee has a certain measure of discretion as to whether to annul an award, even if an annullable error is found').

law under Article 42 of the ICSID Convention'.[255] Yet, 'the error must be "manifest", . . . and a misapprehension (still less mere disagreement) as to the content of a particular rule is not enough'.[256]

The interpretation of certain investment treaty provisions including the necessity defence is a battlefield. Norms can be interpreted and applied in different ways. Arbitrators looking at the same set of facts will not necessarily see one thing. Different people can examine the same phenomenon, disagree and yet be right. The Argentinian crisis, the measures adopted by Argentina to cope with the same and their justification under the relevant international investment treaties between Argentina and other countries have given rise to a stream of diverging awards and decisions of annulment committees. The fact that diverging interpretations are plausible is shown by the different scholarly appreciation of these streams. While some criticise the awards that have considered Argentinian measures as justified, others have criticised the awards which have awarded compensation to foreign companies.[257] Argentina is now liable for hundreds millions of dollars in damages. In borrowing WTO law, *Continental Casualty* was not revolutionary, as earlier arbitral tribunals had similarly referred to WTO law; if there was any error, it was not a manifest error of law and it did not result in the annulment of the award. *Continental Casualty* relied on the complex hermeneutics of the WTO and avoided the legal mistakes of earlier arbitral awards which were subsequently annulled by *ad hoc* committees. In conclusion, while WTO law can be a useful source of macro-comparisons, any comparative analysis must be attentive to textual differences.[258]

Human rights law

Human rights law and international investment law are often juxtaposed for both substantive and procedural reasons.[259] At the

---

[255] *Continental Casualty Company* v. *The Argentine Republic*, Decision on the Application for Partial Annulment, para. 86.

[256] *Ibid.*, para. 87.

[257] See, for example, M. Sornarajah, *The International Law on Foreign Investment*, 3rd ed. (Cambridge: Cambridge University Press, 2010), p. 456.

[258] Kurtz, 'The Use and Abuse of WTO Law in Investor–State Arbitration', 755.

[259] See generally U. Kriebaum and C. Schreuer, 'The Concept of Property in Human Rights Law and International Investment Law', in S. Breitenmoser (ed.), *Liber Amicorum Luzius Wildhaber – Human Rights Democracy and the Rule of Law* (Nomos, 2007), pp. 743–762. See also C. Tomuschat, 'The European Court of Human Rights and Investment Protection', in C. Binder, U. Kriebaum, A. Reinisch, S. Wittich (eds.), *International Investment Law for*

substantive level, human rights law and international investment law provide for analogous standards of protection.[260] The following binary standards are available under international investment law and human rights law, respectively: denial of justice and the right to a fair trial; full protection and certain aspects of the rights to privacy, liberty and life; expropriation and right to property; fair and equitable treatment and due process; non-discrimination and the right to equality.[261] At the procedural level, access to investor–state arbitration shares many characteristics of the direct right of action before human rights courts.[262] While states are the traditional subjects of international law, both human rights law and international investment law empower individuals to bring claims against states before the respective international courts and tribunals.

However, international investment law and human rights law have different aims and procedural features.[263] Different institutional cultures and the pursuit of different objectives – economic/utilitarian interests, on the one hand, and basic human rights, on the other – discourage making any broad analogies. Obligations under international investment law are bilateral and reciprocal; obligations under human rights law are *erga omnes*.[264] This does not mean that there may not be some forms of meaningful overlap as economic development can be a factor in human well-being. While human rights instruments have advocated a human rights-sensitive interpretation of international investment agreements,[265] such an approach can have a dual effect. On the one hand, it can enhance a state's right to regulate in the public interest, thus restricting investors' rights. On the other, it can also reinforce the protection of investors' rights. In

---

the 21st Century: Essays in Honour of Christoph Schreuer (Oxford: Oxford University Press, 2009), p. 636.

[260] See Paparinskis, 'Analogies and Other Regimes of International Law', 8.   [261] *Ibid.*

[262] See C. Reiner and C. Schreuer, 'Human Rights and International Investment Arbitration', in P.-M. Dupuy, F.F. and E.-U. Petersmann (eds.), *Human Rights in International Investment Law and Arbitration* (Oxford: Oxford University Press, 2008), pp. 82–96.

[263] M. Hirsch, 'Investment Tribunals and Human Rights: Divergent Paths', in P.-M. Dupuy, F. Francioni and E.-U. Petersmann (eds.), *Human Rights in International Investment Law and Arbitration* (Oxford: Oxford University Press, 2008), pp. 97–114.

[264] See generally E. de Wet and J. Vidmar (eds), *Hierarchy in International Law: The Place of Human Rights* (Oxford: Oxford University Press, 2012).

[265] See, for example, Economic and Social Council, Commission on Human Rights, Sub-commission on the Promotion and Protection of Human Rights, Report of the High Commissioner for Human Rights, Human Rights, Trade and Investment, E/CN.4 /Sub.2/2003/9, 2 July 2003.

fact, a number of regional human rights instruments protect property rights.[266]

The procedural requirements for having access to investment treaty arbitration differ considerably from those for having access to human rights court. For instance, in human rights law, the exhaustion of local remedies is a procedural requirement for the admissibility of a claim. By contrast, in international investment law, the exhaustion of local remedies is required only with regard to denial of justice claims – that is, the claimant cannot invoke denial of justice without prior exhaustion of local remedies.[267] However, the exhaustion of local remedies may not be necessary for other investment treaty claims; rather, it may be precluded by the fork-in-the-road provision. This provision allows the investor to select the desired venue for filing her claim, but precludes subsequent recourse to other dispute settlement mechanisms. For instance, if an investor opts for investment treaty arbitration, she cannot ask for diplomatic protection afterwards. Only if the host state does not comply with the award rendered by the arbitral tribunal can the investor resort to diplomatic protection.[268] Therefore, arbitral tribunals do not merely constitute an additional forum with respect to state courts (as is the case for all international human rights courts), but they are also an alternative to the latter.

Critical assessment

International investment law and arbitration can be seen through different paradigms, including international commercial arbitration,

---

[266] For instance, property rights have been enshrined in the first Protocol of the European Convention on Human Rights (ECHR), the African Charter on Human Rights and Peoples' Rights as well as the American Declaration on the Rights and Duties of Man and the American Human Rights Convention. European Convention for the Protection of Human Rights and Fundamental Freedoms, 4 November 1950, 213 UNTS 222, Article 1.1 of the First Protocol. See also African Charter on Human and Peoples' Rights, 27 June 1981, in force 21 October 1986, OAU Doc. CAB/LEG/67/3 rev. 5, 21 ILM 58 (1982), Article 14; American Declaration on the Rights and Duties of Man, O.A.S. Res. XXX, adopted by the Ninth International Conference of American States (1948), *reprinted in* Basic Documents Pertaining to Human Rights in the Inter-American System, OEA/Ser.L.V/II.82 doc.6 rev.1 at 17 (1992), Article XXIII. American Convention on Human Rights, 22 November 1969, in force 18 July 1978, OAS Treaty Series 36, Article 21.1.

[267] *Loewen Group, Inc. and Raymond L. Loewen* v. *United States of America*, ICSID Case No. ARB(AF)/98/3, Award, 26 June 2003, para. 150.

[268] ICSID Convention, Article 27(1).

public law and public international law as well as two subsets of the latter: human rights law and international trade law. Questions remain as to the exclusivity or complementarity of the application of each of the paradigms. Some authors have developed a hybrid theory of the investment treaty system, contending that international investment law has distinct characteristics which make it a mixed system.[269] According to these authors, even if several paradigms are available, none fits precisely. Accordingly, the interpreter can rely on different approaches. Other scholars have distinct approaches, considering international investment law and arbitration as either a subsystem of public international law; a different type of international commercial arbitration; or a species of public law.

While some argue that one should adopt a case-by-case approach,[270] others suggest that the elaboration of a hybrid theory could lead to consistent outcomes by sketching out when interpreters should look at different paradigms as relevantly similar and when they should distinguish them as relevantly distinct.[271] Supporting the former approach is the fact that practitioners usually deal with a single issue in a single case. States may have multiple, and sometimes conflicting, interests in given disputes, and this plays a role in determining how their interests are presented in a given scenario. However, adopting an issue-by-issue approach runs a risk of fragmenting discourse and may be conducive to unpredictable outcomes. Rather than helping to depoliticise investor–state disputes, *ad hoc* approaches increase the danger of favouring repeat players and repoliticising these disputes. Hybrid theories of international investment law and arbitration appear more objective and systematic. Yet, they risk unnecessarily complicating the already complicated life of practitioners.[272] The risk is that theories that are too abstract become too complex and too difficult to apply, and thus become detached from legal practice.

Far from being a purely theoretical debate, the identification and application of different paradigms highlight the existence of different approaches to concrete problems. Many legal gaps or contentious problems in investment arbitration all involve the same structural

---

[269] See generally A. Roberts, 'Actors and Analogies in International Investment Law', *American Journal of International Law* 107 (2013), 45–94.
[270] See generally Paparinskis, 'Analogies and Other Regimes of International Law'.
[271] See generally Roberts, 'Actors and Analogies in International Investment Law'.
[272] C. Leben, *The Advancement of International Law* (Oxford: Hart Publishing, 2010), p. 56.

issues concerning the relationship between investors' and states' rights. Depending on the selected approach, the resolution of contentious issues – including the admissibility of countermeasures, the effect of waivers and the permissibility of joint termination with immediate effect – will vary.

For instance, the principle of *iura novit curia* (i.e. 'the court knows the law'), which characterises several national and international *fora*, requires the relevant adjudicators to know the applicable law and apply it, eventually disregarding the different rules invoked by the parties. While the London Court of International Arbitration (LCIA) has an express provision for *iura novit curia*,[273] international investment treaties and the ICSID Convention do not specifically provide for this principle. Yet, a few arbitral tribunals and ICSID annulment committees have held that this principle applies to investment treaty arbitration,[274] and scholars have similarly advocated its use in this context.[275]

---

[273] London Court of International Arbitration, LCIA Arbitration Rules, 1 October 2014, Article 22(1)(3).

[274] *Wena Hotels Ltd.* v. *Arab Republic of Egypt*, ICSID Case No. ARB/98/4, Award, 8 December 2000, 41 ILM 846 (2002), (using compound interest to calculate damages, although neither party argued for compound interest); *Compañia de Aguas del Aconquija S.A. and Vivendi Universal* v. *Argentine Republic*, ICSID Case No. ARB/97/3, Decision on Annulment, 3 July 2002, para. 84 (holding that while the line of reasoning of the underlying award 'came as a surprise to the parties, or at least to some of them ... this would by no means be unprecedented in judicial decision-making' and was not a ground for annulment); *Helnan International Hotels A/S* v. *Arab Republic of Egypt*, ICSID Case No. ARB/05/19, Decision of the Ad hoc Committee, 14 June 2010, para. 23 (quoting the reasoning of the *Vivendi* Tribunal); *BP Exploration Co (Libya) Ltd.* v. *The Government of the Libyan Arab Republic*, Award, 10 October 1973, 53 ILR 297 (1979) (finding that an arbitral tribunal is 'both entitled and compelled to undertake an independent examination of the legal issues deemed relevant by it, and to engage in considerable legal research going beyond the confines of the materials relied upon by the Claimant'). The principle *iura novit curia* is not unlimited. See, for example, *Maritime International Nominees Establishment (MINE)* v. *Government of Guinea*, ICSID Case No. ARB/84/4, Decision of the Annulment Committee, 14 December 1989, para. 6.38 (stating that an arbitral tribunal cannot apply legal authorities outside the law applicable to the dispute); *Mr. Patrick Mitchell* v. *Democratic Republic of Congo*, ICSID Case No. ARB/99/7, Decision on the Application for Annulment, 1 November 2006, para. 57 (holding that the Tribunal was 'not, strictly speaking, subject to any obligation to apply a rule of law that has not been adduced; this is but an option ... '); *CME Czech Republic B.V.* v. *Czech Republic*, Final Award, 14 March 2003, para. 411 (stating that it was not 'bound to research, find and apply national law which has not been argued or referred to by the parties ... ').

[275] Schill, 'Crafting the International Economic Order: The Public Function of Investment Treaty Arbitration and Its Significance for the Role of Arbitrator', 422.

Clearly, *iura novit curia* has nothing to do with adjudication according to principles of equity (*ex aequo et bono*). *Iura novit curia* entails that the adjudicator know and apply the law rather than referring to principles of equity. *Iura novit curia* can also be distinguished by the requirement of *nec ultra petita*, which forbids the adjudicator from adjudicating matters that have not been brought to the attention of the court and on which the court does not have jurisdiction.[276] Rather, *iura novit curia* refers to the application of law: for instance, if the parties offer incomplete argumentation concerning the fair and equitable treatment, by referring to a given line of reasoning without referring to another, the arbitral tribunal is not bound to limit itself to the incomplete analysis of the investment treaty standard offered by the parties.

If investment treaty arbitration is analogised to commercial arbitration, then *iura novit curia* should not apply. In commercial arbitration, arbitrators generally consider only the legal arguments expressly made by the parties (*secundum alligata et probata*) and refrain from the principle *iura novit curia*. Therefore, the application of any building block of norms would ultimately rely upon the will of the parties. Commercial arbitrators cannot render awards based on authorities other than those pleaded by the parties. The principle *nec ultra fines mandati* requires the arbitral tribunal to limit itself to the scope of power allowed. The violation of its mandate by the arbitral tribunal is widely recognised as a cause for the annulment of the international arbitral award.[277]

On the other hand, if one analogises investment treaty arbitration to a(n) (international) public law adjudication, then *iura novit curia* should apply. *Iura novit curia* is a concept that applies in public (international) law. National judges know the applicable law and apply it. International adjudicators take public international law into account according to customary rules of treaty interpretation which *inter alia* require

---

[276] *Klöckner* v. *Cameroon*, ICSID Case No. ARB/81/2, Decision of the Annulment Committee, 3 May 1985, 1 *ICSID Review-Foreign Investment Law Journal* 89 (1986), para. 59 (stating that an ICSID Tribunal cannot 'by formulating its own theory and argument ... go beyond the legal framework established by the claimant and the respondent', for instance, by arbitrating the case 'on the basis of tort while the pleas of the parties were based on contract').

[277] The recognition or enforcement of an award shall be refused under the New York Convention, Article V.1(c) if the award contains decisions on matters beyond the scope of submission to arbitration.

systematic interpretation.[278] Systematic interpretation is characterised by recourse to the context of a given treaty in order to establish the meaning of treaty provisions.[279]

The acceptance of *iura novit curia* in investment arbitration also relates to the role that arbitrators should play in the proceedings. In international commercial arbitration, arbitrators have been regarded as an expression of the parties' autonomy or as private adjudicators of the parties' dispute. The contractual view of the arbitrator as someone who is chosen by two disputing parties to decide the matter stresses the personal basis (*intuitus personae*) which accompanies the choice of the arbitrator and the contractual relationship between the parties and the arbitral body.[280] This view is well suited to international commercial arbitration, which involves international commercial transactions. In this particular context, arbitrators apply the law which is chosen by the parties and consider the legal arguments expressly made by them (*secundum alligata et probata*).

However, investment treaty arbitration differs from international commercial arbitration, as it often involves matters of public law. Furthermore, while the competence for settling commercial disputes arises from an arbitral clause, the competence for settling investment treaty disputes does not merely arise from a contract clause between the foreign investor and the host state, but from treaty text. Arbitrators can be perceived as agents of multiple principals:[281] that is, agents of the investor, the home state, the host state and, in broader terms, the international community as a whole. As Stone Sweet and Grisel point out, 'if the arbitrator is not merely the agent of two contracting principals, but an agent of the greater community, then ... the arbitrator has a responsibility to take into account the community's

---

[278] D. French, 'Treaty Interpretation and the Incorporation of Extraneous Legal Rules', *International & Comparative Law Quarterly* 55 (2006), 281–314; P. Sands, 'Searching for Balance: Concluding Remarks', *New York University Environmental Law Journal* 11 (2002), 198, at 202 (arguing 'those charged with interpreting and applying treaties on the protection of foreign investment need to take into account the values that are reflected in norms that have arisen outside the context of the investment treaty which they are applying').

[279] A. Szpak, 'A Few Reflections on the Interpretation of Treaties in Public International Law', *Hague Yearbook of International Law* 18 (2005), 59–70, 66.

[280] See Y. Jianlong, 'Arbitrators: Private Judges, Service Providers or Both? CIETAC's Perspective', *Stockholm International Arbitration Review* 1 (2007), 9.

[281] See J. Trachtman, *The Economic Structure of International Law* (Cambridge MA: Harvard University Press, 2008), p. 208.

interests in decisions'.[282] The different function and nature of investment treaty arbitration would thus require arbitrators to play a different role, in which arbitrators are assimilated to international 'judges' and have to settle international disputes 'in conformity with principles of justice and international law'.[283] For instance, the ad hoc annulment committee in *RSM Production Corporation* v. *Grenada*[284] held that it had *iura novit curia* powers relying on ICJ decisions.[285] Scholars have also argued that arbitral tribunals have a *iura novit curia* obligation.[286]

In light of the above, the best analogue for investment treaty arbitration is that of public international law. Treaty-makers have shaped the system drawing inspiration from pre-existing systems. Like almost every subsystem of international law, international investment law is a mixture of various norms. This does not mean that international investment law is a self-contained regime. Rather, it is a porous system that borrows from and contributes to other subsystems of public international law thus contributing to the development of the latter. Adopting a public international law paradigm does not entail the complete irrelevance of domestic law.

---

[282] A. Stone Sweet and F. Grisel, 'Transnational Investment Arbitration: From Delegation to Constitutionalization?', in P.M. Dupuy, F. Francioni and E.U. Petersmann (eds.), *Human Rights in International Investment Law and Arbitration* (Oxford: Oxford University Press, 2009), pp. 118–136, p. 125.

[283] VCLT, Preamble.

[284] *RSM Production Corporation* v. *Grenada*, ICSID Case No. ARB/05/14, Decision on RSM Production Corporation's Application for a Preliminary Ruling, 29 October 2009, Decision of the Ad Hoc Annulment Committee, para. 23 (stating that 'Although not cited by the Applicant or the Respondent, there are a number of other arbitral decisions which deal with the power of international courts and tribunals to reopen a case for newly discovered evidence. On the basis of the principle of *jura novit curia*, the Committee is able to consider the relevance of those decisions').

[285] *Fisheries Jurisdiction Case (United Kingdom* v. *Iceland)*, Merits, Judgment of 25 July 1974, [1974] *ICJ Reports* 3, 9 (holding that 'the Court . . . as an international judicial organ, is deemed to take judicial notice of international law, and is therefore required . . . to consider on its own initiative all rules of international law which may be relevant to the settlement of the dispute'), and Case Concerning the *Military and Paramilitary Activities in and against Nicaragua, (Nicaragua* v. *United States of America)*, Merits, Judgment of 27 June 1986 [1986] *ICJ Reports* 14, 24–25 (referring to the 1927 *Lotus* case, adjudicated by the PCIJ, and stating that it was bound to apply *iura novit curia* to establish its jurisdiction).

[286] J. Paulsson, 'International Arbitration and the Generation of Legal Norms: Treaty Arbitration and International Law', *ICCA Congress Series No. 13* (Kluwer, 2007), p. 879.

National law plays an important role in the coalescence of customary international law and general principles of law. Therefore, the public international law paradigm is not detached from a public law approach as it could seem at first glance. In conclusion, the public international law paradigm seems to provide a more consistent explanation for why international investment law and arbitration is the way it is.

Conclusions

International investment law is 'a site for an ongoing and perhaps unresolvable contest of values and interests'.[287] This chapter examined and critically assessed the main sources of analogy for international investment law and arbitration. Each of the mentioned paradigms has a plausible claim to being the most appropriate source for macro-analogy, and each macro-comparison comes with its own distinct logic. The interplay between international investment law and each of the mentioned systems – commercial arbitration, public law and public international law – is complex and multidimensional in that there is potential for mutual cross-fertilisation and cross-judging in such scenarios. However, the selection of the relevant macro-analogy is not neutral and can lead to significantly different results.

These conceptualisations of investment treaty arbitration all have merits and weaknesses and may diverge and converge on specific aspects. Most notably, none of them – but perhaps the international law paradigm due to its comprehensive nature – fully encapsulates the complex phenomenon of investor–state arbitration. These paradigms are not normative; rather, they are descriptive in nature and reflect and emphasise certain aspects of investment treaty arbitration rather than others. While investment treaty arbitration is a relatively recent phenomenon and remains undertheorised, awareness of the existence of different paradigms promotes a better understanding and functioning of the same.

The public international law paradigm constitutes the best source of analogy because international investment arbitration is a creature of, and remains rooted in, public international law. ICSID is based on an

---

[287] Mills, 'Antinomies of Public and Private at the Foundations of International Investment Law and Arbitration', 476.

international treaty and has an international outlook.[288] If there is no agreement between the parties as to the applicable law, ICSID tribunals are to apply 'such rules of international law as may be applicable'.[289] At the same time, it is recognised that other paradigms can be analytically useful and/or complementary. For instance, adopting a public law analysis can help detect the crystallisation of general principles of law and customary law, which are two of the sources of public international law.

---

[288] C. Leben, 'La responsabilité internationale de l'Etat sur le fondement des Traités de promotion et de protection des investissements', *Annuaire Français de Droit International* 50 (2004), 708 (referring to a 'logique internationaliste').

[289] ICSID Convention, Article 42(1).

6

Comparative reasoning in international investment law and arbitration

Challenges and prospects

As long as we understand foreign places as like or unlike home, we cannot begin to fully appreciate them, or ourselves.[1]

Introduction

A conceptual fluidity exists between different legal systems. International investment law and arbitration is not a 'self-contained regime';[2] rather, it has increasingly contributed to the marketplace of ideas importing and exporting a wide range of concepts. In turn, a tension exists between the openness to various inputs from other systems and the autonomy and/or integrity of the importing system.

If used properly, comparative reasoning can offer concrete solutions to interpretative dilemmas and promote consistency within the investment treaty system and, more broadly, within international law. More importantly, the alignment of international investment law with other branches of international law can foster fruitful dialectics: not only do arbitral tribunals import legal concepts, but they also export such items as other

---

[1] G. Frankenberg, 'Critical Comparisons: Re-thinking Comparative Law', *Harvard International Law Journal* 26 (1985), 411–412.

[2] See *Asian Agricultural Products Ltd* v. *Sri Lanka* (*AAPL* v. *Sri Lanka*), ICSID Case ARB/87/3, Award, 27 June 1990, 4 *ICSID Reports* 245 (1997), para. 21 (stating that 'International investment law is "not a self-contained closed legal system" but has to be "envisaged within a wider juridical context in which rules from other sources are integrated through implied incorporation methods, or by direct reference to certain supplementary rules whether of international law character or of domestic law nature"'). The term 'self-contained regime' was first used by the PCIJ in the *Wimbledon* case to determine the relationship between conflicting treaty provisions. *Case of the SS. Wimbledon* (*United Kingdom, France, Italy and Japan* v. *Germany*), Judgment, 17 August 1923, *PCIJ Reports* Series A No. 1. The ICJ used the expression in a different context. *Case Concerning United States Diplomatic and Consular Staff in Tehran* (*United States of America* v. *Iran*), Judgment of 24 May 1980, *ICJ Reports* 1980, p. 3, at para. 86.

courts and tribunals do refer to the jurisprudence of arbitral tribunals. In this manner, international investment arbitration is contributing to the development of international law. Analogies can promote the unity and coherence of international law. Moreover, comparative reasoning can 'increase understanding among peoples and foster the peaceful coexistence of nations'.[3]

If used properly, comparative reasoning can benefit investment treaty arbitration, acting as a legitimising force and facilitating the consideration of the commonweal in the same. Comparative reasoning can help adjudicators in interpreting and applying broad and open-ended investment treaty provisions, facilitating the consideration of the commonweal and contributing to the humanisation of international investment law. Analogies play an important role in and can have a positive impact on shaping the investment law system, promoting awareness of some important values characterising international law, including the equality of states, human rights, human dignity and others. In this regard, a sound circulation of legal models can promote the humanisation of international investment law and the achievement of equilibrium between the promotion of foreign direct investments and the protection of other fundamental interests and values.

However, a more critical approach to the use of comparisons in investment treaty arbitration is needed. Methodology matters; comparative methods are necessary for moving beyond mere juxtaposition and achieving 'genuine, creative recomposition through the search for a synthesis of, or equilibrium between, diverse elements or diverse systems'.[4] According to Delmas-Marty, 'the comparative method has the potential to promote a more pluralist, universal conception of international . . . law, that would neither lead to relativism, nor be based on legal imperialism'.[5]

This chapter proceeds as follows. First, it illustrates the merit of using analogies in international investment law and arbitration, focusing on the coalescence of general principles of law. Second, the chapter considers the perils of analogical reasoning. Third, it explains why a public international law paradigm should be preferred. Fourth, it examines what comparative lawyers and international investment lawyers can

---

[3] R. Sacco, 'Legal Formants: A Dynamic Approach to Comparative Law', *American Journal of Comparative Law* 39 (1991), 1–34, 2.

[4] M. Delmas-Marty, 'The Contribution of Comparative Law to a Pluralist Conception of International Criminal Law', *Journal of International Criminal Justice* 1 (2003), 13–25, 18.

[5] *Ibid.*, at 13.

learn from each other. Fifth, this chapter illustrates what the comparative methods do and how they should be used. Finally, the conclusions will sum up the key findings of the study.

The merit of using analogies in international investment law and arbitration

Analogies are useful means of interpreting and applying vague provisions to ensure consistency among the various subsets of international law. Like other international courts and tribunals, arbitral tribunals are expected to interpret and apply the applicable law. They 'cannot legislate'[6] or render judgment *sub specie legis ferendae*, anticipating the law before the legislator has laid it down.[7] Therefore, interpretation is a fundamental part of the implementing process of international law, as 'only in practice does law come to life'.[8]

However, like other international courts and tribunals, arbitral tribunals also contribute to the development of international law.[9] Whatever the conception of the adjudicative function that arbitrators adopt, it is generally accepted that adjudicators are neither mere *bouche de la loi*, nor authentic lawmakers.[10] As 'agents of legal development',[11] arbitrators have a *maieutic* role, as they identify the applicable rules, clarify their meaning and relate them to the specific facts of the case. According to the International Law Commission, 'the interpretation of documents is to some extent an art, not an exact science'.[12]

---

[6] *Legality of the Threat or Use of Nuclear Weapons*, Advisory Opinion, 8 July 1996, *ICJ Reports* 226, para. 18.

[7] *Fisheries Jurisdiction (Great Britain and Northern Ireland v. Iceland)*, Judgment on the Merits, 25 July 1974, *ICJ Reports* 3, para. 53.

[8] I. Venzke, 'The Role of International Courts as Interpreters and Developers of the Law: Working Out the Jurisgenerative Practice of Interpretation', *Loyola of Los Angeles International and Comparative Law Review* 34 (2011), 99–131, 117.

[9] H. Lauterpacht, *The Development of International Law by the International Court* (London: Stevens & Sons Limited, 1958), p. 42.

[10] See E.-U. Petersmann, 'Introduction and Summary: "Administration of Justice" in International Investment Law and Adjudication?', in P.M. Dupuy, F. Francioni and E.-U. Petersmann (eds.), *Human Rights in International Investment Law and Arbitration* (Oxford: Oxford University Press, 2009), pp. 9–11.

[11] Lauterpacht, *The Development of International Law by the International Court of Justice*, p. 5 (defining international tribunals as 'agencies for the development of international law').

[12] International Law Commission, *Draft Articles on the Law of Treaties: Text as Finally Adopted by the Commission on 18 July 1966*, 2 *Yearbook of the International Law Commission* 218, UN Doc. A/CN.4/190.

Customary rules of treaty interpretation, as restated in the Vienna Convention on the Law of Treaties (VCLT),[13] provide the adjudicators with the necessary conceptual and legal framework to perform their function to settle disputes 'in conformity with the principles of justice and international law'.[14] Customary rules of treaty interpretation are applicable to investment treaties because investment treaties are international law treaties. Furthermore, some investment treaties expressly mention these rules.[15] According to the *general rule of interpretation*, which comprises several subnorms, 'a treaty shall be interpreted in good faith in accordance with the ordinary meaning to be given to the terms of the treaty in their context and in the light of its object and purpose'.[16] As a technique of judicial interpretation, analogies allow adjudicators to broaden their vision and increase the coherence of the system. Reference to other cases of other international courts and tribunals can increase the perceived legitimacy of the system. By cross-pollinating concepts, analogical reasoning can help find the best solutions to common analytical issues.

Where the applicable law is silent on a given issue, arbitrators should fill the gap by using general principles of law. Arbitrators do not create law by using general principles: rather they bring *latent* rules of law to light.[17] For instance, in *SPP* v. *Egypt*, the Tribunal held that even if the applicable law was Egyptian law as the law selected by the parties, this did not exclude the application of general principles of law in order to fill any gap in the domestic law.[18] As Egyptian law did not include any rule for determining the time from which to calculate interest, the tribunal referred to general principles of (international) law.

Some scholars criticised this approach, suggesting that general principles of (national) law should have been used, before resorting to general

---

[13] Vienna Convention on the Law of Treaties, adopted 23 May 1969, in force 27 January 1980, 1155 UNTS 331 (VCLT).

[14] VCLT Preamble.

[15] See, for example, Australia–United States Free Trade Agreement, Article 21.9(2), 18 May 2004, 118 Stat. 919.

[16] VCLT, Article 31(1).

[17] See B. Cheng, *General Principles of Law as Applied by International Courts and Tribunals* (Cambridge: Cambridge University Press, 1953), p. 25.

[18] *Southern Pacific Properties (Middle East) Limited* v. *Arab Republic of Egypt* (*SPP* v. *Egypt*), ICSID Case No. ARB/84/3, Award on the Merits, 20 May 1992, reprinted in *ICSID Review–Foreign Investment Law Journal* 8 (1993), 328. For commentary see G. Delaume, 'The Pyramids Stand – The Pharaohs Can Rest in Peace', *ICSID Review–Foreign Investment Law Journal* 8 (1993), 231.

principles of international law.[19] Yet, one could argue that general principles of international law either encapsulate general principles of (national) law, or, if there is incompatibility, prevail over the latter.[20] On the one hand, general principles of international law are 'rules of law on which the legal systems of [all] states are based'[21] and include 'the norms common to the different legislation of the world'.[22] On the other hand, arbitral awards have acknowledged the precedence of general principles of international law over national rules that might be incompatible with them.[23] In other words, not only can general principles of law complement domestic law, but they can also supplant those rules which conflict with international standards.

Analogies and the coalescence of general principles of law

General principles of law have played a key role in the development of international investment law.[24] General principles of law are one of the sources of international law and fill the gaps left open by customary and treaty law to avoid *non liquet* rulings by international arbitrators.[25] General principles of law also help adjudicators interpret

---

[19] E. Gaillard, 'Use of General Principles of International Law in International Long-Term Contracts', *International Business Lawyer* (1999), 214–224, 220.

[20] *SPP* v. *Egypt*, Award on the Merits, para. 84 (stating that 'when ... international law is violated by the exclusive application of municipal law, the Tribunal is bound ... to apply directly the relevant principles and rules of international law ... [S]uch a process will not involve the confirmation or denial of the validity of the host State's law, but may result in not applying it where that law or action taken under that law violates international law').

[21] *Inceysa Vallisolitana* v. *El Salvador*, ICSID Case No. ARB/03/26, Award, 2 August 2006, para. 227.

[22] *North Sea Continental Shelf (West Germany* v. *Denmark; West Germany* v. *Netherlands)*, Separate Opinion Judge Ammoun, 20 February 1969, 1969 *ICJ Reports* 101, 134 (noting that general principles include 'the norms common to the different legislations of the world, united by the identity of the legal reason therefore, or the *ratio legis*, transposed from the internal legal system to the international legal system').

[23] *Wena Hotels Ltd.* v. *Arab Republic of Egypt*, ICSID Case No. ARB/98/4, Decision on Application for Annulment, 5 February 2002, paras. 40–44, 41 ILM 933 (2002); *Amco* v. *Republic of Indonesia*, ICSID Case No. ARB/81/1, Award, 20 November 1984, para. 40, ICSID Reports 1 (1993) 413 (stating that 'applicable host state laws ... must be checked against international laws, which will prevail in case of conflict').

[24] See generally C. Tams, 'The Sources of International Investment Law', in T. Gazzini and E. De Brabandere (eds.), *International Investment Law: The Sources of Rights and Obligations* (Leiden: Brill, 2012), pp. 319–332.

[25] See, for example, P. Weil, '"The Court Cannot Conclude Definitely ... " *Non Liquet* Revised', *Columbia Journal of Transnational Law* 36 (1997), 109–119 at 110 (stating that

the various sources of international (investment) law, giving concrete meaning to vague provisions and strengthening the reasoning of tribunals 'in conformity with international law'.[26] Some BITs even include express reference to general principles of law for defining treaty standards.[27]

Moreover, the parties may select general principles of law as the applicable law to avoid the law of the host state and to 'mercantilise' investment contracts.[28] Some principles originate in international law, others derive from domestic law, from which they are distilled on a comparative basis. The parties can also select regional principles of law – that is, those principles which are common to a given geographical area – as the law governing the contract. The practice varies: some parties select general principles applicable in a given area (i.e. the European Union) or a particular state and, failing that, general principles of law.[29] For instance, the parties to the *Eurotunnel* case selected 'the principles common to English and French law' and, failing that, 'the principles of international commercial law as they have been applied by national and international tribunals' to govern their contractual relationship.[30] Analogously, in an International Chamber of Commerce (ICC) case, the Arbitral Tribunal applied 'the principles common to the laws of the Arab Republic of Egypt and the United States of America'.[31]

Yet, general principles of law present some structural problems, including the difficulty of determining the content of such rules with any precision. By definition, general principles of *international* law do not indicate purely *national* principles of law or *foreign* principles of

---

'the view prevailing among writers is that there is no room for *non liquet* in international adjudication because there are no *lacunae* in international law').

[26] *Total v. Argentina*, ICSID Case No. ARB/04/1, Decision on Liability, 27 December 2010, at para. 126 (stating that a tribunal should not consider just the BIT 'in isolation or the case law of other arbitral tribunals in investment disputes interpreting and applying similarly worded investment protection treaties, but rather to the content of international law more generally').

[27] See, for example, Article 5(2)(a) of the 2012 US Model BIT (stating that '"fair and equitable treatment" includes the obligation not to deny justice in criminal, civil, or administrative adjudicatory proceedings in accordance with the principle of due process embodied in the principal legal systems of the world . . .').

[28] See Gaillard, 'Use of General Principles of International Law in International Long-Term Contracts', 214–224; B. Goldman, 'The Applicable Law: General Principles of Law – The Lex Mercatoria', in J.D. Lew (ed.), *Contemporary Problems in International Arbitration* (London: Centre for Commercial Law Studies, 1986), p. 113.

[29] Gaillard, 'Use of General Principles of International Law in International Long-Term Contracts', 216.

[30] *Ibid.*, at 215.   [31] ICC case no. 5163.

law.[32] The content of *general* principles can only be ascertained through 'extensive comparative analysis'.[33] Comparative reasoning constitutes 'a fundamental source of general principles of law', examining whether national laws converge on a given issue and thus reflect a general rule.[34] However, there is no single method that can be applied to detect general principles of law.

In order to ascertain the existence of general principles of law, no unanimous or universal acceptance of a rule amongst various legal systems is needed. For instance, in the *South West Africa Cases*, the ICJ rejected the criterion of 'universal acceptance'.[35] Rather, when the ICJ refers to general principles of law, it adopts a pragmatic approach and seems satisfied with a coincidence of opinion amongst its judges. According to Bassiouni, this method seems to grant 'sufficient safeguards', as the judges of the ICJ 'hav[e] been elected so as to ensure "the representation of the main forms of civilization and the principal legal systems of the world" ...'[36] Can this pragmatic approach be applied to international investment law? How have arbitral tribunals ascertained general principles of law?

Arbitral tribunals have addressed these key issues in several awards. No quantitative test for determining whether a particular legal principle is a general principle of law has ever been set up. Rather, a general acceptance of the rule will suffice. For instance, in *Total v. Argentina*,[37] the Arbitral Tribunal acknowledged that reference to 'most legal systems' is sufficient to determine the meaning of given treaty provisions.[38]

What legal systems should be considered? In addition to the legal system of the host country (i.e. the country where the investment takes place), other systems will need to be considered too.[39] Comparative legal

---

[32] Giorgio Del Vecchio, *Sui principi generali del diritto* (Milano: Giuffré, 1958), p. 70.

[33] Gaillard, 'Use of General Principles of International Law in International Long-Term Contracts', 215.

[34] *Ibid.*, at 216.

[35] In his dissenting opinion on other grounds, Judge Tanaka explained that '[t]he recognition of a principle by civilized nations ... does not mean recognition by all civilized nations ...' *South West Africa Cases (Ethiopia v. South Africa; Liberia v. South Africa)*, Judgment, 18 July 1966, *ICJ Reports* 4 (1966) 299, (Judge Tanaka, dissenting).

[36] M.C. Bassiouni, 'A Functional Approach to "General Principles of International Law"', *Michigan Journal of International Law* 11 (1990), 768–818, 783 (referring to Article 9 of the ICJ Statute).

[37] *Total v. Argentina*, ICSID Case No. ARB/04/1, Decision on Liability, 27 December 2010.

[38] *Ibid.*, para. 112.

[39] For instance, in the *North Sea Continental Shelf* case, Judge Lachs, in his dissenting opinion, stated that '[t]he evidence should be sought in the behaviour of a great number of States, possibly the majority of States, in any case the great majority of the interested

research techniques demand the consideration of 'representative states among the world's major legal systems'.[40] In *Total v. Argentina*,[41] the Tribunal considered the fair and equitable treatment standard as deriving from the requirement of good faith, 'which is ... a general principle of law under Article 38(1) of the Statute of the International Court of Justice'.[42] It then conducted 'a comparative analysis of what is considered generally fair or unfair conduct by domestic public authorities in respect of private firms and investors in domestic law' in order 'to identify the legal standards under BITs'.[43] The Tribunal noted that 'the scope and legal basis of the principle varies', but found that 'it has been recognized ... both in civil law and in common law jurisdictions ...'[44] The Tribunal started with the analysis of the legal system of the host state, *in casu* Argentina, because 'factually, the situations and conduct to be evaluated under a BIT occur within the legal system and social, economic and business environment of the host State'.[45] After referring to the law of the host country, German law,[46] and the English common law,[47] the Tribunal examined other regional and international systems,[48] including European human rights law[49] and European Union law. In this regard, the Tribunal stated that

> From a comparative law perspective, the tenets of the legal system of the European Community (now European Union), reflecting the legal traditions of twenty-seven European countries, both civil and common law (including France, the home country of the Claimant) are of relevance, especially since the recognition of the principle of legitimate expectations there has been explicitly based on the international law principle of good faith.[50]

The Tribunal also considered as '[a]dditional criteria for the evaluation of the fairness of national measures of general application as to services' those found in the WTO General Agreement on Trade of Services (GATS).[51] The requirements found in Article VI GATS were considered

---

States'). See *North Sea Continental Shelf* (*West Germany* v. *Denmark; West Germany* v. *Netherlands*), Judgment, 20 February 1969, *ICJ Reports* 101 (1969), 229 (Judge Lachs, dissenting).

[40] Bassiouni, 'Functional Approach to "General Principles"', 789.

[41] *Total* v. *Argentina*, Decision on Liability, para. 111 (internal reference omitted).

[42] *Ibid.*, para. 111.   [43] *Ibid.*, para. 111.   [44] *Ibid.* para. 128.   [45] *Ibid.*

[46] *Ibid.* (stating that 'The concept is considered to have originated in German law where it is extensively used ...').

[47] *Ibid.* (citing a number of cases).   [48] *Ibid.*, para. 127.   [49] *Ibid.*, para. 129.

[50] *Ibid.*, para. 130.   [51] *Ibid.*, para. 124.

'just as "guidance" because it had not been submitted that the GATS [wa]s directly applicable here'.[52]

Analogously, in *Mobil* v. *Venezuela*,[53] in considering the law applicable to abuse of right,[54] the Tribunal observed that 'in all systems of law, whether domestic or international, there are concepts framed in order to avoid misuse of the law'.[55] It then referred to these various concepts and the way they are embedded in public international law, considering rulings of the Permanent Court of International Justice,[56] the ICJ, the Appellate Body of the WTO, ICSID tribunals[57] and the European Court of Justice,[58] as well as different subsets of international law such as the law of the sea, the law of international organisations and European Union law.[59]

International treaties on a particular subject matter also constitute an '[a]uthoritative source of general principles of international law'.[60] The fact that a certain number of states have adopted a rule by signing or ratifying a treaty in which that rule is contained is a clear indicator of the international recognition of such rule'.[61] For instance in *Mobil* v. *Venezuela*, the Tribunal noted the fact that the VCLT mentions the principle of good faith immediately after defining it as a general principle of law.[62]

Scholarly writings are also a useful evidentiary source of general principles of law. Arbitral tribunals refer to monographs and articles to detect general principles of law. For instance, in *Mobil* v. *Venezuela*, reference is made to Hersch Lauterpacht's *Development of International Law by the International Court*[63] to attest the use of the concept of abuse of right in international law.[64] Finally, arbitral tribunals also refer to previous awards and decisions by other international courts and tribunals.

Analogies, legal transplants and their perils

Arbitral tribunals are not consistent across cases in applying comparative methods. While some tribunals have undertaken thorough comparative

---

[52] *Ibid.*

[53] *Mobil* v. *Venezuela*, ICSID Case No. ARB 07/27, Decision on Jurisdiction, 19 June 2010, paras. 169 et seq.

[54] *Ibid.*, para. 168. [55] *Ibid.*, para. 169. [56] *Ibid.*, paras. 173–174. [57] *Ibid.*, para. 170.

[58] *Ibid.*, para. 175. [59] *Ibid.*, para. 171.

[60] Gaillard, 'Use of General Principles of International Law in International Long-Term Contracts', 216.

[61] *Ibid.* [62] *Mobil* v. *Venezuela*, Decision on Jurisdiction, para. 170.

[63] Lauterpacht, *Development of International Law by the International Court.*

[64] *Mobil* v. *Venezuela*, Decision on Jurisdiction, para. 172.

analyses,[65] others have been criticised for carrying out comparisons in a superficial and incomplete manner.[66] In some instances, rather than undertaking a thorough comparative assessment, arbitral tribunals merely refer to the presence or absence of consensus at the international and domestic law levels. In other cases, arbitral tribunals do not clarify why specific sources of comparisons are selected as a default system of reference and which facts provided the basis for their conclusions.[67]

The perils of approximate comparative reasoning and 'the impact of the potential wrong implementation of various legal methodologies' in investment arbitration should not be underestimated; where the risk of incorrect awards is high, 'the legitimacy of the regime is put in doubt, even to the point that withdrawal from particular treaties may be contemplated'.[68] What are the perils of analogies and legal transplants?

First, comparisons are not neutral; rather, the selection of the comparators (*elementa comparationis*) can change the outcome of a given case. To counter the hazard of repoliticising investment disputes, textual differences should be taken into account to prevent arbitral activism and/or free decision-making.

Second, reference to national law must be done with care. Unless the domestic law is the applicable law, or is evidence of customary law and/or general principles of law, reference to it may dilute the international law obligations of states.

Third, when arbitrators refer to the jurisprudence of foreign countries (other than the host state and the home state of the foreign investor), they should briefly explain why and how a given domestic/regional or international experience is selected,[69] eventually referring to scholarly writings. Reference to the case law of other countries may be problematic because of extraterritoriality, legitimacy and/or democracy concerns, as

---

[65] See e.g. *Total* v. *Argentina*, Decision on Liability, para. 111 ff.

[66] See e.g. *Klöckner* v. *Cameroon*, Decision on Annulment, 16 May 1986, 1 *ICSID Reports* 515 (noting that '[The Tribunal's] reasoning [is] limited to postulating and not demonstrating the existence of a principle . . .').

[67] See e.g. *Petroleum Development Ltd.* v. *Sheikh of Abu Dhabi*, International Law Reports 18 (1951), 144, 149–150 (no. 37) (Lord Asquith of Bishoptone, Umpire) (referring to features of 'ecumenical validity' of the English common law).

[68] R. Howse and E. Chalamish, 'The Use and Abuse of WTO Law in Investor–State Arbitration: A Reply to Jürgen Kurtz', *European Journal of International Law* 20 (2009), 1087–1094, 1088.

[69] Frankenberg, 'Critical Comparisons', at 432.

foreign case law does not reflect the will of the people of the host country. Furthermore, the economic, social and cultural conditions of the host country may differ from those of the source country. The risk is that the comparative endeavour leads the investment lawyer to 'the ever-present and idealized home system'.[70] All comparative studies are 'laden with concepts, values and visions' derived from the comparativists' legal culture and experience.[71] There is a risk that the investment lawyer assumes his or her own system as the best paradigm and constructs relevant inquiries on the basis of that system leading to hegemonic or imperialist thinking, potentially fostering North–South critiques and repoliticising investment disputes. Yet, by juxtaposing and/or comparing rules and theories of different systems, investment lawyers can distil the general principles of law.[72]

Finally, in determining which foreign cases to refer to, arbitrators should not 'giv[e] precedence to their personal knowledge (*i.e.*, knowledge of their own or similar legal systems) and otherwise limit their research to data which is immediately available ... in a language that they understand'.[73] Any attempt to mechanically borrow national legal elements should be avoided; rather, comparative methods should lead to the 'gradual decanting of national ... concepts and rules into the international receptacle'.[74]

The most powerful critique to analogic thinking is the argument that law is a manifestation of a given culture and therefore any analogy is bound to fail due to the different contexts involved. Each nation adopts laws that are best suited to its specificities; 'the spirit of the law' varies according to cultural, geographical,[75] and historical factors.[76] In Montesquieu's opinion, only rarely could institutions of one country serve those of another.[77] Others have highlighted the 'organic connection of law with the ... character of the people', comparing domestic law to

---

[70] *Ibid.*, at 433. [71] *Ibid.*, at 442. [72] *Ibid.*, at 433.

[73] Delmas-Marty, 'The Contribution of Comparative Law to a Pluralist Conception of International Criminal Law', 18.

[74] *Ibid.*, at 20.

[75] C. de Secondat Montesquieu, *The Spirit of the Laws* [1748], A.M. Cohler, B.C. Miller and H.S. Stone, eds. and transl. (Cambridge: Cambridge University Press, 1989), pp. 308–333.

[76] *Ibid.* (noting that religion, history and politics shape the essence of a people and influence their laws).

[77] *Ibid.*, Book I, Chapter 3 (stating that 'Les lois politiques et civiles de chaque nation ... doivent être tellement propres au peuple pour lequel elles sont faites, que c'est un grand hasard si celles d'une nation peuvent convenir à une autre').

the national language.[78] More recently, Gunther Teubner famously contended that the process of transplanting concepts from one legal field to another irritates the system and 'cannot be domesticated'.[79] Certainly, legal systems are part of a broader context[80] and express the cultures within which they are situated.[81] While sociologists have pointed out that certain cultures are more conducive to economic growth than others,[82] legal scholars have started investigating the impact of cultural factors on the developments of given approaches to financial, trade and investment law. For instance, in very critical tones, Legrand contended that 'a certain model of capitalism, a ... faith in the natural good of the market, and mercantilism ... posit a collapse of the "cultural" into the "economic"'.[83] In Legrand's view, cultural specificities can constitute 'a resistance to appropriation for domination/exploitation', and the cultural/traditional nature of law should be acknowledged.[84]

This is not to say that analogies are impossible. On the one hand, the importance of differences among legal systems should not be over-stated.[85] On the other hand, if it is true that the comparatists' own systems are never left behind,[86] comparative and investment lawyers 'have to recognize that they are participant observers, therefore their studies have to be ... self-critical'.[87] We participate in one (or more) culture(s) and observe any others: 'instead of pretending to the posture of a neutral, objective, and disinterested observer, the comparativist has to regard herself as being involved ... in a given legal tradition ... and ... in a specific mode of thinking and talking about law'.[88]

---

[78] F.C. von Savigny, *On the Vocation of Our Age for Legislation and Jurisprudence* [1828], A. Hayward transl., (Birmingham, ALA: Legal Classics Library, 1986), p. 27.

[79] G. Teubner, 'Legal Irritants: Good Faith in British Law or How Unifying Law Ends up in New Divergences', *Modern Law Review* 61 (1998), 11, at 12.

[80] J. Ellis, 'General Principles and Comparative Law', *European Journal of International Law* 22 (2011), 971.

[81] S.K. Harding, 'Comparative Reasoning and Judicial Review', *Yale Journal of International Law* 28 (2003), 409, 411. See also P. Legrand, 'On the Singularity of Law', *Harvard International Law Journal* 47 (2006), 517–530, 523 (noting that '[a]ny manifestation of the legal ... must be located in space and situated in time').

[82] M. Weber, *The Protestant Ethic and the Spirit of Capitalism*, 3rd ed. (S. Kalberg ed. and transl.) (Los Angeles, CA: Roxbury Publishing Co., 2002), [*Die protestantische Ethik und der Geist des Kapitalismus* (Tübingen, 1920)], p. 125.

[83] Legrand, 'On the Singularity of Law', 528.   [84] *Ibid.*, at 529–530.

[85] A. Momirov and A. Naudé Fourie, 'Vertical Comparative Methods: Tools for Conceptualising the International Rule of Law', *Erasmus Law Review* 2 (2009), 291–308, 297.

[86] Frankenberg, 'Critical Comparisons', 433.   [87] *Ibid.*, at 441.   [88] *Ibid.*, at 443.

In conclusion, analogies in investment law and arbitration tend to be eclectic as different players in the game have different stakes. This does not mean that any analogy works; rather, one must be aware that analogies do have a political dimension. Investment lawyers are clearly not required to undertake *encyclopedic comparisons* – that is, 'the comparative portrayal of the laws of all peoples, places and times',[89] but they have to be self-critical and adopt a sound methodology.

In order to delineate the contours of a proper methodology, the chapter proceeds as follows. First, the following section addresses the question as to why a public international law paradigm should be preferred. Second, the chapter explores what comparative lawyers and international lawyers can learn from each other. Third, the chapter examines and critically assesses the available methods. The conclusions will sum up the key findings of the chapter.

Why a public international law paradigm should be preferred

Is investment treaty arbitration a legitimate system? Legitimacy has no single definition: it is multidimensional and is used in different fields of study. In political sciences, legitimacy means the acceptance of a legal system.[90] In sociology, 'an entity is considered to be behaving legitimately when it conducts itself in a manner that is accepted as socially appropriate and consistent with widely held values, norms, rules and beliefs'.[91] In international law, the concept of legitimacy is fundamentally related to the question of why state actors obey international law. Compliance with international law is based on the shared belief that international law is legitimate and deserving of compliance. Legitimacy is considered a fundamental condition for governance, without which a régime will face impasse(s) and collapse.

In formal terms, international investment law is a legitimate system as it is based on a network of treaties. States sign and ratify these treaties, expressing their consent to be bound by the same. As many states are representative democracies, their adhesion to given international regimes is based upon the indirect consent of their peoples. The argument goes that the longer the legitimacy chain, the better the legitimacy because it

---

[89] *Ibid.*, at 427.
[90] See J. Locke, *Second Treatise of Government* [1689], C.B. Macpherson (ed.), (Indianapolis, IN: Hackett Publishing, 1980).
[91] K. Sonpar, F. Pazzaglia and J. Kornijenko, 'The Paradox and Constraints of Legitimacy', *Journal of Business Ethics* 95 (2010), 1–21, 1.

goes through different layers of legitimacy. International investment law both is generated by and regulates the international community.[92]

Nevertheless, some scholars claim that investor–state arbitration faces a 'legitimacy crisis'. Such critics advance three essential contentions:[93] (1) arbitral tribunals are biased towards multinational corporations; (2) arbitral awards are often inconsistent; (3) awards can have deep social impact and reallocate wealth. With regard to the first criticism, investors win some cases and lose other cases.[94] Moreover, according to a study, even when investors are awarded damages, they win significantly less than the amount claimed.[95] These findings do not suggest bias against states.[96]

With regard to the second criticism, investment treaty arbitration is a fluid system where arbitral tribunals are not hierarchically ordered but placed on a horizontal plane. Admittedly, this can lead to a chaotic and inconsistent development of the jurisprudence. However, the inconsistency of some arbitral awards often arises because tribunals are responding to the different facts of each case and/or applying a different law. Moreover, some level of inconsistency is not uncommon in other national and international jurisdictions.[97]

With regard to the third criticism, there are concerns that arbitrators do not take the public interest into account, being detached from local needs and values. Certainly, investment treaty arbitration presents *sui generis* features. It constitutes an encounter between global discourse and local particularism.[98] Investment treaty arbitration is at the same time a global and local phenomenon; it is global because it is governed by one or more international treaties and its dispute settlement mechanism is delocalised. It is local because the dispute concerns the investment of foreigners in a given country and the award will be implemented in that given country.[99] International investment law can be a force for good, promoting foreign direct investments, the economic development of the

---

[92] G. Scelle, 'Essai sur les sources formelles du droit international', in *Recueil d'Etudes sur les sources du droit en l'honneur de François Gény*, vol. III, (Paris: Sirey, 1934), pp. 400–30, p. 410 (highlighting the *dédoublement fonctionnel* of states).

[93] See S.M. Schwebel, 'In Defense of Bilateral Investment Treaties', *Columbia FDI Perspectives* n. 135, 24 November 2014.

[94] S. Franck, 'Development and Outcomes of Investment Treaty Arbitration', *Harvard International Law Journal* 50 (2009), 435 (showing that of 144 publicly available awards as of January 2012, states won 87 cases while investors won 57).

[95] *Ibid.*   [96] Schwebel, 'In Defense of Bilateral Investment Treaties', 1.   [97] *Ibid.*

[98] Legrand, 'On the Singularity of Law', at 529-30.   [99] *Ibid.*, at 523 and 529.

host state and the prosperity of investors. This does not mean that there are no areas for improvement. Therefore, further scrutiny is needed.

How can arbitral tribunals reinforce their perceived legitimacy? Investment treaty arbitration should not be looked at in isolation from the rest of international law, as it is a part of the same. Analogies can constitute devices to (re)assert the system's legitimacy. Mapping these analogies can explain the dynamics of the system and influence its future trajectories. Analogies are useful means of interpreting and applying vague provisions to ensure consistency among the various subsets of international law. They allow arbitrators to broaden their vision and increase the coherence of the system. Analogies can be harmonising techniques for defragmenting the alleged fragmentation of international law and cross-pollinating the jurisprudence of international courts and tribunals.[100]

However, there is a risk that analogies delegitimise the investment treaty system. Approximate comparative reasoning can lead to incorrect and inconsistent awards. There is a risk of adopting a Western bias, that is, focusing on those systems arbitrators are more familiar with. There are concerns that analogies can endorse imperialist stances. Therefore, it is crucial to identify the proper source of analogies.

Compelling arguments stand in favour of drawing analogies from international law and its subsystems in international investment law and arbitration. International investment law is an important part of public international law. It 'consists of layers of general international law, of general standards of international economic law and of distinct rules peculiar to its domain'.[101] Investment treaty arbitrations are conducted on the basis of international treaties; their specific function is to settle disputes in conformity with international law.[102] From a functional perspective, 'to some extent, arbitrators are expected to behave like judges in their concern for the public interest'.[103] Not only does

---

[100] See, for example, International Law Commission, *Fragmentation of International Law: Difficulties Arising from the Diversification and Expansion of International Law*, UN Doc. A/CN.4/L.702, 18 July 2006 (encouraging boundary crossings between the subsets of international law by interpretation).

[101] R. Dolzer and C. Schreuer, *Principles of International Investment Law*, II ed. (Oxford: OUP, 2012) p. 3.

[102] S.W. Schill, 'Crafting the International Economic Order: The Public Function of Investment Treaty Arbitration and Its Significance for the Role of the Arbitrator', *Leiden Journal of International Law* 23 (2010) 401–430, 406.

[103] W.W. Park, 'Private Disputes and the Public Good: Explaining Arbitration Law', *American University International Law Review* 20 (2004–2005), at 905.

international law provide for well-established entry points for comparative analysis – including, for instance, ordinary rules of treaty interpretation and the application of general principles of law – but it also provides fertile ground for analogies encompassing a growing number of fields, from international trade law to human rights law.

Arbitral jurisprudence confirms the embeddedness of international investment law in international law. Although previous decisions of other international courts and tribunals are not a source of law, and there is no binding precedent in international (investment) law, arbitral tribunals do frequently refer to these decisions for supporting arguments, enhancing the quality of their awards and fostering their coherence with international practice. In turn, this facilitates the predictability of the awards, enhances the prestige of the arbitral tribunals – who perceive themselves as guardians of international (investment) law and part of the network of international adjudicators – and contributes to their own (perceived) legitimacy.

Rather than being an alternative, comparative public law – that is, comparative law insights from administrative and constitutional law – can complement public international law, as it is useful for discerning general principles of law and state practice, which is an element of customary international law.[104] Adopting a public international law paradigm does not entail the complete irrelevance of domestic law. National law plays an important role in the coalescence of customary international law and general principles of law. Therefore, the public international law paradigm is not detached from a public law approach as it could seem at first glance.

By linking law and the quest for legitimacy, the use of analogies in international investment law and arbitration can provide a useful tool to humanise international investment law, attuning it with public international law. For instance, some have argued that Article 31(3)(c) of the VCLT enables arbitral tribunals to not only apply those human rights treaty obligations to which the host state is subject, but also incorporate human rights rules that might be considered generally applicable among states.[105] Other scholars have argued that crossing regime boundaries can

---

[104] S. Schill, 'International Investment Law and Comparative Public Law – An Introduction', in S. Schill (ed.), *International Investment Law and Comparative Public Law* (Oxford: Oxford University Press, 2010), p. 36.

[105] B. Simma and T. Kill, 'Harmonizing Investment Protection and International Human Rights: First Steps Towards a Methodology', in C. Binder, U. Kriebaum, A. Reinisch and

be a tool for affirming human rights values[106] and conceptualising international law as 'humanity's law'.[107] Certainly, the system must be responsive to the challenges it is facing; comparative analysis can help it adapt and develop harmoniously with public international law.

What can comparative lawyers and international investment lawyers learn from each other?

Both comparative legal studies and international investment law have a 'humanistic outlook' in that, like other legal fields, they centre on our 'common humanity'[108] and 'order our ties to one another'.[109] International investment law governs foreign direct investments, that is, economic activities carried out by individuals establishing their business beyond national borders. International investment law shapes and influences the world in which we live, facilitating transborder economic freedoms for individuals. International investment law can play a strategic role in securing the peace, prosperity and welfare of mankind. Investments should (and at times do) serve human values. At the same time, however, an excessive emphasis on economic considerations can foster a race to the bottom, prevent the adoption of important regulatory measures by the host state and affect a range of human rights of the local population.

In parallel, comparative legal studies provide 'both a window into other cultures as well as a mirror for one's own', broadening the legal horizon and fostering respect for and understanding of other legal cultures.[110] Whereas, historically, one of the prime objectives of comparative studies has been to reach a 'common law of humankind',[111] today comparative reasoning is 'forward-looking', suggesting that we

---

S. Wittich (eds.), *International Investment Law for the 21st Century: Essays in Honour of Christoph Schreuer* (Oxford: Oxford University Press, 2009), p. 678.

[106] J.E. Alvarez, 'Beware: Boundary Crossing', in T. Kahana and A. Scolnicov (eds.), *Boundaries of Rights, Boundaries of State (forthcoming* 2015), p. 11.

[107] R. Teitel, *Humanity's Law* (Oxford: Oxford University Press, 2011).

[108] G. Watt, 'Comparison as Deep Appreciation', in P.G. Monateri (ed.), *Methods of Comparative Law* (Cheltenham, UK: Edward Elgar, 2012), pp. 82–99, p. 85.

[109] L. Rosen, *Law as Culture: An Invitation* (Princeton: Princeton University Press, 2006), pp. 199–200.

[110] R. Dibadj, 'Panglossian Transnationalism', *Stanford Journal of International Law* 44 (2008), 253–299, 297.

[111] A. Wijffels, 'Le droit comparé à la recherche d'un nouvel interface entre ordres juridiques', *Revue de droit international et de droit comparé* 2 (2008), 228–251, 228.

should think out of the box and look for new approaches to legal problems rather than being satisfied with things as they are.[112] Comparative legal research is a social science which is 'not delimited by political frontiers'; rather, 'it contemplates that, while techniques may vary, the problems of justice are basically the same in time and space throughout the world'.[113] Comparative studies can play a role in shedding light on and helping to solve public policy questions that transcend national borders and are of great importance to humanity.

Both international investment law and comparative legal research have traditionally revolved around the nation-state. International investment law is part of international law which, as 'a product of the Westphalian state-centered system of world law', 'maintains that the states are the only subjects of international law ...'[114] In parallel, comparative legal research has traditionally juxtaposed comparable laws of different states. However, the increasing prominence of non-state actors and individuals has required a recalibration of both fields. Investor–state arbitration now offers a level playing field to foreign investors in their disputes against the host states. In turn, comparative legal research has gradually expanded its purview to encompass the relationship between national and transnational regimes and to cover non-state law, including chthonic law.

Yet, both international (investment) law and comparative legal research should have a more comprehensive stance. For instance, the relevance of chthonic law in investment arbitration has recently come to the fore. In the *Grand River* case, a dispute concerning taxation of tobacco products, a Canadian company engaged in exporting tobacco in the United States argued that its investment had been harmed by the US Master Settlement Agreements (MSA) and that the United States had breached, *inter alia*, the fair and equitable treatment standard.[115] According to the claimants, who were members of the Six Nations of Native Americans, Article 1105 of the NAFTA required respect of international law, including indigenous peoples' rights.[116] They contended that customary international law required states to actively

---

[112] H.E. Yntema, 'Comparative Legal Research – Some Remarks on "Looking Out of the Cave"', *Michigan Law Review* 54 (1956), 901–928, 901.
[113] *Ibid.*, at 903. [114] Dibadj, 'Panglossian Transnationalism', 256.
[115] *Grand River Enter. Six Nations, Ltd.* v. *United States of America*, Award, NAFTA Arbitral Tribunal, 12 January 2011, paras. 125 and 173.
[116] *Ibid.*, para. 180.

consult with indigenous peoples before taking regulatory action that would substantially affect their interests.[117]

The Tribunal, with the exception of one member, believed that state legal officers 'acted less than optimally' in developing the proposed regulatory measures and considered that 'the First Nations or tribal governments ... should have been included in these discussions'.[118] The Tribunal also stated: "[i]t may well be, as the Claimants urged, that there does exist a principle of customary international law requiring governmental authorities to consult indigenous peoples on governmental policies or actions ... "[119] Nonetheless, the Tribunal noted that 'the notion of specialized procedural rights protecting some investors, but not others, cannot readily be reconciled with the idea of a minimum customary standard of treatment due to all investments'.[120] Therefore, it held that 'whatever unfair treatment was rendered to [the claimant] or his business enterprise, it did not rise to the level of an infraction of the fair and equitable treatment'.[121] As a matter of applicable law, the Tribunal stated that 'the customary standard of protection of alien investors' investments does not incorporate other legal protections that may be provided investors or classes of investors under other sources of law'.[122] As a matter of interpretation, the Arbitral Tribunal took into account other rules of international law as required by customary norms of treaty interpretation, but reaffirmed it was a 'tribunal of limited jurisdiction; it ha[d] no mandate to decide claims based on treaties other than NAFTA'.[123]

After having examined the commonalities between comparative legal studies and international investment law, this section addresses the question as to what comparative lawyers and international investment lawyers can learn from each other. From an international law perspective, there are different ways through which international law scholars can use comparative reasoning. Analogical reasoning plays an important role in the formation, application and interpretation of international (investment) law. Not only is borrowing from sound comparative surveys critical for ascertaining the existence of customary law and general principles of international (investment) law, but analogical reasoning can facilitate the interpretation and application of vague investment treaty provisions. Comparative reasoning has also offered important insights into how international (investment) law norms become

---

[117] *Ibid.*, para. 182.   [118] *Ibid.*, para. 128.   [119] *Ibid.*, para. 210.   [120] *Ibid.*, para. 213.
[121] *Ibid.*, para. 187.   [122] *Ibid.*, para. 219.   [123] *Ibid.*, para. 71.

domesticated and internalised into domestic law, as well as enforced by domestic courts. By offering insights on how domestic laws address international law issues, comparative investment law can complement international investment law in providing businesses with accurate information on the legal frameworks of host states.

Comparative reasoning can facilitate a greater appreciation of commonalities and differences among competing laws. When sufficient commonality can be found among legal systems, the move from domestic to international law can be implicit, through the recognition of customary international law or general principles of law, or explicit through the drafting of a treaty. In this regard, comparative reasoning can offer 'analytical support to an expansion of the narrow scope of international law'.[124] Conversely, from a comparative law perspective, international investment law constitutes a new field of study to explore and map new interfaces between legal orders.

A comparative practice in search of a methodology

Comparative legal research has long been in search of a method.[125] Method indicates a procedure, technique or planned way of doing something and achieving certain ends. It derives from the Ancient Greek word μέθοδος which literally means 'walking along a path or following a certain route'.[126] Due to the plurality of research questions, there is a variety of comparative methods.[127]

In elaborating a sound methodological design, Husa, an eminent comparativist, identifies five theoretical choices: (1) micro/macro; (2) longitudinal/traverse; (3) multilateral/bilateral; (4) vertical/horizontal; and (5) monocultural/multicultural.[128] The first choice is a matter of scale. On a macro-level, different systems are compared; on the

---

[124] *Ibid.*

[125] See, for example, B. Jaluzot, 'Méthodologie du droit comparé – Bilan et prospective', *Revue Internationale du Droit Comparé* 1 (2005), 29–48, 29; J.C. Reitz, 'How to do Comparative Law', *American Journal of Comparative Law* 46 (1998), 617–636; L.J. Constantinesco, *Traité du droit comparé*, vol. II, *La méthode comparative* (Paris: Librairie générale de droit et de jurisprudence, 1974).

[126] J. Husa, 'Research Designs of Comparative Law – Methodology or Heuristics?', in M. Adams and D. Heirbaut (eds.), *The Method and Culture of Comparative Law* (Oxford and Portland: Hart Publishing, 2014), pp. 53–68, p. 55.

[127] *Ibid.*, p. 56.

[128] Husa, 'Research Designs of Comparative Law – Methodology or Heuristics?', 57.

micro-level, certain issues are compared.[129] The second choice is a matter of time. Usually, analogies are made between modern systems. However, reference can be made to legal systems of the past. The latter type of comparison is called longitudinal comparison.[130] Multilateral comparisons are carried out among a plurality of legal systems, while bilateral comparisons involve only two legal systems. Vertical comparisons involve legal systems belonging to different spheres along the spectrum – national, regional and international.[131] Horizontal comparisons involve legal systems belonging to the same level.[132] Finally, multicultural comparisons are conducted between legal systems which do not belong to the same legal culture.[133] Monocultural comparisons take place between two or more legal systems belonging to the same legal culture.

This book approaches the role of comparative reasoning in international investment law and arbitration. After illustrating some fundamental debates in comparative legal research, the book has applied a combination of the mentioned theoretical choices to elaborate a sound methodological design. In particular, while Chapter 4 examined the use of micro-comparisons in international investment law and arbitration, Chapter 5 illustrated the use of macro-comparisons in the field. Both chapters used a combination of multilateral/bilateral, vertical/horizontal and monocultural/multicultural analogies.

The book demonstrates the need for critical methodological choices in the use of analogies in international investment law and arbitration. Methodology is essential for countering the alleged legitimacy crisis of investment arbitration. Methodological guidelines include the need to pay attention to the context of a given legal analogue, and awareness that the comparativist should not allow her vision to be clouded by the concepts of her own system.[134] Moreover, 'Western ideas of law are no longer automatically accepted as the primary yardstick of legal cultures' and more comprehensive approaches should be adopted.[135] Pluralistic approaches characterising sound comparative methods in the area of international investment law can rebut criticisms of hegemonic thinking and the risk of investment disputes assuming a political rather than legal character. The questions of how to choose which systems to compare; how to measure commonality and differences among systems; and how

---

[129] *Ibid.*, at 58. [130] *Ibid.* [131] *Ibid.* [132] *Ibid.* [133] *Ibid.*, at 59.

[134] S. Glanert, 'Method?', in P.G. Monateri (ed.), *Methods of Comparative Law* (Cheltenham: Edward Elgar, 2012), pp. 61–81, at p. 68.

[135] Husa, 'Research Designs of Comparative Law', 64.

to distil general principles of law are discussed. For instance, a sound comparative methodology in the area of international investment law requires that the concept of general principles of law is broad enough to encompass a meaningful variety of legal systems. The identification of general principles 'requires a truly global comparative exercise'.[136]

Analogies are a frequent phenomenon in international investment law and are in search of a method. Without a proper method, they risk becoming as odd as the famous 'six characters in search of an author' – protagonists of the homonymous play by Pirandello.[137] Attempts to elaborate a comparative method – that is, how to do comparative legal research – have furthered a rich debate in comparative legal studies; a number of approaches have been developed with varied results.[138]

Some scholars have adopted a conceptual or dogmatic method, based on analytical reasoning and the comparison of legal concepts; others have preferred a functional method, focusing on the legal issues to be addressed rather than their categorisation.[139] While some scholars have linked comparative legal research to mathematical tools and game theory,[140] others have linked it to economics,[141] sociology[142] or socio-legal studies.[143] Contextualist approaches conceive law

---

[136] Alvarez, 'Beware: Boundary Crossings', p. 48.

[137] In the play, an acting company was rehearsing a piece, when it was suddenly interrupted by the arrival of six characters in search of an author to complete their story. After the director agrees to stage their play, he is left in doubt as to whether the new play was in fact a play. L. Pirandello, *Sei personaggi in cerca d'autore* [1921], 14 ed. (Milan: Mondadori, 2001).

[138] Jaluzot, 'Méthodologie du droit comparé – Bilan et prospective', 44.

[139] H.A. Schwarz-Liebermann von Wahlendorf, *Droit comparé. Théorie générale et principes* (Paris: Librairie générale de droit et de jurisprudence, 1978), p. 185. For a critical assessment of the functional method, see M.M. Graziadei, 'The Functionalist Heritage', in P. Legrand and R. Munday (eds.), *Comparative Legal Studies: Traditions and Transitions* (Cambridge: Cambridge University Press, 2003), pp. 100–127, and R. Michaels, 'The Functional Method of Comparative Law', in M. Reimann and R. Zimmermann (eds.), *The Oxford Handbook of Comparative Law* (Oxford: Oxford University Press, 2006), pp. 340–380.

[140] See generally M.-L. Izorche, 'Propositions méthodologiques pour la comparaison', *Revue de droit international et de droit comparé* 53 (2001), 289–325.

[141] See generally U. Mattei, *Comparative Law and Economics* (Ann Arbor, MI: University of Michigan Press, 1997).

[142] See G. Winterton, 'Comparative Law Teaching', *American Journal of Comparative Law* 23 (1975), 69–118, 109.

[143] A. Riles, 'Comparative Law and Socio-Legal Studies', in M. Reimann and R. Zimmermann (eds.), *The Oxford Handbook of Comparative Law* (Oxford: Oxford University Press, 2006), pp. 811–812.

in action and emphasise the importance of the economic, social and cultural context of given provisions for drawing sound analogies. Finally, comparative reasoning can have the subversive and/or revolutionary function of improving legal systems,[144] as such reasoning can help the comparativist understand the strengths and weaknesses of her own legal system.[145]

There is no single method of doing comparative research: 'methodology is a means to an end rather than an end in itself, with the result that it can be as good as it is suited to the end being pursued'.[146] This connection between methods and ends entails that 'the politics of these ends will inevitably also be at work in choices of method'.[147] The fact that comparative legal research is question driven requires that the goals and methods of the same research be spelled out explicitly to clarify the researcher's perspective and goals.

Although there is no single methodological model in comparative legal research, two fundamental approaches to the field have emerged: the functional approach and the cultural approach. The functional approach[148] relies on the assumption that law addresses social problems and that all societies confront essentially the same challenges.[149] After posing a functional question (i.e., identifying a given social problem), functionalists investigate how legal systems address the problem, to list, explain and critically assess similarities and differences.[150] Concepts and institutions are compared because of their analogous function. The functional approach tends to presuppose

---

[144] H. Muir-Watt, 'La fonction subversive du droit comparé', *Revue internationale de droit comparé* 52 (2000), 503–527; G.P. Fletcher, 'Comparative Law as a Subversive Discipline', *American Journal of Comparative Law* 46 (1998), 683, 694.

[145] B. Markesinis, 'Unité ou divergence: à la recherche des ressemblances dans le droit européen contemporain', *Revue internationale de droit comparé* 53 (2001), 807–808.

[146] C. Valcke, 'Reflections on Comparative Law Methodology – Getting Inside Contract Law', in M. Adams and J. Bomhoff (eds.), *Practice and Theory in Comparative Law* (Cambridge: Cambridge University Press, 2013).

[147] M. Adams and J. Bomhoff, 'Comparing Law: Practice and Theory', in M. Adams and J. Bomhoff (eds.), *Practice and Theory in Comparative Law* (Cambridge: Cambridge University Press, 2013), pp. 1–21, p. 6.

[148] See, for example, K. Zweigert, 'Méthodologie du droit comparé', in *Mélanges offerts à Jacques Maury*, vol. I (Paris: Dalloz-Sirey, 1960), pp. 579–596; K. Zweigert and H. Kötz, *An Introduction to Comparative Law*, 3rd ed., transl. Tony Weir (Oxford: Oxford University Press, 1998), pp. 32–47.

[149] See, for example, J. Gordley, 'Is Comparative Law a Distinct Discipline?', *American Journal of Comparative Law* 46 (1998), 607–615.

[150] See generally Zweigert and Kötz, *An Introduction to Comparative Law.*

similarity among legal systems (*praesumptio similitudinis*),[151] potentially reflecting 'epistemological optimism', that is, the belief that legal
systems are comparable.[152] Accordingly, a legal concept could be
moved from a context and applied elsewhere, as it would adapt to the
new context.[153] This approach allows a great – yet arguably loose –
methodological freedom.[154]

Cultural or postmodern approaches to comparative reasoning, on the
other hand, reject a purely functionalist vision of law and contend that
law is a cultural phenomenon.[155] Therefore, not only do comparativists
need to consider the functions of legal concepts, but they also have to
contextualise such concepts in their legal matrix and culture of origin.[156]
Meaningful comparisons require understanding the economic, social
and cultural context of legal rules.[157] Cultural differences are presumed
and legal unification is considered an undesirable outcome because law
cannot be separated from its context.[158]

Yet, cultural approaches to comparative reasoning have been criticised for lacking a clear and systematic method. According to their
critics, they do not offer new methods that would match the simplicity
of the functionalist approach.[159] Rather, by stressing differences among
legal systems, cultural approaches to comparative reasoning are analogous to the deconstructivism, namely the development of postmodern
architecture characterised by fragmentation, with non-rectilinear
shapes and dislocated architectural elements in a sort of controlled
chaos.[160] Moreover, if one adopts a too broad understanding of the

---

[151] J. Husa, 'Methodology of Comparative Law Today: From Paradoxes to Flexibility?',
Revue internationale de droit comparé 4 (2006), 1095, 1107.
[152] M. Van Hoecke, 'Deep Level Comparative Law', in M. Van Hoecke (ed.), *Epistemology
and Methodology of Comparative Law* (Oxford: Hart Publishing, 2004), pp. 172–174.
[153] See generally A. Watson, 'Comparative Law and Legal Change', *Cambridge Law Journal*
37 (1978), 313, at 314–315.
[154] Michaels, 'The Functional Method of Comparative Law', p. 340 (stating that 'Th[e]
functional method is a chimera, in both theory and practice of comparative law.')
[155] P. Legrand, 'The Impossibility of Legal Transplants', *Maastricht Journal of European and
Comparative Law* 4 (1997), 111, 111 (suggesting that 'comparing legal systems is
comparing different worldviews').
[156] J.C. Reitz, 'How to do Comparative Law', *American Journal of Comparative Law* 46
(1998), 617, 626.
[157] P. Legrand, 'How to Compare Now?', *Legal Studies* 16 (1996), 232.
[158] O. Kahn-Freund, 'On Uses and Misuses of Comparative Law', *Modern Law Review* 37
(1974), 1–27.
[159] J. Husa, 'About the Methodology of Comparative Law – Some Comments Concerning
the Wonderland . . .', *Maastricht Faculty of Law Working Papers* 5 (2007), 1–18, 10.
[160] See generally D. Libeskind, *Breaking Ground* (New York: Riverhead, 2004).

cultural approach, 'comparative law becomes impossible' as the entire context of law can never be perfectly understood and legal systems become incommensurable.[161]

Despite their differences, however, 'both sides of the debate are simultaneously right and wrong'.[162] On the one hand, the impossibility of legal transplants is contradicted by a number of successful transfers.[163] On the other, 'law is neither completely insulated from, nor completely determined by society'.[164] For example, a vine remains a vine even if it is transplanted from a vineyard to another. However, the vintage will depend on a number of variables such as soil, climate and light.[165]

In light of these debates, the sliding scale of comparative legal methods shares a number of caveats as a common denominator. For instance, borrowing based on inadequately verified information should be avoided. Analogously, the selection of the use of certain countries as examples should be justified. Arbitral tribunals should clarify why they have chosen a particular source of comparison, as the choice of the concrete source is decisive for the outcome of the case.[166] If comparisons are made, these should be explicit rather than implicit. The understanding of the borrowed items should be proper, accurate and contextual. More fundamentally, one should consider whether analogies serve outcomes in compliance with international law and take into account both investor rights and the commonweal of the host country.

Finally, analogies cannot be a mechanical process considering the fact that until recently both comparative legal research and international law used to have a Westphalian[167] – if not Eurocentric – character.[168] For a long time, comparative research focused on European legal systems; the

---

[161] M. Siems, 'The End of Comparative Law', *Journal of Comparative Law* 2 (2007), 133–150, 140–141.

[162] M. Chen-Wishart, 'Legal Transplant and Undue Influence: Lost in Translation or a Working Understanding?', *International & Comparative Law Quarterly* 62 (2013), 1–30, 2.

[163] *Ibid.*   [164] *Ibid.*, at 3.   [165] *Ibid.*, at 2.

[166] See, for instance, in the context of human rights law, M. Ambrus, 'Comparative Law Method in the Jurisprudence of the European Court of Human Rights in the Light of the Rule of Law', *Erasmus Law Review* 2 (2009), 353–371, 365–366.

[167] Treaty of Westphalia: Peace Treaty between the Holy Roman Empire and the King of France and their respective Allies, 24 October 1648, available at http://www.yale.edu/lawweb/avalon/westphal.htm.

[168] W. Twining, 'Globalization and Comparative Law', *Maastricht Journal of European and Comparative Law* 6 (1999), 217–243, 233.

law of former colonies – with the exception of US law – was largely overlooked. By limiting its focus to Western legal traditions, comparative legal research contributed to the legitimisation of an order in which 'peripheral' countries received very limited, if any, recognition for creative contributions to the market of legal ideas.[169] Comparativists assumed that law was almost completely of European making, unfolded through nearly the entire world via colonialism, imperialism and trade. In parallel, the making of international law used to have a predominantly Western character.[170] Some authors have even questioned whether, and just how international international law is.[171]

In the post-colonial era, however, there is an emergent awareness that diffusion of law does not necessarily lead to convergence or unification of laws. On the one hand, scholars have pointed out the multicultural genealogy of the Western legal tradition.[172] On the other hand, the imported laws underwent meaningful transformations once they were implanted into new legal systems. At present, the categorisation of systems into legal families may have become too static and unable to take into account the evolution of law.[173] Economic globalisation has spurred the constant contact and communication among legal cultures, facilitating processes of mutual learning.[174] Many characteristics which define and shape legal families 'are fading or spreading into other systems'.[175] Finally, 'all legal systems are to different degrees hybrids, i.e., cultural and legal mixtures consisting of various elements borrowed from different legal traditions and customs'.[176]

---

[169] J. González-Jácome, 'El uso del derecho comparado como forma de escape de la subordinación colonial', *International Law: Revista Colombiana de Derecho Internacional* 7 (2006), 295–338, 301 (affirming that 'se está contribuyendo a la legitimación de un orden geopolítico en donde a los países periféricos se les atribuye poca posibilidad creativa en el mercado de las ideas jurídicas').

[170] See generally A. Anghie, *Imperialism, Sovereignty and the Making of International Law* (Cambridge: Cambridge University Press, 2005).

[171] K.T. Gaubatz and M. MacArthur, 'How International is International Law?', *Michigan Journal of International Law* 22 (2001), 239.

[172] P.G. Monateri, 'Black Gaius – A Quest for the Multicultural Origins of the "Western Legal Tradition"', *Hastings Law Journal* 51 (1999–2000), 479, 484 (highlighting that Roman law is a multicultural product due to the interaction of different civilisations).

[173] Wijffels, 'Le droit comparé à la recherche d'un nouvel interface entre ordres juridiques', 239.

[174] Ellis, 'General Principles and Comparative Law', 966.

[175] C. Picker, 'International Law's Mixed Heritage: A Common/Civil Law Jurisdiction', *Vanderbilt Journal of Transnational Law* 41 (2008), 1083–1140, 1094.

[176] R. Banakar, 'Power, Culture and Method in Comparative Law', *International Journal of Law in Context* 5 (2009), 69–85, 74.

The key question as to whether (and, if so the extent to which) an international arbitral tribunal may or should draw upon national law concepts and transpose them into investment treaty arbitration is often discussed but remains unsettled. As Cassese famously argued – albeit in the different context of international criminal law – 'notions, legal constructs and terms of art upheld in national law should not be automatically applied at the international level. They cannot be mechanically imported into international ... proceedings.'[177] According to Cassese, 'Reliance on legal notions or concepts as laid down in a national legal system can only be justified if international rules make explicit reference to national law or if such reference is necessarily implied by the very content and nature of the concept.'[178] For instance, in order to ascertain the nationality of a company or an individual, the international judge will refer to the national law of the relevant state.[179] Cassese adds that 'even in the case of international rules embodying national-law notions, an effort must be made to construe those notions in the light of the object and purpose of the international rules or of their general spirit'.[180] Legal concepts lifted from the national level to the international one might well acquire a new dimension, shade and texture. As Bassiouni puts it, 'Is not all international law a process of blending legal concepts in a way that fits the exigencies of the international legal order?'[181] More specifically, unless required by investment treaty provisions, 'it would be inappropriate mechanically to incorporate into international ... proceedings ideas, legal constructs, concepts or terms of art which only belong, and are unique, to a specific group of national legal systems, say common law or civil law systems'.[182] 'Whenever reference to national law is not commanded expressly, or imposed by necessary implication', Cassese adds, 'resort to national legislation is not warranted.'[183]

---

[177] ICTY, *Prosecutor v. Drazen Erdemovic*, Separate and Dissenting Opinion of Judge Cassese, 7 October 1997, para. 2.
[178] *Ibid.*, para. 3.
[179] *Ibid.*, referring to the *Barcelona Traction* Case, *ICJ Reports* 1970, p. 33, para. 36.
[180] *Ibid.*, para. 3.
[181] Bassiouni, 'A Functional Approach to "General Principles of International Law"', 774.
[182] ICTY, *Prosecutor v. Drazen Erdemovic*, Separate and Dissenting Opinion of Judge Cassese, para. 5.
[183] *Ibid.*, para. 3.

Final remarks

International investment and comparative legal research are different fields with distinct aims and methodologies. Their interaction lacks a clear theory; the development of such a theory requires 'concentrated engagement by scholars on both sides of the divide'.[184] Often the legal basis for the interaction between comparative legal research and international investment law is not clearly spelled out by practitioners.

What are then the bridges between the two fields? Both international (investment) law and comparative legal research share 'a passion for looking beyond' traditional political borders.[185] From an international law perspective, there are different approaches through which international law scholars can refer to comparative legal research and benefit from comparative thinking. Under customary rules of treaty interpretation, 'the first duty of the treaty interpreter is fidelity to the treaty regime' in interpreting it, its context and to some extent its negotiating history.[186] Yet, the same rules allow the interpreter to rely on comparisons in a number of different ways. For instance, comparisons inform the creation of customary international law and general principles of law. In order to assess the existence of a general principle of law, one has to ascertain that a number of legal systems have converged on the same solution to a particular problem. Conversely, from a comparative law perspective, international investment law constitutes a new field of study to explore and map new interfaces between legal orders.

To build bridges between international investment law and comparative legal research, however, a number of methodological choices must be made. For instance, 'there is a question of the scale of comparisons to be made'; the role of the cultural context in the making of the compared systems; and the issue as to what objectives a specific research question aims to address.[187]

There is no one comparative legal method; rather, distinct methodological approaches coexist within comparative legal research. Methods

---

[184] A. Roberts, 'Comparative International Law? The Role of National Courts in Creating and Enforcing International Law', *International and Comparative Law Quarterly* 60 (2011), 57–92, 82.

[185] A. Riles, 'Wigmore's Treasure Box: Comparative Law in the Era of Information', *Harvard International Law Journal* 40 (1999), 221–464, 229.

[186] Howse and Chalamish, 'The Use and Abuse of WTO Law in Investor–State Arbitration', 1087–1094.

[187] Riles, 'Wigmore's Treasure Box', 225.

vary depending on the scope and objective of the respective inquiries. All methods have their promises and pitfalls; while functionalism seems to explain why so many legal transplants take place worldwide, cultural approaches elucidate why there remains a consistent legal diversity among legal systems. These methods share more than they realise and 'each group borrows continually from the methodologies of the others'.[188]

---

[188] *Ibid.*, at 231.

~

Conclusions

Le droit est-il une science ou un art?[1]

Analogic reasoning is one of the oldest modes of legal reasoning and plays an important role in international investment law and arbitration. As legal orders face similar issues, lawyers often refer to other systems to identify the best solutions. Just as a type of vine can be transplanted from its native terrain to another, legal concepts can be transplanted across different legal systems. Analogies bring vitality and cross-fertilisation among different systems of law. Analogies can improve the quality of awards, contributing to international judicial dialogue wherein arbitrators evaluate the decisions of other courts and tribunals. Analogies allow arbitral tribunals to confirm results that they have found based on the interpretation of international investment law. Comparative reasoning allows an array of interpretations, reshaping international investment law and arbitration and attuning it to the evolving nature of societies.

Comparative analysis has been seen as the next phase in the theory of international investment law. The emergence of norm creation and enforcement outside the boundaries of the state; the increasingly important role of private actors; and the intermingling of private and public, and national and international dimensions of law which characterise international investment law constitute a new frontier which deserves further scrutiny. In this context, comparative studies may offer a useful lens through which to deepen the analysis of the emerging field of study. These intersections may prove to be a fertile ground for methodological consolidation and offer opportunities for addressing issues in a new fashion.

Yet, to build bridges between international investment law and comparative legal research, a number of methodological choices must be

---

[1] C. Ambroise and H. Capitant, *Cours élémentaire de droit civil français*, vol. 1 (Paris Librairie Dalloz, 1931), p. 6 ('Is law an art or a science?' (author's translation)).

made. For instance, the role of the cultural context in the making of the compared systems, the identification of the best analogues and the method for drawing such analogies raise a number of questions. Methodology is crucial to avoid the danger of cherry-picking, free decision-making and ultimately a *'gouvernement des arbitres'*.[2] The mechanical importation of concepts drawn from one state's law may alter the international character of investment treaty arbitration, repoliticising the dispute. Specific features of national law can get lost in translation. Reference to general principles of law without any serious comparative study can mask arbitrariness. Furthermore, some legal systems predominate in the citation race due to a number of factors such as language, culture, geographical proximity and other variables.

The book examines and critically assesses the role of comparative reasoning in international investment law and arbitration, offering an analytical framework to critically assess the use of analogies in the field. It explores the analogies which characterise the investment law system, investigating the promises and pitfalls of their use in this field of study.

There is no one method of doing comparative legal research; rather there are as many methods as there are research questions. Different methods coexist, converge and diverge, all acknowledging that the context of the law matters. While functional analysis helps in clarifying the multifold uses of comparative reasoning, it risks adopting an ideological approach. On the other hand, a cultural approach to comparative reasoning has the merit of highlighting the unique features of various legal systems. Yet, the extreme version of the cultural approach – contending that each legal culture is unique, culturally contingent and thus incommensurable – entails the impossibility of comparative reasoning. The apparently diametrically opposed methodologies nonetheless converge in stressing the importance of methodological awareness. Whatever the approach adopted by the interpreter, 'transparency and rigor' should accompany her choices.[3]

One could argue that an overly sophisticated methodology risks rendering comparative reasoning unattainable. Yet, the standards of

---

[2] For an analogous point, see V. Grosswald Curran, 'Fear of Formalism: Indications from the Fascist Period in France and Germany on Judicial Methodology's Impact on Substantive Law', *Cornell International Law Journal* 35 (2001–2002), 101, 148.

[3] M. Delmas-Marty, 'Comparative Law and International Law: Methods for Ordering Pluralism', *University of Tokyo Journal of Law and Politics* (2006), 44 ff.

proper comparative research must be maintained. Comparative research is a type of legal research. Therefore, for some aspects, it follows the methodological patterns and adopts the methodological tools of cognate legal disciplines. Yet, for other aspects, it differs from other fields, as it presupposes the comparison between two or more areas of study. In particular, differences between legal systems should be detected and taken into account; the cultural context of given norms should be considered; and, more importantly, the comparatist should be aware of and make explicit her own perspective and selected approach. The reasons for undertaking a comparison should be explicit. For instance, the identification of a general principle of law cannot rely on a handful of legal systems. While there is no common transnational canon to detect general principles of law, certainly, the fact that such principles are general requires a cosmopolitan orientation. In order to assess the existence of a general principle of law, one has to ascertain that a number of legal systems have converged on the same solution to a particular problem.

Moreover, judicial borrowing cannot be an uncritical exercise. Legal norms express a certain political position, being the outcome of historical evolution. Analogously courts and tribunals have different epistemological agendas. While the argument goes that common problems may be addressed by adopting common approaches, the risk of exporting systemic failures is high. Moreover, given approaches may be successful in one system but not necessarily in another. There is a risk of repoliticising investment disputes by referring to given legal systems instead of others. Comparisons are not a neutral phenomenon: depending on the selected perspective, the outcomes can be different. Once aware of perspective, arbitral tribunals and interpreters can make sound use of analogies. Not only would such awareness limit potential abuses of the comparative method, but it would also favour the coherence of the international legal order as a whole.

The use of comparative reasoning in investment treaty law and arbitration is multilayered. *First*, under the label 'comparative investment law', scholars have compared the different legal frameworks which regulate foreign investments at the national level. *Second*, under the label 'comparative arbitration law', scholars have investigated the emergence of a mixed procedural culture in international arbitration. *Third*, investment law scholars have compared specific investment treaty provisions to analogous provisions in international and national regimes. Arbitrators make analogies and resort to judicial borrowing in the light of customary rules of treaty interpretation. The adoption of comparative benchmarks can help adjudicators in interpreting and applying broad and open-ended investment treaty provisions, while restraining their discretion in reviewing state action. Reliance on persuasive precedents of previous arbitral tribunals may lead to an increased coherence of the system. In parallel, the increasing reliance on cases of other international courts and tribunals may increase the perceived legitimacy of the system. This robust dialogue contributes to the unity of international law and can improve the quality of arbitral jurisprudence. Finally, arbitrators may detect international principles of law and/or customary law through the analysis of relevant jurisprudence of other courts and tribunals, in order to clarify the existing law or to avoid *non liquet*.

Fourth, at the macro-level, investment treaty arbitration has been analogised to different legal systems, namely commercial arbitration, public law and public international law. Each of the mentioned systems has a plausible claim to being the most appropriate source for macro-analogy, and each macro-comparison comes with its own distinct logic. These conceptualisations of investment treaty arbitration all have merits and weaknesses and may diverge and converge on specific aspects. Most notably, none of them – but perhaps the international law paradigm due to its comprehensive nature – fully encapsulates the complex phenomenon of investor–state arbitration. These paradigms are not normative; rather they are descriptive in nature and reflect and emphasise certain aspects of investment treaty arbitration rather than others. Awareness of the existence of different paradigms promotes a better understanding and functioning of investment treaty arbitration. However, the selection of the relevant macro-analogy is not neutral and can lead to significantly different results.

The public international law paradigm constitutes the best source of analogy because international investment arbitration is a creature of, and remains rooted in, public international law. At the same time, it is recognised that other paradigms can be analytically useful and/or complementary. For instance, adopting a public law analysis can help detect the crystallisation of general principles of law and customary law, which are two of the sources of public international law. Certainly the migration of ideas from different legal systems to international investment law – and, arguably, from the latter to the former – contributes to building a distinct identity of international investment law as a vibrant and emerging area of international law. In parallel, by looking beyond the boundaries of international investment law, arbitral tribunals are engaged in a dialogue with the world community and position themselves within the cosmopolitan network of international courts and tribunals.

In conclusion, can investment treaty arbitration benefit from a wider use of comparative reasoning? The convergence between comparative legal research and international investment law can illuminate some aspects of both legal fields. On the one hand, the comparative method may have more of a future by penetrating other subjects than by trying to assert its own continued independence. On the other hand, comparing two legal systems will make both clearer by virtue of contrast. While the linkage between comparative legal research and international investment law, as with any use of analogies, is not neutral, comparative reasoning can humanise international investment law, attuning it to the developments of public international law including human rights law and enhancing the perception of its legitimacy. Many of the recent arbitral awards have concerned the determination of the appropriate boundary between two conflicting values: the legitimate sphere for state regulation in the pursuit of public goods, on the one hand, and the protection of foreign investments from state interference, on the other. Comparative reasoning enables 'ordering pluralism', fostering the idea of economic integration that is respectful of cultural differences.

BIBLIOGRAPHY

Books

Adams, M. and Bomhoff, J. 'Comparing Law: Practice and Theory', in M. Adams and J. Bomhoff (eds.), *Practice and Theory in Comparative Law* (Cambridge: Cambridge University Press, 2012), 1–21.

Adams, M. and Bomhoff, J. (eds.). *Practice and Theory in Comparative Law* (Cambridge: Cambridge University Press, 2012).

Adams, M. and Griffiths, J. 'Against "Comparative Method": Explaining Similarities and Differences', in M. Adams and J. Bomhoff (eds.), *Practice and Theory in Comparative Law* (Cambridge: Cambridge University Press, 2012), 279–301.

Aguilar Alvarez, G. and Reisman, W.M. 'How Well are Investment Awards Reasoned?', in G. Aguilar Alvarez and W.M. Reisman (eds.), *The Reasons Requirement in International Investment Arbitration* (Leiden: Martinus Nijhoff Publishers, 2008), 1–31.

Alvarez, J.E. 'Beware: Boundary Crossing', in T. Kahana and A. Scolnicov (eds.), *Boundaries of Rights, Boundaries of State (forthcoming* 2015).

Alvarez, J.E. 'Crossing the Public/Private Divide: Saipem v. Bangladesh and Other "Crossover" Cases', ICCA Congress Series No. 16, Singapore 2012, 2–28.

Alvarez, J.E. 'The Evolving BIT', in I.A. Laird and T. Weiler (eds.), *Investment Treaty Arbitration and International Law* (New York: Juris, 2010), ch. 1.

Alvarez, J.E. *The Public International Law Regime Governing International Investment* (The Hague: Hague Academy of International Law, 2011).

Alvarez, J.E. 'What Are International Judges for? The Main Functions of International Adjudication', in K. Alter, C. Romano and Y. Shany (eds.), *The Oxford Handbook on International Adjudication* (Oxford: Oxford University Press, 2014), 158–176.

Ambroise, C. and Capitant, H. *Cours élémentaire de droit civil français*, vol. I (Paris: Librairie Dalloz, 1931).

Ancel, M. 'Comment aborder le droit comparé (A propos d'une nouvelle "Introduction au droit comparé")', in *Études offertes à René Rodière* (Paris: Dalloz, 1981).

Anghie, A. *Imperialism, Sovereignty and the Making of International Law* (Cambridge: Cambridge University Press, 2005).

Austin, J. *The Province of Jurisprudence Determined* [1832] (Wilfred E. Rumble, ed.) (Cambridge: Cambridge University Press, 1995).

Baetens, F. (ed.). *Investment Law Within International Law: Integrationist Perspectives* (Cambridge: Cambridge University Press, 2013).

Barak, A. *Proportionality Constitutional Rights and Their Limitations* (Cambridge: Cambridge University Press, 2012).

Barak-Erez, D. 'An International Community of Legislatures?', in R.W. Bauman and T. Kahana (eds.), *The Least Examined Branch: The Role of Legislatures in the Constitutional State* (Cambridge: Cambridge University Press, 2006), 532–546.

Baxi, U. 'The Colonialist Heritage', in P. Legrand and R. Munday (eds.), *Comparative Legal Studies: Traditions and Transitions* (Cambridge: Cambridge University Press, 2003), 46–75.

Bederman, D.J. *Custom as a Source of Law* (Cambridge: Cambridge University Press, 2010).

Bell, J. 'Legal Research and the Distinctiveness of Comparative Law', in M. Van Hoecke (ed.), *Methodologies of Legal Research. Which Kind of Method for What Kind of Discipline?* (Oxford: Hart Publishing, 2011), 155–175.

Binder, C., Kriebaum, U., Reinisch, A. and Wittich, S. (eds.). *International Investment Law for the 21st Century* (Oxford: Oxford University Press, 2009).

Bjorklund, A.K. 'Investment Treaty Arbitral Decisions as Jurisprudence Constante', in C. Picker, I. Bunn and D. Arner (eds.), *International Economic Law: The State and Future of the Discipline* (Oxford: Hart Publishing, 2008).

Blackaby, N. 'Investment Arbitration and Commercial Arbitration (or the Tale of the Dolphin and the Shark)', in J.D.M. Lew and L. Mistelis (eds.), *Pervasive Problems in International Arbitration* (The Hague/Boston/London: Kluwer Law International, 2006), 217–233.

Bobbio, N. 'Analogia', in N. Bobbio (ed.), *Contributi a un dizionario giuridico* (Torino: Giappichelli, 1994), 1.

Bobbio, N. *L'analogia nella logica del diritto* (Torino: Istituto Giuridico della Regia Università di Torino, 1938).

Bobek, M. *Comparative Reasoning in European Supreme Courts* (Oxford: Oxford University Press, 2013).

Bobek, M. 'Reasonableness in Administrative Law: A Comparative Reflection on Functional Equivalence', in G. Bongiovanni, G. Sartor and C. Valentini (eds.), *Reasonableness and Law* (Heidelberg: Springer, 2009), 311–326.

Böckstiegel, K.-H. 'Arbitration of Foreign Investment Disputes – An Introduction', in A.J. van den Berg (ed.), *New Horizons in International Commercial Arbitration and Beyond* (Kluwer Law International, 2005), 125–131.

Bogdan, M. *Concise Introduction to Comparative Law* (Amsterdam: Europa Law Publishing, 2013).

Bohlander, M. and Findlay, M. 'The Use of Domestic Sources as a Basis for International Criminal Law Principles', in G.Z. Capaldo (ed.), *The Global*

Community - Yearbook of International Law and Jurisprudence (New York: Oceana Publications, 2002), 3-26.

Bonnitcha, J. 'Outline of a Normative Framework for Evaluating Interpretations of Investment Treaty Protections', in C. Brown and K. Miles (eds.), *Evolution in Investment Treaty Arbitration* (Cambridge: Cambridge University Press, 2011), 117-144.

Born, G.B. and Shenkman, E.G. 'Confidentiality and Transparency in Commercial and Investor–State International Arbitration', in C.A. Rogers and R.P. Alford (eds.), *The Future of Investment Arbitration* (Oxford: Oxford University Press, 2009), 5-42.

Bothe, M. and Ress, G. 'The Comparative Method and Public International Law', in W.E. Butler (ed.), *International Law in Comparative Perspective* (Alphen aan den Rijn: Sijthoff & Noordhoff, 1980), 49-66.

Bourdieu, P. *Distinction - A Social Critique of the Judgment of Taste* (R. Nice, trans., Cambridge, MA: Harvard University Press, 1984).

Brierly, J.L. *The Law of Nations: An Introduction to the International Law of Peace*, 6th ed., (H. Waldock, ed., New York: Oxford University Press, 1963).

Brown, C. *A Common Law of International Adjudication* (Oxford: Oxford University Press, 2007).

Brownlie, I. *Principles of Public International Law* (Oxford: Oxford University Press, 2008).

Brownlie, I. *Principles of Public International Law*, 6th ed., (Oxford: Oxford University Press, 2003).

Bussani, M. and Mattei, U. (eds.). *The Cambridge Companion to Comparative Law* (Cambridge: Cambridge University Press, 2012).

Bussani, M. and Mattei, U. (eds.). *The Common Core of European Private Law - Essays on the Project* (The Hague/London/New York: Kluwer Law International, 2002).

Butler, W., Kresin, O.V. and Shemshuchenko, I.S. *Foundations of Comparative Law: Methods and Typologies* (London: Wildy, Simmonds & Hill Publishing, 2011).

Butler, W.E. 'Comparative Approaches to International Law', *Recueil des Cours* 190 (1985).

Calvino, I. *Le città invisibili* [Torino: Einaudi, 1972] W. Weaver, transl., (London: Penguin, 1997).

Calvino, I. *Il castello dei destini incrociati* (Torino: Einaudi, 1971).

Cannizzaro, E. *Il principio della proporzionalitá nell'ordinamento internazionale* (Milano: Giuffré, 2000).

Cappelletti, M. and Cohen, W. *Comparative Constitutional Law* (Indianapolis, IN: Bobbs Merrill Co., 1979).

Cassese, A. *International Law* (Oxford: Oxford University Press, 2001).

Cassese, A *International Law*, 2nd ed., (Oxford: Oxford University Press, 2005).

Cheng, B. *General Principles of Law as Applied by International Courts and Tribunals* (Cambridge: Cambridge University Press, 1953).

Chiba, M. (ed.), *Asian Indigenous Law in Interaction with Received Law* (London and New York: Kegan Paul International, 1986).

Choudry, S. 'Migration as a New Metaphor in Comparative Constitutional Law', in S. Choudry (ed.), *The Migration of Constitutional Ideas* (Cambridge: Cambridge University Press, 2006), 1–25.

Choudry, S. (ed.), *The Migration of Constitutional Ideas* (Cambridge: Cambridge University Press, 2006).

Collier, J. and Lowe, V. *The Settlement of Disputes in International Law: Institutions and Procedures* (Oxford: Oxford University Press, 1999).

Comeaux, P. and Kinsella, N. *Protecting Foreign Investment under International Law* (New York: Oceana Publications, 1997).

Constantinesco, L.J. *Traité du droit comparé, vol. II, La méthode comparative* (Paris: Librairie générale de droit et de jurisprudence, 1974).

Cordero Moss, G. 'Commercial Arbitration and Investment Arbitration: Fertile Soil for False Friends?', in C. Binder, U. Kriebaum, A. Reinisch and S. Wittich (eds.), *International Investment Law for the 21st Century: Essays in Honour of Christoph Schreuer* (Oxford: Oxford University Press, 2009), 782–800.

Cotterell, R. 'The Concept of Legal Culture', in David Nelken (ed.), *Comparing Legal Cultures* (Aldershot: Dartmouth, 1997).

Cotterell, R. 'Seeking Similarity, Appreciating Difference: Comparative Law and Communities', in A. Harding and E. Örücü (eds.), *Comparative Law in the 21st Century* (The Hague: Kluwer Law International, 2002).

Cotula, L. *Human Rights, Natural Resources and Investment Law in a Globalised World* (London: Routledge, 2013).

Crawford, J. 'International Protection of Foreign Direct Investment: Between Clinical Isolation and Systematic Integration', in R. Hofmann and C.J. Tams (eds.), *International Investment Law and General International Law – from Clinical Isolation to Systemic Integration?* (Baden/Baden: Nomos, 2011), 17–28.

Cross, R. *Precedent in English Law*, 2nd ed., (Oxford: Clarendon Press, 1968).

Cutler, C. *Private Power and Global Authority – Transnational Merchant Law in the Global Political Economy* (New York: Cambridge University Press, 2003).

David, R. *Les grands systèmes de droit contemporains*, 5th ed., (Paris: Dalloz, 1973).

David, R. and Jauffret-Spinosi, C. *Les grands systèmes de droit contemporains*, 11th ed., (Paris: Dalloz, 2002).

De Brabandere, E. and Gazzini, T. (eds.), *International Investment Law: The Sources of Rights and Obligations* (Leiden: Martinus Nijhoff, 2012).

De Bracton, H. *Bracton on the Laws and Customs of England* [1250/1259] (S.E. Thorne, ed.) vol. 2 (Cambridge, MA: Harvard University Press, 1976).

De Cruz, P. *Comparative Law in Changing World* (Abingdon/New York: Routledge-Cavendish, 2007).

Del Vecchio, G. *Sui principi generali del diritto* (Milano: Giuffré, 1958).

De Schutter, O., Swinnen, J. and Wouters, J. (eds.), *Foreign Direct Investment and Human Development* (London: Routledge, 2012).

de Secondat Montesquieu, C. *The Spirit of the Laws*, [1748] (A.M. Cohler, B.C. Miller and H.S. Stone, eds. and transl., Cambridge: Cambridge University Press, 1989), 308–333.

De Sousa Santos, B. and Rodríguez-Garavito, C.A. (eds.), *Law and Globalization from Below. Towards a Cosmopolitan Legality* (Cambridge: Cambridge University Press, 2005).

de Wet, E. and Vidmar, J. (eds), *Hierarchy in International Law: The Place of Human Rights* (Oxford: Oxford University Press, 2012).

Dezalay, Y. and Garth, B. *Dealing in Virtue* (Chicago: University of Chicago, 1996).

Dezalay, Y. and Garth, B.G. (eds.), *Global Prescriptions: The Production, Exportation and Importation of a New Legal Orthodoxy* (Ann Arbor, MI: Michigan University Press, 2002).

Dolzer, R. and Schreuer, C. *Principles of International Investment Law* (Oxford: Oxford University Press, 2008).

Dolzer, R. and Schreuer, C. *Principles of International Investment Law*, 2nd ed., (Oxford: Oxford University Press, 2012).

Douglas, Z. *The International Law of Investment Claims* (Cambridge: Cambridge University Press, 2009).

Drahozal, C.R. and Gibson, C.S. *The Iran–U.S. Claims Tribunal at 25: The Cases Everyone Needs to Know for Investor–State and International Arbitration* (Oxford: Oxford University Press, 2009).

Dugan, C. Rubins, N., Wallace, D., Sabahi, B. *Investor–State Arbitration* (Oxford: Oxford University Press, 2008).

Dupuy, P.-M., Francioni, F. and Petersmann, E.-U. (eds.), *Human Rights in International Investment Law and Arbitration* (Oxford: Oxford University Press, 2009).

Ellis, E. (ed.), *The Principle of Proportionality in the Laws of Europe* (Oxford: Hart Publishing, 1999).

Erlich, E. 'Judicial Freedom of Decision: Its Principles and Objects', in *Science of Legal Method: Selected Essays by Various Authors* [1917] (E. Bruncken and L.B. Register, trans., New York: A.M. Kelley, 1969).

Feldbrugge, F.J.M. 'Sociological Research Methods and Comparative Law', in M. Rotondi (ed.), *Buts et methods du droit comparé/Aims and Methods of Comparative Law* (Padua: CEDAM, 1973).

Feyerabend, P. *Against Method*, 3rd ed., (London: Verso, 1993).

Footer, M.E. 'International Investment Law and Trade: The Relationship that Never Went Away', in F. Baetens (ed.), *Investment Law within International Law: Integrationist Perspectives* (Cambridge: Cambridge University Press, 2013), ch. 12.

Gadamer, H.G. *Truth and Method*, 2nd ed., (J. Weinsheimer and D.G. Marshall, trans., New York: Crossroad, 2004).

Gardiner, R. *Treaty Interpretation* (Oxford: Oxford University Press, 2008).

Gerber, D.J. 'Sculpting the Agenda of Comparative Law: Ernst Rabel and the Façade of Language', in A. Riles (ed.), *Rethinking the Masters of Comparative Law* (Oxford and Portland, Oregon: Hart Publishing, 2001).

Gianformaggio, L. 'L'analogia giuridica', in L. Gianformaggio, *Studi sulla giustificazione giuridica* (Torino: Giappichelli, 1986), 131–147.

Ginsburg, T. 'Written Constitutions and the Administrative State: On the Constitutional Character of Administrative Law', in S. Rose-Ackerman and P.L. Lindseth (eds.), *Comparative Administrative Law* (Cheltenham, UK: Edward Elgar, 2011), 117–127.

Glanert, S. (ed.), *Comparative Law: Engaging Translation* (London: Routledge, 2014).

Glanert, S. 'Method?', in P.G. Monateri (ed.), *Methods of Comparative Law* (Cheltenham: Edward Elgar, 2012), 61–81.

Glanert, S. 'The Challenge of Translation', in M. Palmer (ed.), *ADR and Legal Practice in Comparative Perspective* (Beijing: China University of Political Science and Law Press, 2013), 370–380.

Glenn, H.P. 'Against Method?', in P.G. Monateri (ed.), *Methods of Comparative Law* (Cheltenham, UK: Edward Elgar, 2012) 177–188.

Glenn, H.P. 'Com-paring', in E. Örücü and D. Nelken (eds.), *Comparative Law: A Handbook* (Oxford: Hart Publishing, 2007), 91–108.

Glenn, H.P. *Legal Traditions of the World*, 3rd ed., (Oxford: Oxford University Press, 2007).

Glenn, H.P. *Legal Traditions of the World: Sustainable Diversity in Law*, 4th ed., (Oxford: Oxford University Press, 2010).

Goldman, B. 'The Applicable Law: General Principles of Law – The Lex Mercatoria', in J.D. Lew (ed.), *Contemporary Problems in International Arbitration* (London: Centre for Commercial Law Studies, 1986), 113–125.

Gourgourinis, A. 'Reviewing the Administration of Domestic Regulation in WTO and Investment Law: the International Minimum Standard as "One Standard to Rule them all?"', in F. Baetens (ed.), *Investment Law within International Law Integrationist Perspectives* (Cambridge: Cambridge University Press, 2013), ch. 13.

Graziadei, M. 'Comparative Law as the Study of Transplants and Receptions', in M. Reimann and R. Zimmermann (eds.), *The Oxford Handbook of Comparative Law* (Oxford: Oxford University Press, 2006).

Graziadei, M.M. 'The Functionalist Heritage', in P. Legrand and R. Munday (eds.), *Comparative Legal Studies: Traditions and Transitions* (Cambridge: Cambridge University Press, 2003), 100–127.

Gutteridge, H.C. *Comparative Law: An Introduction to the Comparative Method of Legal Study and Research*, 2nd ed. (Cambridge: Cambridge University Press, 1949).

Hart, H.L.A. *The Concept of Law* (Oxford: Oxford University Press, 1961).

Hirsch, M. 'Investment Tribunals and Human Rights: Divergent Paths', in P.-M. Dupuy, F. Francioni and E.-U. Petersmann (eds.), *Human Rights in International Investment Law and Arbitration* (Oxford: Oxford University Press, 2008), 97–113.

Hirschl, R. *Towards Juristocracy: The Origins and Consequences of the New Constitutionalism* (Boston, MA: Harvard University Press, 2004).

Hofstadter, D. 'Analogy as the Core of Cognition', in D. Gentner, K. Holyoak and B. Kokinov (eds.), *The Analogical Mind: Perspectives from Cognitive Science* (Cambridge, MA: MIT Press/Bradford Book, 2001), 499–538.

Hsu, L. 'Applicability of WTO Law in Regional Trade Agreements: Identifying the Links', in L. Bartels and F. Ortino (eds.), *Regional Trade Agreements and the WTO Legal System* (Oxford: Oxford University Press, 2006), 551.

Husa, J. 'Legal Families', in J. Smit (ed.), *Elgar Encyclopaedia of Comparative Law* (Cheltenham: Edward Elgar, 2010), 491–504.

Husa, J. 'Research Designs of Comparative Law – Methodology or Heuristics?', in M. Adams and D. Heirbaut (eds.), *The Method and Culture of Comparative Law* (Oxford and Portland, OR: Hart Publishing, 2014), 53–68.

Jackson, J. *The World Trading System* (Cambridge, MA: MIT Press, 2002).

Jenks, C.W. *The Common Law of Mankind* (New York: Frederick A. Praeger, 1958).

Kahn-Freund, O. *Comparative Law as an Academic Subject* (Oxford: Clarendon Press, 1965).

Kawharu, A. 'Participation of Non-Governmental Organizations in Investment Arbitration as Amici Curiae', in M. Waibel, A. Kaushal, K.-H.L. Chung and C. Balchin (eds.), *The Blacklash Against Investment Arbitration: Perceptions and Reality* (The Netherlands: Kluwer Law International, 2010), 275–295.

Kingsbury, B. and Schill, S. 'Public Law Concepts to Balance Investors' Rights with State Regulatory Actions in the Public Interest – The Concept of Proportionality', in S. Schill (ed.), *International Investment Law and Comparative Public Law* (Oxford: Oxford University Press, 2010), 75–105.

Kingsbury, B. and Straumann, B. (eds.), *The Roman Foundations of the Law of Nations* (Oxford: Oxford University Press, 2010).

Koschaker, P. *Europa und das römische Recht [1946]*, 2nd ed., (Munich/Berlin: Biederstein Verlag, 1953).

Kriebaum, U. and Schreuer, C. 'The Concept of Property in Human Rights Law and International Investment Law', in S. Breitenmoser (ed.), *Liber Amicorum Luzius Wildhaber – Human Rights Democracy and the Rule of Law* (Berlin: Nomos, 2007), 743–762.

Kuhn, T. *La structure des révolutions scientifiques* (Paris: Flammarion, 1972).

Kulick, A. *Global Public Interest in International Investment Law* (Cambridge: Cambridge University Press, 2013).

Kurtz, J. 'The Merits and Limits of Comparativism: National Treatment in International Investment Law and the WTO', in S. Schill (ed.), *International Investment Law and Comparative Public Law* (Oxford: Oxford University Press, 2010), 243–278.

Lakoff, G. 'Contemporary Theory of Metaphor', in A. Ortony (ed.), *Metaphor and Thought* (Cambridge: Cambridge University Press, 1993), 202–251.

Lalive, P. 'On the Neutrality of the Arbitrator and of the Place of Arbitration', in C. Reymond and E. Bucher (eds.), *Recueil de Travaux Suisses sur l'arbitrage international* (Zürich: Schulthess, 1984), 23–33.

Lalive, P. 'Sur des dimensions culturelles de l'arbitrage international', in J. Makarczyk and K. Skubiszewski (eds.), *Theory of International Law at the Threshold of the 21st Century – Essays in Honour of Krzystof Skubiszewski* (The Hague: Kluwer Law International, 1996).

Landau, T. 'Reasons for Reasons: The Tribunal's Duty in Investor–State Arbitration', in A.J. Van den Berg (ed.), *50 Years of the New York Convention – ICCA International Arbitration Conference ICCA Congress Series No. 14, Dublin Conference, 2008* (The Hague: Kluwer Law International, 2009), 187–205.

Larry, A. and Sherwin, E. *Demystifying Legal Reasoning* (Cambridge: Cambridge University Press, 2008).

Lauterpacht, E. (ed.), *International Law – The Collected Papers of Hersch Lauterpacht*, vol. I, [1970] (London: Cambridge University Press, 2009).

Lauterpacht, H. *Private Law Sources and Analogies of International Law: With Special Reference to International Arbitration* (London and New York: Longmans, Green and Co., Ltd., 1927).

Lauterpacht, H. 'Some Observations on the Prohibition of Non Liquet and the Completeness of the Legal Order', in *Symbolae Verzijl présentées au Professeur J.H.W. Verzijl à l'occasion de son VXXième anniversaire* (The Hague: Martinus Nijhoff, 1958), 196.

Lauterpacht, H. *The Development of International Law by the International Court* (London: Stevens & Sons, 1958).

Leben, C. *The Advancement of International Law* (Oxford: Hart Publishing, 2010).

Legrand, P. *Le droit comparé* (Paris: Presses Universitaires de France, 1999).

Legrand, P. 'What "Legal Transplants"?', in D. Nelken and J. Feest (eds.), *Adapting Legal Cultures* (Oxford: Hart Publishing, 2001), 58.

Legrand, P. and Munday, R. *Comparative Legal Studies: Traditions and Transitions* (Cambridge: Cambridge University Press, 2003).

Lemmens, K. 'Comparative Law as an Act of Modesty: A Pragmatic and Realistic Approach to Comparative Legal Scholarship', in M. Adams and J. Bomhoff (eds.), *Practice and Theory in Comparative Law* (Cambridge: Cambridge University Press, 2012), 302–326.

Levi, E.H. *An Introduction to Legal Reasoning* (Chicago, IL: University of Chicago Press, 1949).

Lew, J.D.M. Mistelis, L.A. and Kröll, S.M. (eds.), *Comparative International Commercial Arbitration* (The Hague: Kluwer Law International, 2003).

Lew, J.D.M. 'The Case for the Publication of Arbitration Awards', in J.C. Schultsz, A.J. van den Berg (eds.), *The Art of Arbitration, Essays on International Arbitration, Liber Amicorum Pieter Sanders* (The Hague: Kluwer Law, 1982), 227.

Libeskind, D. *Breaking Ground* (New York: Riverhead, 2004).

Lloyd, G.E.R. *Polarity and Analogy, Two Types of Argumentation in Early Greek Thought* (Cambridge: Cambridge University Press, 1966).

Locke, J. *Second Treatise of Government* [1689] (C.B. Macpherson, ed.) (Indianapolis, IN: Hackett Publishing, 1980).

Loughlin, M. *The Idea of Public Law* (Oxford: Oxford University Press, 2003).

Lowenfeld, A. *International Economic Law*, 2nd ed. (Oxford: Oxford University Press, 2008).

Mann, H. *International Investment Agreements, Business and Human Rights: Key Issues and Opportunities* (Winnipeg: IISD, 2008).

Mann, H. 'The Right of States to Regulate and International Investment Law: A Comment', in UNCTAD, *The Development Dimension of FDI: Policy and Rule-Making Perspectives* (New York: UN, 2003), 211–223.

Mattei, U. *Comparative Law and Economics* (Ann Arbor, MI: University of Michigan Press, 1997).

McCrudden, C. 'Judicial Comparativism and Human Rights', in E. Örükü and D. Nelken (eds.), *Comparative Law: A Handbook* (Oxford: Hart Publishing, 2007), 371–398.

McLachlan, C., Shore, L. and Weiniger, M. *International Investment Arbitration* (Oxford: Oxford University Press, 2007).

McLaughlin Mitchell, S. and Powell, E.J. *Domestic Law Goes Global* (Cambridge: Cambridge University Press, 2011).

Menski, W. *Comparative Law in a Global Context*, 2nd ed., (Cambridge: Cambridge University Press, 2006).

Merryman, J.H. 'On the Convergence (and Divergence) of the Civil Law and the Common Law', in M. Cappelletti (ed.), *New Perspectives for a Common Law of Europe* (Leyden: Sijthoff, 1978).

Merryman, J.H. 'The Loneliness of the Comparative Lawyer', in J.H. Merryman, *The Loneliness of the Comparative Lawyer And Other Essays in Foreign and Comparative Law* (The Hague/London/Boston: Kluwer Law International, 1999).

Michaels, R. 'The Functional Method of Comparative Law', in M. Reimann and R. Zimmermann (eds.), *The Oxford Handbook of Comparative Law* (Oxford: Oxford University Press, 2006), 340–380.

Miles, K. *The Origins of International Investment Law* (Cambridge: Cambridge University Press, 2013).

Monateri, P.G. (ed.), *Methods of Comparative Law* (Cheltenham: Edward Elgar, 2012).

Montt, S. *State Liability in Investment Treaty Arbitration – Global Constitutional and Administrative Law in the BIT Generation* (Oxford and Portland, OR: Hart Publishing, 2009).

Muchlinski, P. *Multinational Enterprises and the Law*, 2nd ed., (Oxford: Oxford University Press, 2007).

Muchlinski, P. 'The Diplomatic Protection of Foreign Investors: A Tale of Judicial Caution', in C. Binder, U. Kriebaum, A. Reinisch and S. Wittich (eds.), *International Investment Law for the 21st Century: Essays in Honour of Christoph Schreuer* (Oxford: Oxford University Press, 2009), 341–362.

Muir Watt, H. 'Globalization and Comparative Law', in M. Reimann and R. Zimmermann (eds.), *The Oxford Handbook of Comparative Law* (Oxford: Oxford University Press, 2006), 583–606.

Newcombe, A. and Paradell, L. *Law and Practice of Investment Treaties* (Alphen aan den Rijn: Kluwer Law International, 2009).

Nin, A. *Solar Barque* (Ann Arbour, MI: Edwards Brothers, 1958).

Orellana, M.A. 'Science, Risk and Uncertainty: Public Health Measures and Investment Disciplines', in P. Kahn and T.W. Wälde (eds.), *New Aspects of International Investment Law* (Leiden: Martinus Nijhoff, 2007), 671.

Örücü, E. *The Enigma of Comparative Law* (Leiden: Martinus Nijhoff, 2004).

Paparinskis, M. 'Analogies and Other Regimes of International Law', in Z. Douglas, J. Pauwelyn and J.E. Viñuales (eds.), *The Foundations of International Investment Law: Bringing Theory into Practice* (Oxford: Oxford University Press, 2014).

Paparinskis, M. 'Sources of Law and Arbitral Interpretations of *Pari Materia* Investment Protection Rules', in O.K. Fauchald and A. Nollkamper (eds.), *The Practice of International and National Courts and (De-) Fragmentation of International Law* (Portland, OR: Hart Publishing, 2012).

Parra, A. *History of ICSID* (Oxford: Oxford University Press, 2012).

Paulsson, J. *Denial of Justice in International Law* (Cambridge: Cambridge University Press, 2005).

Paulsson, J. 'Avoiding Unintended Consequences', in K. Sauvant and M. Chiswick-Patterson (eds.), *Appeals Mechanism in International Investment Disputes* (Oxford: Oxford University Press, 2008), 241.

Paulsson, J. 'International Arbitration and the Generation of Legal Norms: Treaty Arbitration and International Law', in A.J. Van den Berg (ed.), *International Arbitration 2006: Back to Basics? ICCA Congress Series No. 13* (The Hague: Kluwer Law International, 2007), 879–889.

Perry, A.J. *Legal Systems as Determinant of Foreign Direct Investment: Lessons from Sri Lanka* (London: Kluwer Law, 2001).

Petersmann, E.-U. 'Introduction and Summary: "Administration of Justice" in International Investment Law and Adjudication?', in P.M. Dupuy, F. Francioni and E.-U. Petersmann (eds.), *Human Rights in International Investment Law and Arbitration* (Oxford: Oxford University Press, 2009), 3–43.

Peterson, L.E. *The Global Governance of Foreign Direct Investment: Madly Off in All Directions* (Geneva: Friedrich Ebert Stiftung Publisher, 2005).

Picciotto, S. *Regulating Global Corporate Capitalism* (Cambridge: Cambridge University Press, 2011).

Picker, C. 'International Investment Law: Some Legal Cultural Insights', in L. Trakman and N. Ranieri (eds.), *Regionalism in International Investment Law* (Oxford: Oxford University Press, 2013), 27–58.

Pirandello, L. *Sei personaggi in cerca d'autore* [1921], 14th ed., (Milan: Mondadori, 2001).

Pirker, B. *Proportionality Analysis and Models of Judicial Review* (Groningen: Europa Law Publishing, 2013).

Pizzorusso, A. *Sistemi Giuridici Comparati*, 2d ed., (Milano: Giuffré, 1998).

Porat, I. 'Some Critical Thoughts on Proportionality', in G. Bongiovanni, G. Sartor and C. Valentini (eds.), *Reasonableness and Law* (Heidelberg: Springer, 2009), 243–250.

Posner, R.A. *The Problems of Jurisprudence* (Cambridge, MA: Harvard University Press, 1990).

Posner, R.A. *Overcoming Law* (Cambridge, MA: Harvard University Press, 1995).

Postema, G.J. 'A Similibus ad Similia – Analogical Thinking in Law', in D.E. Edlin (ed.), *Common Law Theory* (Cambridge: Cambridge University Press, 2010), 102–133.

Prott, L.V. *The Latent Power of Culture and the International Judge* (Abingdon: Professional Books Ltd., 1979).

Puvimanasinghe, S.F. *Foreign Investment, Human Rights and the Environment* (Leiden: Martinus Nijhoff, 2007).

Raimondo, F. *General Principles of Law in the Decisions of International Criminal Courts and Tribunals* (Oxford: Oxford University Press, 2008).

Raimondo, F. 'Les principes généraux de droit dans la jurisprudence des Tribunaux ad hoc: une approche functionelle', in M. Delmas-Marty and E. Fronza (eds.), *Les sources du droit international penal: l'expérience des tribunaux pénaux internationaux et le statut de la Cour pénale internationale* (Paris: Societé de législation comparée, 2004), 79.

Rajagopal, B. *International Law from Below – Development, Social Movements and Third World Resistance* (Cambridge: Cambridge University Press, 2003).

Reimann, M. 'Comparative Law and Neighbouring Disciplines', in M. Bussani and U. Mattei (eds.), *The Cambridge Companion to Comparative Law* (Cambridge: Cambridge University Press, 2012), 13–34.

Reimann, M. and Zimmerman, R. (eds.), *The Oxford Handbook of Comparative Law* (Oxford: Oxford University Press, 2006).

Reiner, C. and Schreuer, C. 'Human Rights and International Investment Arbitration', in P.-M. Dupuy, F. Francioni and E.-U. Petersmann (eds.), *Human Rights in International Investment Law and Arbitration* (Oxford: Oxford University Press, 2008), 82–96.

Reinisch, A. *Standards of Investment Protection* (Oxford: Oxford University Press, 2008).

Reisman, W.M. 'Investment and Human Rights Tribunals as Courts of Last Appeal in International Commercial Arbitration', in L. Levy and Y. Derains (eds.), *Liber Amicorum en honneur de Serge Lazareff* (Paris: Pedone, 2011), 521.

Riles, A. 'Comparative Law and Socio-Legal Studies', in M. Reimann and R. Zimmermann (eds.), *The Oxford Handbook of Comparative Law* (Oxford: Oxford University Press, 2006), 811.

Roberts, A. 'Subsequent Agreements and Practice: The Battle over Interpretive Power', in G. Nolte (ed.), *Treaties and Subsequent Practice* (Oxford: Oxford University Press, 2013), chapter 8.

Rodière, R. *Introduction au droit comparé* (Paris: Dalloz, 1979).

Rosen, L. *Law as Culture: An Invitation* (Princeton, NJ: Princeton University Press, 2006), 199–200.

Ross Perry, R. *Common Law Pleading: Its History and Principles* (Boston, MA: Little Brown, 1897).

Sacco, R. *La comparaison juridique au service de la connaissance du droit* (Paris: Economica, 1991).

Sadurski, W. 'Reasonableness and Value Pluralism in Law and Politics', in G. Bongiovanni, G. Sartor and C. Valentini (eds.), *Reasonableness and Law* (Heidelberg: Springer, 2009), 129.

Salacuse, J.W. *The Law of Investment Treaties* (Oxford: Oxford University Press, 2010).

Saleilles, R. 'Conception et Objet de la Science Juridique du Droit Comparé', in *Procès-Verbaux des Séances et Documents du Congrès International de Droit Comparé* 1900, vol. I, (Paris: LGDJ 1905–1907), 173.

Scelle, G. 'Essai sur les sources formelles du droit international', in *Recueil d'Etudes sur les sources du droit en l'honneur de François Gény*, vol. III (Paris: Sirey, 1934), 400–430.

Schill, S. 'General Principles of Law and International Investment Law', in T. Gazzini and E. de Brabandere (eds.), *International Investment Law – The Sources of Rights and Obligations* (Leiden: Martinus Nijhoff, 2012), 133–181.

Schill, S. 'International Investment Law and Comparative Public Law: An Introduction', in S. Schill (ed.), *International Investment Law and Comparative Public Law* (Oxford: Oxford University Press, 2010), 3–38.

Schill, S. (ed.), *International Investment Law and Comparative Public Law* (Oxford: Oxford University Press, 2010).

Schill, S.W. *The Multilateralization of International Investment Law* (Cambridge: Cambridge University Press, 2009).

Schlesinger, R.B. 'The Common Core of Legal Systems – An Emerging Subject of Comparative Study', in K.H. Nadelmann, A.T. von Mehren and J.N. Hazard (eds.), *Twentieth Century Comparative and Conflicts Law – Legal Essays in Honour of Hessel E. Yntema* (Leiden: A. W. Sijthoff, 1961).

Schneiderman, D. *Constitutionalizing Economic Globalization: Investment Rules and Democracy's Premise* (Oxford: Oxford University Press, 2008).

Schreuer, C. *The ICSID Convention: A Commentary* (Cambridge: Cambridge University Press, 2001).

Schreuer, C. and Kriebaum, U. 'The Concept of Property in Human Rights Law and International Investment Law', in S. Breitenmoser, B. Ehrenzeller, M. Sassoli, W. Stoffel and B. Wagner Pfeifer (eds.), *Human Rights, Democracy and the Rule of Law: Liber Amicorum Luzius Wildhaber* (Baden/Baden: Dike, 2007).

Schreuer, C. and Weiniger, M. 'A Doctrine of Precedent?', in P. Muchlinski, F. Ortino and C. Schreuer (eds.), *The Oxford Handbook of International Investment Law* (Oxford: Oxford University Press, 2008), 1191–1196.

Schwarz-Liebermann von Wahlendorf, H.A. *Droit comparé. Théorie générale et principes* (Paris: Librairie générale de droit et de jurisprudence, 1978).

Scobbie, I. 'Wicked Heresies or Legitimate Perspectives? Theory and International Law', in M. Evans (ed.), *International Law* (Oxford: Oxford University Press, 2010), 58–92.

Sen, A. *The Idea of Justice* (Boston, MA: Harvard University Press, 2009).

Shan, W., Simons, P. and Singh, D. (eds.), *Redefining Sovereignty in International Economic Law* (Oxford: Hart Publishing, 2008).

Siems, M.M. 'The Curious Case of Overfitting Legal Transplants', in M. Adams and D. Heirbaut (eds.), *The Method and Culture of Comparative Law: Essays in Honour of Mark Van Hoecke* (Oxford: Hart Publishing, 2014), 133–145.

Siltala, R. *A Theory of Precedent – From Analytical Positivism to a Post-Analytical Philosophy of Law* (Oxford: Hart Publishing, 2000).

Simma, B. and Kill, T. 'Harmonizing Investment Protection and International Human Rights: First Steps Towards a Methodology', in C. Binder, U. Kriebaum, A. Reinisch, S. Wittich (eds.), *International Investment Law for the 21st Century: Essays in Honour of Christoph Schreuer* (Oxford: Oxford University Press, 2009), 678–707.

Sinclair, I. *The Vienna Convention on the Law of Treaties* (Manchester: Manchester University Press, 1984).

Slaughter, A. *A New World Order* (Princeton and Oxford: Princeton University Press, 2004).

Smith, A. *Lectures on Jurisprudence* [1762–1763], R.L. Meek et al. eds., (Oxford: Oxford University Clarendon Press, 1978).

Smits, J. *Elgar Encyclopedia of Comparative Law*, 2nd ed., (Cheltenham, UK: Edward Elgar, 2012).

Sornarajah, M. 'A Coming Crisis: Expansionary Trends in Investment Treaty Arbitration', in K.P. Sauvant (ed.), *Appeals Mechanism in International Investment Disputes Law* (Oxford: Oxford University Press, 2008).

Sornarajah, M. 'Right to Regulate and Safeguards', in UNCTAD, *The Development Dimension of FDI: Policy and Rule Making Perspectives* (New York/Geneva: UN, 2003) 205–210.

Sornarajah, M. *The International Law on Foreign Investment*, 3rd ed., (Cambridge: Cambridge University Press, 2010).

Stern, B. 'In Search of the Frontiers of Indirect Expropriation', in A. Rovine (ed.), *Contemporary Issues in International Arbitration and Mediation* (Leiden: Martinus Nijhoff Publishers, 2008), 29–51.

Stone Sweet, A. and Grisel, F. 'The Evolution of International Arbitration: Delegation, Judicialization, Governance', in W. Mattli and T. Dietz (eds.), *International Arbitration and Global Governance: Contending Theories and Evidence* (Oxford: Oxford University Press, 2014), 22–46.

Stone Sweet, A. and Grisel, F. 'Transnational Investment Arbitration: From Delegation to Constitutionalization?', in P.M. Dupuy, F. Francioni and E.U. Petersmann (eds.), *Human Rights in International Investment Law and Arbitration* (Oxford: Oxford University Press, 2009), 118–136.

Strathern, M. *Partial Connections* (California: Alta Mira Press, 1991).

Subedi, S. *International Investment Law: Reconciling Policy and Principle* (Oxford: Hart Publishing, 2008).

Swanson, G. 'Frameworks for Comparative Research: Structural Anthropology and the Theory of Action', in I. Vallier (ed.), *Comparative Methods in Sociology* (Berkeley, CA: University of California Press, 1971), 141–202.

Swift, J. *Travels into Several Remote Nations of the World. In Four Parts. By Lemuel Gulliver, First a Surgeon, and then a Captain of Several Ships*, [*Gulliver's Travels*] (London: Benjamin Motte, 1726).

Tams, C. 'The Sources of International Investment Law', in T. Gazzini and E. De Brabandere (eds.), *International Investment Law: The Sources of Rights and Obligations* (Leiden: Brill, 2012), 319–332.

Teitel, R. *Humanity's Law* (Oxford: Oxford University Press, 2011).

Teubner, G. 'Global Bukowina: Legal Pluralism in the World Society', in G. Teubner (ed.), *Global Law Without a State* (Aldershot: Dartmouth Publishing, 1997), 3–30.

Tienhaara, K. *The Expropriation of Environmental Governance* (Cambridge: Cambridge University Press, 2009).

Tomuschat, C. 'The European Court of Human Rights and Investment Protection', in C. Binder, U. Kriebaum, A. Reinisch, S. Wittich (eds.), *International Investment*

Law for the 21st Century: Essays in Honour of Christoph Schreuer (Oxford: Oxford University Press, 2009), 636–656.

Trachtman, J. *The Economic Structure of International Law* (Cambridge, MA: Harvard University Press, 2008).

Treves, T., Seatzu, F. and Trevisanut, S. (eds.), *Foreign Investment, International Law and Common Concerns* (London: Routledge, 2014).

Trubek, D. and Santos, A. (eds.), *The New Law and Economic Development* (Cambridge: Cambridge University Press, 2006).

Twining, W. *General Jurisprudence: Understanding Law from a Global Perspective* (Cambridge: Cambridge University Press, 2008).

Vadi, V. *Public Health in International Investment Law and Arbitration* (Abingdon: Routledge, 2012).

Valcke, C. 'Reflections on Comparative Law Methodology – Getting Inside Contract Law', in M. Adams and J. Bomhoff (eds.), *Practice and Theory in Comparative Law* (Cambridge: Cambridge University Press, 2013).

Van den Bossche, P. and Zdouc, W. *The Law and Policy of the World Trade Organization*, 3rd ed. (Cambridge: Cambridge University Press, 2013).

Van Erp, S. 'Comparative Property Law', in M. Reimann and R. Zimmermann (eds.), *The Oxford Handbook of Comparative Law* (Oxford: Oxford University Press, 2006).

Van Harten, G. *Investment Treaty Arbitration and Public Law* (Oxford: Oxford University Press, 2007).

Van Hoecke, M. 'Deep Level Comparative Law', in M. Van Hoecke (ed.), *Epistemology and Methodology of Comparative Law* (Oxford: Hart Publishing, 2004), 165–174.

Van Hoecke, M. (ed.) *Epistemology and Methodology of Comparative Law* (Oxford/Portland: Hart Publishing, 2004).

Velluzzi, V. 'Osservazioni sull'analogia giuridica', in V. Velluzzi, *Tra Teoria e dogmatica* (Pisa: Edizioni ETS, 2012), 65–84.

von Bogdandy, A., Dann, P. and Goldmann, M. 'Developing the Publicness of Public International Law: Towards a Legal Framework for Global Governance Activities', in A. von Bogdandy, R. Wolfrum, J. von Bernstorff, P. Dann, M. Goldmann (eds.), *The Exercise of Public Authority by International Institutions* (Heidelberg: Springer, 2009), 3–32.

von Savigny, F.C. *On the Vocation of Our Age for Legislation and Jurisprudence* [Abraham Hayward, trans., London: Littlewood and Co., 1828] (Birmingham, AL: Legal Classics Library, 1986).

Waibel, M., Kaushal, A., Chung, K.-H.L. and Balchin, C. 'The Blacklash against Investment Arbitration: Perceptions and Reality', in M. Waibel, A. Kaushal, K.-H.L. Chung and C. Balchin (eds.), *The Blacklash against Investment Arbitration: Perceptions and Reality* (The Netherlands: Kluwer Law International, 2010).

Waibel, M., Kaushal, A., Chung, K.-H. and Balchin, C. (eds.), *The Backlash Against Investment Arbitration* (The Netherlands: Kluwer Law International, 2010).

Watson, A. *Legal Transplants: An Approach to Comparative Law* (Edinburgh: Scottish Academic Press, 1974).

Watson, A. *Legal Transplants: An Approach to Comparative Law*, 2nd ed., (Athens; London: University of Georgia Press, 1994).

Watson, A. *The Law of the Ancient Romans* (Dallas: Southern Methodist University, 1970).

Watt, G. 'Comparison as Deep Appreciation', in P.G. Monateri (ed.), *Methods of Comparative Law* (Cheltenham, UK: Edward Elgar, 2012), 82–99.

Weber, M. *The Protestant Ethic and the Spirit of Capitalism [Die protestantische Ethik und der Geist des Kapitalismus (Tübingen, 1920)]*, 3rd ed., (S. Kalberg ed. and trans., Los Angeles, CA: Roxbury Publishing Co., 2002).

Weinreb, L.L. *Legal Reason: The Use of Analogy in Legal Argument* (Cambridge: Cambridge University Press, 2005).

Wigmore, J.H. *A Kaleidoscope of Justice* (Washington, DC: Washington Law Books Co., 1941).

Wittgenstein, L. *Culture and Value* (G.H. Von Wright ed., P. Winch tranl., Oxford: Basil Blackwell, 1980).

Zumbansen, P. 'Transnational Comparisons: Theory and Practice of Comparative Law as a Critique of Global Governance', in M. Adams and J. Bomhoff (eds.), *Practice and Theory in Comparative Law* (Cambridge: Cambridge University Press, 2012), 186–211.

Zweigert, K. 'Méthodologie du droit comparé', in *Mélanges J. Maury* (Paris: Dalloz-Sirey, 1960), 579–596.

Zweigert, K. and Kötz, H. *Introduction to Comparative Law*, 3rd ed., T. Weir transl. (Oxford: Oxford University Press, 1998).

Articles

Aalberts, T.A. 'The Politics of International Law and the Perils and Promises of Interdisciplinarity', *Leiden Journal of International Law* 26 (2013), 503–508.

Akinsanya, A. 'International Protection of Foreign Direct Investments in the Third World', *International and Comparative Law Quarterly* 36 (1987), 58–75.

Allott, P. 'Language, Method and the Nature of International Law', *British Yearbook of International Law* 45 (1971), 79–135.

Alvarez, J.E. 'A BIT on Custom', *New York University Journal of International Law and Politics* (2010), 17–80.

Alvarez, J.E. 'Contemporary Foreign Investment Law: an Empire of Law or the Law of Empire?', *Alabama Law Review* 60 (2009), 943–974.

Alvarez, J.E. 'Contemporary International Law: An "Empire of Law" or "the Law of Empire"?', *American University International Law Review* 24 (2008–2009), 811–842.

Alvarez, J.E. 'The Return of the State', *Minnesota Journal of International Law* 20 (2011), 221–264.

Ambrus, M. 'Comparative Law Method in the Jurisprudence of the European Court of Human Rights in the Light of the Rule of Law', *Erasmus Law Review* 2 (2009), 353–371.

Anderson, J.L. 'Comparative Perspectives on Property Rights', *Journal of Legal Education* 56 (2006), 1–12.

Audit, M. 'The Channel Tunnel Group Ltd and France-Manche SA v. United Kingdom and France', *International and Comparative Law Quarterly* 57 (2008), 724–732.

Banakar, R. 'Power, Culture and Method in Comparative Law', *International Journal of Law in Context* 5 (2009), 69–85.

Barak-Erez, D. 'The Institutional Aspects of Comparative Law', *Columbia Journal of European Law* 15 (2008–2009), 477–492.

Barnes, W.R. 'Contemplating a Civil Law Paradigm for a Future International Commercial Code', *Louisiana Law Review* 65 (2004–2005), 677–774.

Bassiouni, M.C. 'A Functional Approach to General Principles of International Law', *Michigan Journal of International Law* 11 (1990), 768–818.

Bastid Burdeau, G. 'Nouvelles perspectives pour l'arbitrage dans le contentieux economique intéressant l'Etat', *Revue de l'Arbitrage* 1 (1995), 3–38.

Baudenbacher, C. 'Judicial Globalization: New Development or Old Wine in New Bottles?', *Texas International Law Journal* 38 (2003), 505–526.

Bean, V. and Beauvais, J.C. 'The Global Fifth Amendment? NAFTA's Investment Protection and the Misguided Quest for an International Regulatory Takings Doctrine', *New York University Law Review* 78 (2003), 30–143.

Becker, L.C. 'Analogy in Legal Reasoning', *Ethics* 83 (1973), 248–255.

Bénassy-Quéré, A., Coupet, M. and Mayer, T. 'Institutional Determinants of Foreign Direct Investment', *World Economy* 30 (2007), 764–782.

Ben Hamida, W. 'Investment Arbitration and Human Rights', *Transnational Dispute Management* 5 (2007), 1–14.

Benvenisti, E. 'Reclaiming Democracy: The Strategic Uses of Foreign and International Law by National Courts', *American Journal of International Law* 102 (2008), 241–274.

Berman, P.S. 'A Pluralist Approach to International Law', *Yale Journal of International Law* 32 (2007), 301–329.

Berman, F. 'Treaty Interpretation in a Judicial Context', *Yale Journal of International Law* 29 (2004), 315–322.

Bermann, G.A., Glenn, P., Lane Scheppele, K., Shalakany, A., Snyder, D.V. and Zoller, E. 'Comparative Law: Problems and Prospects', *American University International Law Review* 26 (2010–2011), 935–968.

Bhagwati, J. 'Why Multinationals Help Reduce Poverty', *World Economy* 30 (2007), 211–228.

Bjorklund, A. 'The Emerging Civilization of Investment Arbitration', *Penn State Law Review* 113 (2009), 1269–1300.

Böckstiegel, K.-H. 'Commercial and Investment Arbitration: How Different Are They Today?', *Arbitration International* 28 (2012), 577–590.

Böckstiegel, K.-H. 'Enterprise v. State: The New David and Goliath? – The Clayton Utz Lecture', *Arbitration International* 23 (2007), 93–104.

Borsellino, P. 'L'analogia nella logica del diritto: un contributo di Norberto Bobbio alla metodologia giuridica', *Rivista internazionale di filosofia del diritto* LXII (1985), 3–39.

Boughey, J. 'Administrative Law: The Next Frontier for Comparative Law', *International and Comparative Law Quarterly* 62 (2013), 55–95.

Braun, A. 'Burying the Living? The Citation of Legal Writings in English Courts', *American Journal of Comparative Law* 58 (2010), 27–52.

Brewer, T.L. and Young, S. 'Investment Issues at the WTO: The Architecture of Rules and the Settlement of Disputes', *Journal of International Economic Law* (1998), 457–470.

Brower, C.N. 'W(h)ither International Commercial Arbitration?', *Arbitration International* 24 (2008), 181–198.

Brower, C.N. and Schill, S.W. 'Is Arbitration a Threat or a Boon to the Legitimacy of International Investment Law?', *Chicago Journal of International Law* 9 (2008–2009), 471–498.

Brown, C. 'The Use of Precedents of Other International Courts and Tribunals in Investment Treaty Arbitration', *Transnational Dispute Management* 5 (2008), 1–10.

Brown, J., Kudat, A. and McGeeney, K. 'Improving Legislation through Social Analysis: a Case Study in Methodology from the Water Sector in Uzbekistan', *Sustainable Development Law and Policy* 5 (2005), 49–57.

Burke-White, W.W. 'International Legal Pluralism', *Michigan Journal of International Law* 25 (2004), 963–980.

Burke-White, W.W. and Von Staden, A. 'Investment Protection in Extraordinary Times: The Interpretation and Application of Non-Precluded Measures Provisions in Bilateral Investment Treaties', *Virginia Journal of International Law* 48 (2007), 307–411.

Burke-White, W.W. and Von Staden, A. 'Private Litigation in a Public Private Sphere: The Standard of Review in Investor–State Arbitrations', *Yale Journal of International Law* 35 (2010), 283–346.

Cappelletti, M. 'Repudiating Montesquieu? The Expansion and Legitimacy of "Constitutional Justice"', *Catholic University Law Review* 35 (1985), 1–32.

Cassese, S. 'Beyond Legal Comparison', *Annuario di diritto comparato e di studi legislativi* (2012), 387–395.

Chalamish, E. 'The Future of BITs: A De Facto Multilateral Agreement?', *Brooklyn Journal of International Law* 34 (2009), 303–354.

Chen-Wishart, M. 'Legal Transplant and Undue Influence: Lost in Translation or a Working Understanding?', *International and Comparative Law Quarterly* 62 (2013), 1–30.

Chimni, B.S. 'Co-option and Resistance: Two Faces of Global Administrative Law', *New York University Journal of International Law and Politics* 37 (2005), 799–827.

Choudry, S. 'Globalization in Search of a Justification: Toward a Theory of Comparative Constitutional Interpretation', *Indiana Law Journal* 74 (1999), 819–892.

Clark, M. 'Venezuela's Withdrawal from the ICSID Convention', *Association for International Arbitration Bulletin*, October 2012, 2.

Cohen, M. 'Reason-Giving in Court Practice: Decision-Makers at the Crossroads', *Columbia Journal of European Law* 14 (2007–2008), 257–276.

Cohen-Eliya, M. and Porat, I. 'Proportionality and the Culture of Justification', *American Journal of Comparative Law* 59 (2011), 463–490.

Commission, J. 'Precedent in Investment Treaty Arbitration: A Citation Analysis of a Developing Jurisprudence', *Journal of International Arbitration* 24 (2007), 129–158.

Cuniberti, G. 'Parallel Litigation and Foreign Investment Dispute Settlement', *ICSID Review – Foreign Investment Law Journal* 21 (2006), 381–406.

Dattu, R. 'A Journey from Havana to Paris: The Fifty Year Quest for the Elusive Multilateral Agreement on Investment', *Fordham International Law Journal* 24 (2000–2001), 275–316.

David, R. 'Le droit comparé enseignement de culture générale', *Revue internationale de droit comparé* 2 (1950), 682–685.

Davis, F. 'Comparative Law Contributions to the International Legal Order: Common Core Research', *George Washington Law Review* 37 (1969), 615–633.

De Burca, G., Keohane, R.O. and Sabel, C. 'New Modes of Pluralist Global Governance', *New York University Journal of International Law and Politics* 45 (2013), 723–786.

Delaume, G. 'The Pyramids Stand – The Pharaohs can Rest in Peace', *ICSID Review–Foreign Investment Law Journal* 8 (1993), 231–263.

Delmas-Marty, M. 'Comparative Law and International Law: Methods for Ordering Pluralism', *University of Tokyo Journal of Law and Politics* (2006), 43–59.

Delmas-Marty, M. 'The Contribution of Comparative Law to a Pluralist Conception of International Criminal Law', *Journal of International Criminal Justice* 1 (2003), 13–25.

Del Vecchio, G. 'L'Unité de l'Esprit Humain Comme Base de la Comparaison Juridique', *Revue Internationale de Droit Comparé* 2 (1950), 686–691.

Demleitner, N. 'Combating Legal Ethnocentrism: Comparative Law Sets Boundaries', *Arizona State Law Journal* 31 (1999), 737–762.

Dibadj, R. 'Panglossian Transnationalism', *Stanford Journal of International Law* 44 (2008), 253–299.

DiMascio, N. and Pauwelyn, J. 'Nondiscrimination in Trade and Investment Treaties: Worlds Apart or Two Sides of the Same Coin?', *American Journal of International Law* 102 (2008), 48–89.

Dookhun, S. 'Q&A with Professor Pierre Lalive', *Global Arbitration Review* 3 (2008), 5.

Douglas, Z. 'The Hybrid Foundations of Investment Treaty Arbitration', *The British Yearbook of International Law* 74 (2003), 151–289.

Douglas, Z. 'Can a Doctrine of Precedent be Justified in Investment Treaty Arbitration?', *ICSID Review–Foreign Investment Law Journal* 25 (2010), 104–110.

Dworkin, R. 'In Praise of Theory', *Arizona State Law Journal* 29 (1997), 353–376.

Eeckhout, P. 'The Scales of Trade – Reflections on the Growth and Functions of the WTO Adjudicative Branch', *Journal of International Economic Law* 13 (2010), 3–26.

Ehlermann, C.D. 'Six Years on the Bench of the World Trade Court – Some Personal Experiences as Member of the Appellate Body of the WTO', *Journal of World Trade* 36 (2002), 605–639.

Ellickson, R.C. 'Property in Land', *Yale Law Journal* 102 (1993), 1315–1400.

Ellis, J. 'General Principles and Comparative Law', *European Journal of International Law* 22 (2011), 949–971.

Esposito, P. and Martire, J. 'Arbitrating in a World of Communicative Reason', *Arbitration International* 28 (2012), 325–341.

Fletcher, G.P. 'Comparative Law as a Subversive Discipline', *American Journal of Comparative Law* 46 (1998), 683–700.

Fontoura Costa, J.A. 'Comparing WTO Panelists and ICSID Arbitrators: The Creation of International Legal Fields', *Oñati Socio-Legal Series* 1(4) (2011), 1–24.

Fortier, L.Y. and Drymer, S.L. 'Indirect Expropriation in the Law of International Investment: I Know It When I See It, or *Caveat Investor*', *ICSID Review-Foreign Investment Law Journal* 19 (2004), 293–327.

Francioni, F. 'Access to Justice, Denial of Justice, and International Investment Law', *European Journal of International Law* 20 (2009), 729–747.

Franck, S.D. 'Development and Outcomes of Investment Treaty Arbitration', *Harvard International Law Journal* 50 (2009), 435–489.

Franck, S.D. 'The Legitimacy Crisis in Investment Treaty Arbitration: Privatizing Public International Law Through Inconsistent Decisions', *Fordham Law Review* 73 (2005), 1521–1625.

Frankenberg, G. 'Critical Comparisons: Rethinking Comparative Law', *Harvard International Law Journal* 26 (1985), 411–456.

Freeman, E. 'Regulatory Expropriation Under NAFTA Chapter 11: Some Lessons From the European Court of Human Rights', *Columbia Journal of Transnational Law* 42 (2003–2004), 177–215.

Freeman Jalet, F.T. 'The Quest for the General Principles of Law Recognized by Civilized Nations', *UCLA Law Review* 10 (1963), 1041–1086.

French, D. 'Treaty Interpretation and the Incorporation of Extraneous Legal Rules', *International and Comparative Law Quarterly* 55 (2006), 281–314.

Friedmann, W. 'The Uses of "General Principles" in the Development of International Law', *American Journal of International Law* 57 (1963), 279–280.

Fry, J.D. 'International Human Rights Law in Investment Arbitration: Evidence of International Law's Unity', *Duke Journal Comparative and International Law* 18 (2007), 77–150.

Gaillard, E. 'Use of General Principles of International Law in International Long-Term Contracts', *International Business Lawyer* (1999), 214–224.

Gaines, S. 'The WTO's Reading of the GATT Article XX Chapeau: A Disguised Restriction on Environmental Measures', *University of Pennsylvania Journal of International Law* 22 (2001), 739–862.

Gaubatz, K.T. and MacArthur, M. 'How International is International Law?', *Michigan Journal of International Law* 22 (2001), 239–282.

Gerber, D. 'System Dynamics: Toward a Language of Comparative Law?', *American Journal of Comparative Law* 46 (1998), 719–732.

Giliker, P. 'Book Review–*The Enigma of Comparative Law: Variations on a Theme for the Twenty-first Century and Methodology of Comparative Law*' by E. Örücü (Leiden: Martinus Nijhoff Publishers, 2004), *International and Comparative Law Quarterly* 55 (2006), 243–246.

Ginsburg, T. 'The Culture of Arbitration', *Vanderbilt Journal of Transnational Law* 36 (2003), 1335–1346.

Glenn, P. 'Comparative Law: Problems and Prospects', *American University International Law Review* 26 (2010–2011), 935–968.

Glenn, H.P. 'Persuasive Authority', *McGill Law Journal* 32 (1987), 261–298.

Goldhaber, M. 'Wanted: A World Investment Court', *Transnational Dispute Management* 3 (2004), 1–5.

González Jácome, 'El uso del derecho comparado como forma de escape de la subordinación colonial', *International Law: Revista Colombiana de Derecho Internacional* 7 (2006), 295–338.

Gordley, J. 'Is Comparative Law a Distinct Discipline?', *The American Journal of Comparative Law* 46 (1998), 607–615.

Green, L.C. 'Comparative Law as a "Source" of International Law', *Tulane Law Review* 42 (1967–1968), 52–66.

Grosswald Curran, V. 'Comparative Law and the Legal Origins Thesis', *American Journal of Comparative Law* 57 (2009), 863–876.

Grosswald Curran, V. 'Cultural Immersion, Difference and Categories in U.S. Comparative Law', *American Journal of Comparative Law* 46 (1998), 43–92.

Grosswald Curran, V. 'Fear of Formalism: Indications from the Fascist Period in France and Germany of Judicial Methodology's Impact on Substantive Law', *Cornell International Law Journal* 35 (2001–2002), 101–188.

Grosswald Curran, V. 'Romantic Common Law, Enlightened Civil Law: Legal Uniformity and the Homogenization of the European Union', *Columbia Journal European Law* 7 (2001), 63–126.

Gutteridge, H.C. 'Comparative Law and the Law of Nations', *British Yearbook of International Law* 21 (1944), 1–10.

Guzman, A. 'Explaining the Popularity of Bilateral Investment Treaties: Why LDCs Sign Treaties that Hurt Them', *Virginia Journal of Transnational Law* 38 (1997), 639–688.

Haas, P. 'Introduction: Epistemic Communities and International Policy Coordination', *International Organization* 46 (1992), 1–35.

Hallward-Driemeier, M. 'Do Bilateral Investment Treaties Attract Foreign Direct Investment? Only a Bit ... And They Could Bite', Policy Research Working Paper No 3121 (Washington, DC: World Bank, 2003).

Harding, S.K. 'Comparative Reasoning and Judicial Review', *Yale Journal of International Law* 28 (2003), 409–464.

Harlow, C. 'Global Administrative Law: The Quest for Principles and Values', *European Journal of International Law* 17 (2006), 187–214.

Hazard, J.N. 'Briefer Notice', *American Journal of International Law* 63 (1969), 179–180.

Helfer, L.R. 'Constitutional Analogies in the International Legal System', *Loyola Los Angeles Law Review* 37 (2003–2004), 193–237.

Hey, E. and Mak, E. 'Introduction: The Possibilities of Comparative Law Method for Research on the Rule of Law in a Global Context', *Erasmus Law Review* 2 (2009), 287–288.

Higgins, R. 'Policy Considerations and the International Judicial Process', *International and Comparative Law Quarterly* 17 (1968), 58–84.

Hirschl, R. 'The Question of Case Selection in Comparative Constitutional Law', *American Journal of Comparative Law* 53 (2005), 125–156.

Holyoak, K.J. and Thagard, P. 'The Analogical Mind', *American Psychologist* 52 (1997), 35–44.

Horwitz, M.J. 'The History of the Public/Private Distinction', *University of Pennsylvania Law Review* 130 (1982), 1423–1428.

Howse, R. and Chalamish, E. 'The Use and Abuse of WTO Law in Investor-State Arbitration: A Reply to Jürgen Kurtz', *European Journal of International Law* 20 (2009), 1087–1094.

Hsu, L. 'International Investment Disputes: Ideological Fault Lines and an Evolving Zeitgeist', *Journal of World Investment and Trade* 12 (2011), 827–853.

Husa, J. 'Methodology of Comparative Law Today: From Paradoxes to Flexibility?', *Revue internationale de droit comparé* 57 (2006), 1095–1117.

Husa, J. 'Classification of Legal Families Today – Is it Time for Memorial Hymn?', *Revue International de Droit Comparé* 56 (2004), 11–38.

Husa, J. 'About the Methodology of Comparative Law – Some Comments Concerning the Wonderland . . .', *Maastricht Faculty of Law Working Papers* 5 (2007), 1–18.

Izorche, M.-L. 'Propositions méthodologiques pour la comparaison', *Revue internationale de droit comparé* 53 (2001), 289–325.

Jackson, V. 'Constitutional Comparisons: Convergence, Resistance, Engagement', *Harvard Law Review* 119 (2005), 109–129.

Jaluzot, B 'Méthodologie du droit comparé – Bilan et prospective', *Revue internationale de droit comparé* 57 (2005), 29–48.

Jamin, C. 'Saleilles and Lambert's Old Dream Revisited', *American Journal of Comparative Law* 50 (2002), 701–718.

Jans, J. 'Proportionality Revisited', *Legal Issues of Economic Integration* 27 (2000), 239.

Jennings, 'The Judiciary, International and National, and the Development of International Law', *International and Comparative Law Quarterly* 45 (1996), 1–12.

Jianlong, Y. 'Arbitrators: Private Judges, Service Providers or Both? CIETAC's Perspective', *Stockholm International Arbitration Review* 1 (2007), 1–9.

Johnston, A.M. and Trebilcock, M.J. 'Fragmentation in International Trade Law: Insights from the Global Investment Regime', *World Trade Review* 12 (2013), 621–652.

Jouannet, E. 'Universalism and Imperialism: The True False Paradox of International Law?' *European Journal of International Law* 18 (2007), 379–409.

Juthe, A. 'Argument by Analogy', *Argumentation* 19 (2005), 1–27.

Kahn-Freund, O. 'Comparative Law as an Academic Subject', *Law Quarterly Review* 82 (1966), 40–61.

Kahn-Freund, O. 'On Uses and Misuses of Comparative Law', *Modern Law Review* 37 (1974), 1–27.

Kapeliuk, D. 'The Repeat Appointment Factor: Exploring Decision Patterns of Elite Investment Arbitrators', *Cornell Law Review* 96 (2010–2011), 47–90.

Kaplan, N. 'Investment Arbitration's Influence on Practice and Procedure in Commercial Arbitration', *Asian Dispute Review* (2013), 122–125.

Kapterian, G. 'A Critique of the WTO Jurisprudence on Necessity', *International and Comparative Law Quarterly* 59 (2010), 89–127.

Kasirer, N. 'Legal Education as Métissage', *Tulane Law Review* 78 (2003–2004), 481–501.

Kaufmann-Kohler, G. 'Arbitral Precedent: Dream, Necessity or Excuse?', *Arbitration International* 23 (2007), 357–378.

Kaufmann-Kohler, G. 'Globalization of Arbitral Procedure', *Vanderbilt Journal of Transnational Law* 36 (2003), 1313–1334.

Kennedy, D. 'New Approaches to Comparative Law: Comparativism and International Governance', *Utah Law Review* 2 (1997), 545–637.

Kiekbaev, D. 'Comparative Law: Method, Science or Educational Discipline?', *Electronic Journal of Comparative Law* 7 (2003), 1–7.

Kingsbury, B. and Schill, S. 'Investor–State Arbitration as Governance: Fair and Equitable Treatment, Proportionality and the Emerging Global Administrative Law', New York University School of Law, Public Law & Legal Research Theory Research Paper Series, Working Paper No. 09–46 (2009), 1–56.

Kocbek, A. 'Language and Culture in International Legal Communication', *Managing Global Transitions* 4 (2006), 231–247.

Krisch, N. and Kingsbury, B. 'Introduction: Global Governance and Global Administrative Law in the International Legal Order', *European Journal of International Law* 17 (2006), 1–13.

Kurtz, J 'The Use and Abuse of WTO Law in Investor–State Arbitration: Competition and Its Discontents', *European Journal of International Law* 20 (2009), 749–771.

Lachs, M. 'Teachings and Teaching of International Law', *Recueil des Cours de l'Académie de Droit International de la Haye* 151 (1976/III), 161.

Lalive, P. 'On the Reasoning of International Arbitral Awards', *Journal of International Dispute Settlement* 1 (2010), 55–65.

Latty, F. 'Les techniques interprétative du CIRDI', *Revue Générale de Droit International Public* 115 (2011), 459–475.

Lauterpacht, H. 'Decisions of Municipal Courts as a Source of International Law', *British Yearbook of International Law* 10 (1929), 65–95.

Lauterpacht, H. 'Restrictive Interpretation and the Principle of Effectiveness in the Interpretation of Treaties', *British Yearbook of International Law* 26 (1949), 48–85.

Lauterpacht, E. 'The Development of the Law of International Organizations by the Decision of Arbitral Tribunals', *Recueil des Courses* 152 (1976), 396.

Leben, C. 'La responsabilité internationale de l'Etat sur le fondement des Traités de promotion et de protection des investissements', *Annuaire Français de Droit International* 50 (2004), 683–714.

Legrand, P. 'European Legal Systems are not Converging', *International and Comparative Law Quarterly* 45 (1996), 52–81.

Legrand, P. 'How to Compare Now?', *Legal Studies* 16 (1996), 232–242.

Legrand, P. 'On the Singularity of Law', *Harvard International Law Journal* 47 (2006), 517–530.

Legrand, P. 'The Impossibility of Legal Transplants', *Maastricht Journal of European and Comparative Law* 4 (1997), 111–124.

Leonhardsen, E. 'Looking for Legitimacy: Exploring Proportionality Analysis in Investment Treaty Arbitration', *Journal of International Dispute Settlement* 3 (2012), 95–136.

Lévesque, C. 'Influences on the Canadian FIPA Model and the U.S. Model BIT: NAFTA Chapter 11 and Beyond', *Canadian Yearbook of International Law* 44 (2006), 249–298.

Levine, E. '"Amicus Curiae" in International Investment Arbitration: The Implication of an Increase in Third-Party Participation', *Berkeley Journal of International Law* 29 (2011), 200–224.

Lowe, V. 'Regulation or Expropriation?', *Current Legal Problems* 55 (2002), 447–466.

Lowenfeld, A. 'Investment Agreements and International Law', *Columbia Journal of Transnational Law* 42 (2003–2004), 123–130.

Lowenfeld, A. 'The Party-Appointed Arbitrator in International Controversies: Some Reflections', *Texas International Law Journal* 30 (1995), 59–72.

Mamlyuk, B.N. and Mattei, U. 'Comparative International Law', *Brooklyn Journal of International Law* 36 (2010–2011), 385–452.

Maniruzzaman, A.F.M. 'State Contracts in Contemporary International Law: Monist versus Dualist Controversies', *European Journal of International Law* 12 (2001), 309–328.

Marceau, G., Lanovoy, V. and Izaguerri Vila, A. 'A Lighthouse in the Storm of Fragmentation', *Journal of World Trade* 47 (2013), 481–574.

Markesinis, B. 'Unité ou divergence: à la recherche des ressemblances dans le droit européen contemporain', *Revue de droit international et de droit comparé* 53 (2001), 807–808.

Martinez, J.S. 'Towards an International Judicial System', *Stanford Law Review* 56 (2003), 429–530.

Martinez-Fraga, P.J. and Samra, H.J. 'The Role of Precedent in Defining Res Judicata in Investor–State Arbitration', *Northwestern Journal of International Law & Business* 32 (2011–2012), 419–450.

Mattei, U. 'Three Patterns of Law: Taxonomy and Change in the World's Legal Systems', *American Journal of Comparative Law* 45 (1997), 5–45.

Maupin, J.A. 'Public and Private in International Investment Law: An Integrated Systems Approach', *Virginia Journal of International Law* 54 (2013–2014), 267–436.

McCrudden, C. 'A Common Law of Human Rights? Transnational Judicial Conversations on Constitutional Rights', *Oxford Journal of Legal Studies* 20 (2000), 499–532.

McCrudden, C. 'Using Comparative Reasoning in Human Rights Adjudication: The Court of Justice of the European Union and the European Court of Human Rights Compared', *Cambridge Yearbook of European Legal Studies* 15 (2012–2013), 383–415.

McDougal, M.S. 'The Comparative Study of Law for Policy Purposes: Value Clarification as an Instrument of World Order', *American Journal of Comparative Law* 1 (1952), 24–57.

McLachlan, C. 'The Principle of Systemic Integration and Article 31(3)(c) of the Vienna Convention', *International and Comparative Law Quarterly* 54 (2005), 279–320.

Merryman, J.H. 'On the Convergence (and Divergence) of the Civil Law and the Common Law', *Stanford Journal of International Law* 17 (1981), 357–388.

Miller, N. 'An International Jurisprudence? The Operation of "Precedent" Across International Tribunals', *Leiden Journal of International Law* 15 (2002), 483–526.

Mills, A. 'Antinomies of Public and Private at the Foundations of International Investment Law and Arbitration', *Journal of International Economic Law* 14 (2011), 469–503.

Momirov, A. and Naudé Fourie, A. 'Vertical Comparative Methods: Tools for Conceptualising the International Rule of Law', *Erasmus Law Review* 2 (2009), 291–308.

Monateri, P.G. 'Black Gaius – A Quest for the Multicultural Origins of the "Western Legal Tradition"', *Hastings Law Journal* 51 (1999–2000), 479–556.

Mousourakis, G. 'How Comparative Law Can Contribute to the Development of a General Theory on Legal Evolution', *Tilburg Law Review* 14 (2008), 272–297.

Muir Watt, H. 'La fonction subversive du droit comparé', *Revue Internationale de Droit Comparé* 52 (2000), 503–527.

Newcombe, A. 'The Boundaries of Regulatory Expropriation in International Law', *ICSID Review – Foreign Investment Law Journal* 20 (2005), 1–57.

Obiora, L.A. 'Toward an Auspicious Reconciliation of International and Comparative Analyses', *American Journal of Comparative Law* 46 (1998), 669–682.

Olynyk, S. 'A Balanced Approach to Distinguishing Between Legitimate Regulation and Indirect Expropriation in Investor–State Arbitration', *International Trade and Business Law Review* 15 (2012), 254–296.

Oppenheim, L. 'The Science of International Law: Its Task and Method', *American Journal of International Law* 2 (1908), 313–356.

Palmer, V.V. 'From Lerotholi to Lando: Some Examples of Comparative Law Methodology', *American Journal of Comparative Law* 53 (2005), 261–290.

Park, W.W. 'Private Disputes and the Public Good: Explaining Arbitration Law', *American University International Law Review* 20 (2004–2005), 903–906.

Paulsson, J. 'Arbitration Without Privity', *ICSID Review – Foreign Investment Law Journal* 10 (1995), 232–257.

Paulsson, J. 'International Arbitration is not Arbitration', *Stockholm International Arbitration Review* 2 (2008), 1–20.

Pauwelyn J. and Salle, L.E. 'Forum Shopping Before International Tribunals: (Real) Concerns, (Im)possible Solutions', *Cornell International Law Journal* 42 (2009), 77–118.

Peerenboom, R. 'Toward a Methodology for Successful Legal Transplant', *Chinese Journal of Comparative Law* (2013), 1–17.

Pellet, A. 'The Case Law of the ICJ in Investment Arbitration', *ICSID Review – Foreign Investment Law Journal* 28 (2013), 223–240.

Perry, A.J. 'Effective Legal Systems and Foreign Direct Investment: In Search of the Evidence', *International and Comparative Law Quarterly* 49 (2000), 779–799.

Perry-Kessaris, A. 'Finding and Facing Facts about Legal Systems and FDI in South Asia', *Legal Studies* 23 (2003), 649–689.

Peters, A. 'New Approaches to Comparative Law', *American Society of International Law. Proceedings of the Annual Meeting* (1999), 366–369.

Peterson, L.E. 'In Policy Switch, Australia Disavows Need for Investor–State Arbitration Provisions in Trade and Investment Agreements', *Investment Arbitration Reporter* (14 April 2011).

Pfaff, C. 'Alternative Approaches to Foreign Investment Protection', *Transnational Dispute Management* 3 (2006), 1–16.

Pfersmann, O. 'Le droit comparé comme interprétation et comme théorie du droit', *Revue Internationale de Droit Comparé* (2001), 275–288.

Picciotto, S. 'Linkages in International Investment Regulation: The Antinomies of the Draft Multilateral Agreement on Investment', *University of Pennsylvania Journal of International Economic Law* 19 (1998), 731–768.

Picker, C.B. 'International Law's Mixed Heritage: A Common/Civil Law Jurisdiction', *Vanderbilt Journal of Transnational Law* 41 (2008), 1083–1140.

Ponthoreau, M.C. 'Le droit comparé en question(s) entre pragmatism et outil épistémologique', *Revue internationale de droit comparé* 57 (2005), 7–27.

Porat, I. 'Why All Attempts to Make Judicial Review Balancing Principled Fail?', paper presented at the VII World Congress of the International Association of Constitutional Law, Athens, 11–15 June 2007.

Posner, R.A. 'Forward: A Political Court', *Harvard Law Review* 119 (2005), 84–91.

Priem, C. 'International Investment Treaty Arbitration as a Potential Check for Domestic Courts Refusing Enforcement of Foreign Arbitration Awards', *New York University Journal of Law & Business* 10 (2013), 189–221.

Puig, S. 'Emergence and Dynamism in International Organizations: ICSID, Investor-State Arbitration and International Investment Law', *Georgetown Journal of International Law* 44 (2013), 531–608.

Puig, S. 'Social Capital in the Arbitration Market', *European Journal of International Law* 25 (2014), 387–424.

Quint, P.E. 'International Human Rights: The Convergence of Comparative and International Law', *Texas International Law Journal* 36 (2001), 605–610.

Ratner, S. 'Regulatory Takings in Institutional Context: Beyond the Fear of Fragmented International Law', *American Journal of International Law* 102 (2008), 475–528.

Rau, A.S. 'Integrity in Private Judging', *South Texas Law Review* 38 (1997), 485–540.

Raustiala, K. 'Rethinking the Sovereignty Debate in International Economic Law', *Journal of International Economic Law* 6 (2003), 841–878.

Raz, J. 'Why Interpret?', *Ratio Juris* 9 (1996), 349–363.

Reed, L. 'The *De Facto* Precedent Regime in Investment Arbitration: A Case for Proactive Case Management', *ICSID Review – Foreign Investment Law Journal* 25 (2010), 95–103.

Reimann, M. 'Beyond National Systems: A Comparative Law for the International Age', *Tulane Law Review* 75 (2001), 1103–1120.

Reimann, M. 'The End of Comparative Law as an Autonomous Subject', *Tulane European and Civil Law Forum* 11 (1996), 49–72.

Reisman, W.M. 'International Investment Arbitration and ADR: Married but Best Living Apart', *ICSID Review – Foreign Investment Law Journal* 24 (2009), 185–192.

Reitz, J.C. 'How to do Comparative Law', *American Journal of Comparative Law* 46 (1998), 617–636.

Reyntjens, F. 'Note sur l'utilité d'introduire un system juridique "pluraliste" dans la macro-comparaison des droits', *Revue de droit international et droit comparé* 68 (1991), 41–50.

Rheinstein, M. 'Comparative Law and Conflict of Laws in Germany', *The University of Chicago Law Review* 2 (1934), 232–269.

Riles, A. 'Wigmore's Treasure Box: Comparative Law in the Era of Information', *Harvard International Law Journal* 40 (1999), 221–464.

Ripinsky, S. 'Venezuela's Withdrawal from ICSID: What it Does and Does Not Achieve', *Investment Treaty News*, 13 April 2012.

Roach, K. 'The Uses and Audiences of Preambles in Legislation', *McGill Law Journal* 47 (2001), 129–159.

Roberts, A. 'Clash of Paradigms: Actors and Analogies Shaping the Investment Treaty System', *American Journal of International Law* 107 (2013), 45–94.

Roberts, A. 'Comparative International Law? The Role of National Courts in Creating and Enforcing International Law', *International and Comparative Law Quarterly* 60 (2011), 57–92.

Roberts, A. 'State-to-State Investment Treaty Arbitration: A Hybrid Theory of Interdependent Rights and Shared Interpretive Authority', *Harvard International Law Journal* 55 (2014) 1.

Rotondi, M. 'Technique du droit, dogmatique et droit comparé', *Revue internationale de droit comparé* 20 (1968), 5–18.

Sacco, R. 'Legal Formants: A Dynamic Approach to Comparative Law', *American Journal of Comparative Law* 39 (1991), 1–34.

Sacco, R. 'Mute Law', *American Journal of Comparative Law* 43 (1995), 455–468.

Sakellaridou, M. 'La Généalogie de la proportionalité', paper presented at the VII World Congress of the International Association of Constitutional Law, held in Athens, 11–15 June 2007.

Salacuse, J.W. 'The Emerging Global Regime for Investment', *Harvard International Law Journal* 51 (2010), 427–474.

Sands, P. 'Searching for Balance: Concluding Remarks', *New York University Environmental Law Journal* 11 (2002), 198–207.

Sarfatti, M. 'Comparative Law and the Unification of Law', *Tulane Law Review* 26 (1952), 317–323.

Sarooshi, D. 'Investment Treaty Arbitration and the World Trade Organization: What Role for Systemic Values in the Resolution of International Economic Disputes?', *Texas International Law Journal* 49 (2014), 445–467.

Sattorova, M. 'Denial of Justice Disguised?: Investment Arbitration and the Protection of Investors from Judicial Misconduct', *International and Comparative Law Quarterly* 61 (2012), 223–246.

Schachter, O. 'The Invisible College of International Lawyers', *Northwestern University Law Review* 72 (1977), 217–227.

Scheppele, K.L. 'Comparative Law: Problems and Prospects', *American University International Law Review* 26 (2010–2011), 935–968.

Schill, S. 'Enhancing International Investment Law's Legitimacy: Conceptual and Methodological Foundations of a New Public Law Approach', *Virginia Journal of International Law* 52 (2011), 57–102.

Schill, S. 'System Building in Investment Arbitration and Lawmaking', *German Law Journal* 12 (2011), 1083–1110.

Schill, S.W. 'Crafting the International Economic Order: The Public Function of Investment Treaty Arbitration and Its Significance for the Role of the Arbitrator', *Leiden Journal of International Law* 23 (2010), 401–430.

Schill, S.W. 'Fair and Equitable Treatment under Investment Treaties as an Embodiment of the Rule of Law', New York University Law School, International Law & Justice Working Paper No. 6, 2006.

Schill, S.W. 'W(h)ither Fragmentation? On the Literature and Sociology of International Investment Law', *European Journal of International Law* 22 (2011), 875–908.

Schlesinger, R.B. 'Research on the General Principles of Law Recognized by Civilized Nations', *American Journal of International Law* 51 (1957), 734–753.

Schmitthoff, M. 'The Science of Comparative Law', *Cambridge Law Journal* 7 (1939), 94–110.

Schneiderman, D. 'NAFTA's Takings Rule: American Constitutionalism Comes to Canada', *University of Toronto Law Journal* 46 (1996), 499–538.

Schor, M. 'Mapping Comparative Judicial Review', *Washington University Global Studies Law Review* 7 (2008), 257–287.

Schreuer, C. 'The Concept of Expropriation under the ETC and other Investment Protection Treaties', *Transnational Dispute Management* 2 (2005), 1–10.

Schreuer, C. and Weiniger, M. 'Conversations Across Cases – Is There a Doctrine of Precedent in Investment Arbitration?', *Transnational Dispute Management* 5 (2008), 1–15.

Schwarzenberger, G. 'The Inductive Approach to International Law', *Harvard Law Review* 60 (1947), 559–562.

Schwebel, S.M. 'In Defense of Bilateral Investment Treaties', *Columbia FDI Perspectives* 135, 24 November 2014, 1–3.

Sedlak, D. 'ICSID's Resurgence in International Investment Arbitration: Can the Momentum Hold?', *Penn State International Law Review* 23 (2004), 147–171.

Shalakany, A. 'Arbitration and The Third World: A Plea for Reassessing Bias Under the Specter of Neoliberalism', *Harvard International Law Journal* 41 (2000), 419–468.

Shany, Y. 'No Longer a Weak Department of Power? Reflections on the Emergence of a New International Judiciary', *European Journal of International Law* 20 (2009), 73–91.

Siems, M. 'The End of Comparative Law', *Journal of Comparative Law* 2 (2007), 133–150.

Slaughter, A.-M. 'A Global Community of Courts', *Harvard Journal of International Law* 44 (2003), 191–220.

Slaughter, A.-M. 'A Liberal Theory of International Law', *American Society International Law Proceedings* 94 (2000), 240–248.

Slaughter, A.-M. 'Judicial Globalization', *Virginia Journal of International Law* 40 (1999–2000), 1103–1124.

Sonpar, K., Pazzaglia, F. and Kornijenko, J. 'The Paradox and Constraints of Legitimacy', *Journal of Business Ethics* 95 (2010), 1–21.

Sornarajah, M. 'The Clash of Globalizations and the International Law on Foreign Investment', *Canadian Foreign Policy* 12 (2003), 1–32.

Starner, G.M. 'Taking a Constitutional Look: NAFTA Chapter 11 as an Extension of Member States' Constitutional Protection of Property', *Law & Policy in International Law & Business* 33 (2002), 405–436.

Steger, D. 'The Culture of the WTO: Why It Needs to Change', *Journal of International Economic Law* 10 (2007), 483–495.

Steyt, J.-Y. P. 'Comparative Foreign Investment Law: Determinants of the Legal Framework and the Level of Openness and Attractiveness of Host Economies', Cornell Law School, LLM Graduate Research Papers, Paper No. 1 (2006) *available at* http://scholarship.law.cornell.edu/lps_LLMGRP/1/.

Stone, F.F. 'The End to be Served by Comparative Law', *Tulane Law Review* 25 (1950–1951), 325–335.

Stone, J. 'Non Liquet and the Function of Law in the International Community', *British Yearbook of International Law* 35 (1959), 124–161.

Stone Sweet, A. 'Investor–State Arbitration: Proportionality's New Frontier', *Law and Ethics of Human Rights* 4 (2010), 46–76.

Stone Sweet, A. and Mathews, D. 'Proportionality Balancing and Global Constitutionalism', *Columbia Journal of Transnational Law* 47 (2008), 72–164.

Sunstein, C. 'Incommensurability and Valuation in Law', *Michigan Law Review* 92 (1994), 779–861.

Sunstein, C.R. 'On Analogical Reasoning', *Harvard Law Review* 106 (1993), 741–791.

Szpak, A. 'A Few Reflections on the Interpretation of Treaties in Public International Law', *Hague Yearbook of International Law* 18 (2005), 59–70.

Teitel, R. 'Comparative Constitutional Law in a Global Age', *Harvard Law Review* 117 (2004), 2570–2596.

Teubner, G. 'Legal Irritants: Good Faith in British Law or How Unifying Law Ends up in New Divergences', *Modern Law Review* 61 (1998), 11–32.

Thomas, C. 'Does the "Good Governance Policy" of the International Financial Institutions Privilege Markets at the Expense of Democracy?', *Connecticut Journal of International Law* 14 (1999), 551–562.

Titi, C. 'The Arbitrator as a Lawmaker: Jurisgenerative Processes in Investment Arbitration', *Journal of World Investment and Trade* 14 (2013), 829–851.

Tobin, J. and Rose-Ackerman, S. 'Foreign Direct Investment and the Business Environment in Developing Countries: The Impact of Bilateral Investment Treaties', *Yale Law and Economics Research Paper No. 293* (2005), 1–52.

Trachtman, J.P. 'The International Economic Law Revolution', *University of Pennsylvania Journal of International Economic Law* 17 (1996), 33–61.

Traynor, I. 'TTIP Divides a Continent as EU Negotiatiors Cross the Atlantic', *The Guardian*, 8 December 2014.

Tribe, L.H. 'The Curvature of Constitutional Space: What Lawyers can Learn from Modern Physics', *Harvard Law Review* 103 (1989), 1–39.

Trubek, D.M. 'Towards a Social Theory of Law: An Essay on the Study of Law and Development', *Yale Law Journal* 82 (1982), 1–50.

Tushnet, T. 'The Possibilities of Comparative Law', *Yale Law Journal* 108 (1998–1999), 1225–1309.

Twining, W. 'Globalization and Comparative Law', *Maastricht Journal of European and Comparative Law* 6 (1999), 217–243.

Vadi, V. 'Converging Divergences: The Rise of Chinese Outward Foreign Investment and Its Implications for International (Investment) Law', *Yearbook of International Investment Law* (2012), 705–724.

Vadi, V. 'Critical Comparisons: The Role of Comparative Law in Investment Treaty Arbitration', *Denver Journal of International Law and Policy* 39 (2010), 67–100.

Vadi, V. 'The Migration of Constitutional Ideas to Regional and International Economic Law: The Case of Proportionality', *Northwestern Journal of International Law and Business* 35 *(forthcoming* 2015).

Vadi, V. 'Through the Looking Glass: International Investment Law through the Lenses of a Property Theory', *Manchester Journal of International Economic Law* 8 (2011), 22–64.

Van Harten, G. and Loughlin, M. 'Investment Treaty Arbitration as a Species of Global Administrative Law', *European Journal of International Law* 17 (2006), 121–150.

Van Harten, G. 'The Public-Private Distinction in the International Arbitration of Individual Claims Against the State', *International and Comparative Law Quarterly* 56 (2007), 371–394.

Venzke, I. 'The Role of International Courts as Interpreters and Developers of the Law: Working Out the Jurisgenerative Practice of Interpretation', *Loyola of Los Angeles International and Comparative Law Review* 34 (2011), 99–131.

Voeten, E. 'Borrowing and Nonborrowing Among International Courts', *Journal of Legal Studies* 39 (2010), 547–575.

Voigt, C. 'The Role of General Principles in International Law and Their Relationship to Treaty Law', *Retfærd Årgang* 31 (2008), 3–25.

Wälde, T. 'The "Umbrella" (or Sanctity of Contract/Pacta Sunt Servanda) Clause in Investment Arbitration: A Comment on Original Intentions and Recent Cases', *Transnational Dispute Management* 1 (2004), 1–13.

Wälde, T. and Kolo, A. 'Environmental Regulation, Investment Protection and "Regulatory Taking" in International Law', *International and Comparative Law Quarterly* 50 (2001), 811–848.

Waldron, J. 'Foreign Law and the Modern Jus Gentium', *Harvard Law Review* 119 (2005), 129–147.

Walker, H. Jr., 'Modern Treaties of Friendship, Commerce, and Navigation', *Minnesota Law Review* 42 (1957), 805–824.

Watson, A. 'Comparative Law and Legal Change', *The Cambridge Law Journal* 37 (1978), 313–336.

Weil, P. '"The Court Cannot Conclude Definitely ..." Non Liquet Revised', *Columbia Journal of Transnational Law* 36 (1997), 109–119.

Weiler, J.H.H. 'The Rule of Lawyers and the Ethos of Diplomats: Reflections on the Internal and External Legitimacy of WTO Dispute Settlement', Harvard Jean Monnet Working Paper 9/00 (2000), 1–18.

Weiler, T. 'Balancing Human Rights and Investor Protection: A New Approach for a Different Legal Order', *Transnational Dispute Management* 1 (2004), 1–15.

Weiler, T. (ed.), *Intersections: Dissemblance or Convergence between International Trade and Investment Law, Transnational Dispute Management* 3 (2011).

Wijffels, A. 'Le droit comparé à la recherche d'un nouvel interface entre ordres juridiques', *Revue de droit international et de droit comparé* 2 (2008), 228–251.

Winterton, G. 'Comparative Legal Teaching', *American Journal of Comparative Law* 23 (1975), 69–118.

Xiuli, H. 'The Application of the Principle of Proportionality in *Tecmed* v. *Mexico*', *Chinese Journal of International Law* 6 (2007), 635–652.

Yntema, H.E. 'Comparative Research. Some Remarks on "Looking out of the Cave"', *Michigan Law Review* 54 (1956), 899–928.

Yntema, H.E. 'Le droit comparé et l'humanisme', *Revue international de droit comparé* 10 (1958), 693–700.

Zammit Borda, A. 'A Formal Approach to Article 38(1)(d) of the ICJ Statute from the Perspective of the International Criminal Courts and Tribunals', *European Journal of International Law* 24 (2013), 649–661.

Zammit Borda, A. 'Comparative Law and Ad Hoc Tribunals: The Dangers of a Narrow Inquiry', *International Journal of Legal Information* 40 (2012), 22–38.

Zartner, D. 'The Culture of Law: Understanding the Influence of Legal Tradition on Transitional Justice in Post-Conflict Societies', *Indiana International & Comparative Law Review* 22 (2012), 297–316.

Zumbansen, P. 'Comparative Law's Coming of Age? Twenty Years after *Critical Comparisons*', *German Law Journal* 6 (2005), 1073–1084.

Zumbansen, P. 'Transnational Comparisons: Theory and Practice of Comparative Law as a Critique of Global Governance', *Osgoode Hall Law School, Research Paper* No. 1/2012, 1–20.

Documents of International Organizations

International Law Commission, *Draft Articles on the Law of Treaties: Text as Finally Adopted by the Commission on 18 July 1966*, 2 Yearbook of the International Law Commission 218, UN Doc. A/CN.4/190.

International Law Commission, Fragmentation of International Law: Difficulties Arising from the Diversification and Expansion of International Law, Report of the Study Group (Martti Koskenniemi) UN Doc. A/CN.4/L.682, 13 April 2006.

International Law Commission, *Fragmentation of International Law: Difficulties Arising from the Diversification and Expansion of International Law*, UN Doc. A/CN.4/L.702, 18 July 2006.

OECD, 'Indirect Expropriation and the Right to Regulate in International Investment Law', Working Paper on International Investment No. 4 (Paris: OECD, 2004).

UNCTAD, *Bilateral Investment Treaties: 1959–1999* (Geneva: UNCTAD, 2000).

UNCTAD, *World Investment Report 2011* (Switzerland: UN, 2011).

UNCTAD, *World Investment Report 2013 – Global Value Chains: Investment and Trade for Development* (New York and Geneva: UN, 2013).

INDEX

CPSIA information can be obtained
at www.ICGtesting.com
Printed in the USA
LVHW052228070119
603029LV00022B/308